ANNUAL EDITIONS

International Business

Fifteenth Edition

EDITOR

Fred H. Maidment
Western Connecticut State University

Dr. Fred Maidment is a Professor in the Department of Management of the Ancell School of Business at Western Connecticut State University in Danbury, Connecticut. He earned his doctorate from the University of South Carolina, Columbia, his MBA from the Zicklin School of Business of the Baruch College of the City University of New York, and his BS from the Stern School of Business of New York University. He has also been a Visiting Scholar at the Warrington School of Business at the University of Florida, Gainesville. Dr. Maidment lives with his wife in Connecticut and they are the proud parents of four children and three grandchildren.

 **Higher Education**

Boston   Burr Ridge, IL   Dubuque, IA   New York   San Francisco   St. Louis
Bangkok   Bogotá   Caracas   Kuala Lumpur   Lisbon   London   Madrid   Mexico City
Milan   Montreal   New Delhi   Santiago   Seoul   Singapore   Sydney   Taipei   Toronto

Higher Education

ANNUAL EDITIONS: INTERNATIONAL BUSINESS, FIFTEENTH EDITION

Annual Editions® is a registered trademark of The McGraw-Hill Companies, Inc.
Annual Editions is published by the **Contemporary Learning Series** group within the McGraw-Hill Higher Education division.

1 2 3 4 5 6 7 8 9 0 QPD/QPD 0 9 8

ISBN 978–0–07–352851–9
MHID 0–07–352851–X
ISSN 1091–1731

Managing Editor: *Larry Loeppke*
Senior Managing Editor: *Faye Schilling*
Developmental Editor: *Dave Welsh*
Editorial Coordinator: *Mary Foust*
Editorial Assistant: *Nancy Meissner*
Production Service Assistant: *Rita Hingtgen*
Permissions Coordinator: *DeAnna Dausener*
Senior Marketing Manager: *Julie Keck*
Marketing Communications Specialist: *Mary Klein*
Marketing Coordinator: *Alice Link*
Project Manager: *Sandy Wille*
Design Specialist: *Tara McDermott*
Senior Production Supervisor: *Laura Fuller*
Cover Graphics: *Kristine Jubeck*

Compositor: Laserwords Private Limited
Cover Images: © PhotoDisk Imaging/Getty Images (inset); © MaryBeth Thielhelm/Getty (background)

Library in Congress Cataloging-in-Publication Data
Main entry under title: Annual Editions: International Business, 15/e.
1. Management—Periodicals. I. Maidment, Fred H., *comp.* II. Title: International Business.
658'.05

www.mhhe.com

Editors/Advisory Board

Members of the Advisory Board are instrumental in the final selection of articles for each edition of ANNUAL EDITIONS. Their review of articles for content, level, currentness, and appropriateness provides critical direction to the editor and staff. We think that you will find their careful consideration well reflected in this volume.

Preface

In publishing ANNUAL EDITIONS we recognize the enormous role played by the magazines, newspapers, and journals of the public press in providing current, first-rate educational information in a broad spectrum of interest areas. Many of these articles are appropriate for students, researchers, and professionals seeking accurate, current material to help bridge the gap between principles and theories and the real world. These articles, however, become more useful for study when those of lasting value are carefully collected, organized, indexed, and reproduced in a low-cost format, which provides easy and permanent access when the material is needed. That is the role played by ANNUAL EDITIONS.

A lot has occurred in international business and globalization over the years since the first *Annual Editions: International Business* was published. In those days, there was still a Soviet Empire; the Cold War was still going on; China was still, essentially, a closed country; and the twin towers of the World Trade Center still stood. All that now seems like a millennium ago. The world was still round, with barriers, distance and time frequently separating people, countries, cultures, and societies. Today, people, countries, cultures, and societies are no longer separated by barriers, distance, and time. Thanks to technology and the demise of political regimes that repressed the skills, desires and energy of literally billions of people, it is a very different world today; a far more competitive world. A world where the fruits of success will not go to people by virtue of a birthright or an accident of location, but by their ability to remain competitive in this new global market.

This edition of *Annual Editions: International Business* is intended to help students understand this new hyper-competitive, global business environment by providing some of the latest articles available on these topics. The book is designed to present some of the current thinking on international business and help the reader understand the forces at play in the international business environment.

The book begins with an overview of international business that includes an introduction to international business and a unit on the international trade theory. The second unit deals with international institutions and organizations, as well as the international monetary system

and the balance of payments. Global corporations and international organizations, such as the World Bank, are directly addressed in the section. Unit three addresses important factors of international business that includes the legal and political factors; the cultural and social factors; and ethical factors. Unit four, is concerned with strategic management; import/export; foreign direct investment; financial management and accounting; operations, supply chaining and R&D; marketing; human resources; outsourcing and off-shoring. The last unit looks to what the future might be for international business and globalization from the perspective of the overall economy and the individual. It explores some of the things that could happen in the future.

There are many things that could happen in the future, but one thing is certain: the world will continue to change. There is no crystal ball to foretell the future, but one must be prepared for it and be able to welcome it.

Fred Maidment
Editor

Contents

UNIT 1
Overview of International Business

The concepts in bold italics are developed in the article. For further expansion, please refer to the Topic Guide.

UNIT 2
International Institutions and Organizations

The concepts in bold italics are developed in the article. For further expansion, please refer to the Topic Guide.

UNIT 3
Environmental Factors and International Business

The concepts in bold italics are developed in the article. For further expansion, please refer to the Topic Guide.

UNIT 4
International Business Operations

The concepts in bold italics are developed in the article. For further expansion, please refer to the Topic Guide.

UNIT 5
International Business and the Future

The concepts in bold italics are developed in the article. For further expansion, please refer to the Topic Guide.

Correlation Guide

The *Annual Editions* series provides students with convenient, inexpensive access to current, carefully selected articles from the public press. **Annual Editions: International Business, 15/e** is an easy-to-use reader that presents articles on important topics such as *international trade policy, financial markets and exchanges, the monetary system* and many more. For more information on *Annual Editions* and other *McGraw-Hill Contemporary Learning Series* titles, visit www.mhcls.com.

This convenient guide matches the units in **Annual Editions: International Business, 15/e** with the corresponding chapters in three of our best-selling McGraw-Hill International Business textbooks by Hill and Ball et al.

Annual Editions: International Business, 15/e	International Business: Competing in the Global Marketplace, 7/e by Hill	Global Business Today, 6/e by Hill	International Business: The Challenge of Global Competition, 12/e by Ball et al.
Unit 1: Overview of International Business	**Chapter 1:** Globalization **Chapter 5:** International Trade Theory	**Chapter 1:** Globalization **Chapter 5:** International Trade Theory	**Chapter 1:** The Rapid Change of International Business **Chapter 3:** Foreign Direct Investment: Theory and Evidence
Unit 2: International Institutions and Organizations	**Chapter 8:** Regional Economic Integration **Chapter 9:** The Foreign Exchange Market **Chapter 11:** The Global Capital Market	**Chapter 2:** National Differences in Political Economy **Chapter 7:** Foreign Direct Investment **Chapter 10:** The International Monetary System	**Chapter 4:** The Dynamics of International Institutions **Chapter 5:** Sociocultural Forces **Chapter 16:** Export and Import Practices
Unit 3: Environmental Factors and International Business	**Chapter 2:** National Differences in Political Economy **Chapter 3:** Differences in Culture **Chapter 5:** International Trade Theory **Chapter 6:** The Political Economy of International Trade **Chapter 7:** Foreign Direct Investment **Chapter 8:** Regional Economic Integration **Chapter 14:** Entry Strategy and Strategic Alliances **Chapter 15:** Exporting, Importing, and Countertrade **Chapter 16:** Global Production, Outsourcing, and Logistics	**Chapter 3:** National Differences in Culture **Chapter 5:** International Trade Theory **Chapter 6:** The Political Economy of International Trade **Chapter 7:** Foreign Direct Investment **Chapter 8:** Regional Economic Integration **Chapter 11:** The Strategy of International Business **Chapter 12:** Entering Foreign Markets **Chapter 13:** Exporting, Importing, and Countertrade **Chapter 14:** Global Production, Outsourcing, and Logistics	**Chapter 1:** The Rapid Change of International Business **Chapter 2:** International Trade: Theory and Evidence **Chapter 4:** The Dynamics of International Institutions **Chapter 5:** Sociocultural Forces **Chapter 6:** Natural Resources and Environmental Sustainability **Chapter 7:** Economic and Socioeconomic Forces **Chapter 8:** Political Forces **Chapter 9:** Legal Forces **Chapter 10:** Financial Forces **Chapter 11:** Labor Forces **Chapter 14:** Assessing and Analyzing Markets **Chapter 17:** Marketing Internationally
Unit 4: International Business Operations	**Chapter 7:** Foreign Direct Investment **Chapter 11:** The Global Capital Market **Chapter 15:** Exporting, Importing, and Countertrade **Chapter 16:** Global Production, Outsourcing, and Logistics **Chapter 17:** Global Marketing and R&D **Chapter 18:** Global Human Resource Management **Chapter 19:** Accounting in the International Business **Chapter 20:** Financial Management in the International Business	**Chapter 7:** Foreign Direct Investment **Chapter 14:** Global Production, Outsourcing, and Logistics **Chapter 15:** Global Marketing and R&D **Chapter 16:** Global Human Resource Management	**Chapter 12:** International Competitive Strategy **Chapter 13:** Organizational Design and Control **Chapter 14:** Assessing and Analyzing Markets **Chapter 18:** Global Operations and Supply Chain Management **Chapter 19:** Human Resource Management **Chapter 20:** Financial Management
Unit 5: International Business and the Future	**Chapter 1:** Globalization	**Chapter 1:** Globalization	**Chapter 1:** The Rapid Change of International Business

Topic Guide

This topic guide suggests how the selections in this book relate to the subjects covered in your course. You may want to use the topics listed on these pages to search the Web more easily.

On the following pages a number of Web sites have been gathered specifically for this book. They are arranged to reflect the units of this Annual Editions reader. You can link to these sites by going to *http://www.mhcls.com*.

All the articles that relate to each topic are listed below the bold-faced term.

Accounting
8. Are Global Prices Converging or Diverging?
12. The Bretton Woods System
15. Financial Globalization
30. Found in Translation

Consumer behavior
1. Globalization and Its Contents
6. Looking Ahead to Our Place in the Next Economy
16. China's Mobile Maestro
19. Grassroots Diplomacy
21. Is U.S. Business Losing Europe?
22. Can Europe Compete?
24. When Greens Go Corporate
25. Making It in China
32. The Rise of BRIC
41. Globalization and You

Corporate culture
6. Looking Ahead to Our Place in the Next Economy
14. The Challengers
19. Grassroots Diplomacy
21. Is U.S. Business Losing Europe?
24. When Greens Go Corporate
33. International OHS
34. Out of Work
35. Worrying Trends for the Global Outsourcing Industry
36. Roots of Insecurity
40. Going Green

Developing countries
1. Globalization and Its Contents
3. Trading Places
4. Here's the Good News
8. Are Global Prices Converging or Diverging?
9. What One Hand Gives, the Other Takes
10. The World's Banker
11. Helping the Global Economy Stay in Shape
12. The Bretton Woods System
13. Wall Street in the Desert
15. Financial Globalization
16. China's Mobile Maestro
17. The Challengers
18. How Capitalism Is Killing Democracy
19. Grassroots Diplomacy
23. Unequal Access
26. The China Factor
27. A Whiff of New Money
28. BRIC Crumbling?
31. Shaping the Future of Manufacturing
32. The Rise of BRIC
33. International OHS
34. Out of Work
35. Worrying Trends for the Global Outsourcing Industry
38. Oil Frontiers
39. A New World Economy
41. Globalization and You

Economic organizations
2. The Leading Economic Organizations
4. Here's the Good News
5. The Real Global Technology Challenge
9. What One Hand Gives, the Other Takes
10. The World's Banker
11. Helping the Global Economy Stay in Shape
12. The Bretton Woods System
13. Wall Street in the Desert
14. Dollar Doldrums
15. Financial Globalization
17. The Challengers
18. How Capitalism Is Killing Democracy
22. Can Europe Compete?
29. The Brave New World of IFRS
39. A New World Economy
40. Going Green

Ethics and international business
9. What One Hand Gives, the Other Takes
18. How Capitalism Is Killing Democracy
23. Unequal Access
24. When Greens Go Corporate
33. International OHS
34. Out of Work
36. Roots of Insecurity

Export-Import
6. Looking Ahead to Our Place in the Next Economy
7. A Roadmap for the New Trade Landscape
14. Dollar Doldrums
26. The China Factor
31. Shaping the Future of Manufacturing
38. Oil Frontiers

Financial marketing and exchanges
1. Globalization and Its Contents
3. Trading Places
10. The World's Banker
11. Helping the Global Economy Stay in Shape
12. The Bretton Woods System
13. Wall Street in the Desert
14. Dollar Doldrums
15. Financial Globalization
30. Found in Translation
37. Countdown to a Meltdown

Global corporations
1. Globalization and Its Contents
5. The Real Global Technology Challenge
14. Dollar Doldrums
16. China's Mobile Maestro
17. The Challengers
19. Grassroots Diplomacy
21. Is U.S. Business Losing Europe?
24. When Greens Go Corporate
26. The China Factor
27. The Whiff of New Money

Internet References

The following Internet sites have been selected to support the articles found in this reader. These sites were available at the time of publication. However, because Web sites often change their structure and content, the information listed may no longer be available. We invite you to visit http://www.mhcls.com for easy access to these sites.

Annual Editions: International Business 09/10

General Sources

Information Institute: Law About . . . Pages
http://www.law.cornell.edu/topics/index.html

Explore this site's searchable index to learn about a myriad of international legal subjects. Organized by topic, it provides useful summaries with links to key primary source material and off-Net references.

Internet Resources for International Economics & Business
http://dylee.keel.econ.ship.edu/econ/

Dr. Daniel Lee of the College of Business at Shippensburg University maintains this site, which lists Internet resources related to economics and business in general, references, and specific international business topics such as international development.

North American Free Trade Association (NAFTA)
http://www.nafta-sec-alena.org

NAFTA's stated objective is "to provide accurate and timely information to U.S. exporters experiencing market access barriers in Canada or Mexico."

Sales & Marketing Executive International (SME)
http://www.smei.org

Visit this home page of the worldwide association SME. Through this "Digital Resource Mall" you can access research and useful articles on sales and management. You can even listen in as marketing leaders discuss their latest strategies and ideas.

STAT-USA
http://www.stat-usa.gov/stat-usa.html

A service of the U.S. Department of Commerce, this essential site presents daily economic news; a myriad of links to databases, statistical releases, and selected publications; and general information on export and international trade as well as business leads and procurement opportunities.

World Trade Centers Association (WTCA)
http://www.wtca.org

WTCA On-Line presents this site as a news and information service. Members can access the *Dun & Bradstreet Exporters' Encyclopedia* and other valuable sources, and guests to the site can also gain entry to interesting trade-related information.

UNIT 1: Overview of International Business

CIA—The War on Terrorism
http://www.cia.gov/terrorism/

This site is created by the CIA covering news and events inside the intelligence community in the War on Terror. It offers a list of lectures and addresses, plus testimony on terrorism.

America's War Against Terrorism
http://www.lib.umich.edu/govdocs/usterror.html

The University of Michigan created this Web page to gather links and resources covering all aspects of the attacks of September 11, 2001.

UNIT 2: International Institutions and Organizations

Institute of International Bankers (IBB)
http://www.iib.org

Examine this site for information on the Institute of International Bankers, IBB events, and publications in order to become familiar with trends in international banking. The site also features regulatory compliance issues relating to the Year 2000 date change.

International Labour Organization (ILO)
http://www.ilo.org

ILO's home page leads to links that describe the goals of the organization and summarizes international labor standards and human rights. The site's official UN Web site locator can point you to many other useful resources.

Lex Mercatoria: International Trade Law Monitor
http:///lexmercatoria.net

Access a number of resources related to international trade from this site, including data on the European Union and the International Monetary Fund. Among its many links, it addresses such topics as Principles of International Commercial Contracts and UN Arbitration Laws.

Resources for Economists on the Internet
http://rfe.org

This site and its links are essential reading for those interested in learning about the Organization for Economic Cooperation and Development, the World Bank, the International Monetary Fund, and other important international organizations.

WashLaw
http://www.washlaw.edu

This site from the Washburn University School of Law Library Reference Desk can direct you to primary documents related to GATT and other information about the agreement. It also reproduces world constitutions and the text of NAFTA and other major treaties.

UNIT 3: Environmental Factors and International Business

Chambers of Commerce World Network
http://www.worldchambers.com/

This site of the World Chamber Network and Industry describes itself as "the world's first, oldest, and largest business network." Access a global index of Chambers of Commerce & Industry and Chambers for International Business, as well as information on "Strategic Alliance Partners" such as G-7.

India Finance and Investment Guide
http://finance.indiamart.com/

This site is a guide to investing in India, one of the largest markets in the world. It discusses taxation, organizations, capital market investment, and other topics.

Internet References

Foreign Direct Investment Is on the Rise Around the World
http://www.neweconomyindex.org/section1_page04.html

FDI data are a clear indicator of the trend toward globalization, as this report demonstrates.

International Economic Law Web Site
http://www.law.georgetown.edu/iiel/

This site of the International Economic Law Group of the American Society of International Law contains valuable research tools and links to Web resources regarding international law.

United States Trade Representative (USTR)
http://www.ustr.gov

The home page of the U.S. Trade Representative provides links to many other U.S. government resources of value to those interested in international business. It notes important trade-related speeches and agreements and describes the mission of the USTR.

WWW Virtual Library Demography & Population Studies
http://demography.anu.edu.au/VirtualLibrary

Through this Internet guide to demography and population studies, learn about leading information facilities of value and/or significance to researchers in the field of demography. The site is provided by the Australian National University.

UNIT 4: International Business Operations

The Development Gateway
http://www.developmentgateway.org/

The Development Gateway is an interactive portal for information and knowledge sharing on sustainable development and poverty reduction around the world. It includes analysis of business opportunities.

Harvard Business School
http://www.hbs.edu

Harvard Business School's Web site provides useful links to library and research resources, to the *Harvard Business Review,* and to information regarding executive education as well as other topics.

International Business Resources on the WWW
http://globaledge.msu.edu/ibrd/ibrd.asp

Michigan State University's Center for International Business Education and Research provides this site that allows a keyword search and points you to a great deal of trade information and leads, government resources, and related periodicals. It also provides general and specific country and regional information.

UNIT 5: International Business and the Future

The Economic Times
http.//www.The economic times

An online publication focusing on business in India

International Business Times
http.//www.ibtimes.com

"The mission of the International Business Times is to empower readers by bringing clarity and simplicity to global markets."

Private Sector Development Blog of the World Bank
http.//www.psdblog.worldbank.org

"The private sector development blog gathers together news, resources and ideas about the role of private enterprise in fighting poverty. The blog is informal and represents the opinions of the bloggers, not the World Bank."

Outsourcing Center
http.//www.outsourcing center.com

An internet portal on methods for creating competitive advantages. The Outsourcing Center is part of the Everest Group.

UNIT 1

Overview of International Business

Unit Selections

Key Points to Consider

- The world is growing smaller. How do you think this will affect you and your career?

- Do you think the power and importance of the United States will increase or decrease in the coming century?

- What are the challenges the global economy will face in the coming century?

- Are multinational corporations necessarily tied to their home countries to be successful?

- What has been the historic role of foreign aid and how has it been applied?

Student Web Site
www.mhcls.com/online

Internet References
CIA—The War on Terrorism
   http://www.cia.gov/terrorism/
America's War Against Terrorism
   http://www.lib.umich.edu/govdocs/usterror.html

Sixty years ago, at the end of World War II, the U.S. economy stood preeminent in the world. The economies of Europe had been destroyed in the War and Japan was in ruins. Only the United States and the rest of North America had remained essentially untouched by the devastation. As the initial years of the 1950's and 1960's rolled by, the great colonial empires of the European powers eventually disintegrated, leaving the United States and the Soviet Union as the surviving superpowers on the military and political—if not the economic—scene, and eventually, even the Soviet Union collapsed under the weight of its own limitations, corruption, and competition from the United States and its allies. As a result, one would think that the success of American capitalism and democracy over the rest of the competing ideologies of socialism, communism, totalitarianism, and fascism would have put the United States in a position of unchallengeable strength in the world, and that a new "World Order," led by the United States would greet the dawning of the twenty-first century. Unfortunately, however, that has shown to be far from the case.

The prerequisites that led to the eventual success of the United States over the Soviet Union also laid the foundation for the challenges that would confront the United States after the end of the Soviet era. In order to defeat communism and the Soviet Union without starting a World War III, the United States had to engage the Soviets in what became known as the Cold War. The Cold War was not a military conflict. More importantly, it was preventing a military conflict, especially in Europe. Therefore, while military preparedness was certainly a major portion of the Cold War, and some conflicts, such as those in Korea and Viet Nam, did arise, the conflict was primarily fought on political and economic grounds.

From a political perspective, the United States encouraged democracy in those areas where it could, and tolerated and supported friendly tyrants where the alternatives were worse. Today, that policy has come back to haunt the United States in places like Iran and most of the Middle East, as well as through organizations like Al Qaeda.

From an economic perspective, the United States successfully sought to develop the economy of those countries that were aligned with it after World War II against the Soviet Bloc. Programs such as the Marshall Plan were essential in the reconstruction of Europe after the war. These programs of foreign aid helped to reestablish these nations and their economies on a sound economic footing so as to encourage trade and economic development. If anything, these programs were often far more successful than their original planners could have ever hoped, that by the 1960's, Europe and Japan were well on their way to economic prosperity and offering competitive products and services to those made in the United States.

Starting in the 1970's, the industrial economies were faced with the first gas crisis, which was one of the first real shocks to American domination after World War II (the other being the end of the gold standard in 1968 and the beginning of floating currency exchange rates). Americans began to realize that their fate was tied to more than what went on inside their own borders. They started to understand that a group of countries called O. P. E. C. (Organization of Petroleum Exporting Countries) could have an immediate and painful impact on their lives. And there was really very little the United States, with all its military, political and economic might, could do about it. Then it happened again, a second time.

At the same time, technology was advancing. Computers were getting smaller, faster and easier to use. The era of the Internet had started, although nobody at that time really understood what it was or its potential, and where it could take us.

Under the pressure of the United States and its allies, as well as a result of its own internal weaknesses, the Soviet Union collapsed, allow-

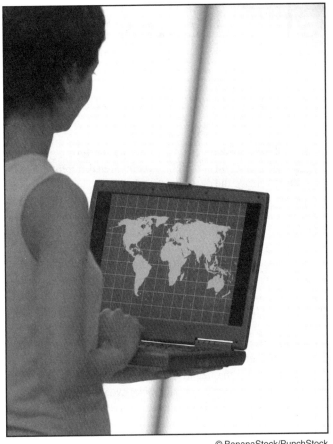

ing the nations of Eastern Europe to become part of Europe and no longer a captive of the Soviet state. In addition, Russia herself started to open to the West. China too opened to the West, which began a period of economic, if not political reform. And so did India, which started to reform its repressive socialist attitudes toward business, and allow the natural energy of the Indian people to blossom into some of the more productive and fastest growing enterprises in the world. These countries, as well as others, are entering the global scene to participate and compete.

Globalization has certainly changed over the years. It has meant different things to people in developed countries and different things to people in developing countries. Generally speaking, people all over the world, with a few exceptions, are better off than their grandparents were fifty years ago. Because of better health care, and organizations like the World Health Organization and the Center for Disease Control, they live longer and healthier lives; and the drugs and other medical techniques that have been developed over the past half century, and improved agriculture has led to fewer people starving. Hunger, today, is usually caused by political, criminal, or military reasons—not by lack of food.

One article, "Trading Places" by Peter Drucker, takes a look at how things are likely to be in the future. Drucker has some ideas on how those changes will take place and why. The article represents a possible road map for the future and attempts to analyze how globalization has changed, and how it will change the lives of every human being on the planet, something which might take time, but is bound to happen.

Globalization and Its Contents

Peter Marber

Ask ten different people to define the term "globalization" and you are likely to receive ten different answers. For many, the meaning of globalization has been shaped largely by media coverage of an angry opposition: from right-wing nationalist xenophobes and left-wing labor leaders who fear rampant economic competition from low-wage countries to social activists who see a conspiracy on the part of multinational corporations to seek profits no matter what the cost to local cultures and economic equality to environmentalists who believe the earth is being systematically ravaged by capitalism run amok. "Globalization"—as if it were a machine that could be turned off—has been presented as fundamentally flawed and dangerous. But "globalization" is a term that encompasses all cross-border interactions, whether economic, political, or cultural. And behind the negative headlines lies a story of human progress and promise that should make even the most pessimistic analysts view globalization in an entirely different light.

Two decades ago, globalization was hardly discussed. At the time, less than 15 percent of the world's population participated in true global trade. Pessimism colored discussions of the Third World, of "lesser developed" or "backward" countries. Pawns in the Cold War's global chess game, these countries conjured images of famine, overpopulation, military dictatorship, and general chaos. At the time, the prospect of the Soviet Union or Communist China integrating economically with the West, or of strongman regimes in Latin America or Asia abandoning central planning, seemed farfetched. The possibility of these countries making meaningful socioeconomic progress and attaining Western standards of living appeared utterly unrealistic. Yet the forces of globalization were already at work.

On average, people are living twice as long as they did a century ago. Moreover, the world's aggregate material infrastructure and productive capabilities are hundreds—if not thousands—of times greater than they were a hundred years ago.[1] Much of this acceleration has occurred since 1950, with a powerful upsurge in the last 25 years. No matter how one measures wealth—whether by means of economic, bio-social, or financial indicators—there have been gains in virtually every meaningful aspect of life in the last two generations, and the trend should continue upward at least through the middle of the twenty-first century.

Most people are living longer, healthier, fuller lives. This is most evident in poor parts of the world. For example, since 1950, life expectancy in emerging markets (countries with less than one-third the per capita income of the United States, or nearly 85 percent of the world's population) has increased by more than 50 percent, reaching levels the West enjoyed only two generations ago. These longevity gains are linked to lower infant mortality, better nutrition (including an 85 percent increase in daily caloric intake), improved sanitation, immunizations, and other public health advances.

Literacy rates in developing countries have also risen dramatically in the last 50 years. In 1950, only a third of the people in Eastern Europe and in parts of Latin living in these countries (roughly 800 million) could read or write; today nearly two-thirds—more than 3.2 billion people—are literate. And while it took the United States and Great Britain more than 120 years to increase average formal education from 2 years in the early nineteenth century to 12 years by the mid-twentieth century, some fast-growing developing countries, like South Korea, have accomplished this feat in fewer than 40 years.

The world now has a far more educated population with greater intellectual capacity than at any other time in history. This is particularly clear in much of Asia, where mass public education has allowed billions of people to increase their productivity and integrate in the global economy as workers and consumers. Similar trends can be seen in Eastern Europe and in parts of Latin America. This increase in human capital has led to historic highs in economic output and financial assets per capita (see chart).

During the twentieth century, economic output in the United States and other West European countries often doubled in less than 30 years, and Japan's postwar economy doubled in less than 16 years. In recent decades, developing country economies have surged so quickly that some—like South Korea in the 1960s and 1970s, or China in recent years—have often doubled productive output in just 7 to 10 years.

We often forget that poverty was the human living standard for most of recorded history. Until approximately two hundred years ago, virtually everyone lived at a subsistence level. As the economist John Maynard Keynes wrote in 1931 in *Essays in Persuasion*: "From the earliest times of which we have record—back, say, to two thousand years before Christ—down to the beginning of the eighteenth century, there was no very great change in the standard life of the average man living in civilized centers of the earth. Ups and downs certainly. Visitation

Measured Global Progress, 1950-2050E			
	1950	2000	2050
Global Output, Per Capita ($)	586	6,666	15,155
Global Financial Market			
Capitalization, Per Capita ($)	158	13,333	75,000
Percent of Global GDP			
Emerging Markets	5	50	55
Industrial Countries	95	75	45
Life Expectancy (years)			
Emerging Markets	41	64	76
Industrial Countries	65	77	82
Daily Caloric Intake			
Emerging Markets	1200	2600	3000
Industrial Countries	2200	3100	3200
Infant Mortality (per 1000)			
Emerging Markets	140	65	10
Industrial Countries	30	8	4
Literacy Rate (per 100)			
Emerging Markets	33	64	90
Industrial Countries	95	98	99

Sources: Bloomberg, World Bank, United Nations, and author's estimates.
Output and financial market capitalization figures are inflation-adjusted.

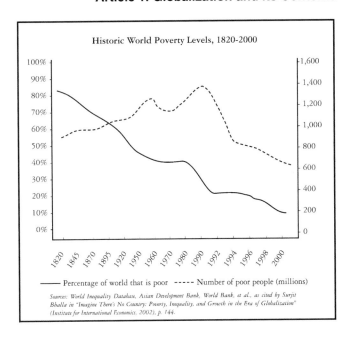

Historic World Poverty Levels, 1820-2000

—— Percentage of world that is poor ----- Number of poor people (millions)

Sources: World Inequality Database, Asian Development Bank, World Bank, et al., as cited by Surjit Bhalla in "Imagine There's No Country: Poverty, Inequality, and Growth in the Era of Globalization" (Institute for International Economics, 2002), p. 144.

of plague, famine, and war. Golden intervals. But no progressive violent change. This slow rate of progress was due to two reasons—to the remarkable absence of technical improvements and the failure of capital to accumulate." Beginning in the early nineteenth century, this picture began to change. The proportion of the world's population living in poverty declined from over 80 percent in 1820 to under 15 percent in 2000; moreover, the actual number of people living in poverty over that period declined, even as the world's population exploded from something over 1 billion to more than 6 billion.

The application of mass production technology, together with excess capital (or "profit") and a free market technologies—is at the root of our modern prosperity. Upon further examination, one can see the virtuous cycle that connects human progress, technology, and globalization. Let's take two countries, one being richer than the other. The richer country has a more educated workforce, with nearly 99 percent literacy, while the poor one has only 50 percent literacy. Due to its less educated workforce and lack of infrastructure, the poor country might only be able to participate in global trade through exporting commodities—let's say fruits and vegetables. The rich country grows fruits and vegetables as well, but it also produces clothing and light manufactured goods such as radios. In the classic Ricardo/Smith models of comparative advantage and free trade, the wealthy country should utilize its skilled workforce to produce more clothing and radios for domestic consumption and export, and it should import more fruits and vegetables from the poorer country. This would, in turn, provide the poorer country with capital to improve education and infrastructure.

As this trade pattern creates profits for both countries, human capital can be mutually developed. Eventually, the poorer country (by boosting literacy and education) should develop its own

ability to produce clothes and radios. Over time, the wealthier country—having reinvested profits in higher education, research and development, etc.—will begin to produce higher-tech goods rather than clothes and radios, perhaps televisions and cars. At this stage, the wealthy country would export its cars and televisions, and import clothes and radios. In turn, the poorer country begins to import agricultural products from an even poorer third country while exporting clothing and radios to both countries. As participating countries make progress through crossborder trade and the continuous upgrading of their workforces, it follows naturally that patterns of labor and employment will evolve over time.

It is sometimes argued that free trade harms economic growth and the poor by causing job losses, particularly in wealthier countries. But trade liberalization works by encouraging a shift of labor and capital from import-competitive sectors to more dynamic export industries where comparative advantages lie. Therefore, the unemployment caused by open trade can be expected to be temporary, being offset by job creation in other export sectors (which often requires some transition time). Output losses due to this transitional unemployment should also be small relative to long-term gains in national income (and lower prices) due to production increases elsewhere. In other words, these short-term labor adjustments should be seen as lesser evils when compared to the costs of continued economic stagnation and isolation that occur without open trade.

The shifting U.S. labor pattern from low-wage agricultural labor to manufacturing to higher-paid office and service employment during the nineteenth and twentieth centuries resulted largely from trade. Similar shifts are now seen all over the globe. In the 1950 and 1960s, the United States imported electronics from Japan, and exported cars and other heavy goods. In the 1970s, we began importing small cars from Japan. In the last 30-odd years, Japan has seen its dominance in electronics and economy cars wither amid competition from China and South Korea. But Japan has made a successful push upmarket into larger, pricier luxury cars and sport utility vehicles. While these markets were shifting over the last three decades, jobs were lost, gained, and relocated in the United States and abroad. But living standards in America, Japan, South Korea, and China have all improved dramatically over that same time.

Working Less, Producing More

There is a growing consensus that international trade has a positive effect on per capita income. A 1999 World Bank study estimates that increasing the ratio of trade to national output by one percentage point raises per capita income by between 0.5 and 2 percent.[2] But the most dramatic illustration of how greater prosperity is spread through globalization is by our increased purchasing power. Ultimately, what determines wealth is the ability to work less and consume more. The time needed for an average American worker to earn the purchase price of various goods and services decreased dramatically during the twentieth century.

In 1919, it took an American worker 30 minutes of labor to earn enough to buy a pound of ground beef. This number dropped to 23 minutes in 1950, 11 minutes in 1975, and 6 minutes in 1997.[3] But this downward trend is even more impressive with respect to manufactured goods and services. For example, in 1895 the list price for an American-made bicycle in the Montgomery Ward catalog was $65. Today an American can buy a Chinese-manufactured 21-speed bike at any mass retailer for the same amount. But an average American needed to work some 260 hours in 1895 to earn the purchase price of the old bicycle, whereas it would take the average worker less than 5 hours to earn enough to buy today's bicycle.[4] In our own lifetimes, the costs of goods and services, everything from televisions to household appliances to telephone calls, computers, and airplane travel have plummeted relative to income—and not just in the United States.

Around the world, both basic commodities and items once considered luxury items now fill store shelves and pantries as increasing output and income have lifted most people above the subsistence level. The 50 most populous countries average more than 95 televisions per 100 households. In the 25 wealthiest countries, there are approximately 450 automobiles per 1,000 people, and China is now among the fastest-growing markets for cars, clothes, computers, cellular phones, and hundreds of household items.

This deflationary effect has also led to a radically improved quality of life. In 1870, the average American worker labored 3,069 hours per year—or six 10-hour days a week. By 1950, the average hours worked had fallen to 2,075.[5] Today, that number is closer to 1,730.[6] This pattern has been repeated around the world. In 1960, the average Japanese worker toiled 2,432 hours a year over a six-day work week; by 1988, this figure had dropped to 2,111 hours a year, and by 2000 it was down to 1,878 hours. There were even more dramatic reductions in European countries like France, Germany, and Sweden.[7] The Nobel Prize–winning economist Robert William Fogel estimates that the average American's lifetime working hours will have declined from 182,100 in 1880 to a projected 75,900 by 2040, with similar trends in other wealthy industrial countries. Fogel notes that while work took up 60 percent of an American's life in 1870, by 1990 it only took up about 30 percent. Between 1880 and 1990, the average American's cumulative lifetime leisure time swelled from 48,300 hours to a remarkable 246,000 hours, or 22 years.[8] This is a pattern of improvement in the human condition that we first saw in the industrialized West and then in Japan, and which is now spreading to dozens of developing countries that are integrating into the global economy.

A Thriving Middle Class

The recent surge in progress is certainly tied to technological advances, but it is also due to the adoption of free-market practices. Cross-border trade has ballooned by a factor of 20 over the past 50 years and now accounts for more than 20 percent of global output, according to the World Bank. Indeed, trade—which grew twice as fast as global output in the 1990s—will continue to drive economic specialization and growth. The global economy is becoming more sophisticated, segmented, and diversified.

The adoption of free-market practices has gone hand-in-hand with greater political freedoms. At the beginning of the twentieth century, less than 10 percent of the world's population had the right to vote, according to Freedom House. By 1950, approximately 35 percent of the global population in less than a quarter of the world's countries enjoyed this right. By 2000, more than two-thirds of the world's countries had implemented universal suffrage.

These symbiotic developments have helped completely recompose the world's "middle class"—those with a per capita income of roughly $10–40 per day, adjusted for inflation and purchasing power parity (PPP). According to the United Nations, in 1960 two-thirds of the world's middle-class citizens lived in the industrialized world—that is, in the United States, Canada, Western Europe, Japan, and Australia. By 1980, over 60 percent of the global middle class lived in developing countries, and by 2000 this number had reached a remarkable 83 percent. It is anticipated that India and China combined could easily produce middle classes of 400–800 million people over the next two generations—roughly the size of the current middle-class populations of the United States, Western Europe, and Japan combined.

A thriving middle class is an important component of economic, political, and social stability that comes with globalization. According to the World Bank, a higher share of income for the middle class is associated with increased national income and growth, improved health, better infrastructure, sounder economic policies, less instability and civil war, and more social modernization and democracy. There are numerous studies that also suggest that increasing wealth promotes gender equality, greater voter participation, income equality, greater concern for the environment, and more transparency in the business and political arenas, all of the quality-of-life issues that concern globalization skeptics.[9]

Measuring Inequality

Even if they concede that the world is wealthier overall, many critics of globalization cite the dangers of growing income inequality. Although the science of analyzing such long-term trends is far from perfect, there are indicators that point toward measurable progress even on this front.[10] The preoccupation with income or gross national product (GNP) as the sole measure of progress is unfortunate. Income is one measure of wealth, but not the only one. And income comparisons do not always reflect informal or unreported economic activity, which tends to be more prevalent in poor countries.

Many social scientists use Gini coefficients (a measure of income dispersion between and within countries) to bolster their arguments about inequality. The lower the Gini figure (between one and zero), the more equal income distribution tends to be. Unfortunately, the Gini index does not take into consideration purchasing power parity, the age dispersion of a population, and other variables that affect the overall picture. When adjusted for PPP, the Gini index for world income distribution decreased from 0.59 to 0.52 between 1965 and 1997, an improvement of nearly 12 percent.[11] Poverty rate trends are also cited by condemners of globalization, but this approach is problematic as well. The impoverished are often defined as those who earn 50 percent less than the median income in a country. But because 50 percent of median American income is very different than 50 percent of median income in Bangladesh, poverty rates may not tell us as much about human progress as we might think.

We can better gauge human progress by examining broader trends in bio-social development than income-centered analyses. A yardstick like the United Nations Development Program's human development index (HDI), for example, which looks at not only income but also life expectancy and education (including literacy and school enrollment), with the higher numbers denoting greater development, provides a clearer picture of global well-being:

	1960	1993	2002
OECD Countries	.80	.91	.91
Developing Countries	.26	.56	.70
Least Developed Countries	.16	.33	.44

What these numbers show is not only that human development has improved overall but that differentials between rich and poor countries are closing. While the HDI figure for wealthy OECD countries in 1960 was five times greater than that for the least developed countries (and three times higher than that for developing countries), those gaps were nearly halved by 1993. And in the most intense period of recent globalization, from 1993 to 2002, these gaps closed even further.

This by no means negates the reality of poverty in many parts of the world. There are still an estimated 1 billion people living in "abject" poverty today, but the World Bank estimates that this number should decline by 50 percent by 2015, if current growth trends hold.

Potholes on the Road to Globalization

The great gains and momentum of the last 25 years should not be seen as sufficient or irreversible. There are still formidable impediments to continued progress, the four most serious being protectionism, armed conflict, environmental stress, and demographic imbalances.

- *Protectionism.* One of the responses to globalization has been the attempt to pull inward, to save traditional industries and cultures, and to expel foreigners and foreign ideas. In India, consumers have protested against McDonald's restaurants for violating Hindu dietary laws. In France, angry farmers have uprooted genetically engineered crops, saying they threatened domestic control over food production.

  Possibly the most harmful protectionism today relates to global agricultural policy. Farming subsidies in wealthy countries now total approximately $350 billion a year, or seven times the $50 billion that such countries provide annually in foreign aid to the developing world.[12] Global trade policies may exclude developing countries from $700 billion in commerce annually, denying them not only needed foreign currency but also the commercial and social interaction necessary to bio-social progress.[13]

  Protectionism in the form of tariffs, rigid labor and immigration laws, capital controls, and regressive tax structures also should be resisted. Wealthy countries should not cling to old industries like apparel or agriculture; it is far more profitable, economically and socially, to look forward and outward, to focus on growing higher-skill industries—like aviation, pharmaceuticals, and entertainment—and to embrace new markets. In turn, poorer countries have generally grown richer through economic interaction with foreign countries, by refocusing nationalistic energies and policies toward future-oriented, internationally engaged commercial activity. The late-twentieth-century march away from closed economies has improved the lives of billions of people. To bow to nationalistic calls for protectionist policies could slow and even reverse this momentum.

- *Armed Conflict.* Countries cannot compete economically, cultivate human capital, or develop financial markets in the midst of armed conflict. According to the Stockholm International Peace Research Institute, there were 57 major armed conflicts in 45 different locations between 1990 and 2001; all but 3 of these were civil wars, which inflict deep economic damage and stunt development. In addition to ongoing civil wars, there are a number of potential cross-border powder kegs (beyond the recent U.S. invasions of Afghanistan and Iraq): Kashmir, over which nuclearized India and Pakistan have been at odds for decades; Taiwan, over which China claims sovereignty; Israel and its Arab neighbors; and the Korean peninsula. The economic, political, and cultural uncertainty surrounding these areas of potential conflict restricts the flow of capital, and paralyzes businesses, investors, and consumers.

To the extent that defense budgets continue to grow in tandem with global tensions and economic resources are used for military purposes, there will be fewer resources devoted to the development of human capital and economic competitiveness.

• *Environmental Stress.* There is no getting around the fact that the success of globalization is underscored by dramatic increases in consumption. With increased consumption comes environmental degradation. Damage to the environment, current or projected, can impede economic progress in many ways. Climatic changes attributed to greenhouse gas emissions and pressure on natural resources are serious problems. Resource scarcity is only one issue we will have to confront as 2–3 billion more people consume like middle-class Americans over the next 50 years. In the face of these environmental dangers, a host of new regulations may be enacted locally or globally. Increased environmental awareness among wealthier populations may lead to domestic policies that will raise costs to businesses and consumers, which in turn could curb economic expansion.

One step in the right direction would be increased public spending on alternative and renewable energy sources in the wealthier countries. The world is clearly underpowered, and the need for diversified energy grows as we speak. The benefits of a burgeoning alternative energy sector could be multiplicative. First, it might spur new economic growth areas for employment in rich countries, supplying them with potential technologies for export while reducing their reliance on foreign oil. Second, it might encourage developing countries that are over-reliant on oil exports to develop and modernize their economies and societies. Third, it would allow developing countries to build their infrastructures with a more diversified, sustainable energy approach than the first wave of industrializing countries.

• *Demographic Imbalances.* There are sharply contrasting population trends around the globe: developing nations are experiencing a youth bulge while industrialized countries are aging rapidly. This divergence may present a variety of challenges to globalization.

In poorer developing countries, the youth bulge equals economic opportunity but is also potentially disruptive. In more than 50 of these countries, 50 percent of the population is under the age of 25. In some cases, half the population is under 20, and in extreme cases, even younger. These developing nations are also among the poorest, the fastest urbanizing, and the least politically or institutionally developed, making them susceptible to violence and instability. The large number of unemployed, disenfranchised young men in these countries may explain the growth of Islamic fundamentalism and the existence of pillaging bands of armed warriors in sub-Saharan Africa. Large young populations may also lead to unregulated, unlawful migration that can create long-lasting instability.[14]

While the youth bulge can cause problems that derail global progress, the richest countries may fall victim to their past success. Prosperity, while providing more lifestyle choices and wellness, also results in lower birth rates and increasing longevity which could dampen long-term economic demand. The aging of wealthier populations also stresses public pension schemes that were conceived under different demographic circumstances—eras of robust population and consumption growth. In economies where populations are stagnant or shrinking, the specter of lengthy "aging recessions"—characterized by vicious cycles of falling demand for consumer goods (and deflation), collapsing asset values (including real estate), shrinking corporate profits, deteriorating household and financial institution balance sheets, weakening currencies, and soaring budget pressures—looms large.

Preparing for the Best, Not the Worst

Globalization and its major engines—burgeoning human capital, freer markets, increasing cross-border interaction—have created a new world order that has incited passionate debate, pro and con. However, both sides have more in common than one might imagine.

First, if human capital is a key component of improved living standards, it is arguable that increased spending on education should become a priority in rich and poor countries alike. Wealthier nations continually need to boost productivity and comparative advantage, while poorer countries need to develop skills to compete in the global economy. By adding to the numbers of the educated, there will be a wider base of workers and consumers to contribute to the virtuous cycle of prosperity we have witnessed in the last 50 years.

Second, boosting human capital in poor countries through increased financial and technical aid should also help broaden the marketplace in terms of workers and consumers. Appropriating an extra $100 billion in aid each year—a drop in the bucket for the 20 richest countries—could help some 2 billion people overcome their daily struggles with malnutrition, HIV/AIDS, malaria, and dirty drinking water, thereby increasing the number of healthy, productive workers and consumers.

Third, reorienting wealthy country subsidies away from low-tech areas like agriculture and mining toward higher-tech industries (including alternative energy development) would accelerate comparative advantage and stimulate greater trade. With wealthy countries focusing on higher-value-added industries for domestic consumption and export, poorer countries could pick up the slack in lower-skilled sectors where they can begin to engage the global economy. Over time, the poorer countries would become larger markets for goods and services. This, along with the two attitudinal and policy shifts mentioned above, could have a positive effect on the well-being of the world's population.

Even with its positive trends, globalization is not a perfect process. It is not a panacea for every problem for every person at every moment in time. It is a messy, complicated web of interdependent relationships, some long-term, some fleeting. But globalization is too often cited as creating a variety of human miseries such as sweatshop labor, civil war, and corruption—as if such ills never existed before 1980. Poverty is more at the root of such miseries. That is why the wholesale rejection of globalization—without acknowledging its tremendously positive record in alleviating poverty—is shortsighted. Indeed, one could see how simply embracing globalization as inevitable—rather than debating its definition and purported shortcomings—could potentially foster more cross-border coordination on a variety of issues such as drug trafficking, ethnic cleansing, illegal immigration, famine, epidemic disease, environmental stress, and terrorism.

Emotion and confusion have unfortunately tainted the globalization debate both in the United States and abroad, and the focus is often on anecdotal successes or failures. Anxieties and economies may ebb and flow in the short run, but the responsibility to manage these progressive evolutions and revolutions—with worldwide human prosperity as the goal—should be our consistent aim in both government and the marketplace.

Notes

Many of the issues and arguments presented here in abbreviated form are examined at greater length in my book, *Money Changes Everything: How Global Prosperity Is Reshaping Out Needs, Values, and Lifestyles* (Upper Saddle River, NJ: FT Prentice Hall, 2003).

1. See Angus Maddison, *Monitoring the World Economy: 1820–1992* (Paris: OECD, 1995).

2. Jeffrey A. Frankel and David Romer, "Does Trade Growth Cause Growth?" *American Economic Review,* vol. 89 (June 1999), pp. 379–99.

3. W. Michael Cox and Richard Alm, *Time Well Spent: The Declining Real Cost of Living in America*, annual report (Dallas: Federal Reserve Bank, 1997), p. 4.

4. Based on average U.S. industrial wages of approximately $15 per hour in 2000.

5. W. Michael Cox and Richard Alm, *These Are the Good Old Days: A Report on US Living Standards*, annual report (Dallas: Federal Reserve Bank, 1994), p. 7.

6. Robert William Fogel, *The Fourth Great Awakening and the Future of Egalitarianism* (Chicago: University of Chicago Press, 2000), p. 185.

7. Ibid., p. 186.

8. Ibid., pp. 184–90.

9. See Marber, *Money Changes Everything*. For more on specific shifts in attitudes and values relative to economic development, the University of Michigan's Ron Inglehart's seminal Human Values Surveys are an invaluable resource.

10. For a balanced study of this subject, see Arne Mechoir, Kjetil Telle, and Henrik Wiig, *Globalisation and Inequality: World Income and Living Standards, 1960–1998,* Norwegian Ministry of Foreign Affairs, Report 6B:2000, October 2000, available at http:// odin.dep.no/archive/udvedlegg/01/01/rev_016.pdf.

11. Ibid., p. 14.

12. James Wolfensohn, "How Rich Countries Keep the Rest of the World in Poverty," *Irish Independent*, September 30, 2002.

13. Ibid.

14. See Michael Teitelbaum, "Are North/South Population Growth Differentials a Prelude to Conflict?" at http://www.csis.org/gai/Graying/speeches/teitelbaum.html.

PETER MARBER is an author, professional money manager, and faculty member at the School of International and Public Affairs at Columbia University.

From *World Policy Journal,* Winter 2004/2005, pp. 29–30, 33–37. Copyright © 2005 by World Policy Institute. Reprinted by permission.

The Leading Economic Organizations at the Beginning of the 21st Century

The largest measured organizations at the beginning of the 21st century are presented which also includes a discussion of the implications of what it means to be counted in this list. Countries, trade associations, and corporations are included. An interesting aspect of the list is the number of corporations is greater than the number of governments. The consequences of this, as well as other observations, are discussed.

FRED MAIDMENT
Western Connecticut State University

Introduction

As the new century begins, it would be useful to look at the major economic organizations at the beginning of the century. The term "economic organization" is used in the broadest possible meaning. It denotes any economic unit that is measured in monetary terms. This would include countries, trade blocs, companies, or national governments.

This information provides a basis for comparison as the century evolves. It will be especially useful in the future to determine how the world economy will change over the next ten, fifty, or even one-hundred years. Certainly, there are names on this list that will have been forgotten in the next hundred years and many names will appear in a hundred years that do not exist today!

It is obvious from the list that:

1. economic activity is concentrated in Europe, Japan and North America;
2. the United States is easily the largest national economy on the planet;
3. corporations make up about one-third of the largest economic organizations on the list.

The various states of the United States have been excluded from the list because if these were included, many of them would be on it.

Importance of the List

Certainly the prior century was one of great change and technological advancement. The poles were conquered; the atom was split; and men walked on the Moon. The world is a much smaller place than it was in 1900, and many of the names that would have appeared on a similar list in 1900 are gone today. There is no British, German, French, or Japanese Empire. Wal-Mart and GM did not exist and some of the countries that are on the list, such as the Philippines, were colonies. 2000 is a different civilization than 1900.

A list of the top 101 measurable economic units at the start of the twenty-first century provides a snapshot of the major players in the global economy so that when the players change, as they will, it can be observed. Trends can be determined. For example, there are now more corporations on the list than there are governments, will this trend continue? Sales of many multinational corporations now rival or exceed the gross domestic product of some of the most populous nations on Earth (Statistical Abstract of the United States, 2001).

What the List Tells Us:

What this means to the world economy and the world's political, military and social circumstances is obvious. To say that there is imbalance in the economic wealth between the developed world and the rest of the world is a gross understatement. The developed world accounts for over eighty percent of the world's GDP, yet represents less than twenty percent of the world's population. The rest of the planet has to subsist on less than twenty percent of the economic production of the global economy.

Consequences of Unequal Distribution

This kind of economic depravation is certain to lead to cultural, social, and political problems. When a society does not have enough economic resources to ensure a reasonable food supply, everything else suffers because people are simply focused on the necessity of getting enough to eat. The basic human needs become paramount, and these societies become ripe for anyone who will promise to deliver them from this situation. Whether it is a military dictator, promising order; or a religious zealot, promising a return of God's kingdom; the people will be receptive to his message if he will promise to provide bread, restore order, and give people at least the promise, if not the reality, of a better life. The twentieth century is littered with these kinds of economic, social, and political disasters.

The Arab World:

There are many nations that are facing similar kinds of choices in the twenty-first century. The most obvious examples are in the Arab world where nearly all of the countries are ruled by some form of undemocratic ruler. This situation has been going on for years in spite of the fact that the western democracies have poured billions of dollars into many of these societies in oil payments. Since 9/11, it has become obvious that the problems in the Middle East are now the problems of the West, and particularly the United States. Organizations like al-Qaeda will continue to thrive in societies that offer little in the way of hope, opportunity or justice. Great wealth that has been transferred to these countries, but little of it has found its way to the average citizen. These societies lag behind the West technologically, economically, and in nearly every important measure of societal growth, except the birth rate.

Saudi Arabia is the world's largest source of oil, but the management of that wealth has not greatly benefited the average Saudi. GDP in Saudi Arabia rose from $156,486 in 1980 to $188,720 million in 2000, a 20.59 percent increase, while the population increased from 7.297 million in 1980 to 21.364 in 2000, or 192 percent. (International Marketing Data and Statistics, 2002). The Saudis have been an important source of funding for a fundamentalist form of Islam, which has been one of the major factors in anti-western, anti-US, developments. The Kingdom is an absolute monarchy where the people have no say in the affairs of the country. The royal family lives at a level of splendor unknown in the rest of the world, while rebellious young men are exported to other countries, where they sometimes fly large airplanes into tall buildings.

South Korea vs. North Korea:

At the end of the Korean War, the Korean economy was a disaster. The entire peninsula was devastated by the war and the people were starving. Fifty years after the armistice. South Korea is a democracy, having gone through a period of dictatorship, but has a constantly growing and evolving economy. In the 1990's the economy did suffer some setbacks, as many of the "Asian Tigers" did during that period of time, but South Korea, as is shown in Table 1, is now the world's twelfth largest national economy with a GDP of $457 billion in 2000.

The differences between South and North Korea are instructive, when determining the reasons why some societies prosper and other do not. Both nations started at virtually zero in 1953. No industry, no food, no infrastructure were in place in either country. Both populations were starving. Today, a dictator rules North Korea. The country cannot feed itself and millions of

people continue to starve. It is the most militarized nation on earth, with a standing army of approximately one million men and reserves to match. The only export the country has is military technology and now seems to be embarked on a program to develop weapons of mass destruction (Ratnesar, R. & Bradford, L., 2003).

Other Considerations:

There are other considerations that become obvious when reviewing the list. The first is the dominance by the American economy. A single country makes up almost 40 percent of the world's GDP. This GDP is produced by a population of just over 4 percent of the world's population (Statistical Abstract of the United States, 2001). While that population makes it the third largest country in the world, it is still relatively small. The other aspect is that the American economy is growing while the rest of the world is either stalled or in decline (Maidment, 2002). During the first several years of the millennium, economic growth in the US did slow and the country did enter a brief, mild recession. The recovery from that recession may not have been particularly strong, but compared to the rest of the world, the US economy is doing rather well.

The continued success of the American economy has formed the basis of continued success in other areas. While other societies and their leaders may privately complain about this American success, it would not be possible without a strong American economy. The American economy makes possible a military that spends as much as the next fifteen countries combined, and is the most sophisticated and educated in history as well as the best equipped, trained and dominant military in the world (Ferguson, Niall, 2003). American technological advancements, fueled by the American economy, make possible the ever increasing productivity of the American worker and the ever increasing dominance of American corporations in key industries for the coming century.

American prosperity continues to form the basis of a culture that is spread throughout the world through American movies, literature, music and television. American culture is so strong that in France, the government has seen fit to place limits on the number of American movies that can be shown in the French cinema (Slalter, Katharine, 1995).

Potential Problems for the US

US dominance in cultural, military and economic affairs can spell trouble for the US. During the Cold War, the old Soviet Union provided a balance to the power of the US. But, now that the Soviets are gone, the United States is a natural concern of other countries seeking their place in the sun and not wishing to be completely dominated by US interests. Even if American motives are friendly, the shear size of the American presence may serve to blot out the distinctiveness of various national cultures. America is so rich, militarily strong, and culturally dynamic that other societies may see themselves in danger of being subsumed by the American juggernaut. This would explain seemingly meaningless anti-American actions on the part of some people in these societies, even when it would appear that the US might be acting

Table 1 The Top 101 Economies in 2000

Rank	Name of Trade Body Corporation/Country Government	GDP/Sales Budget in Billions of US $	Percent of OECD (1) GDP	Rank	Name of Trade Body Corporation/Country Government	GDP/Sales Budget in Billions of US $	Percent of OECD (1) GDP
	World GDP (OECD)	25,228	100	51	Indonesia	153	.60
1	North American (NAFTA)	11,157	44.2	52	Daimler/Chrysler	150	.59
2	United States	9,896	39.2	53	Royal Dutch Petroleum	149	.59
3	Europe	8,720	34.5	54	BP	148	.58
4	Asia and Pacific (2)	8,364	33.1	55	General Electric	129	.51
5	European Union	7,837	32.0	56	Canada Govt Receipts	126	.49
6	Japan	4,750	18.8	57	Mitsubishi	126	.49
7	US Govt All Levels Receipts	3,272	12.9	58	South Africa	123	.48
8	US Fed. Govt Receipts	2,042	8.0	59	Finland	122	.48
9	Germany	1,873	7.4	60	Thailand	122	.48
10	South America & the Caribbean (3)	1,434	5.6	61	Toyota	121	.47
11	United Kingdom	1,414	5.6	62	Venezuela	120	.47
12	Africa and the Middle East (4)	1,394	5.5	63	Mitsui	118	.46
13	France	1,294	5.1	64	Brazil Govt Receipts	116	.45
14	US State and local Govt Receipts	1,230	4.8	65	Greece	112	.44
15	People's Republic of China	1,079	4.2	66	Citigroup	111	.43
16	Italy	1,074	4.2	67	Israel	110	.43
17	Japan Govt Receipts	927	3.6	68	Ihocho	109	.43
18	Canada	689	2.7	69	Spain Govt Receipts	106	.42
19	Brazil	595	2.3	70	Portugal	105	.41
20	Mexico	574	2.2	71	Total Fina	105	.41
21	Spain	559	2.2	72	Nippon T&T	103	.40
22	Germany Govt Receipts	528	2.0	73	Enron	100	.39
23	U.K. Govt Receipts	492	1.9	74	Ireland	94	.37
24	India	471	1.8	75	Egypt	94	.37
25	South Korea	457	1.8	76	South Korea Govt Receipts	93	.36
26	France Govt Receipts	456	1.8	77	Singapore	92	.36
27	Austrailasia	429	1.7	78	AXA	92	.36
28	Australia	392	1.5	79	Sumitomo	91	.36
29	Myanmar	390	1.5	80	Malaysia	89	.35
30	Netherlands	365	1.4	81	IBM	88	.34
31	Iran	307	1.2	82	Sweden Govt Receipts	86	.34
32	Taiwan	289	1.1	83	Belgium Govt Receipts	85	.33
33	Argentina	285	1.1	84	Marabeni	85	.33
34	Italy Govt Receipts	266	1.0	85	Columbia	81	.32
35	Russia	246	.97	86	Volkswagon	78	.30
36	Switzerland	241	.95	87	Australia Govt Receipts	77	.30
37	Belgium	227	.89	88	Hitachi	76	.30
38	Sweden	227	.89	89	Philippines	74	.29
39	Exxon/Mobil	210	.83	90	Siemans	74	.29
40	Turkey	200	.79	91	ING Group	71	.28
41	Wal-Mart	193	.76	92	Allianz	71	.28
42	Austria	190	.75	93	Chile	70	.27
43	General Motors	184	.72	94	Matsushita Electric	69	.27
44	Ford Motor Company	180	.71	95	E.ON	68	.26
45	Saudi Arabia	173	.68	96	Nippon Life	68	.26
46	Denmark	162	.64	97	Duetsche Bank	67	.26
47	Hong Kong	162	.64	98	SONY	66	.26
48	Norway	162	.64	99	AT&T	65	.25
49	China Govt Receipts	161	.63	100	Verizon	64	.25
50	Poland	158	.62	101	US Postal Service	64	.25

Notes:
(1) Organization for Economic Cooperation and Development
(2) Asia/Pacific Excludes: Afghanistan, Nauru, New Caledonia, North Korea, Tajikistan
(3) South America and the Caribbean excludes: Ecuador
(4) Africa and the Middle East excludes: Congo Democratic Republic, Eritrea, Iraq, Liberia, Reunion, Somalia

in their best interests. The example of the French limiting the exposure of American films in movie theaters is a case in point. A minor annoyance to the American film industry, French films do not have to compete with American products. Rather than producing better films that more Frenchmen will want to see, the French government has decided to limit the number of American films available to French audiences. This will probably lead to fewer good French films that fewer French filmgoers will want to see, leading to an ever declining industry.

There are, however, more important consequences to this dominance by the US. The recent activities at the United Nations concerning Iraq would be a case in point. Two allies of the US, France and Germany, lead the attempt to thwart the Security Council's 1441 resolution for Iraq to disarm. It became evident that these actions had much more to do with the United States than they had to do with Iraq. The governments of both countries recognized that even if the UN did not approve military action in the Gulf, the United States would disarm Iraq, militarily, if necessary. They would not have to participate, and a potentially dangerous situation would be eliminated with no cost to either of them. In fact, they may have seen themselves as benefiting from their attempt to thwart American aggression in Iraq. By establishing themselves as the new counter-balance to the American titan, currently being run by a "Texas cowboy", as many in the European press seem so fond of saying, they may be able to reestablish the bi-polar world that ceased to exist when the Soviet Union collapsed.

The problem is that both Germany and France are attempting to become great powers without the necessary resources: their economies are either stalled or in decline; their birth rates are not sufficient to replace the current population (Statistical Abstract of the United States, 2001); their spending on the military and military technology makes them at best a third rate military power; and they cannot even get the rest of Europe to agree with their policies (Asia-Africa Intelligence Wire, 2003). Until and unless these trends in European society are reversed, the likelihood of a Franco-German based European axis being able to compete in a meaningful way with the United States would seem to be remote.

Conclusion

The next hundred years will prove to be interesting. Will the term "Italy" or "Spain" become obsolete as a nation, simply denoting a province in a "United States of Europe" much the way a New York or a California denotes a state in the US? Will the presence of corporations continue to grow from roughly one-third of the world's largest economic units to half or perhaps more? How would that possibility change the relationship between corporations and nation states? No one knows what the future holds. But, to really understand whatever comes, it is necessary to know what is. Surely, the next 100 years will fulfill the ancient Chinese proverb that, "We live in interesting times!"

References

Asia-Africa Intelligence Wire, (2003) Portugal: Bulgaria to support operation against Iraq if inevitable. March 7

European Marketing Data and Statistics. 2002, Euromonitor, London Ferguson, Niall, (2003) Power (Think Again), Foreign Policy, January–February, P18

Global 500 by the Numbers, (2001) Fortune, New York, New York, Time, Inc., July 23, v144, i2, p143

International Marketing Data and Statistics, 2002, Euromonitor, London Maidment, F., (2002) Drifting Apart: American Perceptions of Europe After 9/11

Insights Into A Changing World. Ft. Worth, Texas, Franklin Publishing Company. December

Ratnesar, Romesh & Bradford, Laura, (2003) How dangerous is North Korea? Dictator Kim Jong Il is pushing the world toward a showdown over his nuclear-weapons program, Time, January 13, V161 i2 p22

Slalter, Katharine, (1995) Gual Goal: Infopiketoll: Multimedia restrictions are urged, Variety, January 23, V357 n12 p50

Statistical Abstract of the United States. 2001, United States Government Printing Office, Washington, DC

Trading Places

Peter F. Drucker

The new world economy is fundamentally different from that of the fifty years following World War II. The United States may well remain the political and military leader for decades to come. It is likely also to remain the world's richest and most productive national economy for a long time (though the European Union as a whole is both larger and more productive). But the U.S. economy is no longer the single dominant economy.

The emerging world economy is a pluralist one, with a substantial number of economic "blocs." Eventually there may be six or seven blocs, of which the U.S.-dominated NAFTA is likely to be only one, coexisting and competing with the European Union (EU), MERCOSUR in Latin America, ASEAN in the Far East, and nation-states that are blocs by themselves, China and India. These blocs are neither "free trade" nor "protectionist," but both at the same time.

Even more novel is that what is emerging is not one but *four* world economies: a world economy of information; of money; of multinationals (one no longer dominated by American enterprises); and a mercantilist world economy of goods, services and trade. These world economies overlap and interact with one another. But each is distinct with different members, a different scope, different values and different institutions. Let us examine each in turn.

The World Economy of Information

Information as a concept and a distinct category is an invention of the 18th century—of the newspaper in England and the encyclopedia in France. Within a century, information became global with the development of the modern postal system in the 1830s, followed almost immediately by the electric telegraph and the first computer language, the Morse Code. But unlike the newspaper and the encyclopedia, neither the postal service nor the telegraph made information public. On the contrary, they made it "privileged communication." "Public information" by contrast—newspapers, radio, television—ran one way only, from the publisher to the recipient. The editor rather than the reader decided what was "fit to print."

The Internet, in sharp contrast, makes information both universal and multidirectional rather than keeping it private or one-way. Everyone with a telephone and a personal computer has direct access to every other human being with a phone and a PC. It gives everyone practically limitless access to information. And it gives everyone the ability to create information at minimal cost, that is, to *create* his own website and become a "publisher."

In the long run, the most important implication is probably the impact of information on mentality and awareness. It creates new affinities and new communities. The woman student in Shanghai who taps into the Internet remains Chinese, but she sees herself at the same time as a member of a worldwide, non-national "information society."

Businesses and professional groups such as lawyers and doctors have, of course, had access all along to worldwide information in their own field. But the Internet gives such access to the ultimate customer. In the United States at least (but apparently also in Japan and Europe), the ultimate customer now gets his information about plane schedules and airfares from the Internet rather than from a traditional travel agent. And while a good many book buyers in the United States still pick up and pay for the book of their choice at a bookstore in their neighborhood, an increasing number of them decide what books to buy by reading about them online first. An automobile still has to be serviced by a local dealer. But increasingly, buyers first study both their choice for the new car and their options for trading in their old car online before visiting a dealer.

What is already discernible is that, like all new distribution channels, this new information economy will change not only how customers buy, but what they buy. It will change customers' values and expectations, and with them how to promote goods and services, how to market and sell them, and how to service them online. In other words, Internet customers are becoming a new and distinct market. In the early years of the 21st century, power is shifting to the ultimate consumer.

There is no distance in this world economy. Everything is "local." The potential customers searching for a product do not know—and do not care—where the products come from. This does not eliminate or even curtail protectionism. But it changes it. Tariffs can still determine where a product or service has to be bought. But they are increasingly unable to protect the domestic producers' price.

One example: To get the industrial Midwest with its 140,000 steel workers to vote Republican in congressional elections, President Bush slapped a prohibitive tariff on imports of steel from Europe and Japan in 2001. He got what he wanted: a (bare) Republican majority in the Congress. But while the large steel users (such as automobile makers, railroads and building contractors) were forced by the tariff to buy domestic, they immediately set about cutting their use of steel so as not to spend more on it than they would have had to spend had they been able to buy the imports. Bush's tariff action thus only accelerated the long-term decline of the traditional midwestern steel producers and the jobs they generate. Tariffs, in other words, can still force users to buy domestic, but they are no longer capable of protecting the domestic producers' prices. Those are set through information and on the world-market level.

This development underlies the steady shift in protectionism: from tariffs—the traditional way—to protection through rules, regulations and especially export subsidies. World trade has grown spectacularly in the last fifty years. The largest growth has been in subsidized farm exports from the developed world: western and central Europe, Australia, Canada and the United States. Farm subsidies are now the only net income of French farmers, as their crops produce nothing but net losses and are grown only as the entitlement for the subsidies. These subsidies are in fact a major—perhaps the major—cement of the Franco-German alliance, and with it, of the European Union.

The international organization designed to set world economic policy is the World Trade Organization (WTO). But its meetings and agreements deal less and less with trade and tariffs, and instead with rules, regulations and subsidies. The discipline of international economics still, in large measure, concerns itself with international trade—that is, with the flow of money, goods and services. But the essence of the new world economy is that it is, above all, an economy of information and truly a global economy.

The Global Oligopoly of Money

The next major economic crisis will most probably be a crisis of the U.S. dollar in the world economy. It will put to a severe test the oligopoly of the central banks of the developed countries that now rules over the world financial economy.

Sixty years ago, in the Bretton Woods meetings of 1944, which tried to refashion a world economy that had been devastated by depression and war, John Maynard Keynes, the 20th century's greatest economist, proposed a supra-national central bank. It was vetoed by the United States. The two institutions that Bretton Woods established instead, the Bank for International Development (World Bank) and the International Monetary Fund (IMF), are, despite their impressive names, auxiliary rather than central—the former mainly financing development projects, the latter providing financial first aid to governments in distress.

The Bretton Woods system was never the stable, "non-political" system Keynes wanted. It could not and did not prevent currencies from being overvalued or undervalued. Still, although it limped from one crisis to the next, the Bretton Woods system worked for most of the half-century after World War II. And there was only one reason why it worked (however poorly): the commitment to it of the United States and the strength of the U.S. dollar as the world's key currency.

The dollar is still the world's key currency. But the Bretton Woods system is being killed by the U.S. government deficit, which is fast becoming the sinkhole of the world financial economy. The persistent U.S. deficit creates a persistent deficit in the U.S. balance of payments, which make both the U.S. economy and the government increasingly dependent on massive injections of short-term and panic-prone money from abroad. The U.S. savings rate is barely high enough to finance the minimum capital needs of industry. It could, in all likelihood, be raised considerably by raising interest rates. But that is not only politically almost impossible; it would also require that a larger share of incomes go into savings rather than into consumption, with an inevitable collapse of an economy based on consumer spending and low interest rates, as for instance, the U.S. housing market.

The government deficit is therefore being financed almost in its entirety by foreign investments in the United States, mostly in government securities like short-term treasury notes and medium-term bonds. The Japanese are converting most, if not all, of their trade surplus with the United States into dollar-denominated U.S. government securities and have thus become the largest U.S. creditor.

It is often argued, especially in Washington, that the deficit is mostly an accounting mirage. Defense spending—the main cause of the deficit—enables other free countries to keep their own defense spending low, which then generates the surpluses these countries invest in U.S. government securities. But this is a political argument. The *economic* fact is that the United States increasingly borrows short term (U.S. securities can be sold overnight) to invest long term and with very limited liquidity. This, needless to say, is an unstable and volatile system. It would collapse if the foreign holders of U.S. government securities (above all, the Japanese) were for whatever reason (such as a crash in their own economy) to dump their holdings of U.S. government securities. It certainly cannot be extended indefinitely, which, among other serious drawbacks, calls into question the long-term viability of the Bush Doctrine's goal of defending and extending the "zone of freedom" around the world.

The World Economy of the Multinationals

There were 7,258 multinational companies worldwide in 1969. Thirty-one years later, in 2000, the number had increased ninefold to more than 63,000. By that year, multinationals accounted for 80 percent of the world's industrial production.

But what is a multinational? Most Americans would answer: a big American manufacturer with foreign subsidiaries. That is wrong in almost every particular.

American-based multinationals are only a fraction—and a diminishing one—of all multinationals. Only 185 of the world's 500 largest multinationals—fewer than 40 percent—are headquartered in the United States (the European Union has 126, Japan 108). And multinationals are growing much faster outside the United States, especially in Japan, Mexico, and lately, Brazil.

Furthermore, most multinationals are not big. Rather, they are mostly small- to medium-sized enterprises. Typical perhaps is a German manufacturer of specialized surgical instruments who, with $20 million in sales and with plants in eleven countries, has around 60 percent of the world market in the field. And only a fraction of multinationals are manufacturers. Banks are probably the largest single group of multinationals, followed by insurance companies such as Germany's Allianz, financial-services institutions such as GE Finance Corporation and Merrill Lynch, wholesale distributors (especially in pharmaceuticals), and retailers like Japan's Ito Yokado.

The traditional multinational was indeed a domestic company with foreign subsidiaries, like Coca-Cola. But the new multinationals are increasingly being managed as one integrated business regardless of national boundaries, and the managers of the "foreign subsidiaries" are seen and treated as just another group of "division managers" rather than as top managements of semi-autonomous businesses. Internally, new multinationals are often not even organized by geography, but worldwide by products or services, such as one worldwide division for cleaning products or short-term inventory loans. They are increasingly organized by "markets": fully-developed markets (such as western and northern Europe or Japan); "developing markets" (eastern Europe, Latin America and parts of East Asia); and the "underdeveloped markets" and big "blocs" (China, Russia and India)—each with different objectives and strategies.

Finally, the new multinationals are increasingly not domestic companies with foreign subsidiaries, but are more likely to be domestic companies with foreign partners. They are being built through alliances, know-how agreements, marketing agreements, joint research, joint management development programs and so on. They require very different management skills; they must persuade, not command. The typical old multinational began planning with the questions: "What do we want to achieve? What are our objectives?" The first question in the new multinational is likely to be: "What do our partners value? What do they want to achieve? What are their competencies?" And in turn: "What do they need to know about our values, our goals, our competencies?"

We have almost no data on the world economy of the multinationals. Our statistics are primarily domestic. Nor do we truly understand the multinational and how it is being managed. How, for instance, does a multinational pharmaceutical company decide in what country first to introduce a new drug? How does a medium-sized multinational, like the German surgical-instrument maker mentioned earlier, decide whether to keep importing into the United States? To buy a small American competitor who has become available? To build its own plant in the United States and to start manufacturing there? Our dominant economic theories—both Keynes and Friedman's monetarism—assume that any but the smallest national economy can be managed in isolation from world economy and world society. With an estimated 30 percent of the U.S. workforce affected by foreign trade (and a much higher percentage in most European countries), this is patently absurd. But an economic theory of the world economy exists so far only in fragments. It is badly needed. In the meantime, however, the world economy of multinationals has become a truly global one, rather than one dominated by America and by U.S. companies.

The New Mercantilism

The modern state was invented by the French political philosopher Jean Bodin in his 1576 book *Six Livres de la Republique*. He invented the state for one purpose only: to generate the cash needed to pay the soldiers defending France against a Spanish army financed by silver from the New World—the first standing army since the Romans' more than a thousand years earlier. Mercenaries have to be paid in cash, and the only way to obtain a large and reliable cash income over any period—at a time when domestic economies had not yet been fully monetized and could therefore not yield a permanent tax—was a revenue obtained through keeping imports low while pushing exports and subsidizing them.

It took 300 years—the time until the unification of Germany and Italy in the 19th century—before Bodin's political invention, the nation-state, came to dominate Europe. But his mercantilism was adopted almost immediately by every European government, large or small. It remained the reigning philosophy until Adam Smith showed the absurdity of believing (as mercantilism does) that a nation can get rich by robbing its neighbors. Twenty-five years after Smith, mercantilism was still the doctrine that underlay America's first and most important work in political theory, *The Report on Manufacturers* (1791) by Alexander Hamilton. And almost a century later, in the second half of the 19th century, Bismarck based the new German Empire on Bodin's mercantilism as adapted to Europe by Hamilton's great German admirer, Friedrich List, in his 1841 book, *The National System of Political Economy*. However discredited as economic theory, mercantilism, not Adam Smith's free trade, thus became the policy and practice of governments virtually everywhere (except for one century in the UK).

But mercantilism is increasingly becoming the policy of "blocs" rather than of individual nation-states. These blocs—with the European Union the most structured one, and the U.S.-dominated NAFTA trying to embrace the entire Western Hemisphere (or at least North and Central America)—are becoming the integrating units of the new world economy. Each bloc is trying to establish free trade internally and to abolish within the bloc all hurdles, restrictions and impediments, first to the movement of goods and money and ultimately to the movement of people. The United States, for instance, has proposed extending NAFTA to embrace all of Central America.

At the same time, each bloc is becoming more protectionist against the outside. The most extreme protectionism, as already discussed, consists of rules with respect to agriculture and the protection of farm incomes. But similar protectionism is certain to develop for blue-collar workers in the manufacturing industry, and for the same reason: They are becoming an endangered species, the victims of productivity. In the United States for instance, manufacturing production increased in volume by at least 30 percent during the 1990s. It has at least doubled since 1960, and may even have tripled. (We have only money figures and have to guess at volume.) But manual workers in industrial production in the same period decreased from some 35 percent of the work force to barely more than 13 percent—and their numbers are still going down. Total employment in the manufacturing industry has remained the same proportion of the work force—it probably has even gone up. But the growth has been in white-collar work rather than the manual kind.

A mercantilist world economy, however, faces the same problems that led to the ultimate collapse of mercantilist national policies: It is impossible to export unless someone imports. This means, as Adam Smith showed 250 years ago, that the blocs must concentrate on those areas in which they have comparative advantages. In today's technology and world economy, that means concentrating on an area of knowledge work. Such concentration is already beginning. India is emerging as a world leader in applied-knowledge work—its comparative advantage is the 150 million well-educated Indians whose main language is English. China may similarly attain leadership through its world-class competence in manufacturing management—the legacy of the communist emphasis on output and production.

And just as it was for the mercantilists of 17th- and 18th-century Europe, an adequate home market (or access to one, as the Swiss and Dutch had to the markets of Germany and central Europe in the 19th century) is the most effective base for being competitive in the world economy. This "home market"—small enough to be protected and big enough to be competitive—is what the "blocs" provide.

Thus, the European Union is already in the process of creating the institutions for its bloc to be effective in this world economy: a European Parliament, a European Central Bank, a European Cartel Office and so on. Even the French, reluctantly, are integrating their economy and their industries—and even their agriculture—into the economy, the industries and the agriculture of the EU (provided that the Germans foot the bill). The United States, of course, has been a genuine bloc *and* a nation-state all along. Its economic institutions have been federal, at least since the creation of the Interstate Commerce Commission and the Federal Reserve Banking System. U.S. institutions like the Federal Reserve Bank of New York also act, in emergencies (such as the recent collapse of the Mexican peso) as the agent of NAFTA.

What, then, is likely to be the future relationship between these two blocs? The United States has openly announced its policy of extending NAFTA to all of Latin America. And while NAFTA means free trade within the bloc, it also means high protection externally, and especially high protection against Europe. Officially, the United States is still committed to worldwide free trade. But the actual result of its policies is that a zone of preferential trade agreements is gradually emerging around the United States—not unlike the bloc that is the EU. The world economy is thus fast coming to look far more like the mercantilism of Alexander Hamilton than like Adam Smith's free trade. It is fast becoming an "interzonal" rather than an "international" world economy.

But a new kind of mercantilist rivalry is emerging in this new economy—one in which the United States suffers from little-noticed disadvantages. For instance, the EU is seeking to export its regulations (and to impose its high regulatory costs on the United States) through international agreements, the reinterpretation of WTO rules, and the growing acceptance of EU standards in third markets.[1] It is also promoting its new currency, the euro, as a rival and alternative to the dollar as the world's reserve currency—a step that, if it succeeded, would greatly reduce the U.S. government's ability to attract foreign funds to finance its deficit and thus maintain the Bush Doctrine. Nor can the United States be certain of maintaining the solidarity of its own bloc in competition with the EU. Several Latin American states are going slow on the negotiations to extend NAFTA for political reasons. The EU is itself seeking closer trade and economic relationships with Latin America through partnership talks with MERCOSUR. And the recent trend of Latin American politics has been to drift away from "neo-liberalism" and towards a Left perennially tempted by anti-*yanquí* protectionism. What is different today is that the EU offers these political forces the ability to choose free trade while simultaneously resisting U.S. "hegemony." The United States could therefore find itself with a smaller "home market" than rival blocs, but with the same high-cost regulations, in a world of intense mercantilist competition.

For thirty years after World War II, the U.S. economy dominated practically without serious competition. For another twenty years it was clearly the world's foremost economy and especially the undisputed leader in technology and innovation. Though the United States today still dominates the world economy of information, it is only one major player in the three other world economies of money, multinationals and trade. And it is facing rivals that, either singly or in combination, could conceivably make America Number Two.

Note

1. For more, see Lawrence Kogan, "Exporting Europe's Protectionism", The National Interest (Fall 2004).

PETER F. DRUCKER is a writer, consultant and teacher. His most recent book is *Managing the Next Society (2002)*.

Here's the Good News

Forget headlines—the world economy has never been better.

BARRETT SHERIDAN AND DANIEL GROSS

There's been little cheer in the global economic news since the subprime-mortgage meltdown started last spring, and now, it seems, we're entering a winter of discontent. Credit problems have spread like a virus throughout the American and European financial systems. Holiday sales at U.S. malls and British high-street shops are tepid. Sky-high food and oil prices are crimping household budgets and furrowing the brows of inflation-phobic central bankers. The dollar has entered a Britney Spears-like downward spiral. And banks are engaged in a race to notch the biggest write-downs on bad debt, with the implied promise of more to come. Dismal politics, from the growing pains of Gordon Brown to the singularly downlifting pageant of the U.S. presidential primaries, only adds to the malaise. To aggravate matters, the Hollywood writers' strike has deprived many television viewers of their comic relief.

It seems things are as bad as they've been in recent memory. Except that if you look beyond temporal market fluctuations to how the real global economy is doing, things have never been better. For the past four years, the world has grown at a 5.2 percent annual rate—a full 2 percentage points higher than in the '80s and '90s—thanks in large part to booming emerging markets. While the United States and many parts of Europe are lagging, most of the rest of the planet is soaring. Consider that between 1980 and 2000, the number of countries growing at 5 percent or more hovered around 50. In 2006, 104 nations grew at that rate. When asked to think of a few countries besides China and India that have shown strong growth, World Bank economist Andrew Burns replies: "It's hard to think of somebody who hasn't." In fact, this year the economies of only three countries—Zimbabwe, Fiji and Tonga—are contracting. Two are highly isolated archipelagoes and the former is a hugely dysfunctional dictatorship. Harvard's Ken Rogoff, a former chief economist at the IMF, sums it up simply: "We're in a boom."

Who knew? The ranks of fast growers go way beyond the usual suspects. Cambodia, still recovering from a generation of genocide, civil war and political turmoil, is completing its ninth straight year of growth above 6 percent (one of 27 such countries on a similar streak). Slovakia, which got mostly jobless masses and entrenched communists when it was severed from Czechoslovakia in 1992, hit 9 percent growth in 2007. Unemployment—a formerly intractable problem for this nation of 5 million—has plunged to record lows, thanks to tax and business reforms that have made the country an export dynamo. Turkey is another pleasant surprise. Growth has averaged 6.9 percent for six years, despite a restive Kurdish population and a war raging just beyond its 331-kilometer border with Iraq. The tide is lifting even the long-moored boats of Africa, where growth has topped 5 percent since 2004, driven by oil states but also by expanding agricultural economies like Tanzania. This broad boom is reflected in emerging-market stock indexes, up 40 percent this year, versus a measly 5 percent for the S&P 500.

It's the polar opposite of the 1990s, when rolling economic crises caused serious problems in emerging economies like Malaysia, Turkey and Russia—countries with fragile political and monetary institutions. Prior to that, the 1980s had become known as Latin America's "lost decade," a period when countries like Mexico, Brazil and Argentina tanked after years of excessive borrowing and a sudden spike in interest rates. Ironically, financial instability today seems to be a phenomenon largely confined to the developed world. Even as Western consumers have fudged on retirement savings in favor of flat-screen TVs, and Western governments have skimped on education and infrastructure, emerging nations have been paying back debt, taming inflation, strengthening their institutions, diversifying their economies and generally behaving like responsible global citizens. The result has been a huge range of benefits: fewer hungry children in Tanzania, increased political stability in Brazil and a more balanced global financial system, in which nations previously labeled unstable debtors are now extending credit to richer countries.

There's no denying that a large chunk of the good news is commodity-driven. The exploding demand from China has driven up prices for everything from oil to corn to platinum. But while past commodity booms have done little to spread the wealth, this time many countries have taken advantage of the chance to build up cash reserves and pay down once crippling debt. "They've done exactly the opposite of American homeowners," says the World Bank's Burns. In 2006, Russia paid back $22 billion to the Paris Club, a group of rich-country lenders. Algeria, Indonesia and Argentina each paid back more than $8 billion to various aid groups. The retiring loans provoked something of an existential crisis for the IMF, which saw more than 82 percent of its outstanding loans paid back between 2003 and March 2007. Free of debts, developing nations have been able to invest more in health, education and infrastructure, boosting economic growth. And this time growth has not unleashed inflation, for a simple reason. "Central banks around the world are much more professionally run than they used to be," says Harvard's Rogoff.

For all the scared talk about how nations like Russia, Iran and Venezuela are growing fast under authoritarian regimes, they are the political exceptions, not the rule. "Africa has gone from having three democracies to 23 democracies over the last 10 years," says Homi Kharas, the former World Bank chief economist for Asia, now at the Wolfensohn Center for Development. "That's one of the reasons why people feel much more optimistic about fundamentals today. They're not just economic fundamentals, they're also institutional fundamentals." While these new democracies are far from perfect, leaders are now more accountable for their actions—and nothing makes voters angrier than seeing their savings wiped out through political incompetence.

Smarter policy has led to growth-building moves like export diversification (copper went from roughly 80 to 40 percent of Chilean export value between 1980 and 2000) and the taming of inflation. The latter is particularly essential, says Lawrence Goodman, Bank of America's head of emerging-markets strategy, as it "provides a backdrop for these economies to deepen their capital markets and have more certainty around planning." Brazil, for example, suffered years of hyperinflation: in 1994, prices climbed more than 2,000 percent. Today inflation is below 4 percent, a key factor in encouraging a tenfold jump in foreign direct investment since 1994. Likewise, global foreign direct investment more than doubled from 2003 to 2006, to $1.3 trillion, largely reflecting a new trust in emerging economies.

Competition has been a huge growth catalyst, too. Eastern European nations jockeying for EU accession have done much to clean up their balance sheets. And the success of China has been a motivator for numerous would-be emerging-market giants, most notably India. "There's no question that India has been influenced by China," says Rogoff. "When India was telling its people that 5 percent growth would be great, and Indian businessmen took tours of China and saw that growth could be much higher, that had a big influence." The

	Growth	GDP per Capita	Inflation	Current Account Balance*
Chile	5.9%	$9,698	3.9%*	3.7%*
Turkey	5.0%	$6,548	8.2%	−7.5%
Egypt	7.1%	$1,739	10.9%	−1.4%
Kenya	6.4%	$851	6.9%	−3.7%

*As share of GDP

specter of China has forced others, like the Vietnamese, to improve productivity, bolster infrastructure, and encourage entrepreneurship. The result is that the economy has grown by more than 8 percent for the last three years.

Among economists, of course, no narrative would be complete without a series of "buts." Perhaps the biggest question: is 5 percent enough? Some say yes—former Mexican foreign minister Jorge Castañeda, now a professor at New York University, believes that 5 to 6 percent growth in Mexico could solve the U.S.-Mexican immigration problems. Still, it's no accident that countries like China and India get the most ink—after all, their trend growth (11 and 9 percent, respectively) and size put them in a different league, even from other emerging markets. Countries like Cambodia are starting from such a low level that it will take a few decades of really supercharged growth to raise living standards significantly. In some places, problems like unemployment and low productivity are severe enough that a few years of 5 percent growth won't make much of a dent. In the Middle East and North Africa, for example, high fertility rates have created a cascade of young people who will be joining the work force over the next decade or so, requiring 4.5 million new jobs a year—but recent growth has been capable of generating only 3 million new jobs annually, according to the World Bank. Income inequality is another problem. If an economy grows at 8 percent annually, but the gains flow disproportionately to the elite, the lot of the typical citizen won't improve much.

Meanwhile, many emerging economies are about to hit some speed bumps. In China, the impact of the breakneck pursuit of profits and development—pollution, rising food prices—is spurring a backlash. In places like Vietnam and India, where the buildup of factories or call centers hasn't been matched by investment in ports and roads, poor infrastructure is a clear impediment to future growth. In sub-Saharan Africa, things viewed as essential for business—streets, Internet access, telecommunications networks, functioning railways—are still on the drawing board.

Yet there's still plenty of cause for optimism. Emerging nations are no longer just extracting resources and supplying cheap labor, but growing their own massive middle classes, breeding world-beating companies and becoming players on the global financial stage. Such developments—the prospect of China suddenly being a major source of investment capital, cash-rich Latin American countries banding together to lend to one another, Russia emerging as the top luxury-car market—have defied the predictions of the world's collective economic wisdom. And that's not surprising. Back in the post-dotcom-bubble days of 2001 and 2002, few economists predicted that the global economy would enjoy the expansion it has. Several years into this new phase of growth, it's still somewhat unclear what it all means. Could emerging markets really carry the global economy through a massive downturn in the United States? Have rich and poor nations really "decoupled"? Will multinational firms leave New York and London for Mumbai en masse? Whatever happens, the dismal scientists and the rest of us will have to learn to cope with the truth—things, for now anyway, are really pretty good.

The Real Global Technology Challenge

LEONARD LYNN AND HAROLD SALZMAN

At one of the renowned Indian Institutes of Technology, we recently asked a class of 80 engineering and science undergraduates how many wanted to go to the United States for graduate school or a job. A decade ago nearly everyone in the classroom would have a hand in the air. Now, not a single hand was raised. "Why go to the U.S.," they asked, "when all the opportunity is in India?"

In China when we visited software, telecommunications, and heavy-equipment companies owned by U.S. multinational corporations, we met managers born and raised in Asia but with U.S. engineering degrees. They had expected to spend their entire working lives in the United States. So why had they gone back to China? Because these days not only were the new career opportunities there as good as those in the U.S., but the technology-development projects were even more challenging.

Clearly the U.S. is no longer the universally preferred home for the global technology elite. Increasing numbers of scientists and engineers who were educated and have built successful careers here are returning to China, India, and other countries. Many in the younger generation never come here in the first place.

Noting these trends, the policy and technology communities are sounding the alarm about an impending U.S. fall from scientific and technological dominance. Compounding the loss of international talent, they say, is the declining appeal of science and engineering for American students, even as the tide of engineers and scientists trained in China and India rises. Recent policy reports and popular press stories claim that each of these countries is graduating around 600,000 engineers a year, compared to about 100,000 in the United States.

Leading policy groups fear that this combination of a decline in science and engineering prowess and the rising strength of China and India will leave the United States a much-diminished technology power, one that will have to concede leadership to the emerging economies. The American Electronics Association warns that "the United States can no longer take its technological dominance for granted;" the National Academy of Sciences fears that the "scientific and technological building blocks critical to our economic leadership are eroding at a time when many other nations are gathering strength;" the Business Roundtable exhorts us to "not disregard our history" of scientific and technological superiority, "nor forget who we are;" and the Council on Competitiveness foresees "a fall from leadership [that will] threaten the security of the nation and the prosperity of its citizens."

The Numbers Game

Well, *should* the U.S. worry if China and India each graduates about five times as many engineers as we do? First of all, there is good reason to doubt the numbers. Only a few thousand new engineers are coming out of the Indian Institutes of Technology (IIT) or the premier Chinese universities each year. Many others are graduating from universities with poor or marginal facilities where students have little exposure to innovative engineering and science. And frankly, the numbers being reported seem to overestimate actual graduation rates by a factor of four or five.

But let's not quibble. Surely, even if India and China only graduate two or three times as many engineers as we do, as no doubt they will over the next decade, shouldn't we think through the ramifications of this fact? Well, yes. But perhaps we should first ask what all these engineers in China and India *do* after they graduate. Those of us with long memories may recall that when the U.S.S.R. launched the first satellite in 1957, policy observers warned that that nation was graduating far more engineers than we were. The feared corollary of Russian domination of space was military domination on earth. Later, in the 1980s, when Japanese businesses seemed unstoppable in every industry from steelmaking to consumer electronics, critics complained that the brightest Japanese went into engineering while the brightest Americans got M.B.A.s and law degrees. The inevitable consequence seemed to be that we would soon fall under Japanese economic domination. U.S. education and industry did rise to the international challenge, but not by cajoling twice as many of our young people to major in engineering. It turned out that the key to military and economic success based on technology was not the *number* of engineers but how they were educated and used.

Let's go back to our class at the elite Indian Institutes of Technology, part of the research we conducted for a study funded by the National Science Foundation and the Kauffman Foundation. When we asked the students about their career aspirations, two-thirds said they had no intention of going into a science or engineering career. The opportunity they saw in India was in starting a new business or rising through the management ranks of a multinational (and rising more quickly at the Indian office than they would in the firm's U.S. or European office). But, we asked, why spend four years in a grueling engineering or science curriculum if they wanted to go into business? "Branding" was the reply. Two-thirds of U.S. science and engineering students abandon a strictly scientific or engineering career path upon graduation, and Indian students seem to be planning similar career trajectories and strategies for success.

In our view the key question is not how many engineers graduate in a country; rather, it is how they are educated, how many are used in the development of innovative technology, how they are used, and how well they are supported by a country's innovation policy.

So the U.S. economy is not threatened by the increase in the numbers of scientists and engineers in China and India. Nevertheless, our research in the U.S., Europe, China, and India does find plenty for us to be worried about, as well as pointing to what kinds of public policy could address those concerns. Unfortunately, the spurious data on numbers of engineers are a distraction that may cause us to devote our resources to the solution of false problems, while neglecting those that are real. That neglect is due in part to our failure to appreciate how the world is changing and how the role of the United States in the new global economy will have to change if we are to continue to prosper.

"Sea Turtles" and the End of U.S. Technological Hegemony

All the best opportunities for science and technology were located in the United States as recently as five or six years ago. We had the best universities, the best technical facilities, and the companies that offered the most exciting technical careers. We offered the best opportunities for entrepreneurs using advanced technology to start new companies. Indian engineering students competed desperately for opportunities to attend U.S. universities and to make careers here after graduation. Chinese nationals with good jobs at major firms here never would have dreamt of going back to China. Silicon Valley and its ilk were the engines of the American innovation system, powered by a unique elixir of intellectual and financial fuel, and coupled with the opportunity and openness inherent in the United States culture and economy. A key ingredient was our ability to attract some of the most dynamic technological entrepreneurs from India, China, and other countries.

Clearly this is no longer the case.

China has welcomed nearly 200,000 returning scientists, engineers, managers, entrepreneurs, and other Western-educated Chinese in recent years, according to a count by the Chinese Ministry of Education. Known as *hai gui*, sea turtles returning home, they are representative of a shift in the high-skill migration tide away from the West and toward emerging and transitional economies around the globe. Perhaps even more significant is that with the return and retention of scientists and engineers, venture capital, multinational collaborators, and other components necessary to build global enterprises follow this tide. Many successful Indian and Chinese entrepreneurs are moving their existing companies to their countries of birth. We were also surprised to discover how many small technology firms in India have recently been founded by expatriate Indians returning after 20-, 30-, or even 40-year careers at large firms in the U.S.

An American has to ask: What causes someone in a secure, well-paid position—with long-time residency and often citizenship in the world's richest country—to begin anew with a risky venture in a country with a spotty infrastructure and some of the world's worst pockets of poverty? The answer, in brief, is the promise—which used to be uniquely American—of opportunity.

In Guangzhou we interviewed a 35-year-old entrepreneur from Taiwan and toured one of his plants, a facility producing zinc and brass components for U.S. and European multinationals, components that are used in a variety of products ranging from plumbing fixtures to communications equipment. A dozen years ago he had gone to the U.S. to get an M.B.A., and he had planned to make his career here as well. But when he graduated in the late 1990s, his father called him back to take over the family business and expand it into mainland China. The firm had 150 employees then. Now it has more than 5,000 at several sites in China. A U.S. engineer who first visited the plant in Guangzhou six or seven years ago told us that at that time the plant was using 1920s technology. Now, he tells us, it is more advanced than any comparable facility in the U.S.

And if the U.S. is less and less regarded as the "land of technological opportunity" for bright technologists and entrepreneurs from China and India, China and India are increasingly seen as the lands of technological opportunity by multinational corporations, both American and foreign. Multinationals from the U.S., Europe, Taiwan, Singapore, Japan, and Korea increasingly populate the new technology parks of China and India.

Meanwhile, back home in the United States "foreign" firms like Toyota, Honda, Hyundai, and BMW are now hiring American autoworkers. And the U.S. has become the center of design, with every leading auto manufacturer in the world establishing a design center in this country, although nearly all are in California, not Detroit. So while we do not believe that the rise of global competitors will make the U.S. a science and engineering rust belt, this country *is* facing a difficult transition as the opportunities, challenges, and companies are changing.

The United States' "Technology Problem"

We need to understand both the economies and the sentiments beyond our borders in order to develop policy that will support the future economic and technological health of the United States. Unfortunately, U.S. policymakers have not fully grasped that need. Their talk of a "science and engineering gap" based on numbers of engineers misses the point.

Policies that have been proposed to shore up the U.S. technological position in the world include investing more in basic research; revamping the visa system to re-establish our attractiveness to the smartest foreign students, scientists, and engineers; improving the pre-university education in science and math; and enticing more young Americans to major in science and engineering. While we certainly favor doing a better job of increasing our store of knowledge through research and our human capital by attracting the best and brightest from around the world, we do not believe these approaches fully address the major challenge now facing the United States.

Nor does merely increasing the quantity and quality of American science and math education. Just as comparing the numbers of engineering graduates in the United States to those in China and India is misleading, so too is attributing our newly vulnerable position to a collapse of the U.S. education system based on the low international ranking of our students' senior-year science and math scores. While our schools can always do better and are woefully inadequate in serving certain groups and areas in the nation, a science and math deficit is not the major driver of our technology problem. When only a third of qualified four-year college graduates in science and engineering continue in those fields, we should turn our attention to market demand.

Why produce more types of workers that firms have no intention of hiring? When we asked U.S. engineers and engineering managers what careers they wanted for their children, none mentioned engineering. And it was not because they hadn't had a great ride in their careers, but rather it was because they thought the ride was over for the next generation. The U.S. technology problem, we would argue, is that the technology needs of the growth markets—for both consumer products and capital goods that require new types of technology or innovation (ranging from low-cost laptops to more efficient heating technology to less-polluting manufacturing technology)—are not being met by U.S. engineering or science or the current direction of public policy. This is the crux of the *real* science and engineering gap in the U.S.

Science and Engineering Jobs Have Changed

Today's engineering or science firm looks little like one of just a decade ago, when nearly all software development was done by teams in the United States or Europe. Now, as one U.S. manager explained from the half-vacant offices of his IT company, the jobs of programmers and even systems analysts previously employed by the company now are being done abroad. His and other companies currently are hiring only experienced project managers. Among the IT firms we've studied, the latest projects will have only 10 to 20 percent of the work done in the U.S. or Europe. The rest will be done in India and soon China.

Shortages of certain types of engineers in the United States may occasionally be a factor in the decision of U.S. firms to offshore their technology development, but more common reasons are 1) to serve customers in the fastest-growing markets, 2) to take advantage of lower wages for professionals (although this is declining in importance), and 3) to increase the capacity and deployment of their science and technology workforce. Some offshoring has taken place because the substance of engineering work has changed and, in some cases, technology innovation is different from what it was just a few years ago.

In office software, for example, innovation now comes from improvement in the process, not the functionality of the product. Standard office-suite products such as word processing, spreadsheets, and presentation slides have been relatively static in the past few years (with the addition of a new feature or two

to sell new products). In the past eight years, perhaps the most important productivity innovation in office software has been the reduction of failures, namely fewer system crashes. Now, the most critical need for software innovation is to increase user productivity by addressing the problems of ever-new bugs, security threats, and difficulty in supporting and maintaining software—much of which depends on building *better* products rather than new products. This, in turn, depends on improving the process of development software.

But while important to users, improvements for stability and maintainability are hardly the stuff of pioneering discovery and invention or great IPO potential. One only needs to talk to the current crop of computer engineers and entrepreneurs in the U.S. or Europe to gauge their lack of interest in devoting their careers to developing more secure, stable, and maintainable versions of existing software. These improvements are increasingly the result of innovation in the methods and process of software development, of using structured methods and systems. The current wave of software development is flowing to the locus of *process innovation*, which is offshore. Under the aegis of low-cost and legacy work, Indian software firms have been focused on work that addresses the real needs of industry and, at least for the moment, there are many bright science and engineering graduates in India and China who are anxious to work on these problems for a good salary. Ramping up the number of our young people majoring in software engineering will not re-create the IT heyday of the past decade.

So, will these trends continue until all technology development has left the United States? Of course not. Indeed, we believe there will be some reversal. There is substantial evidence that a lot of the offshoring of technical work has taken place because of a kind of "bandwagon" effect. A perception exists that major savings can be made by offshoring, so Wall Street analysts ask CEOs about their offshoring policies. Thus, pressures to outsource are driven down into organizations from the top levels. Engineering managers are allowed to expand their headcount of employees, but not in the United States. Naturally, they go global.

But this strategy may not be cost effective. Our interviews at multinationals suggest, for example, that the strategy of having teams on both sides of the globe is often based on a mythical 24-hour workday. The coordination problems working across time zones can cost as much as outsourcing saves in salary costs. With actual total cost savings (not just salary differences) estimated at 15 percent—among other things, offshore productivity is about three-fifths of onshore productivity in our estimates—the benefit can be small if cost is the only reason for going offshore. Sending a team manager to visit his or her team in India can easily cost $10,000 to $15,000 a trip, and for strategic operations, frequent trips are a necessity.

Moreover, salaries for qualified engineers and engineering managers in India and China are rising fast. One multinational manager in Shanghai commented that he has trouble keeping good engineers for more than a year, and to attract qualified replacements, he must pay significantly more. There is also an emerging shortage of Chinese and Indian engineering managers who can work effectively within multinationals.

China, Russia, and other Eastern Bloc economies once tried to out-compete the West by setting ever-higher quotas for the production of steel and other products. The result was scrap yards piled high with steel and other products that were neither needed nor usable. We should expect the same kind of result if we concentrate on setting quotas for the production of engineers. Our educational institutions should instead focus on educating the *types* of technologists and innovators that the markets will demand, through gaining better understanding of changing job requirements and employer needs, rather than relying on their longstanding curricula and programs. And in their role of promoting the U.S. public good, policymakers can play a pivotal role in guiding human-resource investment, with the aim not to restore national technological hegemony but rather to ensure us a rewarding place in the newly developing global technology system.

Techno-Nationalism versus Collaborative Advantage

Globalism is permeating the U.S. economy at every level. The Chinese and Indian economies are growing faster than the typical 3.5 percent annual growth rate in the U.S. and other "advanced economies," and their markets are much larger than ours. This means that the emerging world economies are not only producing producers of technology—they are also producing consumers. Already, U.S.-based firms have made their top priorities developing products for the emerging economies. If those products also sell in the U.S., all the better—but the needs of the American market will no longer be the sole driver of the technologies of the future.

As a mature market, the bulk of U.S. consumption can be satisfied with older products and technology. Not so in the emerging economies. Heating technology developed for the U.S. market and U.S. energy prices will gain little market share in China. With relatively low energy costs and well-established technologies, the U.S. market has less demand for new low-cost and highly efficient technologies than do the emerging markets. Similarly, the SUVs and large automobiles developed for maximum profitability in the United States market may find a niche among the wealthy and status-conscious in the emerging economies, but they are unlikely to meet the far greater demand from the expanding middle classes in those countries.

In some cases, technological and scientific priorities will suggest that work should be done elsewhere. For example, a pharmaceutical firm we visited in Europe centers its research on infectious diseases in India. That's where they can find top scientists who are highly motivated to work on this problem, and that's where scientists have the most experience with it. But U.S. scientists can collaborate with their Indian counterparts to extend the resulting knowledge to other parts of the world. It is challenges like these that are the stuff of pioneering discoveries and IPO potential. Clearly, an understanding that local science leads to global science is already re-orienting corporate strategies.

So what sort of engineers and engineering managers will we need in this new environment? When we examine actual hiring practices of firms, we find that although they are looking for technical competence, they want much more than that. An engineering manager at a major multinational we visited was trying to decide between two candidates to lead an engineering team. One had a stellar academic record and work history while the other had a strong but not exceptional record. Who was hired? The second candidate—because he wanted to travel, felt comfortable in the company of different types of people, and spoke a second language. This firm, like most of the 25 multinationals we visited, needs managers who have not just sufficient understanding of the technology but also excellent skills in developing and managing globally collaborative project teams.

A new class of engineers and engineering managers is emerging who will pioneer the new engineering and science framework necessary for global innovation. These people are not only engineers or managers or marketers; they also have a combination of skills, knowledge, and education that go beyond traditional engineering and science training. They have mixed allegiances to the various countries of their birth, education, citizenship, and residence. They manage their multiple identities while working comfortably across organizational, cultural, and disciplinary boundaries and dealing with the special situations of emerging economies. They have the linguistic ability to conduct negotiations in local languages and the cultural sensitivity to work in a variety of environments. There are not nearly enough of them. And hardly any of them were born in the United States, though most were educated here.

There are a small but growing number of initiatives to broaden science and engineering education to include academic work designed to develop the broad, multidisciplinary skills and knowledge necessary to produce global innovation. Our system allows considerable local experimentation, and these experiments should be strongly supported. It is the openness and breadth of the American education system that provide a comparative advantage over highly technical programs in other countries.

U.S. innovation policy could help in this effort. It could support more exchange and study-abroad opportunities for our engineering students. It could encourage and support the development of new curricula at engineering schools and promote a broad, rather than a narrowly technical, education for engineers. It could exploit the U.S.'s advantage in having a growing proportion of its college population made up of ethnic and racial minorities.

An important first step, however, is for policymakers to stop talking in terms of threats and competition, which is likely to alienate those with whom we need to work and to prevent us from seeing opportunities for collaboration. Anachronistic, zero-sum nationalist policies are ill-suited for the global economy. Worse, they encourage other countries to compete with us and to look for non-U.S. partners instead of cooperating with us for mutual gain.

The theory of comparative advantage postulates that countries gain when they concentrate on what they do best and trade that expertise to others. In collaborative advantage, mutual gain comes from the strength of interdependencies. Other countries may have comparative advantage in the sheer number of engineers they can devote to problems, in their motivation to develop certain technologies, or because of different approaches to engineering. Our hope of a prosperous national future may well rest on our capacity to work for collaborative advantage with global partners. Rather than compete with other countries on the numbers, we need to educate the kinds of engineers and scientists who can to work with them to our mutual advantage. We should focus on crafting policies that support the development and work of this new breed.

LEONARD LYNN is a professor of management policy at Case Western Reserve University. HAL SALZMAN is a sociologist and senior research associate at the Urban Institute in Washington, D.C. Over the past five years, Lynn and Salzman have led several multinational teams in a series of projects looking at the impacts of the globalization of technology on emerging and first-world economies, multinational enterprises, entrepreneurs, and education systems. From *The Real Global Technology Challenge* by Leonard Lynn and Harold Salzman, Change, July/August 2007, pages 8–13.

Looking Ahead to Our Place in the Next Economy

Matthew Budman

When we hear about manufacturing jobs moving overseas—whether in steel, cotton, textiles, or Buicks—it doesn't sting all that much anymore, unless, of course, a family member is among the pink-slipped unlucky. Somehow it seems inevitable—progress, even: *The United States is continuing its forward movement, leaving behind the remnants of the Industrial Age and bringing its diverse workforce into the Information Age, ready to lead the way.*

But news of software-programming and radiology positions being outsourced to Romania and India has a more visceral impact. Few knowledge workers—and aren't we all supposed to be knowledge workers now?—foresaw their livelihoods being jeopardized by the same free-market principles that have devastated U.S. manufacturing.

Yet technology and toppling trade barriers have left white-collar jobs as vulnerable to overseas migration as those in blue-collar industries. And U.S. workers may not even be the first choice to run call centers or manage the information that is the new economy's lifeblood: Americans are expensive, what with 401(k)s, ergonomics requirements, health care, vacation days, and life insurance, and most have little educational or training advantage over their foreign counterparts.

"I'm nervous," says the ordinarily buoyant management guru Tom Peters. "I don't think there's any job that's safe right now."

"Is the anxiety justified? Absolutely," says Dow Chemical ideation leader Andy Hines. "We're facing a real challenge."

After all, notes USC management professor Ian Mitroff, "if finance and engineering-design jobs can be moved offshore, what *can't* be moved?"

If you find the trend disquieting in principle, check out the numbers: A recent U.C. Berkeley study estimated that some 14 million U.S. white-collar jobs—11 percent of *all* jobs—are at risk of being outsourced, anytime employers want to make the move. That's significantly higher than the widely reported Forrester Research forecast of 3.3 million jobs lost over the next 15 years, not to mention the 2.5 million manufacturing jobs lost in the last three years. And who can blame U.S. companies for looking east for lower personnel costs? The Berkeley researchers, Ashok Deo Bardhan and Cynthia A. Kroll, note that Indian telephone operators earn under $1 an hour, payroll clerks just $2, paralegals $8 or less.

The baby boomers' retirement will stave off any true white-collar crisis for a few years—employers will be scrambling for warm bodies, and anyone who fits that description will probably get by. But for far-thinking organizations, the coming demographic shift is another argument for moving operations offshore even faster. In five or 10 or 20 years, will there be any work for knowledge workers—or their supervisors—to do?

Of course, few forecast a future as bleak as all that—U.S. workers have survived every previous disruption, major and minor, and they'll survive this one. It's the disruption's severity and duration that are in question—and whether top-tier workers will be able to maintain their position in the global economy.

Granted, not everything can be outsourced. Despite improvements in videoconferencing and the ubiquity of cell phones, plenty of jobs—even white-collar jobs—require face-to-face contact. We haven't—and won't—become "a nation of burger-flippers," as Lee Iacocca once feared; the service economy hasn't trumped the information age. Whatever the Internet's reach, society can't function without doctors, social workers, and police officers. The economy will continue to need trainers and researchers and economists and teachers and lawyers and editors—and executives to manage them all.

And there's the not-unimportant fact that work will always be here because here is where workers want to be. The United States remains the world's top destination spot for both well-off emigrants and destitute refugees, all seeking a dynamic, vibrant society as well as economic prosperity. Sure, the cost of living is far lower in the developing world, but America is where people want to come—and stay. It may be cheaper to start a software-development firm in Ghana or the Philippines, but how many U.S. entrepreneurs would gladly relocate their families from Ohio or Massachusetts?

So should we be worried about our prospects a decade or two down the line? What will it take to stave off downward mobility—individual and collective—and decline both economic and social? We asked some thought leaders with their eyes on the future, including a few who proudly call themselves futurists, to peer at what's ahead for American executives and knowledge workers.

Applaud the Job Exodus?

We already know what *won't* work: protectionist efforts to keep jobs here. It hasn't worked with manufacturing—the latest example, George W. Bush's clumsily enacted and globally rejected steel tariffs, ended up costing more jobs than they saved. And no program of tax-based carrots and sticks is likely to keep data-entry and accounting functions on these shores.

Anyway, creative destruction of jobs is hardly news in any industrialized nation. Each economic era has seen massive displacement of workers, of families, of entire industries. No one called it retraining, but all those cobblers and subsistence farmers and, yes, buggy-whip factories needed to transform into something else—something unforeseen.

"The loss of manufacturing jobs is just another chapter of technological progress in our economy," insists Christopher Meyer, former director of the Center for Business Innovation, who says that the ongoing white-collar volatility, like economic upheavals before it, is absolutely necessary. He sees the job exodus as "part of a long-term trend of manufacturing jobs leaving this economy—and we should applaud it." A country advances by replacing lower-level jobs: "That's how economic growth happens—the new jobs have to have higher value-added, higher productivity. It's like when automation replaced blue-collar jobs—we look at most of the jobs it displaced as brutish and short: mining coal, or having your internal organs cooked by the infrared radiation from a ladle of steel. These adjustments will allow more people to do *what* they want to do, not what they *have* to do."

"The issue is, 'Does the United States represent the front end of the pipeline?' "

Business thinker Stan Davis, Meyer's frequent co-author, uses a pipeline metaphor to describe the pattern of job creation and motion. "I'm not concerned about U.S. job losses so long as we're feeding the front end of the pipeline with growth and innovation," he says. "As each new innovation creates new jobs and new sectors mature, those jobs migrate down the global food chain. The issue is, 'Does the United States represent the front end of the pipeline?' It's a question of how long we stay healthy and grow and innovate and create new sectors."

And no matter how many call centers and programmers head overseas, the United States has a head start in invention and innovation, according to Glen Hiemstra, founder of Futurist.com: "Our biggest competitive advantage will remain creativity and innovative thinking—as compared to routine churning out of information—because of the innovative history of the country, because of the cross-cultural mix that leads to fertility of thinking," he says.

U.S. companies and workers also benefit—though they won't do so forever—from ease and familiarity of communication, language, and organization. Futurist Watts Wacker, CEO of FirstMatter LLC, points out that no emphasis on efficiency will obviate the need for human contact—"You can't Six Sigma relationships," he says—or for unusually valuable personnel. "There will always be a premium for people who are better than others."

The question is whether U.S. workers will always be better than their foreign competitors. Meyer emphasizes that workers must stress distinctiveness over superiority: "Either U.S. income will fall to the level of those in other countries who have the same skills, or we have to have different skills," he says. "So what are those different skills going to be?"

The effort to develop those different skills must be a priority for not just individuals but entire economic sectors, says Dow Chemical's Andy Hines, who also chairs the Association of Professional Futurists. "Look at what's happened to unions," he points out. "They've had a very similar kind of challenge—in their case, with physical labor migrating overseas—and they've responded not by trying to improve what they brought to the table but by staying static and trying to hold on tight. When someone else can do the job for one-sixth the price, you're going to lose no matter how hard you fight. It's a losing game, and knowledge workers can lose too—if they stay at the same skill level as somebody in India."

Staying Ahead of the Curve

Keeping U.S. workers on the cutting edge will require efforts both individual and national. It won't just *happen.* Hines calls it a national imperative: "If we stand still, there will be up-and-coming economies that will take the things that we're doing now," he says.

Hiemstra cites "two critical things that we need to do" on a national scale. First: We must move quickly to bring a high-speed Internet connection "into every home and every business location," he says. "Other countries are moving in that direction as a matter of national policy, through a mixture of public initiative and privatization. We ought to be looking at the Korean model, and at what's happening with the telecommunications infrastructure in China and India, which are moving much faster than we are on a percentage basis. This ought to be a top national priority for us, and currently it's seen only as something that would be nice—if the telecommunications companies could make money doing it.

"Second," he continues, "to maintain our innovation lead, we need to push for more people receiving advanced math, science, and technology education. Grad schools in those areas are dominated by foreign students. We're just not generating enough people with the kind of high-level technical knowledge to do the innovation in the new technologies and in the realms of innovation that are going to be dominant in the next quarter-century."

USC's Ian Mitroff also sees education as key. "We haven't done a good job of teaching critical thinking and creative problem-solving," he says. "People find critical thinking difficult because it's a radical switch from their 20 years of education in solving well-structured problems. We've produced a nation of certainty junkies, where if you can't define a problem with precision and certainty, people go crazy. Well, welcome to the real world. The game has changed. Problems change as fast as you're working on them." Indeed, they change *because* you're working on them—or *not* working on them.

For Corporate America as a whole, if CEOs needed any more incentive to pay more attention to long-range planning and encourage entrepreneurial thinking within organizations, the offshoring trend should provide a convincing kick in the pants. "For most organizations," Mitroff says, "most of the traditional management functions get in the way of innovation. That doesn't mean that a company shouldn't have a CFO, but you have to have a different *kind* of CFO—an interdisciplinary CFO."

"You have to have a different kind of CFO— an interdisciplinary CFO."

Hines argues that companies that want to stay vital—not to mention in business—must encourage creative thinking in the workforce as well as on an organizational level. "It's not just the jobs that are going overseas—it's the corporate functions," he says. "If you're going up against a European-headquartered company, your only value-add is going to be being creative, innovative, and forward-looking."

Keeping Up on Your Own

You've seen all those articles warning knowledge workers to upgrade their skills or get left behind? Time to start photocopying them for your staff.

"Knowledge workers should be working to acquire more knowledge," Hiemstra counsels. "You've got to keep learning in new areas and improving your skills as much as you can. You've got to keep asking yourself, 'What will I be learning in the next six months?' And you need to look for opportunities to be more innovative in the settings you're in."

Both Meyer and Mitroff believe that tomorrow's successful knowledge worker will be the one who can cope with an increasingly unstable world. "Don't look for a job that's well-defined, with a lot of work rules and specifications," Meyer says. "Look for jobs where your task is to make change rather than to continually deliver the same thing—not to *do* but to *innovate*. Conceive of your job as entrepreneurial."

Mitroff insists that top workers must "be comfortable with huge amounts of uncertainty. That's part of the new skill set. They will have to learn how to solve ill-defined problems, to retool and regear, to learn inter- and trans-disciplinary education, to make connections between problems and issues. Everyone will have to learn systems thinking, what the properties are of complex systems and how that can be used as a problem-solving skill. People are going to have to learn the art of problem formulation. They're going to have to learn how to question assumptions—in fact, a whole discipline for challenging assumptions. They're going to have to grapple with complex, fuzzy issues that are often in conflict, that are contradictory. It's a totally different philosophy of inquiry."

"We have become a nation of spoiled brats! America is not about certainty."

Tom Peters echoes Mitroff's emphasis on uncertainty, in somewhat less academic language. "We have become a nation of spoiled brats!" he exclaims. "America is not about certainty. The fundamental Pilgrim-father myth may be mostly nonsense, but that myth—which has served us quite well for over 300 years—is that America is about taking chances and reinventing ourselves. We have become security junkies, and to hell with that."

For Peters, white-collar workers who can demonstrate discrete, concrete achievement are most likely to beat out their peers, domestic or foreign. Some, naturally, generate tangible results in the normal course of their work: "I give a bunch of speeches—people like 'em or don't like 'em," he says. "I write a bunch of books—people like 'em or don't like 'em. I write a bunch of articles—people like 'em or don't like 'em. Whatever. They're *stuff*." But most workers and executives are unaccustomed to thinking in those terms. "It's far more difficult if you are a purchasing manager, HR manager, or finance manager, even if you are at the $100,000-a-year level," Peters says. If asked to provide evidence of their accomplishments, "to some extent, the most that those people could say is, 'I came to work every day; I showed up; I did good work; the company is still around.'" Successful 21st-century career management—including planning for that career's next phase—demands less passivity.

"Your responsibility is to be continually upscaling," Hines says. "You need a work/life plan in which you're constantly raising your own bar. If you do that, you'll always be ahead of the outsourcing wave. It's not as though everything stands still—there's a demand for more advanced activities, and if you've been keeping yourself in professional shape, you'll go up the curve with it." He argues that, more than ever, it's crucial for workers to not leave their careers in their employers' hands. "I have a responsibility to maintain my own skill level, and I can't just get stale in one place and hope I'll be taken care of, because I won't be. I'm not sure that most people have quite that level of personal responsibility yet."

Top executives in particular, of course, face broader issues than their own careers—and are, if anything, at greater risk than front-line white-collar workers of losing their place in the next economy. If all the positions you used to supervise are 8,000 miles away, and your salary is now *thousands* of times higher than theirs, you're affordable only if you can offer something truly extraordinary.

The futurists' key advice: Expand your scope of knowledge and vision. "Put your head up," Hiemstra urges, "and start seeing what's happening. I speak frequently to groups of executives in various industries, and I ask them, 'How many know something about nanotechnology?' The typical percentage is 5 to 10 percent who've even *heard* of it, which always floors me. Then I ask how many know what's happening with global population, and even though it's become a big news item, almost no executives know about the impending decline in global population in significant parts of the world—the fact that Europe will see a population decline of 80 million people in the next 50 years. Since population and social trends are primary drivers of business, I'm always surprised that executives are barely familiar with these things."

Where Will the Jobs Come From?

As Watts Wacker puts it, the U.S. economy has evolved "from agricultural to manufacturing to social to information to mental." But the consensus is that the transition to the "mental"—a "Creative Age," in the phrase of Carnegie Mellon professor Richard Florida—remains a ways off. Hiemstra insists that "we're still in the early stages of the information age," if you date the age from the emergence of the World Wide Web.

"I think we're about two-thirds through the knowledge wave," says Andy Hines, who's excited about the prospects for the last third: "This is the part where it gets good and interesting. It takes a really long time to institutionalize and incorporate and get used to working with big innovations, like electricity and information. And now it's so routine—such a part of everyday life—that we're really figuring out how to use it."

Hiemstra looks to biotech, energy, and nanotechnology for the next boom, and Davis agrees, calling biology the "parent science" of the next economic era—one that is bottom-up and rule-based rather than top-down and law-based, as physics is.

Wacker agrees and emphasizes business process as well: "The information age has been about disintermediation; the next age will be about reintermediation," he says. "It's not that we don't need middlemen—we just need different *kinds* of middlemen, and that's where the new jobs will be."

And Hines sees the next economic wave being driven by sustainability—"the triple-bottom-line idea." In the next decade or two, "sustainability will be a driving force of what we're going to use this knowledge and innovation and creativity for." The push for increased consciousness in issues of ethics, the environment, and economic justice will come from developing countries, NGOs, and knowledge workers themselves, he predicts. "A growing number of those workers *want* to be socially responsible and environmentally responsible, and they haven't been able to express that. The demand for the triple bottom line, which used to be from the crazy NGOs and the fringe, is going to come from *us*.

"At Dow Chemical," Hines continues, "sustainability is a very important part of our company. The message has thoroughly permeated—of course, you can't measure how much everyone *believes* it, but you start to see that this is what people really want to do. It's sometimes hard in the business climate to act on what you believe, but I think we're going to see more of it: Talented workers are going to go places that let them express what they want to express."

But predictions of what the next economy will focus on, or what its "energy source" will be, or even what its unofficial name will be, don't—*can't*—point definitively to the next job sector. The tech explosion came out of nowhere and rescued the U.S. economy by boosting productivity; will the next new sector do the same? We can only guess what it will be—or what impact it may have. It's not enough to study demographics and forecast that Generation Y, in its entirety, will be staffing nursing homes for retired boomers.

Peters is fast losing faith: "I'm unnerved by this jobless recovery; I'm a lot less confident than I was 18 months ago," he

Silver Lining

Does overseas migration of American knowledge jobs directly benefit the United States and its workers? Definitely: As countries such as India and Ghana begin taking—and creating—high-value jobs, those countries will see an irresistible incentive to invest more in education and other human-capital expenditures, and to de-emphasize repressive policies and military escalation. And other nations will surely follow their example: If Romania can do it, why not us? That human-capital investment, Christopher Meyer points out, is "a prerequisite for sustained economic development."

Of course, the United States, in its current antagonistic attitude, is more concerned with security than in other nations' economic health—and the white-collar transfer aids that goal as well. "High-value jobs give countries a stake in free trade and orderly economic life, which is the best anti-terror campaign that we could devise," Meyer says, noting that in addition, exporting of opportunity tends to reduce disparities in personal income—a healthy outcome by any measure: "Within a society and across the globe, there may be no more divisive force than income inequality."

says. "For 15 years, this was the pattern: We lost a manufacturing job to Mexico; we added a service job in New York—or better yet, 1.5 service jobs. I'm uncomfortable with that simplistic notion, now that we are losing high-paying jobs at an unprecedented rate—especially those damn tech jobs that we got only five years ago. It's not clear to me where the replacement jobs will come from. I think we have every right to be worried."

The Next Organization

It's practically a truism: The command-and-control era is dead; long live the age of empowerment and self-governed teams and decentralization and knowledge-sharing. And yet charismatic CEOs are still superstars, and plenty of old-style, top-down organizations are not only hanging tough but thriving. Top executives aren't the only ones content with the status quo: "We still have a lot of workers, a large sector of the economy, who want to spend their careers with one company, and who don't want to go anywhere—who have no intention of going anywhere," says Michele Bowman, senior VP of Global Foresight Associates and a founding member of the Association of Professional Futurists.

So will every company be *forced* to change how it does business in the next decade or two? Of course not. Some don't have to change and sure as hell don't want to. Others simply can't face that degree of disruption. Plenty will make incremental changes, and only under duress. And many of all these holdouts will get along just fine in the next economy.

But the rest of you—start thinking about new systems of thinking and organization. We mean it this time.

"For those whose business model currently is not threatened the way it is in music and telecommunications, I would not rest easy," Davis says. "I would be looking to figure out how my current model is creaky. What are the business models for the future? We don't have them yet. The dotcom bubble bursting is a perfect example of the wrong answer for the right question—the question being, 'What's your business model?' We'll figure out the models within the next decade or so, and they'll probably be bottom-up models."

Those models may come from the unlikeliest of sources. "On Sept. 11," Peters points out, "a virtual organization attacked a real organization, and at least in the short term, the virtual organization made idiots out of us."

"What are the business models for the future? We don't have them yet."

Mitroff invokes the same unsettling example. "Al Qaeda has a 21st-century network node organization, and we're fighting them with a 19th-century bureaucracy," he says. "The war on terrorism is not just a military war—it's an organizational war. People have been educated to solve problems that say, 'Here I am—solve me,' and we don't live in that world anymore. Sept. 11 also showed that the oceans are no longer protective moats—we don't have a magic bubble around this country." The lesson applies to work as well: "The white-collar crisis represents a radical transformation of the nature of work. You now have to be able to make connections between your job—however limited it is—and an unlimited, unbounded world."

Not everyone is apprehensive about participating in an unbounded world. "Our borders keep expanding; this is really the second or third era of globalization," Bowman says. "Twenty years from now, will we have employee ideologies that reflect industry-based perspectives more than geographically based perspectives? Absolutely." She looks ahead to a world largely populated by "electronic immigrants"—workers who take jobs in other countries without actually changing residence, much less citizenship.

Hiemstra believes that spreading globalization will occasion re-examinations of corporate social responsibility. "In the next quarter-century, more and more kinds of work will be eligible to be done anywhere in the world by people who are skilled enough to do them," he says. "Companies of all kinds will be forced to ask, 'What is our obligation to, commitment to, interest in the community and our workers? What are we really here for?' I don't know what the answers will be. They may say that the only things that matter are survival of the company and shareholder value, or they'll have a more complex answer. But companies will have to sit down and decide what is really important and what that means in terms of moving the work or not moving the work."

With American workers in mind, Peters is not especially optimistic about what choices companies will make—or even about the prospects for those companies' survival. "I think we're entering a 50-, 60-, 70-, 80-year period of instability, where I can well imagine the great American economy being surpassed by the Chinese or the Indians," he says. "The certainty is gone—which suggests that workers don't have that long to screw around. You've got to figure out what you have to sell in a global economy—and then sell the hell out of it."

MATTHEW BUDMAN is managing editor of *Across the Board*. He wrote "With Fresh Eyes" in the Nov/Dec 2003 issue.

A Roadmap for the New Trade Landscape

Putting a Face on Trade

Patty Murray

Good morning and thank you so much. It is wonderful to be here. I appreciate the warm welcome. It's really hard for me to believe that this is my twelfth year co-hosting this conference, but it is great to be here with all of you again.

Every year, the Washington Council on International Trade (WCIT) provides a great forum for all of us to talk about the most pressing trade issues, and I really want to take a second and thank Kate Wilson for the tremendous job she is doing for WCIT today. I want to thank her staff members, who have worked so hard to make today possible, all of the other speakers that you're going to enjoy hearing from today. And I want to join Kate in thanking all of our sponsors.

This year, your topic is "Choosing China or India." Well, I hope you'll forgive me, but I am not going to choose between the two largest countries in the world. I'd just rather not start my speech by upsetting a billion people this early in the morning. [audience laughs]

But there's another reason why I'm not going to focus on India, or on China, as I did last year. And that's because there's a much larger and more urgent challenge that we need to address. Now, standing up here today, I could focus on the happy news. I could say, "We signed the Panama and South Korea trade deals a few days ago. And we can all pat ourselves on the back."

But there is a hard truth all of us have to face, and that's why I'm here. The truth is that the trade landscape in Washington, D.C.—and really across the entire country—has changed dramatically in the past few years, and those of us who support trade have to adjust to this new reality. The old pro-trade consensus that once existed in the Senate is not there. The old arguments about trade that we've been using since NAFTA don't work anymore. And the days when we could talk about the benefits of trade—without addressing the downsides—are history.

Unless we change how we look at trade, how we talk about it, and how we engage, we will find ourselves standing alone on the margins while the trade debate moves forward without us.

Friends, I believe we cannot let that happen to our country or to our state. As the most trade-dependent state in the nation, we have too much to lose in jobs and economic opportunity if

America turns away from trade. And as a country, we have too much to lose if we turn inward and let other countries write the rules of trade without us at the table.

We are living in a new trade landscape. I see it every day in the United States Senate. This morning, I want to help you understand it: where it's coming from—and most important—how we need to change to have an impact. In that spirit, I want to offer a roadmap to the new trade landscape.

Two months ago, a number of you came to Washington, D.C., and we talked about the trade climate. I mentioned to you that support has really fallen since I first arrived in the Senate back in 1993.

Back then, you will remember, WCIT members were in D.C.—it seemed to me like every week. Everyone was talking about what trade agreements would accomplish. We were bringing Washington state apples over to the White House in great celebration. Al Gore was debating Ross Perot on national TV. Everyone was talking about it. Every day I was hearing from farmers, from workers, from businesses, and from the Administration about trade. And it wasn't just that the U.S. Trade Representative and Cabinet secretaries came to my office in Washington, D.C. They were out in our states—talking with our constituents, talking to people here at home and every state across the nation about the importance of trade.

So what's the landscape today? Well, consider this: on Saturday night (6/30/07), the President's Trade Promotion Authority expired. And how did it end? As T.S. Eliot might say, "Not with a bang, but a whimper." Actually, there wasn't even a whimper. It was more like the last episode of the *Sopranos*. It just ended. [audience laughs]

I never even got a phone call from the Administration saying they were concerned about this. Certainly this weekend, as I went about my schedule and went to the grocery store, no one mentioned it to me. For me, that "lack of volume" speaks volumes about how much the trade landscape has changed. Years ago, there was a general consensus that increased trade was good for America. Today that consensus has faded. But we cannot give up.

We all know our state depends on trade. The vitality of this region depends on whether or not we can export our airplanes, or our apples, and or our operating systems. We know that trade can mean more good-paying, family-wage jobs here at home, and a better standard of living. We also know that trade has to work for everyone, and that trade agreements need bipartisan support.

So what is this new trade climate? How did we get here? And what can we do about it so our state and our country don't suffer? To understand this new trade reality, I think you need to understand two things—the new center and the new standard.

The New Center

The landscape has moved, and what was once "on the periphery" is now "the new center." Let me give you two clear examples. In 1993, when NAFTA passed, there were two side agreements—one on labor, and one on the environment. That was 14 years ago. Last week, when the trade agreement with Panama was signed, labor and the environment were not extras added on separately. They were part of the core, underlying agreement. What was once on the periphery is now the new center.

There is also a new political center around trade in the U.S. Congress. The members of Congress who were once strong advocates for trade are now skeptics. And the people who were once skeptical are now hostile. The landscape has shifted dramatically, and in Congress we have a new center of gravity in the trade debate.

The New Standard

The second big feature of this new environment is the new standard by which we now evaluate trade deals. It used to be that, "What's good for General Motors is good for America." Well, those days are gone. Now the standard has two questions: Is it good for American workers? And is it good for America's long-term growth?

During the push for NAFTA, businesses came in and talked about how it was important for them. And that was enough. But today—if they don't talk about the impact for their workers—they will have a very tough time having a credible voice in the debate.

Trade Skepticism Is Bipartisan

I want to add that the skepticism about trade is bipartisan. For a long time, it was just assumed that it was the Democratic side of the aisle that was most skeptical about trade. Well, believe me there are a lot of strong skeptics in our Democratic caucus today. But consider this: The main bill on China's currency was written by 4 senators—two Democrats, two Republicans. Two years ago, the Central American Free Trade Agreement faced opposition from whom? Southern Republicans who were concerned about the sugar industry. Last year on the trade agreement with Vietnam, it was Republicans who were concerned about their local textile industry. Today the concern about trade is both intense and bipartisan.

Why Trade Support Is Fading

As we try to adjust to this new landscape, we have to ask—why has support for trade begun to evaporate? There are many reasons. Mainly, I think the American people have been more directly exposed to the negative impacts of trade than to the positive ones.

There's a big gap between the way we experience the upsides and the downsides of trade. It's the difference between a summer breeze and a tornado. The benefits of trade are gradual, diffuse and subtle. They carry you forward slowly. But trade's downsides are more like a tornado—strong, sharp and localized. People feel the impact of the downsides in a very direct and personal way.

There's another reason for the shift. Our government has done a lousy job of enforcing trade deals. We have not made other countries live up to their agreements. And that's one of the reasons why we see support for trade among farmers slipping dramatically. Now, I have to say, in recent years, USTR has been pushing on the aerospace sector and on intellectual property, but everyone agrees we have a long way to go.

And it is not an underestimation to say that American workers don't feel secure today. They see trade as part of the problem rather than part of the solution. In March, a poll by *The Wall Street Journal* and NBC News found that 46 percent of Americans feel trade agreements have hurt the United States. Only 28 percent feel trade agreements have helped our country.

And the numbers are even worse when you ask people about the impact on jobs. A major study by the Pew Research Center in December of 2006 found that 48 percent of Americans believe that free trade agreements cost jobs. Only 12 percent believe they create jobs.

So what is behind these numbers?

Our promises about trade have slammed into some of the negative realities of trade, and people have felt it. For example, we've seen outsourcing move up the job ladder from call center operators to computer programmers and engineers. So today when you say "trade," many Americans don't think of new markets, they wonder if their jobs will be shipped overseas. They worry that one day they'll call 911, and they'll get an operator in Bangalore.

People don't feel secure today, and in a climate of fear, people don't look for opportunities. They look for security. So when you talk about a new trade agreement, they're not focused on what they can win. They're focused on what they're going to lose. That viewpoint has some very loud and strong proponents. Need I say the name "Lou Dobbs"? He is reflecting that insecurity, and he is amplifying it. Believe me, I have been on his show and, trust me, when he has an opinion, you know it. [audience laughs]

So that is the new landscape that we live in and how it came to be. The next question really is—what can we do about it? So let me offer you today a roadmap of five strategies that I think will help us move forward in the new trade landscape.

A Roadmap for the New Trade Landscape

- **First of all, we have to engage in today's trade debate—not the one from 14 years ago.** We've been saying "trade is good" ever since NAFTA. In the meantime, real people have been hurt by trade, and we're still saying the words "trade is good." We need to acknowledge the downsides of trade, and we need to address and work on those downsides.
- **Secondly, we need to put a human face on the benefits of trade.** When a trade deal is coming up, we need to

share the personal stories of how it will tangibly help real families. No longer can businesses make the case just based on growth lines and projections of their markets. You have to tell the story about how it really affects people, and you have to help those of us in Congress find and tell those stories.

- **Third, you've got to help people see that they have a personal stake in trade.** That's a challenge even here in Washington state. We always throw out that statistic—"1 in 3 jobs in Washington state relies on international trade." And it's true. But I bet if I went out on the street and asked 100 people—"Does your job rely on international trade?" Maybe one person would say yes. We've got to get the other 32 people—whose jobs really do rely on trade—to see they have a personal stake in the outcome.
- **Fourth, you've got to talk to the people who are not on your dance card.** We've got to talk to more than the usual suspects because the center of gravity on trade has shifted. It used to be that when you came to Washington, D.C., if you met with the Washington state congressional delegation and USTR, you'd covered your bases. Not anymore. Now the people we need to reach out to are people who've never heard of WCIT. You need to find a way to reach them. In your industry, look for associations that can help you get in the door to the movers and shakers who you've never met.

And finally—here's the most challenging one—we need to equip American workers to win in a global market, and trade advocates need to be leading that fight.

Equipping Americans to Win Through Trade

It's not enough to push for your own bottom line. Trade advocates need to become the new champions of American workers—because unless we can show that Americans will win in open markets we won't get open markets.

And this isn't about lip service. It's about investing. It's about training workers here instead of looking for cheap labor overseas. It's about pushing to improve our workforce investment system. It's about being in our high schools and making sure we're producing the next generation of scientists and engineers. It's a full-court press—not for rhetoric—but for results.

And that's one of the things I'm really focused on in the United States Senate. I've been working on education for years in the classroom and in the Congress, and I know it starts with early childhood education. In the Senate last month, we passed a new Head Start bill that really improves early education and complements the strong work our state has begun.

Next, we've also got to build the New American High School—a place where students get the skills they need to graduate and succeed in college, careers, and life. Bill Gates has said that our high schools are "obsolete." What can we do about it?

We need to target reading, math and graduation. Four years ago, I introduced the PASS Act to reform America's high schools. My bill invests in reading and math, helps students and their families plan for graduation, and helps schools that are struggling. I've been pushing it every year, and I'm proud to say that this year, the Bush Administration and others have finally agreed that high school reform will be the central idea as we update No Child Left Behind. So it starts in our schools.

The next step is helping workers get the skills they need to fill the jobs that are in demand. We've got 87,000 job openings here in Washington state, and 145,000 people looking for work. We've got more than enough people to fill those jobs, but they don't have right skills. It's about priorities and reversing the trends.

Unfortunately, since 2001 the Bush Administration has cut workforce training by a billion dollars. That's the wrong priority. That's why in the Senate, as chairman of the Senate Employment and Workplace Safety Subcommittee, I'm leading the fight to update the Workforce Investment Act for today's realities.

And finally, we need to help the workers who have been hurt by trade. That's why I support expanding Trade Adjustment Assistance, so it covers workers in more fields and offers more types of training and assistance.

Friends, I need your help to turn all of those proposals—the PASS Act, the Workforce Investment Act and Trade Adjustment Assistance reform—into law. If businesses lead the fight to help American workers, they'll win credibility to argue for more trade agreements in the future.

So friends, in conclusion, we do face a new trade landscape. It's contentious, and it's been tempered by the reality that workers have experienced since the 1990s. We have to change the way we think and the way we engage. We have to make the benefits of trade real, and trade advocates must become the new champions for American workers.

I know that sounds like a tall order, but Washington state has done it before. It was our own Senator Warren Magnuson who saw the importance of trade with China before many others. It was our state that welcomed the first trading ships from China. It was our state's tech industry that has transformed how we work and communicate.

I'm convinced we can build a stronger future for our kids and grandkids through trade. We've got the roadmap. Now let's get to work.

Address by **Patty Murray**, U.S. Senator from Washington State. Delivered at the 12th Annual Senators Trade Conference, Washington Council on International Trade, Seattle, Washington, July 2, 2007.

As Seen in *Vital Speeches of the Day*, by Patty Murray. October 2007. Delivered at the 12th Annual Senators Trade Conference on International Trade, Seattle, Washington, July 2, 2007.

Are Global Prices Converging or Diverging?

REUVEN GLICK

Most people barely think twice anymore when they discover that their toothbrush was made in China, their tee-shirt was made in Honduras, and their car was made in Germany. With an increasing volume of goods and services flowing around the world, it is natural to assume that the marketplace has become "global," which is to say, much more integrated. One implication of greater integration among the world's markets is that prices for equivalent goods and services from country to country should tend to converge.

This *Economic Letter* reports on recent research that analyzes trends in global prices over the past decade and a half (Bergin and Glick 2007). It finds that, in fact, according to one measure, there was a trend of convergence from 1990 through 1997, which is consistent with the view that the world has become increasingly more trade-integrated over time, due to fewer governmental barriers and declining costs for transportation and communication. Somewhat surprisingly, however, it also finds that this trend was interrupted and then reversed in subsequent years, implying a general U-shaped pattern over the past one and a half decades. In exploring possible factors accounting for this reversal, a likely suspect turns out to be the hike in oil prices in recent years, which has raised transportation costs.

Data

Our measure of price dispersion is constructed from data on actual price levels obtained from the *Worldwide Cost of Living Survey* conducted by the Economist Intelligence Unit (EIU), which records local prices for over 160 individual goods and services in more than 120 cities worldwide. The goods are narrowly defined—for example, "apples (1 kg)," "men's raincoats (Burberry type)," and "light bulbs (2, 60 watt)." All prices are recorded in local currency and converted into dollars.

The EIU database does not contain a price quote for all goods and cities in every year. Since we are interested in how prices vary both from country to country and over time, we assembled data for the same set of tradable products for cities where generally no more than 30% of the observations were missing in any given year. The resulting panel consists of price data on 101 tradable products in 108 cities in 70 countries for the period 1990 to 2005, the last year for which we have data.

We use these data to compare price level differences across cities in different locations and countries. For example, for a given pair of cities, say, London and New York, we compute the difference in the dollar price level of each good, such as tomatoes (specifically, the log of the ratio of the price levels of tomatoes in the two locations). We then define price dispersion for each pair of cities as the mean of squared price differences across all 101 traded goods. (We square the price differences before calculating the mean because we care only about the magnitude of price differences, not whether prices are higher or lower in one country than in another.)

The solid line in Figure 1 presents our measure of price dispersion averaged over all city-pairs on a year-by-year basis over the period 1990 to 2005; a rough U-shaped pattern is apparent, with dispersion falling from 1990 to 1997 and then gradually rising through 2005. The dotted line plots results that exclude city pairs within the same country, and clearly, the pattern is little changed. The fact that this line is somewhat higher implies that price dispersion is less among cities within the same borders.

Further analysis (not shown) indicates that the U-shape applies broadly across various subgroupings of countries, that is, for city pairs where both are in industrial countries, both are in developing countries, and one city is in an industrial country and the other is in a developing country. For city pairs within the eurozone alone and for U.S. pairs, the degree of "U-ness" is shallower, but it still holds. In addition, as shown in Figure 2, the U-pattern is present when we break the data into particular commodity groups. (For comparison, we also show the pattern of price dispersion for a set of nontraded goods.) While there are clear differences between commodity groups in terms of average levels of price dispersion—high dispersion among perishable food items, and low dispersion among household supplies—the U-shaped pattern over time is consistent across almost all of the commodity groups, with falling levels of dispersion until 1997 and rising dispersion afterward.

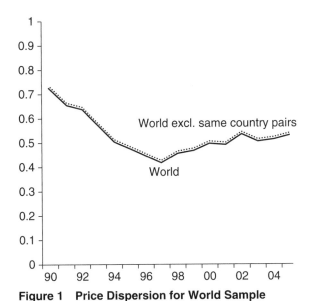

Figure 1 Price Dispersion for World Sample

Note: Dotted line omits city pairs where both cities are in the same country.

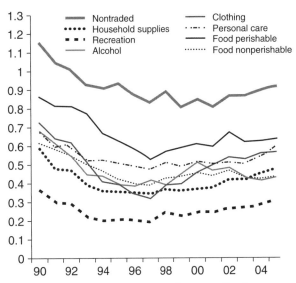

Figure 2 Price Dispersion by Commodity Groups

Determinants of Price Dispersion

To explore further the determinants of the pattern of price dispersion in our sample, we conducted a formal statistical analysis. Specifically, we modeled price dispersion between any two cities as a function of standard trade friction determinants, such as the distance between the cities, language differences, adjacent national borders, tariff barriers, and institutional arrangements, including membership in regional trade agreements or currency unions. Also included are city and year dummy variables to capture factors that may affect the dispersion in prices between cities and over time that are not otherwise modeled.

Regression results for the full world data set indicate that price dispersion increases with distance and tariffs, and it decreases when the cities are in the same country, when they share a border, and when they share a language. In addition, price dispersion declines when countries participate in a regional trade agreement or in a currency union. However, the U-shaped pattern over time remains, indicating that it is not attributable to the "usual suspect" variables studied in past research. (The U-shaped time pattern is captured in the regression by the estimated coefficients for the time variable dummies.)

Therefore, we considered several other factors. One is exchange rate variability, as measured by the nominal exchange rate volatility or the occurrence of a currency crisis. If exchange rate variability has increased in recent years, this might have contributed to the greater price dispersion observed in the data. In fact, we found that neither measure of exchange rate variability is time-varying in a way that is helpful in explaining the U-shaped pattern of price dispersion. The yearly means of exchange rate volatility and the occurrence of currency crises across the pairs in the sample take on large values in several points during our sample period (1992, 1997–1998, and 2002), but no U-shape is evident. This is confirmed by regressions, which find that greater price dispersion is associated with greater exchange rate variability, but the latter does not account for the U-shaped time variation in price dispersion.

Another avenue we explored is whether the relationship between our explanatory factors and price dispersion has shifted over time. For example, there is some evidence that the pass-through of exchange rate movements to import prices has fallen over time, so that a given depreciation of a country's currency leads to a smaller increase in import prices in the local currency. Lower pass-through implies that price changes in one country are less likely to lead to price changes in other countries, and therefore to more price divergence. While we do find statistically significant variation over time in the sensitivity of price dispersion to exchange rate volatility, this variation does not appear to correspond much with the U-shaped pattern in price dispersion.

However, in a similar exercise examining the variation in the sensitivity of price dispersion to distance, we find a rough U-shape is apparent, with the sensitivity to distance first declining and then rising. This suggests that some common factor affecting the cost of transporting goods a given distance may be at work.

Oil and Transport Costs

Pursuing this possibility, we search for additional variables that vary over time and that are related to distance. An obvious candidate is the price of oil, which has varied significantly over time and affects transportation costs. If oil prices raise transportation costs, they should increase differences in the prices of imported goods, raising average price dispersion. In addition, they should raise costs proportionately more for countries farther apart.

In fact, a plot of oil prices (relative to the U.S. Consumer Price Index, CPI) in Figure 3 shows that it is time-varying in a manner that roughly coincides with the pattern in price dispersion, in that the price of oil reached a low point in the sample shortly after 1997 and rose gradually in subsequent years. For comparison, the figure also plots measures of U.S. air and freight transport costs, which also rose at the end of the sample. In the

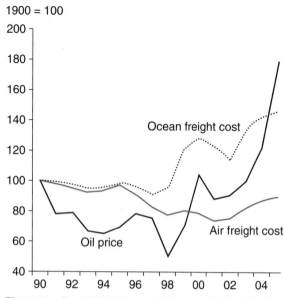

1900 = 100

Figure 3   Real Oil Price and Transportation Costs

Note: All series are expressed relative to the U.S. CPI.

absence of a general measure of world transport costs, we use oil prices to proxy for trends in such costs in regressions. We find this variable is highly significant and associated with increased price dispersion. We also find that a rise in the price of oil has a bigger impact on price dispersion if two countries are far apart. This clearly lends support to the transportation cost story.

The basic findings of our analysis hold under a variety of alternative formulations, namely, omitting any city without data for all 15 years of the sample period, including only one city per country, using different measures of price dispersion, and considering additional control variables, such as international differences in GDP per capita, GDP, or wages.

Conclusion

Our analysis finds significant variation over time in the degree of global price convergence over the past 15 years. In particular, there appears to be a general U-shaped pattern with rising price dispersion in recent years, a pattern which is remarkably robust across country groupings and commodity groups. This time-variation is difficult to explain in terms of the explanatory factors common in the literature, as these tend not to vary much over time. However, regression analysis indicates that this time-varying pattern coincides well with oil price and transport cost fluctuations, which clearly vary over time and have risen in recent years.

Reference

Bergin, Paul, and Reuven Glick. 2007. "Global Price Dispersion: Are Prices Converging or Diverging?" *Journal of International Money and Finance* 26(5) pp. 703–729 (September).

Reprinted with permission from the *FRBSF Economic Letter*, August 10, 2007, by Reuven Glick. The opinions expressed in this article do not necessarily reflect the views of the management of the Federal Reserve Bank of San Francisco, or of the Board of Governors of the Federal Reserve System.

What One Hand Gives, the Other Takes

Industrial Countries' Policy Coherence for Development

Rich countries' policies in areas such as trade, the environment, investment, migration, security, and technology could either bolster or blunt the effectiveness of their own aid policies to poor countries, depending on whether and to what extent all these policies are coherent or contradictory. Too often they are not coherent. But the main message of this author is that policy coherence for development cannot be determined by the rich industrial countries alone. Meaningful developing-country participation is essential in forming coherent, constructive policies.

RONALD MENDOZA

Rich countries' foreign aid policies are intended to help poor countries develop. But their policies in other areas—spanning trade, the environment, investment, migration, security, and technology—could be just as (if not more) important in attaining that goal. If these other policies are contradictory to foreign aid, they could blunt the latter's effectiveness and hinder development in poor countries. Rich countries' policy contradictions are myriad, and a number of them could have serious implications for poor countries' development prospects.[1]

"Tying" foreign aid is one case in point. Essentially, this policy requires that part of the aid is spent to purchase inputs from the donor country. Designed to generate economic benefits for the donor by promoting its domestic commercial and trade interests, this policy often comes at the cost of aid effectiveness—tying aid could contradict aid itself. Studies suggest that "tying" could raise aid project costs by about 15–30 percent, effectively reducing aid value by 15 percent or over, and it could also result in a misallocation of resources and the use of inappropriate technologies (Jepma 1994). At present, only about 42 percent of official development assistance by rich countries is untied (OECD 2006).

Some trade promotion policies of rich countries could also prove contradictory to their own development assistance efforts and detrimental to development. A specific example is the Norwegian Ship Export Campaign of 1976–1980, which resulted in the export of vessels and equipment to a number of developing countries. Financed through the Norwegian Guarantee Institute for Export Credits (GIEK), these projects proved to be economically unsustainable, so that government counter-guarantees on the part of the developing countries were triggered, and the Norwegian government became a creditor. A subsequent evaluation of the program by the Norwegian government concluded that there was a lack of needs analyses and risk assessments that would have revealed how this project was contradictory to the development of the countries participating in it. In October 2006, Norway took what many in the development community saw as a groundbreaking step: unilaterally declaring as "illegitimate" about $80 million in debt related to the ship export campaign that was owed to it by Egypt, Ecuador, Peru, Jamaica, and Sierra Leone. As a way of sharing responsibility for this failure, Norway canceled this debt and, taking a further step, chose not to declare this move as a contribution to Official Development Assistance (ODA).[2]

Norway's debt cancellation is but one of many fairly recent examples of industrial countries' recognizing and acting on instances of their own policy incoherence vis-à-vis their broader efforts to contribute to development. This paper seeks to shed light on this issue and its growing importance. "Policy coherence" is defined herein as the mutual consistency of policies, and it could be viewed either proactively, requiring coherent policies to be mutually supportive, or as a minimum condition, requiring that policies at least not be contradictory. Thus there are two main levels of coherence: one where the policies are reinforcing in their effects (i.e., a strong form of coherence) and another where "at least no harm is done" (i.e., a weak form of coherence). Understanding this issue in these terms is especially useful when policies with different objectives are analyzed. The hierarchy of policy objectives is not always well defined nationally, let alone internationally. And there is often no easy way to prioritize among myriad, often competing, policy objectives and their beneficiaries.[3] Under these circumstances, "weak form coherence" is often the best that policymakers can aim for.

Why raise this issue now? Increasing emphasis on aid effectiveness, growing recognition that aid alone is insufficient for development, and increasing globalization and its resulting policy externalities are some of the principal reasons that enhancing rich countries' policy coherence for development is emerging as one of the key challenges for public policy today. The present discussions on this topic, however, have been largely rich-country–centric. This paper briefly scans some of the key ideas on policy coherence for development, and it argues that, in addition, it would be important to examine its distributional and regime aspects. The point made here is that policy coherence for development cannot simply be "supplied" by industrial countries. Proactive developing-country participation is essential to forging agreement on in what forms and to what extent policy coherence for development will take shape.

Why the Growing Interest in Policy Coherence?

Increasing interest in industrial countries' policy coherence for development results from perhaps three main factors: increasing emphasis on aid effectiveness; growing recognition that aid alone is insufficient for development; and increasing globalization and its resulting policy externalities.

More Bang for the Foreign Aid Buck

Growing interest in policy coherence could be traced in part to donor countries' heightened efforts to increase aid effectiveness and accomplish more with their aid. Even as many donor countries face their own domestic challenges that could tighten the fiscal purse strings further, they are nevertheless expected to live up to their aid commitments and contribute to internationally agreed policy objectives in part embodied in the Millennium Development Goals (MDGs).[4] Significant resources are required to achieve these goals—the United Nations Millennium Project (2005, 240) estimates that about $73 billion in 2006, rising to $135 billion in 2015, would be required to meet the MDGs in all poor countries. Yet, increases in ODA in recent years have been modest when compared to the needed resources, and part of these flows has been focused mostly on only certain countries.[5] This places even more emphasis on aid effectiveness—that no aid is wasted and that available resources are put to best use for development.

Trade, Not Aid

There is also stronger recognition of the fact that development assistance or aid alone is insufficient in achieving development—echoing, in part, the decades-old call for "trade, not aid" in many parts of the developing world. This is reflected in part in Millennium Development Goal 8, which calls for a global partnership for development, including taking steps such as further developing an open trading and financial system and dealing comprehensively with developing countries' debt problems. Growing attention is given to ensuring "development friendliness" in other areas to reinforce aid. For instance, Birdsall et al. (2005, 150) note that a scheme for temporary work visas amounting to no more than 3 percent of the rich countries' total labor force could easily yield $200 billion annually for the citizens of developing countries. Furthermore, liberalization of industrial

countries' markets as well as investments in trade facilitation in developing countries[6] could create welfare gains for low- and middle-income countries of about another $150 billion per year (Hertel 2004, 23–24). Hence, it has been argued that policies in international trade and migration as well as in other areas, such as investment, environment, security, and technology, could be critical in improving the development prospects of poor countries. Within, as well as across, each of these areas, policy coherence could bolster development objectives.

Your Policy, My Backyard

The preponderance of policy externalities—policy effects stretching across borders—has also placed the onus on more coherent policymaking. Externalities emerge as a by-product of many economic activities that in certain cases are directly facilitated (or condoned) by public policy. This outcome could, of course, be true for any country; however, by virtue of their (individual and collective) economic size, the industrial countries are often among the primary generators of many of these externalities. From a development perspective, one could judge these externalities as being positive (promoting development) or negative (obstructing development). For instance, positive worldwide externalities could emerge from sound monetary policies and robust financial regulations in industrial countries—home to some of the largest financial centers in the world.

However, some of their domestic policies also produce border-transgressing negative externalities. Domestic agricultural protection policies in these countries, for example, tend to depress world prices and limit the revenue opportunities for many developing-country farmers (Baffes 2006), as well as create possible inefficiencies in the subsidizing country itself (see Box 1). In 2004, tariff and budget-based support to agriculture in Organization for Economic Cooperation and Development (OECD) countries reached about $350 billion, with about $280 billion going directly to producers. Developing-country farmers are at a significant disadvantage, as illustrated, for example, in the case of the sugar sector, where total support in OECD countries of about $6.4 billion per annum is roughly equal to the entire annual sugar exports of developing countries (Newfarmer 2006, 17). Hence, enhanced policy coherence is often required in order to promote more activities that generate positive externalities and to mitigate incidences of negative externalities.

Policy Coherence from an Industrial Country Viewpoint

An industrial country perspective on policy coherence reveals important insights, particularly as these countries' individual and collective policies often have widespread and relatively larger effects across borders and on the developing world. A growing number of studies have been undertaken on the topic (see, for instance, Forster and Stokke 1999; OECD 2004a). The policies examined in these coherence-related studies could be roughly categorized into two broad types: external policies (i.e., those explicitly directed across borders) and domestic policies that have cross-border consequences (i.e., international exter-

Box 1
On U.S. Agricultural Policy

"[C]urrent agriculture policies are not sufficient for addressing the challenges facing farmers and the nation as a whole. Federal farm programs, while remaining popular with many producers, are not serving U.S. agriculture as well as in the past and are having unintended consequences. These programs have traditionally been justified as a way to provide insulation against market fluctuations and keep more small farms in business. Current programs do, in fact, increase incomes and provide some protection against sharp market changes. But rather than keep smaller farmers on the land, they have contributed to farm consolidation and higher land prices. This, in turn, makes it more difficult for younger farmers to enter farming. In many cases the programs also discourage producers of program commodities from switching crops as markets change and undermine the incentive to innovate and develop the specialty products today's consumers want.

Continued U.S. backing of our current farm programs is also one of the major reasons for the recent collapse of the World Trade Organization's (WTO) Doha Round of negotiations. The view of this as a positive development by some U.S. farm groups is shortsighted. If it can be restarted, the Doha Round could be a catalyst for expanding markets for U.S. food and agricultural products. Additionally, our current farm programs are vulnerable to WTO litigation for breaking current international trade rules. We run the risk of losing these programs through litigation without receiving the benefits that a negotiated Doha Round agreement would provide. Farm programs that serve a smaller and smaller portion of farmers may also be vulnerable to Congressional budget-cutting because of their continuing high cost and perceived inequity at a time of historic deficits. To be efficient and environmentally sustainable, agricultural production must be flexible and responsive to market opportunities. The biggest opportunity for American farmers today is in the new markets created by dramatically changing patterns of demand: Economic growth in developing countries; population growth and evolving consumption patterns in both the United States and developing countries; the expanding role of agriculture in energy production. To secure these new markets, farm production must reorient itself to today's changing world, and public policy must support this goal."

Source: Bertini et al. (2006, 4–5).

Assessments of policy coherence for development could determine whether and to what extent policies reinforce (or contradict) each other. Ideally, these conclusions could be reached by assessing policy impact and then comparing the results directly against the various stated goals of development, such as the Millennium Development Goals. However, given the measurement difficulties, present discussions on this topic have generally not focused on the final development impact of industrial-country policies. For practical and pragmatic reasons, alternative approaches have been taken, and proxies for "impact" have been used. These include assessing resource flows, policy effort, and institutional reforms implemented. One could think of these factors simply as different possible "units of measure" that could help indicate the extent to which policy coherence is being (or can be) enhanced.

Resource Flows

Estimating resource flows is one alternative to evaluating policy impact. Capital scarcity is seen as one of the most critical impediments to growth and development in poor countries. Increasing resource flows to the developing world is therefore a critical policy objective that feeds into final development outcomes like poverty reduction, increased education, and better health. Policies that, explicitly or inadvertently, shrink resources in the developing world could be deemed incoherent with the policies that seek to facilitate these resource flows in support of development. Resource flows are obviously rough indicators, given that there are myriad other factors that jointly determine how these flows affect development.[7]

Various studies, notably a few on aid and trade, have tried to assess net resource flows into developing countries. Some juxtapose aid to certain countries with the unrealized export revenues due to agricultural support policies in industrial countries (see Table 1). Here, aid is intended to benefit developing countries by increasing resource flows to them; on the other hand, agricultural support policies are intended to benefit domestic producers, and in the process diminish trade revenues in developing countries. Using resource flows as a "unit of measure" for policy coherence, it often appears that "what one hand gives, the other takes."

However, trade revenues are not equivalent to foreign aid flows. The nature and motivations behind these two flows are inherently different. Development assistance, or foreign aid, is ideally a form of "giving" where the development of the recipient is the primary objective. Trade revenues, on the other hand, are the result of a mutually beneficial exchange, or a *quid pro quo*. Hence, these assessments often attempt to suggest—but in fact do not necessarily measure—some notion of "net benefit" by showing the opposing direction of these flows. At an intuitive level, the figures in Table 1 nevertheless underscore possible contradictory policies.

Policy Effort

A relatively more direct alternative could be to assess the policies themselves—to examine the "policy effort" that countries individually undertake toward enhanced policy coherence. That is, one could "grade" industrial countries on the presence,

nalities). Examples of the former include official development assistance and international trade and financial policies, whereas examples of the latter include studies of domestic agricultural support policies and domestic environmental policies. Each of these policies affects the developing world in distinct ways, and understanding their possible interactions and effectiveness are clearly among industrial country policymakers' concerns.

Table 1 What One Hand Gives, the Other Takes

- In 2001, Mali received $38 million in U.S. aid . . .
  . . . but lost $43 million in cotton export earnings due to U.S. subsidies.
- Burkina Faso received $27 million in heavily indebted poor countries (HIPC) debt relief . . .
  . . . but lost $28 million in cotton export earnings due to U.S. subsidies.
- Mozambique received $136 million in EU aid . . .
  . . . but lost $106 million in sugar export earnings due to EU subsidies.
- In 2002, EU aid to Brazil, Thailand, South Africa, and India were $10 million, $14.6 million, $121.8 million, and $13 million respectively[a] . . .
  . . . but that same year, EU sugar policies cost Brazil $494 million, Thailand $151 million, and South Africa and India around $60 million each.
- In 2003, U.S. subsidies to its cotton growers totaled $2.3 billion—about 1.5 times higher than its foreign aid to Africa that year. These subsidies contribute to depressing world prices, leading to income losses for near-subsistence cotton farmers in West Africa and Central and South Asia. In West Africa alone, rich-country subsidies lead to income losses in excess of about $150 million per year.[b]
- In 2004, for every $3 of EU aid to Mozambique, the EU "takes back" $1 through restrictions on access to the EU sugar market.
- In 2004, U.S. tariffs on imports from India, Indonesia, Sri Lanka, and Thailand brought in $1.87 billion in revenues—twice the amount the U.S. committed for tsunami relief to these same countries.[c]

Sources: Unless otherwise stated, data are from OXFAM International (2002a; 2002b; 2004).
a. External aid financed from the general budget of the Commission and the European Development Fund (in euros) taken from EC (2002, 177–80). Dollar values calculated using the 2002 average exchange rate of €1.06 = $1.
b. Baffes (2006, 121–24).
c. Roodman (2005a, 3).

extent, and quality of their policies in areas that are deemed crucial to development. The Commitment to Development Index (CDI) of the Center for Global Development and *Foreign Policy* magazine has pioneered this approach.[8]

Intended to generate widespread interest and debate on industrial countries' policies and their effects on development, the CDI is an annual index calculated for each of twenty-one OECD Development Assistance Committee (DAC) member countries (except Luxembourg). The CDI is composed of indicators in seven policy areas (called "policy domains"): official development assistance or aid, trade, investment, migration, environment, security, and technology. One of the main rationales behind the CDI is that foreign aid policies need to be complemented and reinforced by policies in these other areas to achieve development, thus alluding to the need for *strong form* policy coherence (i.e., policies that reinforce each other in support of development in poor countries). Table 2 summarizes the components of the indicators in each area and notes some of the key features in the construction of the CDI.

The index is so far a unique attempt to evaluate and rank the industrial countries on the "development friendliness" of their policies. All twenty-one countries are given scores based on indicators in each of the seven policy areas. These indicators are based partly on the availability of data and the extent to which they represent the key policies within each area. To illustrate, the index score on aid is based first on aid totals with principal and interest payments on debt netted out in order to more closely reflect net transfers to recipients (akin to the resource-flows approach discussed earlier). A penalty is applied to the score if the country has policies that tend to diminish the impact of aid, such as through "tying" and the tendency to

fund many small projects or "project proliferation." Thus, these specific forms of policy incoherence are penalized, and result in a lower score.[9]

On the other hand, strong form coherence is also rewarded. The score is increased by accounting for the private giving to developing countries caused by fiscal policy (e.g., tax incentives). Furthermore, a "selectivity weight" is applied to reflect the recipient country's appropriateness for aid, based on its quality of governance and need. Thus, a donor country that gives aid to better governed and poorer countries (instead of using aid for nondevelopment—i.e., geopolitical—purposes) will tend to get a higher score on the aid policy area.

Thus, the final score is meant to reflect the "quality adjusted aid quantity" (Roodman 2005b). All these features of the index provide a fuller picture of not just the level of resources channeled to poor countries, but also the ways these resources are channeled, which could be equally important in ensuring strong development outcomes.

Because the scores in aid (and in the other areas where necessary) are weighted for differences in country size (e.g., wealth), countries could be ranked within each policy area. For instance, the United States with income roughly twenty times that of Spain could give a greater volume of aid than the latter. However, based on the methodology of the CDI, the measured "efforts" of these two countries in pursuing coherent development assistance policies are presently not dramatically different, after scaling for size and discounting for contradictory policies.[10] Furthermore, across policy areas, countries could rank very differently. Denmark, for example, ranks first in aid in 2005, but only fifth in trade (tied with four other countries) and ninth in investment (tied with three others). Ranking therefore depends

Table 2 Summary Description of the Commitment to Development Index

Policy Domain	Components	Some Key Features
Aid	Index based on gross aid totals with the following adjustments: • Debt service from developing countries on concessional loans deducted. • Three aspects of "aid quality" factored in as discounts or penalties: tying, (lack of) selectivity, and the tendency to fund many small projects. • Portion of private charitable giving is credited to government tax policies.	"Selectivity weight" is intended to reflect the recipient country's appropriateness for aid, based on a combination of governance (i.e., aid is more effective where there is good governance) and poverty (i.e., need). Emergency aid is exempted from selectivity weighting to reflect that some types of aid may be more valuable in countries with very poor governance.
Trade	Index based on measure of barriers to goods exports from developing countries, composed of: • Index measuring combined effect of tariffs, nontariff measures, and domestic subsidies. • Indicator of "revealed openness" (i.e., imports from developing countries as a share of importer's GDP).	• The indicator of "revealed openness" was included in order to take account of unmeasured (tacit) barriers. • The tariff data refer to upper bound rates committed in the WTO and do not factor in the preferences granted to poor countries, such as through the U.S. Africa Growth and Opportunity Act and the European Everything But Arms Initiative.
Investment	Index based on qualitative survey of government policies in the following areas: • Provision of quasi-political risk insurance. • Procedures to prevent double taxation. • Actions to prevent bribery and other corruption. • Measures to support foreign investors moving to developing countries. • Policies that affect portfolio flows (e.g., restrictions on pension fund investment in developing countries).	Improves on 2003 index, which used foreign direct investment (i.e., an outcome rather than a policy).
Migration	Index based on weighted indicators of: • Immigrant flows, i.e., gross non-DAC immigrant inflow/total immigrant inflow multiplied by net immigrant inflow over five years/receiving country population. • Share of foreign students that are from non-DAC countries. • Index measuring countries' contributions to aiding refugees and asylum seekers.	• The original migration index contained two additional indicators that were dropped. The ratio of gross non-DAC immigrant inflow to receiving-country population was dropped due to overlap with two other indicators (i.e., the first two). The difference between the unemployment rates of natives and of immigrants was also dropped as an indicator due to possible ambiguity in its beneficiality (i.e., high unemployment among immigrants could be a good sign of more openness to immigration). • This policy area suffers from lack of disaggregated data on remittances and still very little understanding of the linkages between policies and actual migration flows. Furthermore, illegal migration remains largely unresearched.
Environment	Index based on weighted measures of: • Depletion of shared commons. • Contributions to international efforts and government cooperation.	Some proportion of the index weight goes to outcome measures with non-policy elements.
Security	Index based on contributions to international peacekeeping and forcible human interventions (e.g., Australian-led intervention in East Timor in 1999).	The index is different from the 2003 version due to: • Expansion in scope to include forcible human interventions. • Expansion of timeframe from 2 to 10 years, in recognition that interventions do not occur often.
Technology	Index based on government financial support for research and development, counting government funding and tax incentives.	• The index reflects only technology generation, but not technology diffusion. • The current system of intellectual property rights protection based on the Agreement on Trade Related Aspects of Intellectual Property Rights (TRIPS) is not reflected by the index.

Note: The interested reader may wish to refer to Roodman (2004; 2005b) for further details on the construction of the CDI.

Box 2
Are Rich-Country Policies in Aid and Trade Becoming Less Coherent?

The components of the Commitment to Development Index could be used to monitor trends in policy areas over time, indicating whether policy efforts are progressing positively and in unison (mutually supportive), regressing (both becoming worse), or might be contradictory (one improving and the other regressing). One way to do this would be to estimate the changes in the components of the index—say for aid and trade—and then construct a cross-plot each year. Each index component is constructed so that increases reflect greater development friendliness; thus positive changes in each component (and in the overall index) over time reflect improvement.

To illustrate, comparing changes in the aid[a] and trade[b] components, for example, policy efforts in these areas were generally moving in a coherent—mutually supportive—direction in 2004 for a few countries (see Figure 1, quadrant 1). However, a caveat to consider is that the aid and trade policies of a number of countries were moving in unison, but in a regressive (non-development-friendly) direction (quadrant 3). That year, about seven countries' aid and trade policies may have moved in contradictory directions (quadrants 2 and 4).

For 2005, changes in the aid and trade components of several rich countries seem to suggest more pronounced contradictions in their policies, compared to the year before, as indicated by the more negative slope in the scatter plot

as well as the presence of a dozen countries in Figure 2, quadrant 2 (where there is progress in the trade component but regress in the aid component). This seems to have grown worse in 2006, with even fewer countries located in quadrant 1 (only two in 2006, as compared with eight in 2005, and seven in 2004). The trend for 2006 (see Figure 3) also seems to indicate that most rich countries' aid and trade policies are either moving in generally opposite directions (quadrants 2 and 4), or are *simultaneously* regressing (quadrant 3).

Source: Author's calculations based on data from the Center for Global Development's Commitment to Development Index, www. cgdev.org/section/initiatives/_active/cdi/.

a. The aid component is primarily based on the quantity of aid governments give, factoring in quality indicators such as penalizing donors for giving aid to rich or corrupt governments, for overburdening recipients with lots of small aid projects, or for "tying" aid, which forces recipients to spend it on the donor country's own goods rather than shopping around for the lowest price. A higher aid index score suggests that the country's aid policies are more development friendly.

b. The trade component essentially reflects how open rich countries are to trading with poor countries. It uses data on main types of barriers: tariffs on imports and agricultural subsidies. It rewards tax deductions and credits that support private charity and penalizes countries for erecting barriers to imports of crops, clothing, and other goods from poor nations. A higher trade index score suggests that the country's trade policies are more development friendly.

on how a country compares with its peers within each of these policy areas. Finally, the country's scores in each area are then aggregated (using equal weights for each score) to arrive at the final index, which again lends itself to a cross-country ranking. In 2006, for example, the Netherlands ranked only fourth in aid but placed in the top half of ranked countries in all seven components of the CDI so that it received the highest overall ranking for commitment to development that year.

While the CDI is clearly still a work in progress,[11] its approach offers certain benefits. The index focuses on the policies themselves, which are relatively easier to measure and update, allowing the index to be reported every year. Policies are also the most pragmatic starting point for discussions on enhancing policy coherence, making "policy effort" a useful bellwether indicator of what policy actions have been (or can be) taken. The CDI also provides an "across-policy-area scorecard" that is comparable across countries and across years. Drawing from our definition earlier, we could view this scorecard as an indicator for how actively an industrial country pursues *strong form* coherence compared to its peers. Changes in the components of the index—for instance, for aid and trade—could also be monitored, revealing whether rich countries are moving in the direction of greater or lesser coherence (see Box 2). Over time, this index could possibly serve as an effective incentive, particularly for countries on both ends of the ranking—leaders would want to stay on top, and laggards would want to improve their ranking. In fact, the Netherlands has already taken the lead by

adopting the CDI as a performance indicator for its own policy coherence for development (Van Ardenne 2003).

Institutional Reforms

The lack of cooperation, coordination, and discussion across different government agencies and entities in the policy design and implementation stages could also clearly produce incoherent policies. Hence, another "unit of measure" for policy coherence could try to reflect the organizational, legal, and political dimensions of facilitating coherence. Some studies have assessed the extent to which coherence-enhancing institutional reforms and innovations have been undertaken. One should take note that these reforms need not focus on policy coherence for development alone—that is, they could simply be part of broader efforts to improve policy coherence in general within countries. These reforms could take the form of laws enacted or international agreements signed in order to bind countries to policy coherence objectives, specific coordinating functions or agencies created to ensure coherence across different line ministries, or the development of analytical capacity to evaluate policy impact.[12] Focusing more specifically on policy coherence for development, Table 3 lists some of the institutional reforms tailored for this purpose. Sweden, for example, is the first nation in the world to pass a law on an integrated global development policy—requiring its agriculture, environment, migration, trade, and other policies to align to fight poverty and promote sustainable development.

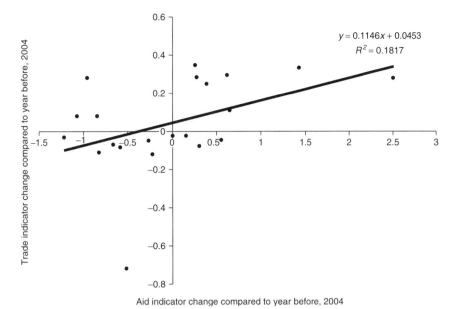

Figure 1   Changes in Aid and Trade Policy Indicators, 2004

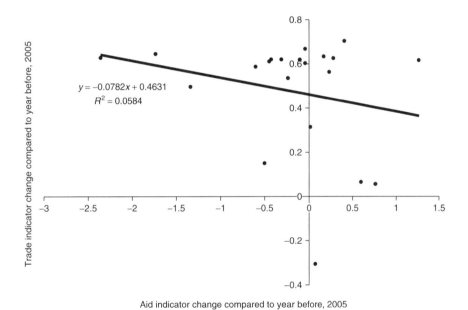

Figure 2   Changes in Aid and Trade Policy Indicators, 2005

Assessments that focus on institutional reforms are, for the most part, qualitative.[13] Incoherence could be the result of "missing" policy inputs, which in this case are embodied in institutional reforms. Various agencies and institutions of government have their specific function, mandate, and policy objectives. For very obvious reasons, if these agencies do not discuss or coordinate policies, they are unlikely to achieve policy coherence, particularly when faced with multiple, and possibly competing, objectives. For instance, how would the Agriculture Ministry know that some of its projects and policies to help domestic farmers could in fact counteract some of the projects and policies of the Aid Ministry? More importantly, once such policy incoherence is discovered, what would be the process to resolve it? The analytical tools and the institutional and organizational

framework for discussion, as well as the legal mandate for such coordination to take place, are therefore critical in weeding out institutional and organizational causes of incoherence. Critics could note that these elements might not necessarily ensure policy coherence, but at the very least they are probably necessary preconditions.

Policy Coherence from a Developing-Country Viewpoint

While resource flows, policy effort, and institutional reforms are important dimensions of policy coherence, notably from an industrial country perspective, additional important dimensions

41

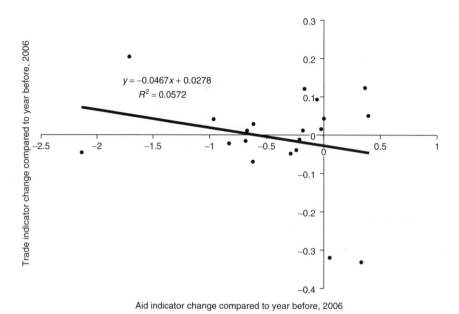

$$y = -0.0467x + 0.0278$$
$$R^2 = 0.0572$$

Aid indicator change compared to year before, 2006

Figure 3 Changes in Aid and Trade Policy Indicators, 2006

Table 3 Examples of Institutional Reforms for Enhanced Policy Coherence

Country (or group of countries)	Reform	Function
European Union	Maastricht Treaty	The 1992 treaty stipulates in Article C that the external policies of the Union should be consistent with each other; and in Article 130V it requires that the European Community (EC) take into account development policy objectives in its other policies.
	Interservice Quality Support Group	Established since 2001, and serving under the Development Commissioner, the IQSG contributes to policy coherence by acting as a single monitoring entity for all Country Strategy Papers (CSPs) for EC aid recipient countries.
Germany	Extended Right of Review by the BMZ of all legislation	Since 2000 as part of the Joint Standing Orders (GGO) of the Federal Ministries, this regulation requires all legislation to be reviewed by the Ministry of Economic Cooperation and Development (BMZ).
Netherlands	Policy Coherence Unit Within the Ministry of Foreign Affairs	Created in 2002 and directly positioned under the Director-General for International Cooperation, this unit ensures coherence across government agencies and operates in project teams with key players from other divisions in the ministry and other departments.
Spain	Law on International Development Cooperation	Passed in 1998, this law states that the principles and objectives of Spanish development cooperation should be reflected in all other policies affecting developing countries.
Sweden	Bill on Integrated Development Policy	Passed in 2003, the bill calls for the alignment of aid, trade, agriculture, environment, migration, security, and other policies with the objectives of reducing poverty and promoting sustainable development.
Over 100 countries and organizations	Paris Declaration on Aid Effectiveness	Endorsed in March 2005, the Paris Declaration is an international agreement to which over 100 ministers, heads of agencies, and other senior officials adhered and committed their countries and organizations to continue to increase efforts in harmonization, alignment, and managing aid for results with a set of monitorable actions and indicators.

Sources: Ministry of Foreign Affairs of the Netherlands (2004); Ministry of Foreign Affairs of Sweden (2003); OECD (2004a); and the Paris Declaration on Aid Effectiveness (see www.oecd.org/dataoecd/11/41/34428351.pdf).

could be revealed by taking a developing-country perspective on the topic—notably the distributional and regime aspects of policy coherence for development. Each reveals how policy coherence in many respects is not only an industrial-country issue to be handled internally or in industrial-country forums—developing countries can and should play a crucial role.

Distributional Aspects

One important additional aspect of policy impact pertains to its distributional dimension. Industrial countries could work toward enhanced policy coherence in various areas of critical interest to the developing world, but how would different developing countries be affected by these efforts? Would countries in Africa, for instance, benefit from further trade liberalization in industrial countries? The evidence suggests uneven country performance, as low-income countries have had meager success in penetrating global markets. Between 1990 and 2003, low-income countries managed only a 0.5 percent increase in their share of global non-oil trade, while middle-income countries snapped up a hefty 14 percent (Newfarmer and Nowak 2006, 373). In addition, various scholars have argued that some countries in Africa could actually be harmed (Panagariya 2004; Polaski 2006). Further liberalization in industrial countries is expected to erode the trade preferences given to some of the least developed countries (LDCs), a number of which are in that region. A few net food-importing LDCs could stand to lose from the elimination of Northern agricultural subsidies, since this would tend to drive up world agricultural prices.

Assessing the distributional dimension of policy coherence for development in any one policy area is therefore of critical interest to all developing countries since not all of them will necessarily benefit (nor benefit to the same degree). A more disaggregated analysis could better reveal how different countries—and different sectors within these countries—stand to lose or gain from enhanced policy coherence. Indeed such an analysis could also enable a closer approximation of the impact on development, since it could often be country and/or sector specific.

In addition, enhanced policy coherence is not always good for all. Drawing still from the example of eliminating agricultural subsidies, if some net-food-importing developing countries could actually be harmed, then more insight on the distribution dimension would allow policymakers to consider and more systematically evaluate the appropriateness of additional policies, such as possible compensating arrangements, in order to ensure, as a minimum condition, weak-form coherence (i.e., "at least no harm is done").

Regime Dimension

Increasingly, industrial country policies are becoming embedded in international regimes. In such cases, it would also be critical to assess policy coherence for development for these policies. Should they be found to be incoherent, then the appropriate entry point for reform might no longer be at the industrial-country level but at the regime level. This signals the growing importance of various international regimes that are taking shape as a result of international agreement on certain policies. Analyses of the design or "architecture" of various international (i.e., bilateral or multilateral) regimes have in fact been undertaken quite extensively across various disciplines, including environmental economics, international finance and trade, and international relations, to name a few.[14] The underlying logic behind many of these studies is also one of coherence: Are the various rules or components of a regime coherent with respect to its objectives, and are those objectives coherent with development?

For instance, Bradford and Lawrence (2004) examined policy options that could be unilaterally considered by each of the eight industrialized countries they studied. They found that Japan, for example, could decide to further liberalize its domestic markets in its own—as well as the developing world's—interest.[15] Such policy reforms would therefore be within its discretion. However, broader liberalization policies could be the result of further negotiations at the World Trade Organization (WTO).

From another angle, regimes could also have a direct impact on development that is distinct from industrial country policies. The WTO Agreement on Trade Related Aspects of Intellectual Property Rights (TRIPS) is an example. By triggering the enforcement of stronger intellectual property rights (IPRs) laws across countries, TRIPS could benefit predominantly technology-exporting countries at the expense of predominantly technology-importing countries. Here, it is not industrial country policies per se, but the international harmonization of certain rules that could harm developing countries, which largely fall under the latter technology-importing group. This would therefore not be captured by assessments of industrial country policies.

One way to evaluate this regime would be to again assess its effect on resource flows to the developing world. In terms of net transfers, Maskus (2000) used an index of patent rights for a sample of countries to measure the possible effects on patent values of harmonizing these rights. The forecasted effects on net transfers are illustrated in Figure 4.[16]

With the implementation of stronger laws on IPRs, the United States, Germany, and France are expected to gain substantially from net transfers—sourced mainly from some industrial and many developing countries that are net consumers of patented products and technologies. Note that the United States alone is projected to gain some $6 billion, while Brazil is expected to experience negative net transfers of roughly $2 billion. Regimes such as TRIPS could trigger government policy actions as well as responses among various market actors, which in turn could affect resource flows, welfare, and, more broadly, development in poor countries. Hence, possibilities for enhanced policy coherence for development could sometimes require an entry point for reforms within regimes. Developing countries should, ideally, play a proactive role in pressing for these regime reforms, when and where those are necessary.

Quo Vadis?

This paper, no doubt, only scratches the surface of the issue of policy coherence for development. However, based on the foregoing discussion, several concrete steps could already be considered in moving forward.

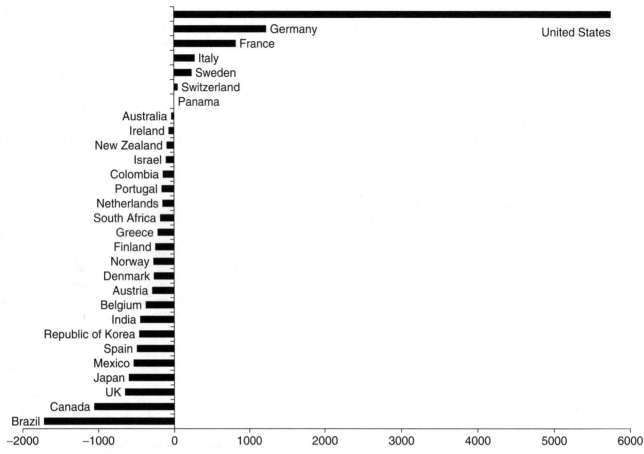

Figure 4   Estimated Net Rent Transfers from TRIPS-Induced Strengthening of 1988 Patent Laws in Selected Countries

Source: Maskus (2000, 184, table 6.1).
Note: Figures in 1995 $ millions.

First, assessments of policy impact, while crucial and necessary, are also quite likely to be insufficient and need to be complemented. This paper suggests that assessing the distributional aspect is also important, because enhanced policy coherence across different policy areas affects various developing countries in different ways. To highlight this distributional dimension, it could be useful to undertake analyses of industrial countries' policy coherence for development not only from their perspective (e.g., Forster and Stokke 1999; OECD 2004a), but also from the perspective of specific developing countries. For example, recent studies by the OECD examined the role of industrial countries' policies notably from the 1960s to the 1990s in the development takeoff of a number of East Asian countries (see Fukusaku et al. 2005). Such studies therefore offer a useful lens to clarify factors that might be specific to only some developing countries and regions (also perhaps certain time periods). In addition to taking a developing-country perspective, it could be useful to undertake more distribution-sensitive analyses of the expected spillover effects from various industrial country policies.

Assessing the coherence of policies already embedded in regimes could also provide important insights. In these assessments, it would be useful to differentiate the policies that are subject to each country's discretion from those policies that are embedded in international regimes. For instance, in the absence of an international migration regime, policies in this area are still largely within the discretion of industrial countries. Thus they could be "graded" as the Commitment to Development Index does on how "development friendly" they are in this policy area. However, in the case of international rules on IPRs, it would not be appropriate to follow this approach. Reforms in this policy area require specific focus on the TRIPS regime and the World Trade Organization. Here, the entry point for policy reforms would no longer be within the discretion of industrial countries. International collective agreement, rather than the actions of any one industrial country, would be crucial in facilitating any reforms thought to be necessary.

Some consensus on policy coherence therefore deserves examination, since establishing an agreed-upon target for it is also critical. As noted earlier, policy coherence is also a matter of degree. Incremental steps toward enhanced policy coherence could be taken, but how would one judge whether those would be enough? There is an urgent need to develop joint North-South, consensus-driven goalposts of policy coherence for development. Policy coherence, at the end of the day, is about managing different objectives. The outcomes from this "management" depend crucially on how balance is struck across different objectives and, most likely, also different beneficiary groups. Achieving enhanced coherence therefore requires that developing countries also exert their views in policy discussions and debate.

Notes

1. This is not to say that poor countries do not themselves have policy contradictions, many of which hamper their own development. These have been analyzed extensively in the literature on economic reforms and development policy and will not be the focus of this paper. Instead, the main interest here is on rich countries' other policies—in addition to foreign aid—in an effort to contribute to the still nascent literature in this area.

2. For further information, see EURODAD (2006) and Royal Norwegian Ministry of Foreign Affairs (2006).

3. In addition, in some cases the exact direction and degree of impact of some policies may be impossible to predict ex ante. Policy coherence also thus tends to follow an incremental process. There is an extensive literature in organizational theory and notably on incrementalism, which becomes relevant when considering the complex issues here. It is beyond the scope of this paper to treat this aspect, but it is flagged here for the interested reader.

4. For further information on the MDGs, see www.un.org/millenniumgoals/.

5. Net ODA in 2003 increased by 3.9 percent in real terms from the year-before level. Of the $2.3 billion net increase, $2 billion was focused on the start of reconstruction in Iraq. In 2004, net ODA rose by about $7.7 billion, and about a third of this went to Afghanistan and Iraq. In 2005 and 2006, a temporary spike in aid levels was expected because of major debt relief for Iraq and Nigeria (i.e., $19 billion in 2005 and $11 billion in 2006). Preliminary data for 2006 suggest that development aid from Organization for Economic Cooperation and Development (OECD) countries fell by about 5 percent in 2006. See OECD (2004b; 2005; 2006; 2007).

6. For instance, investments in port efficiency, customs environments, regulatory environment, and electronic commerce.

7. For instance, in terms of aid flows, different ways and channels of giving aid could also have an impact on its effectiveness. Some of these features are addressed by the Commitment to Development Index (CDI), a policy-coherence indicator that focuses on "policy effort" and is discussed in the next subsection.

8. See www.cgdev.org/rankingtherich/home.html.

9. When and where available and appropriate, the method of discounting draws on empirical evidence on the countereffects of these other policies. For instance, "tying" is expected to raise aid project costs by about 15–30 percent, reducing aid value by some 15–23 percent (Jepma 1994). The CDI scores for aid therefore discounts "tied" aid by 20 percent.

10. The 2005 scores on aid policy were 1.9 and 2.6 for the United States and Spain respectively. In 2006, the scores were 2.2 for the United States and 2.5 for Spain. See www.cgdev.org/section/initiatives/_active/cdi.

11. Some methodological issues in the CDI remain, including the method of scaling and weighting within and across the various policy areas. At present, across-policy-area scores are equally weighted in the CDI, yet some policy areas (such as that of international trade or labor migration) may have a potentially much larger impact and therefore might merit greater weight. There is no straightforward way to deal with this issue, however. In addition, with the availability of more data, each of the indicators could be further improved. As a final point, "policy effort" as a unit of measure also does not reflect whether the steps toward enhanced policy coherence are "sufficient." That is, the index does not reflect whether development objectives are achieved, or how much different countries benefit from enhanced policy coherence. The implicit assumption is simply that more "coherence" (in more policy areas) is better for development (and developing countries in general) than less. The interested reader may wish to turn to Roodman (2004; 2005b) and Sawada et al. (2004) for a discussion of further possible improvements in the CDI methodology.

12. More broadly, Hilker (2004) expands on past work by the OECD and develops an analytical framework specifically for institutional mechanisms to promote policy coherence for development. She examines several elements: (a) government/institutional structures; (b) political context, commitment, and leadership; (c) policy frameworks/statements; (d) stakeholder analysis/consultation; (e) analytical capacity and knowledge management; (f) policy coordination mechanisms; (g) working practices and policymaking processes; and (h) monitoring, accountability, and lesson learning.

13. For some examples, the interested reader may wish to refer to the country case studies contained in the edited volume of Forster and Stokke (1999), *Policy Coherence in Development Co-operation*. The peer reviews of the Organization for Economic Cooperation and Development also include a section on policy coherence that contains detailed discussion on institutional reforms. See OECD (2004a).

14. It is beyond the scope of this paper to discuss these; the interested reader may wish to refer to the studies of international regimes in Hasenclever et al. (1997).

15. If Japan alone were to take steps toward enhanced policy coherence for development by removing its barriers to trade, Bradford and Lawrence (2004, 11–12) estimate that it could generate about $41 billion in welfare gains for the developing world, not to mention about $135 billion for itself. Such a reform would enhance policy coherence in two ways. First it would enhance coherence within Japan's policies to promote its own welfare. In addition, it would enhance coherence between Japan's trade and development (i.e., official development assistance) policies.

16. The counterfactual in this exercise was to evaluate what the additional net present value of patents would have been in 1988 had each country in the sample satisfied its TRIPS commitments. Innovation and patent rights were held constant, thus resulting in a static calculation of how rents would be shifted. This builds on earlier work on this topic by McCalman (1999).

References

Baffes, John. 2006. "Cotton and the Developing Countries: Implications for Development." In *Trade, Doha and Development: A Window into the Issues*, ed. Richard Newfarmer. Washington, DC: World Bank.

Bertini, Catherine, August Schumacher, and Robert Thompson. 2006. *Modernizing America's Farm and Food Policy: Vision for a New Direction.* Report of the Task Force on U.S.

Agriculture Policy. Chicago: Chicago Council on Global Affairs. Available at www.thechicagocouncil.org/UserFiles/File/Task%20Force%20Reports/Agriculture%20Task%20Force%20report.pdf.

Birdsall, Nancy, Dani Rodrik, and Arvind Subramanian. 2005. "How to Help Poor Countries." *Foreign Affairs* 84, no. 4: 136–52.

Bradford, Scott C., and Robert Lawrence. 2004. *Has Globalization Gone Far Enough? The Costs of Fragmented Markets.* Washington, DC: Institute for International Economics.

EURODAD (European Network on Debt and Development). 2006. "Norway Makes Groundbreaking Decision to Cancel Illegitimate Debt." October 3, 2006. Brussels. Available at www.eurodad.org/articles/default.aspx?id=737/.

Forster, Jacques, and Olav Stokke, ed. 1999. *Policy Coherence in Development Co-operation.* European Association of Development Research and Training Institutes (EADI) Book Series 22. London: Frank Cass.

Fukusaku, Kiichiro, Masahiro Kawai, Michael G. Plummer, and Alexandra TrzeciakDuval. 2005. *Policy Coherence Towards East Asia: Development Challenges for OECD Countries.* Paris: OECD.

Hasenclever, Andreas, Peter Mayer, and Volker Rittberger. 1997. *Theories of International Regimes.* Cambridge: Cambridge University Press.

Hertel, Thomas. 2004. "Assessing the Provision of International Trade as a Global Public Good." Background paper for *The New Public Finance: Responding to Global Challenges.* Available at www.thenewpublicfinance.org/background/hertel.pdf.

Hilker, Lyndsay McLean. 2004. "A Comparative Analysis of Institutional Mechanisms to Promote Coherence for Development: Case Study Synthesis of the EU, US, and Japan." Paper presented at the OECD Policy Workshop on Institutional Approaches to Policy Coherence for Development, May 18–19, Paris. Available at www.oecd.org/dataoecd/0/31/31659769.pdf.

Jepma, Catrinus J. 1994. Inter-Nation Policy Co-Ordination and Untying of Aid. Brookfield, VT: Ashgate.

Maskus, Keith. 2000. *Intellectual Property Rights in the Global Economy.* Washington, DC: Institute for International Economics.

McCalman, Phillip. 1999. "Reaping What You Sow: An Empirical Analysis of International Patent Harmonization." Working Paper in Economics and Econometrics 374. Canberra: Australian National University.

Ministry of Foreign Affairs of the Netherlands. 2004. "Millennium Development Goal 8: Developing a Global Partnership for Development, Progress Report by the Netherlands." The Hague: Ministry of Foreign Affairs. Available at www.minbuza.nl/default.asp?CMS_ITEM=6625AAAB61534816875BD52E1E0117F9X3X50352X73/.

Ministry of Foreign Affairs of Sweden. 2003. "Sweden, First in the World with Cohesive Development Policy." Ministry of Foreign Affairs, Stockholm. Available at www.sweden.se/templates/News_7578.asp.

Newfarmer, Richard. 2006. "Through the Window: Beacons for a Pro-Poor World Trading System." In *Trade, Doha and Development: A Window into the Issues*, ed. Richard Newfarmer, pp. 15–26. Washington, DC: World Bank.

Newfarmer, Richard, and Dorota Nowak. 2006. "The World Bank in Trade: The New Trade Agenda." In *Trade, Doha and Development*, pp. 371–82.

Organization for Economic Cooperation and Development (OECD). 2004a. "Extracts from the Development Cooperation Review Series Concerning Policy Coherence." Paris. Available at www.oecd.org/dataoecd/23/16/25497010.pdf.

———. 2004b. "Modest Increase in Development Aid in 2003." Paris: OECD. Available at www.oecd.org/document/22/0,2340,en_2649_33721_31504022_1_1_1_1,00.html.

———. 2005. "Aid Rising Sharply, According to Final ODA Figures for 2004." Paris. Available at www.oecd.org/dataoecd/0/41/35842562.pdf.

———. 2006. OECD DAC Development Co-operation Report 2005. Paris.

———. 2007. "Development Aid from OECD Countries Fell 5.1% in 2006." Available at www.oecd.org/document/17/0,2340,en_2649_33721_38341265_1_1_1_1,00.html.

OXFAM. 2002a. "The Great EU Sugar Scam: How Europe's Sugar Regime Is Devastating Livelihoods in the Developing World." OXFAM Briefing Paper 27. Available at www.oxfam.org/eng/pdfs/pr022508_eu_sugar_scam.pdf.

———. 2002b. "Cultivating Poverty: The Impact of US Cotton Subsidies on Africa." OXFAM Briefing Paper 30. Available at www.oxfam.org/eng/pdfs/pp020925_cotton.pdf.

———. 2004. "Dumping on the World: How EU Sugar Policies Hurt Poor Countries." OXFAM Briefing Paper 61. Available at www.oxfam.org.uk/what_we_do/issues/trade/bp61_sugar_dumping.htm.

Panagariya, Arvind. 2004. "Tide of Free Trade Will Not Lift All Boats." *Financial Times*, August 2, 2004.

Polaski, Sandra. 2006. "Winners and Losers: Impact of the Doha Round on Developing Countries." Carnegie Endowment for International Peace, New York. Available at www.carnegieendowment.org/files/Winners.Losers.fina12.pdf.

Roodman, David. 2004. "The Commitment to Development Index: 2004 Edition." Center for Global Development, Washington, DC. Available at www.cgdev.org/rankingtherich/docs/Technical_description_2004.pdf.

———. 2005a. "The 2005 Commitment to Development Index: Components and Results." Center for Global Development, Washington, DC. Available at www.cgdev.org/files/3647_file_Commitment_to_Development_Index_Brief.pdf.

———. 2005b. "The Commitment to Development Index: 2005 Edition." Center for Global Development, Washington, DC. Available at www.cgdev.org/doc/cdi/technicaldescrip05.pdf.

Royal Norwegian Ministry of Foreign Affairs. 2006. "Cancellation of Debts Incurred as a Result of the Norwegian Ship Export Campaign (1976–1980)." Available at www.regjeringen.no/en/dep/ud/Documents/Reports-programmes-of-action-and-plans/Reports/2006/Cancellation-of-debts-incurred-as-a-result-of-the-Norwegian-Ship-Export-Campaign-1976–80.html?id=420457/.

Sawada, Yasuyuki, Hirohisa Kohama, Hisaki Kono, and Munenobu Ikegami. 2004. "Commitment to Development Index (CDI): Critical Comments." FASID Discussion Paper on Development Assistance no. 1. Tokyo. Available at www.fasid.or.jp/english/publication/discussion/pdf/DP_1_E.pdf.

United Nations Millennium Project. 2005. *Investing in Development: A Practical Plan to Achieve the Millennium Development Goals.* New York: United Nations Development Programme. Available at www.unmillenniumproject.org/documents/MainReportComplete-lowres.pdf.

Van Ardenne, Agnes. 2003. "Statement by the Minister for Development Co-operation of The Netherlands, representing the constituency consisting of Armenia, Bosnia and Herzegovina, Bulgaria, Croatia, Cyprus, Georgia, Israel, Republic of Macedonia, Moldova, The Netherlands, Romania, and Ukraine." 68th Meeting of the Development Committee, Dubai, September 22, World Bank, Washington, DC. Available at http://siteresources.worldbank.org/DEVCOMMINT/ Documentation/20128823/DCS2003–0052-vanArdenne.pdf.

RONALD MENDOZA is a policy analyst and economist with the Office of Development Studies, United Nations Development Programme (UNDP). The views expressed herein do not necessarily reflect the views and policies of the UNDP. The author thanks Chandrika Bahadur, Pedro Conceição, Paola Deles, and Inge Kaul for very helpful discussions on the topic, and Jeff Madrick, David Roodman, and Yanchun Zhang for their comments on an earlier draft. All remaining errors are his.

UNIT 2
International Institutions and Organizations

Unit Selections

Key Points to Consider

- What do you think should be the role of the World Bank and the IMF?

- The world's financial markets are no longer restricted to New York, London and Tokyo. What do you think of the developments that has taken place in other nations?

- The U.S. trade deficit is a cause for great concern. No nation in history has been able to sustain such a deficit for an extended period of time without severe economic consequences. What do you think could or should be done about it?

- Large, multinational corporations are not just restricted to the developed countries but are now being born and nurtured in developing countries as well. What do you think of this development? Has it changed the competitive landscape?

Student Web Site
www.mhcls.com/online

Internet References
Institute of International Bankers (IBB)
   http://www.iib.org
International Labour Organization (ILO)
   http://www.ilo.org
Lex Mercatoria: International Trade Law Monitor
   http://lexmercatoria.net
Resources for Economists on the Internet
   http://rfe.org
WashLaw
   http://www.washlaw.edu

© Flying Colours Ltd/Getty Images

Global trade is facilitated by a number of different organizations that have been devised for the purpose of encouraging and engaging in international trade and commerce. The first of these international institutions includes those that were initially established as a result of the Bretton Woods Agreement at the end of World War II and also includes the World Bank and the International Monetary Fund (IMF). Both of these organizations work to stabilize and promote world trade, and encourage investment in the developed and the developing world, as discussed in, "Helping the Global Economy Stay in Shape" and "The Bretton Woods System". Other important international trade organizations designed to promote trade would include the World Trade Organization (WTO), which is the successor to the General Agreement on Tariffs and Trade (GATT), as well as regional trade organizations such as the European Union (EU) and the North American Free Trade Agreement (NAFTA). The EU and NAFTA are specifically designed to encourage trade among a select and limited number of nations, unlike the IMF or the WTO, which are designed to encourage these trends among

virtually all countries. These organizations have proven to be successful in developing global trade among different countries, and helping to make goods and services from all countries competitive in the global market.

International financial markets and exchanges now play a major role in the promotion of global business. The first and most important reason for this has to do with the easy means of communication available today and the nature of the global markets. It is indeed a twenty-four-hour world. The major financial markets of the world in New York, Tokyo and London literally straddle the globe making around-the-clock trading a reality. Once the markets close in London, they are well-underway in New York and the slack is soon picked up in Tokyo. In addition, the trading in these markets reflect their results in more minor markets in Hong Kong, Paris, Rome, and now, even Dubai as may be seen in "Wall Street in the Desert." The business of international finance is literally a twenty-four hour occupation, where new developments can happen overnight and be immediately reflected in the markets, whereby, by the time the markets open in New York or London, the damage or gain has already been accounted for.

The international financial scenario represents several different types of markets. The first is the regular security and commodity market such as the New York Stock Exchange or the Chicago Board of Trade. While these are often thought of as domestic markets, there is a great deal of foreign money at play in these institutions. There is nothing really stopping someone from France or Japan from purchasing shares in IBM, U.S. Government Bonds, or from buying pork bellies. The second type of financial market that is, almost by definition, an international market, is the currency exchange market. It is in this market where the relative value of currencies is allowed to fluctuate against other currencies. The Dollar may go up against the Euro or it may go down. In this market, national currencies are little more than commodities to be bought and sold, and their price is based on the law of supply and demand. If there are too many Pounds offered for a limited number of Yen, then the price of the pound goes down relative to the Yen. Or, another way to put it is that the price of the Yen goes up relative to the Pound. It is very difficult to negotiate in these markets and it requires a great deal of expertise to function successfully. These markets are important to organizations because they have a direct impact on the profitability of organizations. Many organizations have had good years, overseas, turned into bad years because of currency exchange transactions, as discussed in "Dollar Doldrums".

The balance of payments is a major issue that faces the United States and other nations. For the past twenty years, the United States has been running an increasing balance of payments deficit in hundreds of billions of dollars. This is a change in the historic role of the United States as a creditor nation into a debtor nation. Simply put, Americans are buying more from overseas than they are selling overseas. The difference is reflected in the balance of payments. This represents a transfer of wealth on an unprecedented scale, hundreds of billions of dollars, annually, and trillions over time. This debt is being held mostly by foreign banks in the form of U.S. government bonds, by countries such as China and Japan that have set up their economies for export, and their primary export market is the United States. The purchases Americans are making are being financed by the people who are selling the goods to them. This is not a situation that is sustainable for a long time.

Global corporations represent the most significant development of the twentieth century in international commerce. These are huge corporations with operations in many parts of the world that are often larger than the economy of the countries they operate in. For example, if Wal-Mart's annual sales are compared to the gross domestic product of countries, it would be among the top twenty-five largest economies in the world. As it is, it is China's sixth largest trading partner. Whether they are called global corporations or multinational corporations (MNC), they have a tremendous impact on world commerce, the society and culture. While many of the MNC's are American in origin, there are also a number of them that have originated from different parts of the world. Any location can be the birthplace of a global corporation, as seen in the article, "The Challengers." But historically, the most fertile ground has been the United States, Europe, and Japan—the developed world. Corporations in Mexico, India, and China are now active participants in the global economy, as the Chinese recent purchase of IBM's personal computer business for over $1 billion will attest. These companies represent the future of world trade, they play a decisive role not only between nations, but within the domestic economy of individual nations as well. All these organizations and institutions will be major participants in the future.

The World's Banker

Paul Wolfowitz is an inspired choice.

DAVID FRUM

Say this for President Bush: The man has a sense of style. Critic after critic howls for the heads of the architects of the Iraq war, and above all for the head of the man the European media call "Paul Vulfovitz," as though he were a villain in a John Buchan novel. So what does the president do? He names this Vulfovitz to run the World Bank—a job that the world's do-gooders and bleeding hearts have long regarded as their exclusive domain. Take that!

And just to add extra torque to the nomination, there is this irony: Even the president's detractors have been constrained to admit that Wolfowitz is likely to prove an excellent choice—maybe more excellent than is entirely comfortable either for the bank, for its clients in the underdeveloped world, or for its constituencies in the advanced industrial democracies.

The foreign-aid industry has long been under fire from the free-market Right. The great Hungarian-born economist Peter Bauer published his searing essay "Dissent on Development" all the way back in 1971. Bauer's work was bitterly controversial at the time, but in the three and a half decades since, it has evolved into something close to orthodoxy: Bauer himself ended his days as a member of the British House of Lords.

In the 1990s, the old attack from the Right was reinforced by a new challenge from the anti-globalist Left. This new wave of protesters objected to the World Bank's record of supporting dams, mines, highways, and airports rather than the traditional life of primitive villages—and to its even more alarming habit of expecting its loans to be repaid. In the face of this unexpected onslaught, the bank's image-conscious chairman James Wolfensohn hastily retreated. He gave speeches declaring that he shared the protesters' goals. He promised to consult environmental activists before funding future dams. He declared that poverty reduction would replace traditional big-project development as the bank's main priority.

These lofty words did not, alas, translate into actual progress against poverty. In a fascinating and important new book about Wolfensohn, *The World's Banker,* Sebastian Mallaby of the *Washington Post* observes that the condition of the poor in much of the world actually deteriorated in the 1990s. Between 1987 and 1998, the number of people living on less than $1 per day increased by 100 million. The growing population of desperately disadvantaged was obscured, however, by a counterbalancing statistic: Over those same years, the number of Chinese living on less than $1 per day declined by about 100 million. Net-net, as the bankers say, there was global progress—but only because one smashing success story could be set against disappointment throughout much of the rest of the poor world.

In the 1960s and 1970s, the World Bank justified its role by arguing that only a subsidized multinational lender like the bank could be counted on to fund essential projects in the developing world. The experience of the 1990s discredited that old claim. In the post-1989 globalization boom, capital flooded into Latin America and East Asia. And despite shocks, disappointments, and crises, the money keeps coming: Developing countries attracted $255 billion in foreign direct investment in 2004, 42 percent of all foreign direct investment that year—the highest level since 1994.

When the developing world offers opportunities, entrepreneurs and investors will eagerly seize them. The trouble of course is that much of the developing world does not offer opportunities. And the reason for that glaring lack is politics, bad politics: war, civil strife, corruption, oppression, and lawless government. Why is Zimbabwe plunging into famine? Not for lack of fertile land or willing workers—but because of a greedy and brutal dictator, Robert Mugabe. Variants of this story can be told from West Africa to Andean South America—and throughout too much of the Islamic world, from Mali to Pakistan.

If Paul Wolfowitz is known for any one thing, it is his insistence that Middle Eastern terrorism can be traced back to Middle Eastern tyranny—that the region cannot know security until it enjoys freedom. This insight has, if possible, even more relevance to the problems of global poverty and Third World development.

The World Bank has in the past eschewed such political thinking. It is after all an institution owned and controlled by governments. The United States is the bank's single biggest funder and accordingly holds the most votes—about 16.4 percent—but bank management cannot easily avoid responding to other large shareholders such as France (4.3 percent) or China, Russia, and Saudi Arabia (2.78 percent each). Any suggestion that tyranny is an important cause of poverty can be counted on to offend large voting blocs.

No wonder then that the Wolfowitz nomination has stirred the pot. But isn't it long past time that this particular pot be stirred? Fifty-plus years since the World Bank went into business, there is precious little verifiable evidence that it has as yet done its supposed beneficiaries any real or enduring good—and considerable evidence that its willingness to underwrite projects that flunk the market test has done real and enduring harm. If the day should ever come, though, when the bank reinvents itself as a force for clean and representative government in the Third World; if it could offer incentives to encourage peace and stability in conflict-wracked places like Sierra Leone or Iraq; if it could be a force for democracy-led development: then its long disappointing record would at last change for the better. Paul Wolfowitz is heart and soul committed to this task—and so is the president who has again defied international complacency to give Wolfowitz his backing. It's a great choice by a gutsy president who stands by friends—and has the right enemies.

Mr. Frum is the author, most recently, of *An End to Evil: How to Win the War on Terror* (with Richard Perle) and *The Right Man: The Surprise Presidency of George W. Bush.*

Helping the Global Economy Stay in Shape

CARLO COTTARELLI AND ISABELLE MATEOS Y LAGO

From an economic perspective, no country is an island. The policy decisions of one country often have consequences for neighboring ones. And when it comes to the policies of large countries, an entire region or even the whole world may be affected. This is more true today than ever. Trade links have increased, and capital markets are now able to magnify and transmit shocks across borders at extraordinary speed. Often, these dynamics are benign. But in the late 1990s, the Asian crisis showed us how powerful economic forces have the ability to wreak havoc across borders, with a crisis in one country spreading like wildfire to other economies that had been perceived as sound until then. Although awareness of these global dynamics is growing, national policymakers are inherently ill equipped to deal with them.

The IMF adopts a new framework for monitoring countries' economic performance.

This is where the IMF comes into the picture. The IMF was set up in the wake of the Second World War—an event that many historians consider rooted, in part, in the Great Depression—to help ensure global monetary stability. The founding fathers were particularly keen to avoid competitive devaluations, which had worsened the crisis and helped make it global. While this basic goal remains the same today—exchange rates have again become the subject of often-heated international debate—the way the IMF goes about promoting global economic stability has evolved in response to the new landscape of international trade and finance.

In recent decades, the IMF was often seen as a global financial firefighter or aid catalyst. But providing financial assistance to countries in need has always been a means to an end. Today, the IMF's business model is undergoing a wide-ranging reexamination to ensure that it can continue to fulfill its core mandate of promoting international financial stability.

A Universal Code of Conduct

In 1945, the emphasis was on avoiding the competitive devaluations that had marred the 1930s. Under the Bretton Woods system, this objective was achieved through fixed but adjustable exchange rates—a key pillar of the original code of conduct that countries were encouraged to follow when they joined the IMF. Changes in exchange rate parities exceeding 10 percent could take place only with the IMF's approval. When the United States broke the dollar's link to gold in 1971, this system broke down. As a result, a new code of conduct had to be agreed upon. The outcome of those deliberations was a revision of Article IV of the IMF's Articles of Agreement, which became effective in 1978 and is still in force.

Under the revised Article IV, countries pledged not to run their policies in blind pursuit of their own short-term interests, disregarding the effects of their policies on neighbors or indeed on their own longer-term stability. In particular, the new code of conduct encouraged member countries to promote economic growth while maintaining reasonable price stability and orderly financial conditions. It also directed member countries not to manipulate their exchange rate for balance of payments purposes, for instance to gain an unfair competitive advantage, and called on them to pursue exchange rate policies that were compatible with domestic and external stability.

As for the IMF's own obligations, the revised Article IV mandated the organization to assess whether country policies were consistent with the code of conduct and to provide advice on economic policy. This process has come to be known as country, or bilateral, surveillance, and it applies to all member countries regardless of size and economic health. Article IV also requires the IMF to oversee the functioning of the international monetary system to ensure its effective operation—a mandate known as multilateral surveillance.

Targeted Policy Advice

Through surveillance, the IMF provides an expert assessment of economic conditions in member countries and identifies risks to stability and growth. This analysis is packaged into policy advice delivered in high-level discussions with policymakers in each member country and in written reports, most of which are accessible on the IMF's website. Of course, there are many other sources of assessment and advice, but the IMF has distinct comparative advantages. These include access to economic policymakers and all the data needed for thorough economic analysis; a perspective free of national, political, or commercial bias that reflects the interests of the international community as a whole; and the ability to draw on a vast stock of knowledge, comprising not only a bird's-eye view of global economic and financial conditions but also the accumulated experience of 185 member countries in figuring out which policies work best in what circumstances.

The process of surveillance has the added benefit of giving all 185 member countries—represented by 24 Executive Directors that sit on the IMF's Executive Board—the opportunity to comment on each other's economic policies. The views of the Board are communicated to the country's authorities after the meeting.

Surveillance in the Spotlight

The IMF's surveillance work has generally attracted much less public attention than its external financing packages and the sometimes-controversial policy conditionality attached to its loans. But in recent years, countries' external financing needs have receded, putting surveillance in the spotlight. The resulting scrutiny has led to a recognition that IMF surveillance faces significant challenges to its effectiveness. Some of these are long-standing whereas others are more recent.

Persuasion. Surveillance is based on persuasion through dialogue and peer pressure, not on penalties. Thus, it lacks the "teeth" that policy conditionality gives to IMF-supported programs. This has led many observers to ask whether surveillance can be effective at all when it lacks a proper enforcement mechanism. This is a long-standing challenge, inherent in the modus operandi of surveillance.

Leverage. The IMF has also suffered from a perception that it has more leverage over some member countries than others—reflecting differences either in the likelihood of countries having to resort to IMF financing down the road or in countries' sensitivity to opinions voiced by the IMF about their future access to financial markets. A related concern is a perception that the IMF may not be as candid with its larger members as with the smaller ones. Regardless of whether such perceptions are valid, the fact that these views are out there is in itself a challenge to the institution's effectiveness.

Higher expectations. The world has changed in ways that raise the bar for IMF surveillance to add value. For example, the IMF can no longer claim a monopoly in providing macroeconomic analysis and advice. Every day, financial institutions flood markets—and policymakers—with new analysis of economic developments, and an array of experts are on hand to offer advice. And although 20 years ago many countries had to rely on external advice on macroeconomic matters, most have now developed their own talent. Moreover, there is an ever-growing number of regional and international organizations—including the European Union and the OECD to mention but two—that allow countries to tap many different sources of multilateral

policy advice. Finally, the world economy itself has changed significantly, the most striking development being the enormous expansion of international capital markets and the subsequent increase in cross-border capital flows. Although the global economy presents countries with a host of new opportunities, it has also created new risks to stability. These risks often elude clear diagnosis because of their complexity and a lack of data, and are therefore difficult to contain.

Taking Action

All these challenges have increased the urgency of adapting surveillance to the new realities of the 21st century. Making surveillance more effective is a key goal of the IMF's Medium-Term Strategy (MTS), launched by Managing Director Rodrigo de Rato in April 2005. The MTS encompasses ambitious reforms in areas ranging from governance to lending. Reforms pertaining to surveillance have centered on seeking clearer goals, better advice, and better delivery.

Clearer goals. The idea behind the first set of reforms mirrors the one behind public sector reforms introduced in recent years in many countries—namely, that clearly spelling out the objectives expected to be achieved will improve effectiveness and accountability in two ways: first, by focusing on what is critical; second, by allowing various stakeholders to monitor progress. In the case of surveillance, this clarification is taking place at several levels.

- At the highest level, the IMF has just completed a major update of its policy framework by adopting a new Decision on Bilateral Surveillance to replace one that for 30 years, together with Article IV, provided the main legal foundation for surveillance (see box). As a result, the IMF now has, for the first time, a clear and detailed statement, endorsed by its membership, of what constitutes best practice in surveillance.
- One level down, the IMF has been considering the introduction of a statement of time-bound surveillance priorities (a three-year horizon has been mentioned as one possibility) that would help focus its work, clarify responsibilities, and better integrate bilateral and multilateral surveillance. These priorities would include both operational objectives (such as improving the IMF's analysis of exchange rate issues) and economic objectives (such as contributing to the reduction of current global imbalances).
- At the country level, the IMF recently introduced surveillance agendas, a list of priority objectives that surveillance will promote over the next three years for each member country, and a work plan for achieving these objectives.

Better Advice. The second set of reforms aims at improving the quality of IMF analysis in core areas, including exchange rate policies and developments, cross-country spillovers, financial sector surveillance, and the vulnerabilities in emerging market countries. A number of initiatives are under way.

A New Framework for Surveillance

As part of a number of initiatives to strengthen its surveillance framework, the IMF's Executive Board approved in June 2007 a new Decision on Bilateral Surveillance, replacing its predecessor adopted 30 years ago.

The new decision is the first comprehensive policy statement on surveillance. By clarifying expectations about the best practice of surveillance, it will ensure that the policy dialogue between the IMF and its member countries is more focused and more effective. It provides an up-to-date and comprehensive framework for the regular "health checks" of national economies and encourages candor and even-handed treatment of all countries. It reaffirms that country surveillance should be focused on assessing whether countries' policies promote external stability (see box chart). And it spells out what is and what is not acceptable to the international community in terms of how countries run their exchange rate policies, including by defining what is meant by exchange rate manipulation and indicating the type of situations when discussions with the country may be in order.

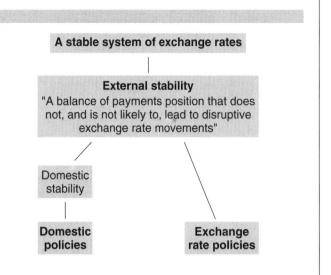

Clarifying the Goals The new decision on surveillance spells out how countries should run their economic policies.

Source: IMF staff

The main area of emphasis has been exchange rate analysis. A recent study by the IMF's Independent Evaluation Office (IEO) identified an effectiveness gap in this crucial area during 1999–2005. The IEO pointed to insufficient analysis of exchange rate levels, scope for greater clarity in discussing de facto exchange rate regimes, and inadequate attention to spillover effects and coordination issues. The MTS also focused on improving exchange rate analysis. In fact, the IMF had already begun to strengthen exchange rate surveillance in the very areas identified by the IEO as needing improvement when that report was published.

Many efforts are under way, but a particularly noteworthy change has been the strengthening of analytical tools to assess exchange rate misalignments. In particular, a growing set of countries benefit from assessments of their exchange rates performed in a multilateral analytical framework (see chart).

New ground is being broken in other areas as well. Analytical tools are increasingly being applied to capture cross-country spillovers—how one country's policies may inadvertently affect other countries. Tools are also being developed to better integrate financial sector and capital markets analysis into macroeconomic assessments. These new approaches will put the IMF in a better position to assess the impact of the financial sector on the economy as a whole and will enable it to assess the multifaceted risks that may originate from this increasingly important sector. The methodology used by IMF staff to assess underlying vulnerabilities and crisis risks in emerging markets has also been revamped.

Better delivery. The third set of reforms relates to the IMF's interaction with policymakers. The most far-reaching of these reforms is the introduction of multilateral consultations. The IMF has long had tools for multilateral surveillance, including its biannual World Economic Outlook and Global Financial Stability Report, but these are based mainly on IMF research and do not involve detailed policy discussions with countries. However, some problems—and their solutions—involve many countries at the same time.

The multilateral consultations provide a new forum for discussing issues of global or regional interest among the countries that are most directly affected by them. The talks further a common understanding of what the problems are and provide a platform to address them. The role of the IMF in this exercise is essentially to facilitate the discussions and provide analytical input, including by identifying any synergies or inconsistencies between the policies of different member countries. The first multilateral consultation started in 2006. It covered the issue of global payments imbalances and involved China, the euro area, Japan, Saudi Arabia, and the United States. The discussions resulted in a public statement in April 2007 in which each of the participants committed to a set of policies that will help reduce imbalances. The IMF will follow up on implementation in its regular surveillance work.

Additional reforms are under way—more mundane but no less important in practice, given that they affect the delivery of surveillance throughout the IMF's membership. Looking beyond closed-door interactions with officials, the IMF is enhancing its outreach and communications efforts to make sure the messages of surveillance inform the domestic policy debates in the broadest possible way. And more focused consultations have been introduced for countries for which only a few issues need to be discussed, allowing for a more thorough analysis.

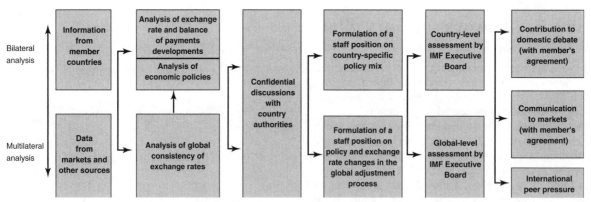

How It Works   The IMF's analysis of its member countries' policies takes into account global as well as country-specific factors.

Source: IMF staff

In Sum

Multifaceted reforms are under way to adapt surveillance to the current realities and ensure that the IMF continues to deliver on its mandate of supporting global monetary stability. Will these reforms enable surveillance to fix all the problems in the world economy and guarantee everlasting stability? Of course not. No matter how sophisticated its advice and analysis, the IMF does not control the policy levers that ultimately determine economic policies around the world. But there is no doubt that these reforms are timely—the global economic environment remains benign, providing the IMF with a great opportunity to step back and rethink the way it operates.

What is going to be the effect of all these reforms? It is too early to tell with any certainty, but change is perceptible already in the way the IMF goes about its work. Ultimately, the hope is that these reforms will help ensure that the IMF's advice remains highly relevant and sought after, and that its voice is both heard and heeded. Provided the IMF adjusts to the demands of the global economy and keeps chasing the highest standards of analysis and communication, surveillance can make a unique and critical contribution to helping the global economy work better. In so doing, it will give member countries reasons to keep believing in the spirit of multilateralism—the force that was behind the creation of the IMF.

CARLO COTTARELLI is a Deputy Director and **ISABELLE MATEOS Y LAGO** is a Deputy Division Chief in the IMF's Policy Development and Review Department.

The Bretton Woods System

Are We Experiencing a Revival?

REUVEN GLICK AND MARK SPIEGEL

At the center of this symposium was a presentation by Michael Dooley (University of California at Santa Cruz and Deutschebank) and Peter Garber (Deutschebank) based on their papers with David Folkerts-Landau (2003a, b, 2004). Dooley and Garber presented their views on the current international exchange rate system, the sustainability of global trade imbalances, and the implications for development by emerging markets, such as China. Other participants presented papers that questioned the bases of their arguments and the extent to which those arguments account for current developments.

A Revival of Bretton Woods?

Dooley, Folkerts-Landau, and Garber (DFG 2003b) argue that the current international exchange rate system operates much like the Bretton Woods system of fixed exchange rates that prevailed for nearly a quarter of a century, from the end of World War II until the early 1970s. Under Bretton Woods, foreign currencies were pegged to the dollar at fixed parities, and the dollar was pegged to gold at $35 an ounce. The system was abandoned when foreign governments perceived that guarantees of currency conversion at fixed rates were no longer credible.

Although the current international exchange rate regime carries no guarantees of fixed parities in terms of gold or the dollar, DFG argue that many countries, particularly those in Asia, do limit exchange rate fluctuations against the dollar to varying degrees. For example, Japan often has conducted foreign exchange intervention—selling yen for dollars, which pushes the yen down against the dollar—in order to maintain its export competitiveness. As a result, Japan has been a net accumulator of dollar-denominated assets; indeed, it ranks first among official reserve holders of U.S. Treasury securities.

China's policy of keeping exchange rates low relative to the dollar is also related to a desire to boost exports. In addition, according to DFG, China has also been motivated by a desire to attract foreign direct investment by multinational firms as well as the technical expertise that usually comes with it. As a result, China also has been a net accumulator of dollar-denominated assets and is second only to Japan among official reserve holders of U.S. Treasury securities.

This result is surprising, however. Given that China is a rapidly growing developing country, one might expect it to be a net international borrower, as capital presumably enjoys a higher rate of return there than in the U.S. Naturally, this question also arises with other developing economies that may peg their exchange rates to varying degrees to the dollar. Whether this issue is a valid point or not, DFG (2004) have an answer. They argue that developing nations like China need to accumulate U.S. Treasury securities, because they provide a form of "collateral" against concerns about possible future expropriation of the assets of U.S. foreign direct investors.

This argument has implications for the U.S. trade deficit. The exchange rate policies discussed have been accompanied by large trade surpluses in most Asian countries vis-à-vis the U.S., as well as by a corresponding need by the U.S. to borrow to finance its purchases of net imports. This implies that, insofar as developing countries like China continue to accumulate these U.S. assets, the U.S. will see ongoing trade deficits.

Perhaps the biggest question facing DFG's world view is whether the current system is sustainable as the U.S. current account deficit continues to grow. DFG (2003a) argue that the system is sustainable in the near term (though their estimates of what the "near term" is varies from three to ten years or more) as long as Asian countries are willing to finance the growing U.S. current account deficit by purchasing additional U.S. securities.

Does China Fit the Story?

Several symposium participants questioned the merits and viability of a strategy of deliberate currency undervaluation by developing countries, particularly in the case of China.

For example, Nicholas Lardy (Institute of International Economics), in his paper with Morris Goldstein, pointed out that more than half of China's exports go to markets other than the U.S. or to countries with currencies not pegged to the dollar. Thus, a strategy of undervaluation by China to boost its exports should depend not just on the renminbi's exchange rate against the dollar but also on its effective rate against the currencies of all of its trading partners. In fact, between 1994 and 2001 the renminbi's real trade-weighted exchange rate (adjusted for inflation differences across countries) appreciated by 30% before falling by 13% since 2001. Lardy also disagreed with DFG's argument that the undervaluation contributed significantly to increasing foreign direct investment in China and the growth of China's capital stock. In his view, this argument ignores the fact that foreign direct investment in China has financed less than 5% of fixed asset investment over the past few years.

Barry Eichengreen (University of California at Berkeley) dismissed the purported role of U.S. assets as collateral that justify U.S. multinational firms' decisions to invest in China. For one thing, he argues that the timing is wrong: rising U.S. foreign direct investment in China began around 1992, whereas China's massive reserve accumulation came a decade later. In addition, he doubts that political conditions would support U.S. expropriation of Chinese claims, invalidating the collateral role these claims are purported to play. Finally, he points out that in recent years the U.S. has accounted for less than 10% of China's inward foreign direct investment.

Steven Kamin (Board of Governors) agreed with DFG that the authorities in developing economies other than China have been acting to maintain the competitiveness of their exports by limiting currency appreciation. However, he argues that the recent large current account surpluses in the region mainly reflect the special, ongoing effects of a decline in investment and domestic demand following the Asian financial crisis of 1997–1998. He attributes this fall in investment to factors such as the presence of considerable excess capacity after the crisis and the near collapse of domestic banking systems in the region. To be sure, immediately after the Asian financial crisis, the desire to rebuild foreign exchange reserves was another reason that authorities in the region intervened in foreign exchange markets to acquire dollar assets, but this motive has diminished in importance as reserves have grown. He believes that, over time, Asian investment spending will revive, that the authorities will be more comfortable in allowing their currencies to strengthen, and that their trade surpluses will narrow.

Will the System Last?

Barry Eichengreen and Ted Truman (Institute of International Economics) argue that DFG make a false analogy between the current international foreign exchange system and Bretton Woods. In particular, they argue that the U.S. is now no longer a net saver with current account surpluses, as it was in the years immediately after World War II. In addition, domestic financial systems are more liberalized, capital accounts are more open, and exchange rates are more flexible, for both industrial and emerging market economies. These differences make it harder to sustain undervalued exchange rates indefinitely.

Nouriel Roubini (New York University) and Brad Setser (Roubini Global International) also questioned the sustainability of efforts to limit dollar appreciation, arguing that the scale of the financing required is increasing faster than the willingness of the world's central banks to build up their dollar reserves. In addition, the enormous reserve growth in these countries has

become increasingly harder to sterilize fully, particularly in China, where the resulting increase in the money supply is fueling a lending boom and an asset-price bubble. Lardy and Roubini both suggest an earlier rather than a later end of China's peg to the dollar. Eichengreen argues that China has good reason to abandon its peg soon, while confidence is strong, capital is still flowing in, and reserves are still being accumulated.

DFG suggest that because the euro area has borne a large and disproportionate share of the adjustment of the U.S. trade imbalance, the European Central Bank will be compelled to engage in large-scale currency intervention to resist further euro appreciation. However, Roubini and Setser and Truman all argue that the European Central Bank is unlikely to do so, in part because of its conviction that the recent massive Japanese intervention had limited effectiveness. The implication is that there will be continuing downward pressure on the dollar against floating currencies until the overall adjustment is consistent with a lower U.S. current account deficit.

Might global imbalances spark a sharp decline in the dollar? Maurice Obstfeld (University of California at Berkeley) discusses the likelihood that the U.S. might face an emerging markets-style "sudden stop" crisis. In his work with Kenneth Rogoff, he questions the sustainability of U.S. current account imbalances, and suggests that a large depreciation of the dollar is indeed very likely.

Ron McKinnon (Stanford University) agrees with DFG that it is in China's interest to maintain a dollar peg, but his argument is different. He argues that a stable exchange rate is an important way for China to anchor low inflation expectations. Accordingly, he provides three arguments for why it is not a good idea for China to allow the renminbi to appreciate. First, an appreciation of the renminbi would not necessarily improve the U.S. trade balance; for example, it could lead to reduced world demand for China's exports, thus slowing China's economic growth, which, in turn, could lead to significant declines in Chinese demand for U.S. products. Second, it may create deflationary pressure in China. Third, it would encourage more speculative capital inflows.

Conclusion

One way to assess the arguments of DFG and their critics may be to examine the implications of the revaluation of the Chinese renminbi in July 2005, five months after the symposium took place. On one hand, it is clear that the Chinese have adjusted their currency by revaluing against the dollar and announced that they would move towards more flexibility in the future. These developments would seem to portend changes that conflict with the DFG vision of Asian countries' ongoing willingness to finance ever-increasing U.S. deficits in the interest of maintaining their trade balance surpluses.

On the other hand, it must be acknowledged that DFG's first works on this subject were published in 2003, and the imminent sharp adjustment in the dollar that was predicted by many has yet to take place. Indeed, so far, the renminbi has adjusted by less than 3%. As such, the DFG framework has already lasted for a notably long duration in today's volatile international financial markets.

Symposium papers

Eichengreen, Barry. "Global Imbalances and the Lessons of Bretton Woods"

Goldstein, Morris, and Nicholas R. Lardy. "China's Role in the Revived Bretton Woods System: A Case of Mistaken Identity."

Kamin, Steven."The Revived Bretton Woods System: Does It Explain Developments in Non-China Developing Asia?"

McKinnon, Ronald. "Exchange Rates,Wages, and International Adjustment: Japan and China versus the United States."

Obstfeld, Maurice, and Kenneth Rogoff. "The Unsustainable U.S. Current Account Position Revisited."

Roubini, Nouriel, and Brad Setser. "Will the Bretton Woods 2 Regime Unravel Soon? The Risk of a Hard Landing in 2005–2006."

Truman, Edwin. "The U.S. Current Account Deficit and the Euro Area."

References

Dooley, Michael, David Folkerts-Landau, and Peter Garber. 2003a. "Dollars and Deficits: Where Do We Go from Here?" Deutsche Bank Global Markets Research Newsletter, June 18, 2003.

Dooley, Michael, David Folkerts-Landau, and Peter Garber. 2003b. "An Essay on the Revived Bretton Woods System." NBER Working Paper 9971 (September).

Dooley, Michael, David Folkerts-Landau, and Peter Garber. 2004. "The U.S. Current Account Deficit and Economic Development: Collateral for a Total Return Swap." NBER Working Paper 10727 (August).

REUVEN GLICK, Group Vice President and **MARK SPIEGEL**, Vice President and Director, Center for Pacific Basin Studies.

Reprinted with permission from the *FRBSF Economic Letter,* November 25, 2005, by Reuven Glick and Mark Spiegel. The opinions expressed in this article do not necessarily reflect the views of the management of the Federal Reserve Bank of San Francisco, or of the Board of Governors of the Federal Reserve System.

Wall Street in the Desert?

Dubai's deal to buy into Swedish exchange OMX and NASDAQ furthers its ambitions to be the money center of the Middle East.

STANLEY REED

Ramadan is usually a quiet month across the Middle East. Businesses close their doors in the early afternoon, commerce slows to a crawl, and with virtually everyone fasting until sundown, few people have much energy for globetrotting and dealmaking. So how to explain Soud Ba'alawy's brutal travel schedule in the past two weeks? Since Ramadan began on Sept. 13, he has been to New York, London, Milan, and Stockholm—missing *Iftars*, the traditional breaking of the fast every evening, back home in Dubai.

The reason: Ba'alawy is one of the key drivers of Dubai's effort to become a global financial hub. As executive chairman of Dubai Group—a big investment arm of the emirate's ruler, Mohammed bin Rashid al Maktoum—Ba'alawy was instrumental in forging a complex $6.5 billion deal involving Borse Dubai, NASDAQ, the Swedish exchange operator OMX Group, and the London Stock Exchange. The series of transactions would result in NASDAQ Stock Market Inc. taking over the Swedish group, Borse Dubai holding a 20% stake in NASDAQ, and the U.S. exchange owning a third of a Borse Dubai subsidiary. On Sept. 26 the deal took a step closer to completion as investors owning 47% of OMX shares indicated their support. In a related transaction, Borse Dubai will take over a 28% stake NASDAQ holds in the LSE.

In a stroke, NASDAQ got an entrée into the booming Gulf region and a partner that may yet help it get its hands on the London bourse. OMX, which owns exchanges in Europe and—more important—has developed trading software used at 60 bourses around the world, got extra firepower in its efforts to sell that technology. And Dubai found a powerful ally to bolster its bid to become the regional money hub.

The transaction highlights the ambitions of Dubai and al Maktoum. With only modest oil resources, the sheikh has long nurtured non-energy industries such as shipping and high tech. And using both his own money and growing piles of debt, he has built a multibillion-dollar investment portfolio that includes top hotels such as New York's Essex House and London's Carlton Tower, extensive real estate holdings, and big stakes in international bank HSBC and European planemaker EADS. Now he sees opportunity in creating a regional banking and trading hub, hoping to cash in on the trillions of dollars that have flowed to the Gulf in recent years. "If we develop a strong financial market, it will change the region," Ba'alawy says.

To make that happen, Sheikh Mohammed has assembled a team of top finance talent. Ba'alawy, 46, spent a decade at Citigroup, working his way up the ranks in risk management until finally taking over as treasurer for the bank's operations in the Gulf region. Now, Ba'alawy has 130 people in five countries scouting for investments around the world. His chief executive at Dubai Group, Thomas S. Volpe, is a former head of San Francisco-based investment bank Hambrecht & Quist Inc. And Per E. Larsson, the former boss of OMX' predecessor, is now chief of Borse Dubai. "Sheikh Mohammed's main concern is making sure this city competes quickly with New York," says Mohamed Ali Alabbar, chairman of developer Emaar Properties and a close adviser to al Maktoum.

The sheikh isn't alone among Gulf rulers in recognizing the potential in financial markets. Some 250 miles to the west in Doha, Qatar, Sheikh Hamad bin Khalifa Al-Thani has adopted a similar strategy, earmarking some $40 billion for projects that might reduce the emirate's dependence on oil and gas. Giving Dubai a poke in the eye, Qatar in 2005 hired as its chief financial regulator Phillip Thorpe, who had been fired from a similar job in Dubai after a flap over dealmaking by local officials. The Qataris were interested in NASDAQ's stake in the LSE, and industry insiders say they were furious when Borse Dubai and NASDAQ got together. Qatar quickly responded by purchasing 20% of the LSE and 10% of OMX. Qatar officials declined to comment, but their bid for OMX forced Borse Dubai to raise its offer by some $700 million.

Sheikh's Mandate

Still, Dubai has the upper hand in the competition. Just about every major bank on earth has set up shop in or near the polished stone complex called the Dubai International Financial Center, aiming for work on mergers and acquisitions, Islamic finance, and lending for projects ranging from oil refineries to luxury hotels. Qatar's financial industry, by contrast, is largely focused on the local market, though it will likely get a boost from growing cooperation with the LSE. "I think I'm the only investment banker in Doha," quips Kapil Chadda, head of investment banking for HSBC in Qatar.

Central to Dubai's efforts are Ba'alawy and Essa Kazim, a 44-year-old with an M.A. in economics from the University of Iowa.

Why No Outrage from Washington

When the Dubai Group and NASDAQ announced the complex deal on Sept. 20 that would give Borse Dubai a 20% stake in the U.S. exchange, the Washington reaction was surprisingly calm. No one denounced the deal, and most lawmakers took a "wait-and-see" attitude in judging whether it posed a national security risk.

It was a far cry from the firestorm that greeted Dubai Ports World when it tried to buy a handful of U.S. ports in 2006. That deal fell apart amid vehement criticism that key ports would end up in the hands of a state-owned company from a country with links to the September 11 hijackers.

The more measured reaction was no accident. In part, that's because a stake in NASDAQ doesn't stir up the same visceral fears of terrorism that the ports did. But Dubai and the United Arab Emirates—the loose federation of states to which Dubai belongs—also learned a hard lesson from the collapse of the earlier bid. And over the past 18 months they've launched a multimillion-dollar lobbying push to boost their image in the states and prevent another fiasco.

Those efforts went into overdrive in the days leading up to the NASDAQ deal, as a handful of Washington lobbyists led by George Salem, a senior adviser to the law firm DLA Piper and a past president of the National Association of Arab Americans, scrambled to ensure a smoother reception. Dubai executives believe that a big reason the ports deal ran aground was that they didn't give lawmakers advance warning or explain their perspective on the deal early enough. So this time, they made sure they got to key members of the Administration and Congress before the news broke and attitudes hardened.

Dubai paid more than $3 million to lobbying firms

In the days before the deal was disclosed, for example, a high-ranking Dubai official flew to Washington for a series of confidential briefings. And as soon as the markets closed on Sept. 19, Salem and his team hit the phones. According to a Capitol Hill source, NASDAQ Chief Executive Robert Greifeld personally called Senator Chuck Schumer (D-N.Y.), who had been a ringleader in the fight over the ports deal. The basic message, says one Dubai lobbyist: This deal is good for U.S. financial markets because it will give NASDAQ access to rich Mideast pockets. To counter terrorism fears, the lobbyists argue that the UAE and Dubai are among America's strongest allies in the region. All told, they rang up some 120 Beltway power players in the first 24 hours.

The rapid-fire round of diplomacy came against a backdrop of intense effort to bolster ties to Washington. Dubai alone has paid more than $3 million to three different lobbying firms, which have spent much of the past year talking up the tiny nation in meetings with aides to everyone from Barack Obama (D-Ill.) to Vice-President Dick Cheney. And earlier this year, the UAE budgeted an additional $5 million to lobbying firm Harbour Group to launch a new body, the U.S.-Emirates Alliance, to help shape public opinion. The alliance has quietly contributed more than $100,000 to the Center for Strategic & International Studies, a foreign policy think tank, to support Mideast programs—though Jon B. Alterman, who heads the center's Middle East research, says its programs aren't influenced by funding. The alliance has also sent Reem Al-Hashimy, the UAE's Boston University-educated deputy chief of mission, to a dozen U.S. cities since July to meet with civic and business leaders.

Such moves appear to be working. Hill staffers say the NASDAQ briefings were clearly effective. A senior aide at the Senate Banking Committee says the talks kept people from "jumping to conclusions about the nature of the investment." While Schumer has raised questions, the betting is that the deal will pass national security review. "The fact that people haven't rushed in behind [Schumer] suggests that the proposal hasn't created the instinctive negative reaction" that the ports deal did, says Joseph Dennin, a trade attorney at McKenna Long & Aldridge.

—Eamon Javers and Dawn Kopecki

In August the sheikh merged the successful local exchange with the two-year-old Dubai International Financial Exchange (DIFX), a bourse with British-style regulation aimed at international investors that has been something of a flop. Al Maktoum named Ba'alawy vice-chairman and Kazim chairman of the merged company, Borse Dubai. And he gave them a mandate to cut deals that would boost the emirate's profile in global finance. Ba'alawy is the strategist and diplomat, close to Mohamed al Gergawi, the ruler's right-hand man, and on good terms with outside players such as LSE boss Clara Furse. Kazim, on the other hand, has won wide respect for his work in building the local bourse into a big moneymaker.

Ba'alawy and Kazim quickly singled out OMX. So last spring the Dubai moneymen offered to buy 30% of the Swedish outfit but were brushed off. When NASDAQ on May 25 announced a $3.7 billion offer for OMX, Borse Dubai countered with its own bid of $4 billion. With the help of bankers at JPMorgan Chase & Co. and HSBC (which is providing nearly all the financing for the deal), the two teams kicked off a series of meetings in London and New York. NASDAQ CEO Bob Greifeld—who will also become vice-chairman of the DIFX—says he was reassured by the Dubai executives' "organized and methodical" approach. He decided that the two groups didn't need to be adversaries. NASDAQ saw OMX as a way to expand into northern Europe, while Dubai wanted OMX's technology to use in emerging markets, especially around the Gulf. "We went after OMX," Kazim says, "and we wound up with a better brand."

Dollar Doldrums

How American Companies Are Beating the Currency

S<small>ARAH</small> G<small>OLDSTEIN</small>

Since last fall, when it sank to a record low against the euro, the dollar has been stuck in a torpor, showing few signs of life. And no one knows when the greenback—which also has been hovering at a 30-year low against the Canadian dollar and a 26-year low against the British pound—will rebound. That's bad news for many American businesses, especially those that collect revenue in dollars but buy supplies and pay salaries overseas. It's not all doom and gloom, of course—some exporters are experiencing their biggest gains in years, a phenomenon that was largely responsible for the sizable GDP increase in the third quarter of 2007. But other companies have had to relocate operations, switch to U.S. suppliers, and cut costs wherever they could. Here's how four companies are dealing with the fallout of the currency crunch—some more successfully than others.

Selling French Wine to the French
The Company: WineCommune,
Oakland, California

The problem: WineCommune, which was No. 35 on the Inc. 500 last year, sells imported and American wine, mostly online. Wine from France—which is 50 percent of its inventory—has become much more expensive, and the company hasn't passed all of those cost increases on to its customers, says CEO Michael Stajer. WineCommune's sales doubled in 2007, to $17 million, and margins are up—but not as much as they would have been had the dollar stayed strong.

The fix WineCommune has limited its losses by hedging. Stajer entered into a forward contract in fall 2006, locking in an exchange rate when the euro was worth about $1.25. When he actually bought the wine the following spring, the euro had risen to $1.36, so he saved about 8 percent.

In one of the stranger twists to come out of the currency crunch, customers in France are turning to the States to buy French wine. In fact, the very people from whom WineCommune originally bought the wine are buying it back. In France, a negociant acts as the middleman between the vintner and

retailer, in this case WineCommune. As negociants have sold out their own stock, which they cannot refill until next season, they have started buying some of the wine they originally sold to WineCommune. Even with shipping costs, and even with WineCommune as an additional middleman taking profits of its own, the negociants can still sell the wine at a profit in France.

The French aren't the only oenophiles who have discovered that bargain prices can be found in the U.S. Sales to foreign markets have more than tripled; they now account for about 7 percent of the company's revenue. The company is hiring a full-time sales rep for the Asian market (the dollar has fallen against a number of Asian currencies), and Stajer says it's not hard to imagine opening an office in China in 12 months, to satisfy the thirsts of newly affluent Chinese and reach out to other Asian markets. Stajer says now is the perfect time to build up relationships with Asian distributors.

Getting a Break from Vendors
The Company: SaltWorks,
Woodinville, Washington

The problem: The company peddles everything salt: pink kitchen salt from the Himalayas, bath salt from the Dead Sea, and even 24 varieties that come in a bamboo box. To buy the stuff, SaltWorks does business in about a dozen currencies. The company is doing well—revenue nearly doubled in 2007, to about $7 million. But profits dropped 5 percent, partly because of the weak dollar, according to co-founder Naomi Novotny.

The fix: Novotny says SaltWorks' European vendors are sympathetic and have been willing to renegotiate contracts. One vendor even agreed to not boost prices because SaltWorks couldn't afford it. Most of the company's vendors have been flexible about payment schedules as well, which has allowed SaltWorks to lock in more favorable exchange rates. "If the euro is really high, we'll ask if we can hold off a couple of days or a week until it goes back down a bit," says Novotny. "Even if the difference is pennies, when you're dealing with hundreds of thousands of dollars, every last one counts." If the euro doesn't move in SaltWorks' favor, it eats the loss and pays the vendor, rather than squandering goodwill. But the weak currency has still eroded profits, and SaltWorks is considering raising prices this year.

Hedging Up to a Year in Advance
The Company: People to People Ambassador Programs, Spokane, Washington

The problem: People to People sends tour groups around the U.S. and the world, and its customers typically reserve their spaces—and lock in their prices—months in advance. As a result, by the time an excursion begins, the real cost of the trip to People to People could have increased 10 percent or more because of exchange rates.

The fix: The company hedges its currency expenditures 12 to 18 months in advance. People to People consults with a foreign exchange advisory firm, HiFX, about the economic factors affecting currency prices and the optimal times to buy. For the 2008 travel season, People to People first started hedging in January 2007, when the euro was worth about $1.30. The company entered into several other forward contracts over the year. In early summer, consultants at HiFX advised People to People to finish its hedging soon instead of waiting until the end of 2007, as the company had planned. The experts on the foreign exchange desk at People to People's bank said the same thing. People to People took the advice and was glad for it: By the end of the year the euro had risen to $1.47. But even with hedging, the weak dollar was a major factor behind the company's 10 percent price hikes this year. Luckily, domestic trips have been on the rise, thanks in part to the exchange rate, and that has helped bolster profits.

Seeking American Suppliers
The Company: Rainbow Packaging, Chandler, Arizona

The problem: Rainbow is a distributor; the company buys packaging machines from two German suppliers and resells them to customers in the U.S., including Hallmark Cards. CEO Wes Henriksen has had to raise prices as the machines, which encase products like DVDs and stationery in plastic packaging, have become more expensive for him to buy. The calls from customers started slowing down 11 months ago, when the euro hit $1.35—today it's $1.48. The machines have always cost more than their American counterparts, but now they cost close to $100,000 more—far too expensive to compete, Henriksen says.

The fix: It was an eerily quiet year for Rainbow, which saw revenue fall from about $3 million in 2006 to $275,000 in 2007—or, as Henriksen says, "$3 million to retired." Though he avoided laying off either of his two employees, he had to dig into cash reserves to pay their salaries. Toward the end of last year, Rainbow began buying packaging machines from domestic manufacturers. "It's like starting from scratch," says Henriksen. "It's 10 years out the window." Nonetheless, he is adamant about continuing to work with his German suppliers, whose product, he says, is superior, and will find its market once the dollar rebounds.

GOLDSTEIN, SARAH. "Dollar doldrums: how American companies are beating the currency crunch.(GLOBAL BUSINESS)." *Inc.* 30.3 (March 2008): 45(2). *General Reference Center Gold*. Gale. Western Connecticut State University. 3 Mar. 2008 <http://0-find.galegroup.com.csulib.ctstateu.edu:80/itx/start.do?prodId=GRGM>.

For more on how companies can weather the weak dollar, listen to a podcast with Inc. associate editor Hannah Clark Steiman at www.inc.com/keyword/mar08.

Financial Globalization

Beyond the Blame Game

A new way of looking at financial globalization reexamines its costs and benefits.

M. AYHAN KOSE ET AL.

Financial globalization—the phenomenon of rising cross-border financial flows—is often blamed for the string of damaging economic crises that rocked a number of emerging markets in the late 1980s in Latin America and in the 1990s in Mexico and a handful of Asian countries. The market turmoil and resulting bankruptcies prompted a rash of finger-pointing by those who suggested that developing countries had dismantled capital controls too hastily—leaving themselves vulnerable to the harsh dictates of rapid capital movements and market herd effects. Some were openly critical of international institutions they saw as promoting capital account liberalization without stressing the necessity of building up the strong institutions needed to steer markets through bad times.

In contrast to the growing consensus among academic economists that trade liberalization is, by and large, beneficial for both industrial and developing economies, debate rages among academics and practitioners about the costs and benefits of financial globalization. Some economists (for example, Dani Rodrik, Jagdish Bhagwati, and Joseph Stiglitz) view unfettered capital flows as disruptive to global financial stability, leading to calls for capital controls and other curbs on international asset trade. Others (including Stanley Fischer and Lawrence Summers) argue that increased openness to capital flows has, in general, proved essential for countries seeking to rise from lower- to middle-income status and that it has strengthened stability among industrial countries. This debate clearly has considerable relevance for economic policy, especially given that major economies like China and India have recently taken steps to open up their capital accounts.

To get beyond the polemics, we put together a framework for analyzing the vast and growing body of studies about the costs and benefits of financial globalization. Our framework offers a fresh perspective on the macroeconomic effects of global financial flows, in terms of both growth and volatility. We systematically sift through various pieces of evidence on whether developing countries can benefit from financial globalization and whether financial globalization, in itself, leads to economic crises. Our findings suggest that financial globalization appears to be neither a magic bullet to spur growth, as some proponents would claim, nor an unmanageable risk, as others have sought to portray it.

Unanswered Questions

The recent wave of financial globalization began in earnest in the mid-1980s, spurred by the liberalization of capital controls in many countries in anticipation of the better growth outcomes and increased stability of consumption that cross-border flows would bring. It was presumed that these benefits would be large, especially for developing countries, which tend to be more capital-poor and have more volatile income growth than other countries.

Emerging market economies, the group of developing countries that have actively participated in financial globalization, have clearly registered better growth outcomes, on average, than those countries that have not participated (see Chart 1). Yet the majority of studies using cross-country growth regressions to analyze the relationship between growth and financial openness have been unable to show that capital account liberalization produces measurable growth benefits. One reason may be traced to the difficulty of measuring financial openness. For example, widely used measures of capital controls (restrictions on capital account transactions) fail to capture how effectively countries enforce those controls and do not always reflect the actual degree of an economy's integration with international capital markets. In recent years, considerable progress has been made on developing better measures of capital controls and better data on flows and stocks of international assets and liabilities. Studies that are based on these improved measures of financial integration are beginning to find evidence of positive

(per capita GDP, weighted by purchasing power parity; 1970=100)

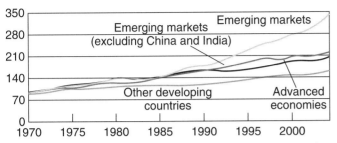

Chart 1 Against the Odds Despite crises in some emerging market countries, this group has outperformed other groups over the past three decades.

Sources: IMF, *World Economic Outlook*; World Bank, *World Development Indicators.*

(composition or gross flows to emerging markets, percent of total)

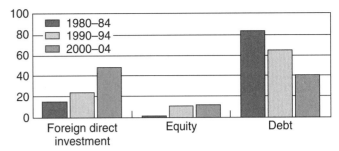

Chart 2 On the Rise Emerging markets now attract more FDI than other types of flows.

Source: External Wealth of Nations database from Philip R. Lane and Gian Maria Milesi-Ferretti.

"The External Wealth of Nations Mark II: Revised and Extended Estimates of Foreign Assets and Liabilities, 1970–2004," IMF Working Paper No. 06/69 (Washington Monetary Fund, 2006).

growth effects of financial integration. The evidence, however, is still far from conclusive.

Nor is there systematic evidence that financial integration is the proximate determinant of financial crises. Authors who have looked at different manifestations of such crises—including sudden stops of capital inflows, current account reversals, and banking crises—have found no evidence that countries that are more open to financial flows tend to have a higher incidence of crises than those that are less open.

Although crisis episodes receive most of the attention, they are just particularly sharp manifestations of the more general phenomenon of macroeconomic volatility. On that score, the results are less favorable: financial globalization has not delivered on the promised benefit of improved international risk sharing and reduced volatility of consumption for developing countries.

In sum, the effects of financial globalization have not been conclusively determined. Although there is little formal empirical evidence to support the oft-cited claims that financial globalization has *caused* the financial crises that the world has seen over the past three decades, the existence of robust macroeconomic evidence of the benefits of financial globalization is elusive, too. Given the shortcomings of cross-country growth regressions, is there another approach that can shed light on the effects of financial globalization?

Not Created Equal

An alternative perspective on the growth and volatility effects of financial globalization is based on differentiating among various types of capital flows. This is particularly relevant because the composition of international financial flows has changed markedly over time.

Foreign direct investment (FDI) has now become the dominant source of private capital flows to emerging market economies (see Chart 2); *equity flows* have also risen in importance, whereas *debt flows* have declined. FDI and portfolio equity flows are presumed to be more stable and less prone to reversals and are believed to bring with them many of the indirect benefits of financial globalization, such as transfers of managerial and technological expertise. Debt

flows, by contrast, are widely accepted as being riskier; in particular, the fact that they are procyclical and highly volatile can magnify the adverse impact of negative shocks on economic growth.

The increasing importance of portfolio equity flows to emerging markets has motivated a number of studies examining the growth effects of equity market liberalizations. These papers uniformly suggest that these liberalizations have a significant, positive impact on output growth. Whether the estimated growth effects could be picking up the effects of other factors—especially other reforms that tend to accompany these liberalizations—remains, in our view, an open question. On the other hand, the body of microeconomic evidence (using industry- and firm-level data) supporting the macro evidence of the benefits of equity liberalizations is growing. Some of these papers also document the empirical relevance of various theoretical channels that link equity market liberalization to economic growth, including through increases in investment and total factor productivity growth.

Interestingly, despite the general consensus that FDI is most likely to spin off positive growth benefits, these benefits are harder to detect in aggregate data than those associated with equity flows. Fortunately, recent research using micro data is starting to confirm that FDI flows do have significant spillover effects on output and productivity growth.

From the evidence we have reviewed thus far, a key theme emerges: many of the benefits of financial openness seem to be masked in cross-country analysis using macroeconomic data but are more apparent in disaggregated analyses using micro data. An approach based on micro data also has a better chance of disentangling causal effects and capturing the relative importance of different channels through which financial integration affects growth.

Some economists have used micro data to estimate the costs of capital controls. Such controls seem to cause distortions in the behavior of firms (and individuals), which adjust their behavior to evade capital controls. By insulating an economy from competitive forces, capital controls may also reduce market discipline. Thus, their existence appears to result in significant efficiency costs at the level of individual firms or sectors.

Financial globalization yields collateral benefits...

Traditional view

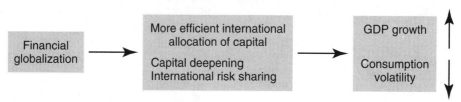

The traditional view focuses on the importance of channels through which capital flows could directly increase GDP growth and reduce consumption volatility.

A different perspective

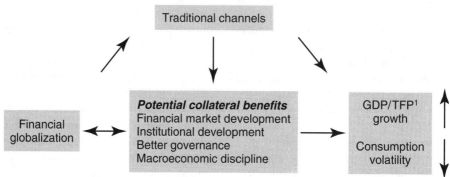

Chart 3 Our perspective acknowledges the relevance of the traditional channels but argues that the role of financial globalization as a catalyst for certain "collateral benefits" may be more important in increasing GDP/TFP growth and reducing consumption volatility.

1. Total factor productivity.

Making Sense of the Evidence

We now introduce a conceptual framework that assembles these disparate strands of evidence in order to shed some light on why empirical evidence at different levels of disaggregation reaches different conclusions.

A basic building block of our framework is the notion that successful financial globalization does not simply enhance access to financing for domestic investment but that its benefits are catalytic and indirect. Far more important than the direct growth effects of access to more capital is how capital flows generate what we label financial integration's potential *collateral benefits* (so called because they may not be countries' primary motivations for undertaking financial integration). A growing number of studies are showing that financial openness can promote development of the domestic financial sector, impose discipline on macroeconomic policies, generate efficiency gains among domestic firms by exposing them to competition from foreign entrants, and unleash forces that result in better government and corporate governance. These collateral benefits could enhance efficiency and, by extension, total factor productivity growth.

The notion that financial globalization influences growth mainly through indirect channels has powerful implications for an empirical analysis of its benefits. Building institutions, enhancing market discipline, and deepening the financial sector take time, as does the realization of growth benefits from such channels. This may explain why, over relatively short periods, it seems much easier to detect the costs but not the benefits of financial globalization. More fundamentally, even over long horizons, it may be difficult to detect the productivity-enhancing benefits of financial globalization in empirical work if one includes structural, institutional, and macroeconomic policy variables in cross-country regressions that attempt to explain growth. After all, it is through these very channels that financial integration generates growth (see Chart 3).

> "Given the difficulties that we have identified in interpreting the cross-country growth evidence, it is encouraging to see that financial market integration seems to be operating through some of the indirect channels."

One should not, of course, overstate the case that financial integration generates collateral benefits. It is equally plausible that, all else being equal, more foreign capital tends to flow to countries with better-developed financial markets and institutions. We also do not dismiss the importance of traditional channels—that financial integration can increase investment by relaxing the constraints imposed by low levels of domestic saving and reducing the cost of capital. But our view is that these traditional channels may have been overemphasized in previous research.

Is there empirical merit to our conceptual framework? We now turn our attention to marshalling the evidence for a key piece of our argument—that financial globalization has significant collateral benefits.

Financial Integration's Indirect Benefits

The potential indirect benefits of financial globalization are likely to be important in three key areas: financial sector development, institutional quality, and macroeconomic policies.

A good deal of research suggests that international financial flows serve as an important catalyst for domestic *financial market development*, as reflected both in straightforward measures of the size of the banking sector and equity markets and in broader concepts of financial market development, including supervision and regulation.

Research based on a variety of techniques, including country case studies, supports the notion that the larger the presence of foreign banks in a country, the better the quality of its financial services and the greater the efficiency of financial intermediation. As for equity markets, the overwhelming theoretical presumption is that foreign entry increases efficiency, and the evidence seems to support this. Stock markets do, in fact, tend to become larger and more liquid after equity market liberalizations.

The empirical evidence suggests that financial globalization has induced a number of countries to adjust their corporate governance structures in response to foreign competition and demands from international investors. Moreover, financial sector FDI from well-regulated and well-supervised source countries tends to support *institutional development and governance* in emerging market economies.

Capital account liberalization, by increasing the potential costs associated with weak policies and enhancing the benefits associated with good ones, should also impose discipline on macroeconomic policies. Precisely because capital account liberalization makes a country more vulnerable to sudden shifts in global investor sentiment, it can signal the country's commitment to better *macroeconomic policies* as a way of mitigating the likelihood of such shifts and their adverse effects. Although the empirical evidence on this point is suggestive, it is sparse. Countries with higher levels of financial openness appear more likely to generate better monetary policy outcomes in terms of lower inflation, but there is no evidence of a systematic relationship between financial openness and better fiscal policies.

The evidence that we have surveyed in this section is hardly decisive, but it does consistently point to international financial integration as a catalyst for a variety of productivity-enhancing benefits. Given the difficulties that we have identified in interpreting the cross-country growth evidence, it is encouraging to see that financial market integration seems to be operating through some of the indirect channels.

A Complication: Thresholds

Some related studies have tackled the question of what initial conditions are necessary if financial openness is to generate good growth benefits for a country while lowering the risks of a crisis. What are these conditions?

Financial sector development, in particular, is a key determinant of the extent of the growth and stability benefits financial globalization can bring. The more developed a country's financial sector, the greater the growth benefits of capital inflows and the lower the country's vulnerability to crises, through both direct and indirect channels.

Another benefit of greater financial sector development is that it has a positive effect on macroeconomic stability, which, in turn, has implications for the volume and composition of capital flows. In developing countries that lack deep financial sectors, sudden changes in the direction of capital flows tend to induce or exacerbate boom-bust cycles. Furthermore, inadequate or mismanaged domestic financial sector liberalizations have contributed to many crises that may be associated with financial integration.

Institutional quality appears to play an important role in determining not just the outcomes of financial integration but the actual level of integration. It also appears to strongly influence the composition of inflows into developing economies, which is another way it affects macroeconomic outcomes. Better institutional quality helps tilt a country's capital structure toward FDI and portfolio equity flows, which tend to bring more of the collateral benefits of financial integration.

The *quality of domestic macroeconomic policies* also appears to influence the level and composition of inflows, as well as a country's vulnerability to crises. Sound fiscal and monetary policies increase the growth benefits of capital account liberalization and help avert crises in countries with open capital accounts. Moreover, for economies with weak financial systems, an open capital account and a fixed exchange rate regime are not an auspicious combination. A compelling case can be made that rigid exchange rate regimes can make a country more vulnerable to crises when it opens its capital markets.

Trade integration improves the cost-benefit trade-off associated with financial integration. It also reduces the probability of crises associated with financial openness and mitigates the costs of such crises if they do occur. Thus, recent studies strengthen the case made by the old sequencing literature that argued in favor of putting trade liberalization ahead of capital account liberalization.

This discussion suggests that there are some basic supporting conditions, or thresholds, that determine where on the continuum of potential costs and benefits a country ends up. It is the

...but initial, or threshold, conditions are a complication

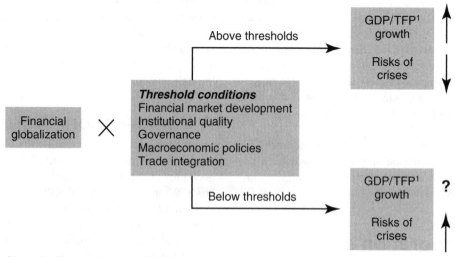

Chart 4 Financial globalization leads to better macroeconomic outcomes when certain threshold conditions are met. This generates tension because many of the threshold conditions are similar to the collateral benefits.

1. Total factor productivity.

interaction between financial globalization and this set of initial conditions that determines growth and volatility outcomes (see Chart 4).

A comparison of Charts 3 and 4 highlights a fundamental tension between the costs and benefits of financial globalization. Many of the threshold conditions are similar to the collateral benefits. In other words, financial globalization is a catalyst for a number of important collateral benefits but can greatly elevate the risk-to-benefit ratio if the initial conditions in these dimensions are inadequate.

A different threshold is related to the level of integration itself. Industrial economies, which are far more integrated with global financial markets, clearly do a better job than emerging markets of using international capital flows to allocate capital efficiently, thereby accruing productivity gains and sharing income risk. Does this mean that, to realize the collateral benefits, developing countries' only hope is to attain a level of financial integration similar to that of industrial economies and that the risks they encounter along the way are unavoidable? After all, if the short-term costs take the form of crises, they could have persistent negative effects that detract from the long-term growth benefits. Furthermore, the distributional effects associated with these short-term consequences can be particularly painful for low-income countries.

Risk-Benefit Calculus

Our synthesis of the literature on financial globalization, while guardedly positive about its overall benefit, suggests that as countries make the transition from being less integrated to being more integrated with global financial markets, they are likely to encounter major complications. For developing countries, financial globalization appears to have the potential to generate an array of collateral benefits that may help boost long-run

growth and welfare. At the same time, if a country opens its capital account without having some basic supporting conditions in place, the benefits can be delayed and the country can be more vulnerable to sudden stops of capital flows. This is a fundamental tension between the costs and benefits of financial globalization that may be difficult to avoid.

Does this imply that a country that wants the collateral benefits of financial globalization has no alternative but to expose itself to substantial risks of crises? Or, alternatively, would developing countries do best to shield themselves from external influences while trying to improve the quality of their domestic policies and institutions to some acceptable level? Our view is that, although the risks can never be totally avoided, there are ways to improve the benefit-risk calculus of financial globalization. There is, however, unlikely to be a uniform approach to opening the capital account that will work well for all countries.

> "Some of the more extreme polemic claims made about the effects of financial globalization on developing countries, both pro and con, are far less easy to substantiate than either side generally cares to admit."

The collateral benefits perspective may provide a way for moving forward on capital account liberalization that takes into account individual country circumstances (initial conditions), as well as the relative priorities of different collateral benefits for that country. Depending on a country's internal distortions—particularly those related to the domestic financial sector—one can, in principle, design an approach to capital account liberalization that could generate specific benefits while minimizing the associated risks. Although we have laid out a framework for thinking about these issues, further research is clearly needed in a number of areas before one can derive strong policy conclusions about the specifics of such an approach.

Meanwhile, we should recognize that some of the more extreme polemic claims made about the effects of financial globalization on developing countries, both pro and con, are far less easy to substantiate than either side generally cares to admit.

M. Ayhan Kose is an Economist and Shang-Jin Wei is a Division Chief in the IMF's Research Department. Eswar Prasad is the Nandlal P. Tolani Senior Professor of Trade Policy at Cornell University. Kenneth Rogoff is the Thomas D. Cabot Professor of Public Policy and Professor of Economics at Harvard University.

This article is based on IMF Working Paper No. 06/189, "Financial Globalization: A Reappraisal." See that paper for a detailed list of references to the literature on this topic and for the primary sources from which some of the material in this article is drawn.

China's Mobile Maestro

China mobile, the world's largest wireless company, has 332 million subscribers, thousands of shareholders, and one communist party to please. That's not an easy job for its CEO.

Clay Chandler

In New York city last year for a meeting with news Corp.'s Rupert Murdoch, Wang Jianzhou, CEO of China's largest mobile-phone company, came across an ad for Cingular Wireless that gave him pause. Touting low dropped-call rates and a vast web of base stations-"over 47,000 cell sites, more than any other wireless network"—the ad proclaimed Cingular, then the largest U.S. mobile operator, "the only true leader in wireless." Wang wouldn't dream of making such a boast; he'd be too embarrassed. His company, China Mobile, has a network of more than 230,000 base stations and is spending furiously to put up more. When you run the biggest mobile-phone network in the world's most populous country, you operate on a different scale.

And what a scale it is. With 332 million subscribers as of July, China Mobile serves five times as many customers as AT&T, the largest U.S. carrier since acquiring Cingular last year, and continues to sign five million new users a month. In China's largest cities, where mobile penetration rates match those in the U.S. and Europe, China Mobile offers a dizzying array of non-voice services including Internet search, ringtones, and music downloads. It has struck content deals with domestic and foreign providers, including News Corp., MTV Networks, Yahoo, and the National Basketball Association, and transmits 1.2 billion text messages every day. In rural China, home to two-thirds of China's 1.3 billion people, the carrier has launched an aggressive expansion drive, joining with government agricultural bureaus to beam farmers in remote hamlets advice on improving harvests and where to get the best prices for their crops. China Mobile's wireless network now stretches from Hong Kong to the Himalayas, offering mobile coverage to 97% of China's citizens. Its signal comes in strong on the Beijing subway, inside Shanghai elevators, in Guangxi rice paddies—even atop Mount Everest.

So far, this breakneck growth hasn't come at the expense of profit. Far from it: In the first half of 2007 the company reported net profits of $5 billion, up 25% from the previous year, on sales of $21.1 billion. As of early August its shares traded at $57 on the New York Stock Exchange, an eightfold increase since their October 1997 debut, lifting China Mobile's market capi-

talization to $218 billion. The result? China, a country where only two decades ago fixed-line phones were a privilege of the Communist elite, now claims the most valuable mobile-phone company in the world.

But running this behemoth is no cinch. Wang, an unassuming 58-year-old engineer who started his career three decades ago as a bureaucrat in the Ministry of Post and Telecommunications, may have one of the trickiest jobs of any FORTUNE Global 500 CEO. It's hard to imagine another chief who answers to as many masters. First and foremost, he must heed the wishes of the Chinese government, China Mobile's regulator and its controlling shareholder. Beijing wants China Mobile, which has a 73% market share, to become a global powerhouse, but without beating up too badly on China Unicom, China's other mobile carrier. Government planners have prodded China Mobile to take an active approach to foreign acquisitions, as it did this year when parent company China Mobile Communications, which Wang also heads, snapped up Paktel, Pakistan's fifth-largest wireless company, for $460 million. They've also ordered China Mobile to take the lead in developing a Chinese standard for third-generation mobile services rather than rely on existing technologies from the U.S., Japan, or Europe.

But investors, who own 25% of China Mobile's shares, fret that Beijing's national policy goals threaten the bottom line. They worry that Wang will be encouraged to overpay for foreign acquisitions he doesn't need, forced to overspend on unproven homegrown 3G technologies less efficient than those already available, and discouraged from seizing opportunities in his home market for fear of becoming too dominant. And then there are all those customers: on the one hand, hip, young urbanites demanding worldclass mobile services, and on the other, farmers clamoring for lower prices. How to reconcile these divergent interests? Wang insists he isn't fazed. "I don't think it's so difficult to find the balance," he says at China Mobile's imposing headquarters in Beijing's new financial district. "As head of a state-owned enterprise, my duty is to maximize the value of state assets. As CEO of a listed company, my job is to enhance value for our shareholders."

TOP TEN MOBILE COMPANIES	COUNTRY	2006 WORLDWIDE SUBSCRIBERS (MILLIONS)
CHINA MOBILE	China	291
VODAFONE	Britain	199
CHINA UNICOM	China	142
TELEFÓNICA	Spain	126
AMÉRICA MÓVIL	Mexico	117
DEUTSCHE TELEKOM	Germany	99
FRANCE TÉLÉCOM	France	98
TELENOR	Norway	68
AT&T	U.S.	64
TELECOM ITALIA	Italy	60

Source: Cowen & Co.

Improbably, Wang has hatched a growth strategy that, for now at least, is keeping everyone happy. The secret to his balancing act can be found in places like Wuzhubi, a village of about 250 families nestled deep in the mountains of Yunnan province not far from the Tibet border. Until last year only a handful of Wuzhubi's residents owned a mobile phone. And little wonder: To pick up a signal, would-be callers had to hike to the top of a ridge several miles away. But all that changed in March, when China Mobile erected a transmission tower atop a nearby hill. Hundreds of residents purchased handsets. Dozens invested in wireless terminals on which they can make unlimited calls within the village at a monthly rate of less than $2.

He Wanyong, Wuzhubi's 39-year-old chief, marvels at the speed with which mobile phones have transformed life in his isolated village. Now, when He wants to convene a meeting of Wuzhubi's 20-member council, he just rings them up or shoots them text messages. In the pre-wireless era, he recalls, he had to spend an entire morning walking house to house to let folks know. For He, who also serves as village grocer and pharmacist, the arrival of the China Mobile tower has made it easier to restock cigarettes and dispense medicine. "To do all the things I do now," he says, "I used to need three heads and six arms."

North of Wuzhubi, beyond the towering rock cliffs of Tiger Leaping Gorge, ethnic Tibetans, who live in rough-hewn homes and dress much as they have for centuries, have embraced the mobile phone as an invaluable tool. In the tiny hamlet of Dala, residents use mobile phones to track fluctuations in the price of wild pine-ear mushrooms. In the late 1980s they learned from Japanese visitors, much to their astonishment, that the mushrooms—known as *songrong* in China and *matsutake* in Japan—could fetch hundreds of dollars a kilogram in Tokyo. But before wireless coverage, locals were at the mercy of a handful of mushroom brokers who cheated them on price. With mobile phones, they can call around. "Mushroom prices can fluctuate a lot, even in a single day," says Nongbu Qilin, Dala's village chief. "You might get 200 yuan per kilogram in the morning but 500 yuan at night. You really need to know the right time to sell."

Dala lies near the center of a sparsely populated county that changed its name a decade ago to Shangri-la in a bid to draw tourists. The cobalt skies, rugged terrain, and proximity to Tibet evoke the hidden paradise described by James Hilton in his 1933 novel *Lost Horizon*. These days the horizon is dotted with transmission towers: Even in Shangri-la, there are few spots where the China Mobile signal can't find potential customers.

That has revolutionized one of the region's oldest trades, yak herding. In a makeshift hut on a ridge thousands of feet above Dala, 73-year-old Nongnu says he and his wife, Xizha, 71, use their mobile phone to ask family members below for supplies, let them know they've collected enough yak milk for churning, and alert them if a yak has wandered off. Until China Mobile's signal came to their mountaintop three years ago, Nongnu's grandchildren had to trek two hours up the mountain every couple of days to check on them. Now they come only every five days, although lately the interval is shrinking. It seems Nongnu and his wife spend so much time on the phone that they often run down their one battery after a few days, requiring someone to hike up for the battery, hike down to recharge, then hike back up again. (China Mobile says it's developing an affordable solar-powered battery recharger.)

Nongbu, the village chief, bought his first mobile phone when he was a salesman at a sawmill. It cost him 6,000 yuan, more than many families made in a year. But it was worth it, he says, assuring that he never missed sales and could keep his customers happy. Now that handsets are cheaper, he changes models every three or four months. He uses the phones to manage village affairs, keep tabs on the truck he rents out for cargo jobs, dispatch his duties as secretary general of a local transport cooperative, stay in touch with his mother—and, as he demonstrates during a visit, follow the NBA. "I really love LeBron James," he says. "He's better than Yao Ming." In a flash, he rings a friend in town to find out that the Cavs won a playoff game by one point.

Bringing mobile-phone service to Dala and Wuzhubi is part of an ambitious rural expansion drive launched by China Mobile in 2004, when Wang was named CEO. Last year rural subscribers accounted for more than half of China Mobile's 53 million new subscribers. Given that rural China has a mobile-phone penetration rate of only 17%—compared with more than 60% in major urban centers—Wang figures rural growth can continue at its current pace for years to come.

In its early stages, this rural buildout was dismissed by foreign analysts as an effort to win Brownie points with China's Communist leadership. Certainly the strategy was consistent with the goals espoused by President Hu Jintao, who has emphasized the need for policies to close the gap between rural and urban living standards. But the decision to take wireless services to the rural masses also made good business sense. While China's urban markets had reached the saturation point, rural China was wide open. Signing new customers in the countryside is far less expensive than trying to lure them away from China Unicom in the cities—not least because regulators allow Unicom to offer its services for as much as 10% less than China Mobile's. There's less need to shell out for TV commercials or billboard space; in many villages, China Mobile can promote its brand for little more than the cost of the bucket of paint required to emblazon its logo on the side of a shed. Adding cell sites is cheaper too. A new transmission tower in rural areas costs less than $65,000, on average, a fraction of what it takes to build a tower in Beijing.

True, rural customers have far less to spend on mobile-phone services than their urban counterparts and aren't much interested in music downloads, the latest ringtones, or games. But it turns out they use their phones for voice and text messaging more frequently than anyone imagined. To attract more rural customers, China Mobile has gradually lowered rates, but only to the extent that reductions are offset by increased usage. Average revenue per user—the favorite benchmark of telecom analysts—has held steady at around $11 a month in the first half of this year, down less than two percentage points from 2004, when the rural expansion drive began.

Before wireless coverage, locals were at the mercy of mushroom brokers who cheated them. With mobile phones, they can call around.

Wang, a fan of Insead management professors W. Chan Kim and Renée Mauborgne, talks about China's hinterland as a classic "blue-ocean market," where the company can cast its net widely without worrying about getting tangled up with the nets of rivals. To be sure, the fish are tiny: In many of China's rural communities, per capita income is less than $50 a month. But China Mobile's low cost structure assures comfortable margins serving such small fry. In that sense the company's strategy reflects the wisdom of another popular management guru, C.K. Prahalad, who promises that big corporations capable of serving the world's aspiring poor will discover a "fortune at the bottom of the pyramid."

Wang chuckles as he recalls the frosty reception he received from analysts three years ago when he unveiled his rural strategy. "Analysts and investors, managers of large institutional funds, all thought China Mobile's years of high growth were over," he says. "They thought we were a good company, but they considered us a big, slow elephant. I went around asking why, and always the answer was this: 'You can still add to your subscriber base, but from now on all your customers will be low-end users. You'll run up big capital expenditures to reach them and high operational costs to serve them, but they won't bring you much profit.' But I had worked in this industry many years. I knew the numbers. I knew what kind of returns we could see on those investments. I told skeptics, 'You are absolutely wrong.'"

Great Northern Telegraph, a Danish firm, opened China's first telephone office in Shanghai in 1882. One hundred years later, Wang says, the country had no more than 2.3 million fixed-line phones. But in his early years as a bureaucrat there was no need to think about consumers, and the only marketing skill required was an ability to persuade people to be a little more patient. Wang didn't get a phone for his family until 1987, after he'd toiled in the ministry for more than a decade.

Wang's own marketing skills have improved considerably since then. He is arguably the most polished CEO at any of China's state-owned giants. He speaks English fluently, is well versed in the latest management literature, works at building relationships with global telecom leaders, and has gone to great lengths to meet foreign analysts and investors.

Still, Beijing keeps even its most talented executives on a short leash—something made clear in 2004, when the State Assets Supervision and Administration Commission (SASAC), which holds ultimate control over China's two fixed-line and two mobile carriers, rotated the CEOs of three of the four companies into one another's jobs. Wang, then president of China Unicom, was ordered to clear out his desk and report for duty at China Mobile. Wang says he took his 2004 transfer in stride, although he admits it caught him by surprise. "I don't talk about my old job," he says.

At the end of his workday, Wang says, he enjoys using his own mobile phone to surf the Internet. "The search engine is very useful for me," he says. "On my way home from work, I'll sit in the back of the car and put my name into Baidu or Google to look for the daily news reports about myself." And why not? For now at least, the news about Wang and China Mobile is pretty good.

But the pressure on Wang can only increase. Beijing has decreed that China will deploy its own 3G standard, known as TD-SCDMA, to compete with CDMA2000, the dominant U.S. protocol, and W-CDMA, favored in Europe and Japan. They have also vowed to have 3G networks up and running in at least ten cities by next summer, when tens of thousands of athletes, journalists, dignitaries, and tourists descend on China for the Olympics. China Mobile's parent has been tasked with developing the standard, and China Mobile has been ordered to roll out the service in eight cities. Whether the new standard is ready for prime time remains one of China's most guarded state secrets. Wang won't comment, but earlier this year a top official declared TD-SCDMA "commercially mature."

Analysts remain skeptical, as regulators have been promising a 3G rollout for years. But they are paying close attention because many believe the rollout, when it comes, will occasion an industry revamp. Officials have repeatedly said China's telecom sector is out of balance. In the wireless segment, China Mobile dominates. And the fixed-line carriers, while big, are far less profitable than the mobile carriers. Among the possible scenarios: The state will break up China Unicom and parcel out its mobile networks to the fixed-line operators, creating two much stronger competitors to slug it out with China Mobile.

"Analysts all thought China mobile's years of high growth were over," Wang says. "I told skeptics, 'you are absolutely wrong.'"

Some analysts are betting 3G will be put on hold until after the Olympics, reasoning that Beijing is too proud to roll out TD-SCDMA before it's perfect. Plans for China Mobile to list shares on Shanghai's stock exchange—a development expected as early as August—may add to regulators' aversion to risk. But Goldman Sachs analyst Helen Zhu predicts 3G will be up and running and the industry shaken up well before the Olympics, arguing that it won't be possible to work the bugs out of TD-SCDMA without loading "substantial numbers of subscribers on the network" and rolling out on a commercial basis.

Regardless of timing, restructuring is sure to make life tougher for Wang, which explains why he's moving so aggressively to stake his claim in rural China. "The longer regulators wait to restructure," says BDA International research director Zhang Dongming, "the more subscribers China Mobile can load onto its network. This is an old-fashioned land grab: China Mobile is trying to lock up the countryside while it can." Mobilizing rural masses is a time-honored strategy in China; after all, it worked for Chairman Mao. For China's newly connected farmers, the results of this campaign may prove no less revolutionary.

Reporter Associates Dan Chinoy; Joan L. Levinstein and Zhang Dan.

The Challengers

A New Breed of Multinational Company Has Emerged

When Ford Motor Company bought Jaguar in 1989 and Land Rover 11 years later, it marked a low point for Britain's ailing industrial heritage. Last year Ford concluded that it could not make money from the illustrious British marques—equally a sign of its waning fortunes. The two firms shortlisted to take the prize come from India. Their ambition and confidence is a sign of something new in global business: the arrival in force of emerging-market multinationals.

Tata Motors, the carmaking bit of Tata Group, India's biggest industrial conglomerate, has edged ahead of Mahindra & Mahindra, a sprawling group that makes tractors and off-road vehicles, to become the preferred bidder. Ford told Jaguar workers this month that it was "in substantive discussions" with Tata. The future of these two grand old badges will be shaped not in Coventry, cradle of the British motor industry, but in Pune, home of Tata Motors.

Another indication of this newcomer's growing strength was the unveiling this week of the revolutionary, cheap "one lakh" car, which will sell in India and South-East Asia for the equivalent of $2,500. Thus the Indian company, which launched its first saloon car barely ten years ago, is beating the industry's established giants in a new market segment in which sales will surely grow fast.

Tata is certainly not the only company from an emerging economy striding onto the global stage. A study by Boston Consulting Group (BCG) found 100 companies from emerging markets with total assets in 2006 of $520 billion, more than the world's top 20 car companies. By 2004 the UN Conference on Trade and Development (UNCTAD) even noted that five companies from emerging Asia had made it into the list of the world's 100 biggest multinationals measured by overseas assets; ten more emerging-economy firms made it into the top 200.

By 2006 foreign direct investment (including mergers and acquisitions) from developing economies had reached $174 billion, 14% of the world's total, giving such countries a 13% share (worth $1.6 trillion) of the stock of global FDI. In 1990 emerging economies accounted for just 5% of the flow (see chart 1) and 8% of the stock. Their slice of global cross-border M&A has been climbing. It reached 14% in value terms in 2006 (chart 2). That year they spent $123 billion in more than 1,000 cross-border deals.

Since UNCTAD's first analysis in the early 1970s there has been concern about the power wielded by companies from rich

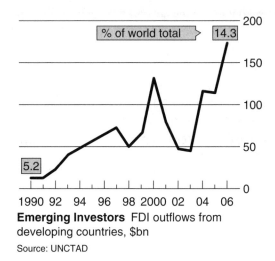

Emerging Investors FDI outflows from developing countries, $bn

Source: UNCTAD

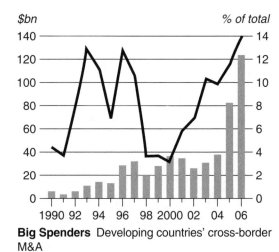

Big Spenders Developing countries' cross-border M&A

Source: UNCTAD

countries in poorer ones. Developed countries have had their bouts of anxiety too. In the 1960s the French fretted about *le défi américain*, as IBM, Ford, General Motors, Dow Chemical and ITT spread their tentacles across Europe; in the 1980s it was America's turn to squirm as Japanese firms bought up Hollywood and Manhattan.

The latest trend reflects a new, fundamental shift. In a more open world, emerging economies are spawning their own giants.

UNCTAD is turning its attention to the new shape of global business: investment now flows increasingly from south to north and south to south, as emerging economies invest both in the rich world and in less developed countries.

Meet the New Boys

The rest of the world has woken up to the newcomers in the past couple of years thanks to some huge cross-border deals. In early 2006 Arcelor, a steelmaker of French, Luxembourgeois and Spanish extraction and Europe's biggest, faced a bid from Mittal, an international steel group largely owned by the family of Lakshmi Mittal, an expatriate Indian based in London. Mr Mittal and his son, Aditya, had cooked up the deal two days before Christmas 2005, during their annual skiing holiday in St Moritz. When the French government heard about the deal in January, recalls Mr Mittal, ministers wondered whether his company was Indian or American. Arcelor turned to another emerging-economy steelmaker, Russia's Severstal, as a possible white knight, before eventually succumbing to Mittal six months later. Thus was born Arcelor Mittal, the first steel company with an annual output of more than 100m tonnes.

The confusion over Mittal's origins among French government ministers reflects the novelty of the group. Unable to expand the family's steel business in stuffy, over-regulated India, Mr Mittal took off to lead an international wing, with a steel mill in Indonesia, which soon prospered "under the noses of the Japanese" as he gleefully recalls. His reputation there led to a contract to turn around the state-owned steel industry in Trinidad, which he later acquired. Next was Mexico, where he bought steel plants in the country's 1990s privatisation wave, before buying Inland Steel and International Steel in America, as traditional steelmakers there wilted in the rust-belt meltdown. Then he snapped up old state steel firms in eastern Europe.

Even before Mr Mittal bought Arcelor, Corus, an Anglo-Dutch steel firm, had approached Ratan Tata, head of Tata Group, about joining forces with Tata Steel, which owned plants in Singapore and elsewhere in South-East Asia as well as in India. Months of discussion led to the conclusion that the only efficient way to combine would be for the Indian firm to take over Corus (most Tata group companies are separately quoted, with the holding company having about 20% of the shares). This agreement led to another dramatic demonstration of power: a bidding war for Corus between Tata Steel and Brazil's CSN group, which broke out in late 2006. Tata eventually secured its prize in an all-night auction organised by the takeover panel in London a year ago.

Besides the companies making such big deals, a whole squad of well-known new multinationals from developing countries have been growing organically and through smaller deals. The Indian trio of Wipro, Infosys and Tata Consultancy Services (TCS) have built an IT outsourcing industry that has moved upmarket, has gone global and is chasing rich-country leaders such as Accenture and IBM. China has Lenovo, which bought IBM's PC business, the Haier and Hisense groups in domestic appliances and consumer electronics, and BYD, the world's largest maker of nickel-cadmium batteries.

Others now being watched by western analysts include Chery Automobile, China's leading car exporter, which aims to build plants in eastern Europe, the Middle East and South America. Johnson Electric, of Hong Kong, has cornered half the world's market for tiny electric motors. Cemex, a Mexican cement company, has already taken over a big British group, RMC. Embraer of Brazil has become the world's third-largest aircraft company, specialising in regional jets. Half the sales of Sadia and Perdigão, two Brazilian food companies, which amount to around $6 billion combined, are exports.

India's Bharat Forge, now the world's second-largest forging company and a leading supplier to the motor industry around the world, recently tied up with a French company to get close to PSA Peugeot Citroën. Indian private-equity groups have been eyeing this tactic and aim to take over small European car-parts companies. Their motivation is not to own assets in France or Germany, but to acquire relationships with manufacturers. "We are not really buying factories," says such an investor. "We are buying orders, which we can eventually fulfil with cheaper supplies from India."

The Rationale

According to BCG, thousands of companies like these are expanding sales and production internationally. Their home markets offer several advantages. Rapid growth gives companies scale and spare cash to invest abroad. Costs are low. The difficulties of operating in an emerging market may make managers adaptable and resilient. Finally, gradual liberalisation in their home markets—as in India since the early 1990s—has exposed them to competition from multinationals. The threat to their domestic dominance has encouraged their managers to hone their skills, exposed them to best international practice and spurred them to seek growth abroad to compensate for lost market share at home.

Ratan Tata spent his first ten years at the helm of the family company tidying up its rambling and often decrepit Indian businesses before turning his attention to foreign markets in the late 1990s. When the Indian market opened up, he recalls, Indian companies thought they would all have to merge with each other, because years of protection had made them too weak to face the new foreign competition. That soon passed as other industries saw the success of Indian IT and outsourcing, textile and pharmaceutical companies; Ranbaxy was on the way to becoming one of the world's leading makers of generic drugs, just as the boom in such products was taking off in the mid-1990s.

While Tata's IT business, TCS, was cutting a swathe through North America, Mr Tata was planning other international moves. He bought Tetley Tea, an English brand, and NatSteel Asia, based in Singapore, whose rolling mills could use the slab steel produced in Tata's Indian plants. He also bought Daewoo trucks, after the stricken South Korean *chaebol* had to be broken up. Mr Tata says that he looks beyond sheer size in search of a strategic fit when he acquires companies.

The new brigades are fanning out around the world using a selection of five strategies, according to BCG. The first is taking brands from local to global. China's Hisense, a $3.3 billion consumer-electronics group, is a prime example. With over 10% of the market for TV sets at home, it has turned its attention to the wider world with a product range that includes air conditioners, PCs and telecoms equipment. It manufactures in Algeria, Hungary, Iran, Pakistan and South Africa. It now sells over 10m TVs and 3m air conditioners a year in more than 40 countries. Hisense owns the best-selling brand of flat-screen TVs in France. The home Chinese market gives the company a vast, cheap manufacturing base, to which it adds other advantages such as stylish design and a world-class R&D centre.

Bajaj Auto, based like Tata Motors in Pune, is another developing-country brand going global. It is India's biggest maker of two- and three-wheeled vehicles. Its sales have more than doubled since 2000, to $2.3 billion. Under the former boss, Rahul Bajaj, the company was typical of a stratum of Indian entrepreneurs, known as the Bombay club, who wanted to keep foreign competition at bay with tariff walls and domestic mergers. Now, under Rahul's son, Rajiv, Bajaj has taken its own first steps onto the global stage with organic growth of exports, mostly to South-East Asia.

A second strategy is to turn local engineering excellence into innovation on a global scale, as Embraer has done. Supported by the Brazilian government and later largely privatised, Embraer has overtaken Canada's Bombardier to become the world's leading maker of regional jets. It has timed its push to take advantage of regional airlines' desire to replace traditional, noisy turbo-prop aircraft with sleeker, faster small jets. By 2006 over 95% of its $3.8 billion sales were outside Brazil. It is one of Brazil's biggest exporters, combining low-cost manufacturing with advanced R&D. In addition, Embraer has a joint venture with China Aviation Industry Corporation II. In this it was even ahead of Boeing and Airbus, both now scrambling to transform themselves from rich-world exporters into global producers, with long, difficult-to-manage supply chains spanning the world.

The third path to international success is going for global leadership in a narrow product category. Two Chinese companies are notable for taking this route. One is BYD, the battery-maker. It uses a more labour-intensive production system than the Japanese firms it competes with to take advantage of low labour costs. The other is Johnson Electric, which though based in Hong Kong now produces chiefly in mainland China. It makes tiny electric motors for products such as cameras or cars. A BMW 5 series, for instance, has over 100 tiny motors (of less than one horsepower) to move the wing mirrors, adjust the seats, open the sun roof and so on. Johnson churns out 3m a day, most of them for export. Manufacturers prefer to have them designed to their specifications than to buy them off the shelf. Johnson has landed its half-share of the market by catering to these requirements.

In this way an industry that used to be in the hands of American or European companies, with factories in the Midwest, the English Midlands or Germany's industrial heartland, has moved to China. That said, Johnson has built its strength partly through well-timed acquisitions (including parts of America's Lear and ArvinMeritor) in target markets to get closer to customers. It now has plants in America and western Europe and R&D centres in Israel, Italy, Japan and America.

Brazil's Sadia and Perdigão exemplify the fourth strategy: taking advantage of natural resources at home, and boosting them with first-class marketing and distribution. They have built sales organisations around the world to make the most of the abundant resources for producing pork, poultry and grain in Brazil, complemented by ideal growing conditions and low labour costs. Another Brazilian firm, Vale, has exploited its home country's huge, cheap sources of iron ore to become one of the world's leading suppliers.

The fifth strategy is to have a new or better business model to roll out to many different markets. This is the approach of Mexico's Cemex, one of the world's biggest suppliers of ready-mixed concrete. Its annual sales topped $18 billion in 2006.

Industries such as cement and other building materials are usually considered "territorial goods", meaning they are bulky, basic and too expensive to transport long distances. But now this wisdom is being stood on its head: though it may not be worth shipping cement from Mexico to Europe, know-how and investment can be swiftly poured into any market. Whereas rich-world companies, such as Lafarge and Saint-Gobain, are investing in developing countries to increase sales of their cement and building products, Cemex is showing that the same thing can flow in reverse.

Few in Europe had taken much note of Cemex until it swooped to buy RMC in 2005. But by that time four-fifths of its revenue was already coming from beyond Mexico's borders. It had bought or built businesses in Colombia, Panama, Venezuela, Indonesia, the Philippines, Thailand and the United States before it set its sights on Europe.

The secret of the company's success is the rigorous development of its own style of managing acquisitions, which it calls "the Cemex way". A British manager who left RMC, somewhat discomfited, shortly after its purchase by the Mexicans nevertheless praises their approach. "They have their own systems, very heavily dependent on standardised procedures built around highly developed IT systems," he concedes.

The new multinationals have some distinct advantages in their sprint to the fore of global business. They are often family-owned or family-controlled (even when they are public companies), which helps them to make decisions quickly. They often enjoy cheap finance from state banks. But they also face particular problems, because they are trying to break into a world economy in which globalisation is already well advanced.

When rich-world companies were going international, everything moved at a slower pace. Now, as Gordon Orr, who works in McKinsey's Shanghai office points out, the prizes go to the top few firms in any industry. Organic growth is generally too slow to turn companies into winners.

Tariffs and anti-dumping actions can also prevent developing-country companies from getting into the rich world. Firms may be ignorant of the markets they are entering. Their brands, though well established at home, are unknown in Europe or America. They may lack the necessary management talent. Pay structures are hard to devise when middle managers in rich-world subsidiaries expect to earn more than their seniors in head office.

The Future Is Mittalic

But the new boys have often leapt these hurdles impressively. TCL, a Chinese consumer-electronics company, broke into Europe by buying the French Thomson TV brand. Cemex started investing in America when its cement exports were hit by anti-dumping suits: it became the market leader. Lenovo bought IBM's PC business partly to acquire management talent, and went on to create a firm that blended the best of the two businesses. Sunil Kakkad of LG, a London-based business-law firm, says that Indian multinationals are reversing the usual brain-drain by sucking non-resident Indians back from branch offices in America and Europe, where they have gained experience that could be useful at the centre.

Possibly, more newcomers will not build out from home markets but will amass businesses in all parts of the world, as Mr Mittal's group has done. He likes to point out that having a strong base in both developing and rich countries gives his company a balanced portfolio. "I see plenty of scope for growth in developing countries and plenty of opportunities for consolidation in developed countries," he beams in his office overlooking London's Berkeley Square.

Success in one developing country led Mr Mittal to opportunities on the other side of the world. Family ownership helped with quick decisions to outsmart competitors. There will be more Mittals: not just Tatas or Cherys, emerging from giant, booming domestic markets; but new creatures, bursting out of nowhere to take the world by storm.

UNIT 3

Environmental Factors and International Business

Unit Selections

Key Points to Consider

- What are the rights of the indigenous people in today's world? Can they be removed from their native land where they have lived for generations for the sake of obtaining resources?

- Capitalism and democracy have been said to go hand in hand, but that is apparently not the case. What if one can preclude the other? What are the consequences? And what can be done in such a case?

- Europe and the United States seem to be going in different directions. It is not just about the War in Iraq, but there are many other fundamental differences and trends in between the two. How do you see this playing out?

- The developing world is suffering from many problems and not all of them are imposed by the developed world; many of them have to do with their own customs and traditions. What can be done to overcome centuries of those social traditions and culture that are restrictive in order to provide people with a better life?

Student Web Site

www.mhcls.com/online

Internet References

Chambers of Commerce World Network
  http://www.worldchambers.com/
India Finance and Investment Guide
  http://finance.indiamart.com/
Foreign Direct Investment Is on the Rise Around the World
  http://www.neweconomyindex.org/section1_page04.html
International Economic Law Web Site
  http://www.law.georgetown.edu/iiel/
United States Trade Representative (USTR)
  http://www.ustr.gov
WWW Virtual Library Demography & Population Studies
  http://demography.anu.edu.au/VirtualLibrary

The environment of international business is one that is rapidly changing with the advent of computers and the Internet. Cities that were once on the other side of the world in terms of time and distance are now, for all intents and purposes, as close as New York is to Philadelphia. Documents can be sent electronically to any place in the world in a matter of seconds. Indeed, anything that can be digitized, including tax returns and medical X rays, can be sent around the world for processing, and returned after they have been processed, at the same speed back to the originator, whether the originator is across the street or across the globe.

This has led to changes in the political and legal environment of business and has brought about certain changes in laws relating to trade and business. The advancement in technology that has highly enhanced communication has made it much more difficult to hide crimes than it was a hundred years ago. Acts of mass genocide cannot be easily hidden and forgotten as was the case then. Today, while such acts may still go on, they can no longer be hidden as they once were.

Corporations too must learn to deal with the new international environment. Offshore corporations (OFC's) are now far more common than they were just a few years ago and their number is growing. More organizations are taking advantage of this arrangement for tax purposes as well as for meeting public reporting requirements that have become stricter, especially in the United States after Sarbanes-Oxley. The companies number in thousands in the British Virgin Islands alone, and there are other havens including the Cayman Islands and Bermuda. Corporate lawyers, companies and governments are going to have to learn how to deal with OFC's in the future.

The cultural and social environment that organizations find themselves in will always play a major role in the success of any firm, especially when it ventures outside of its home market. Today, given the unpopularity of American foreign policy in many parts of the world, companies that are easily identified as American, along with American business people working overseas have been put on the defensive. In some instances, American executives have been put in the position of acting as ambassadors for the United States, in an attempt to try to explain what is happening in the country, so that the anti-Americanism does not spill over onto their company and its products, as explained in "Is U.S. Business Losing Europe?" Some companies have responded differently to this situation by using more nationals in the positions that were once held by American executives. This has been done to lower the American profile of the company in the host market by putting a more local face on the organization. While this may or may not help the situation in the short run, it deprives the American executives of valuable international experience, and it also makes the American viewpoint, whether pro or con to the current administration's policy, less available to Europeans, and thereby further widening the gulf.

Cultural aspects play a major role in the development of any society. This can be said of both the developed and the developing world. Two of the articles in this collection draw this contrast. "Can Europe Compete?" looks at the problems affecting the competitive balance in Europe, and how culture plays a major role in determining the ability of Europeans to be able to compete in the global marketplace. "Unequal Access" looks at India and how it needs to deal with the outlawed but culturally ingrained caste system that is holding back the country's competitiveness and ability to participate effectively in the global forum. This cultural aspect of Indian society is keeping the majority of Indians from participating in the economic expansion of the rest of Indian society and has long-term consequences for the Indian nation as a whole.

Developing countries also depend on their social and cultural environment to be able to expand. The old factory-town model that was once prevalent in the United States in the mining industry is still being used in some of the lesser developed countries. Many of the raw materials and agricultural goods that find their way to the developed nations of the world are produced in some of these factory-like mines and plantations including the "Bananas" on your kitchen table.

Ethical conduct in international business is a problematic issue. What is considered perfectly ethical in some societies might be considered unethical in others, in some cases, even illegal. But, there are certain things that would be considered at least unethical, if not criminal in most societies. The U.S. Government has made gambling on the Internet illegal, but that has not stopped people from doing it. The problem of the Internet is that no one organization truly controls it. People can set-up shops almost anywhere in the world and they are not subject to the laws of any jurisdiction except the one in which they are located. The U.S. Congress can pass any law it likes, but it does not have much of an impact on people doing business in New Zealand or Kenya, as discussed in "Bootleggers on the Internet."

Environmentalism also raises some ethical questions for the corporations and the environmentalist NGO's (Non-Government Organizations) that are involved with corporations. Just what is the relationship between these organizations? Corporations give money to environmentalist NGO's and the NGO's lend/endorse the activities of the companies. The NGO's then use the money to advance their agenda and the companies use the relationship with the NGO's to advance their agenda. But, what exactly, are the companies buying? And are the NGO's making a deal with the Devil? Are the NGO's making the classic Faustian bargain of doing good with the powers of the Devil at the cost of their soul? This question is analyzed in "When Greens Go Corporate."

How Capitalism Is Killing Democracy

Free markets were supposed to lead to free societies. Instead, today's supercharged global economy is eroding the power of the people in democracies around the globe. Welcome to a world where the bottom line trumps the common good and government takes a back seat to big business.

ROBERT B. REICH

It was supposed to be a match made in heaven. Capitalism and democracy, we've long been told, are the twin ideological pillars capable of bringing unprecedented prosperity and freedom to the world. In recent decades, the duo has shared a common ascent. By almost any measure, global capitalism is triumphant. Most nations around the world are today part of a single, integrated, and turbocharged global market. Democracy has enjoyed a similar renaissance. Three decades ago, a third of the world's nations held free elections; today, nearly two thirds do.

Conventional wisdom holds that where either capitalism or democracy flourishes, the other must soon follow. Yet today, their fortunes are beginning to diverge. Capitalism, long sold as the yin to democracy's yang, is thriving, while democracy is struggling to keep up. China, poised to become the world's third largest capitalist nation this year after the United States and Japan, has embraced market freedom, but not political freedom. Many economically successful nations—from Russia to Mexico—are democracies in name only. They are encumbered by the same problems that have hobbled American democracy in recent years, allowing corporations and elites buoyed by runaway economic success to undermine the government's capacity to respond to citizens' concerns.

Of course, democracy means much more than the process of free and fair elections. It is a system for accomplishing what can only be achieved by citizens joining together to further the common good. But though free markets have brought unprecedented prosperity to many, they have been accompanied by widening inequalities of income and wealth, heightened job insecurity, and environmental hazards such as global warming. Democracy is designed to allow citizens to address these very issues in constructive ways. And yet a sense of political powerlessness is on the rise among citizens in Europe, Japan, and the United States, even as consumers and investors feel more empowered. In short, no democratic nation is effectively coping with capitalism's negative side effects.

This fact is not, however, a failing of capitalism. As these two forces have spread around the world, we have blurred their responsibilities, to the detriment of our democratic duties. Capitalism's role is to increase the economic pie, nothing more. And while capitalism has become remarkably responsive to what people want as individual consumers, democracies have struggled to perform their own basic functions: to articulate and act upon the common good, and to help societies achieve both growth and equity. Democracy, at its best, enables citizens to debate collectively how the slices of the pie should be divided and to determine which rules apply to private goods and which to public goods. Today, those tasks are increasingly being left to the market. What is desperately needed is a clear delineation of the boundary between global capitalism and democracy—between the economic game, on the one hand, and how its rules are set, on the other. If the purpose of capitalism is to allow corporations to play the market as aggressively as possible, the challenge for citizens is to stop these economic entities from being the authors of the rules by which we live.

The Cost of Doing Business

Most people are of two minds: As consumers and investors, we want the bargains and high returns that the global economy provides. As citizens, we don't like many of the social consequences that flow from these transactions. We like to blame corporations for the ills that follow, but in truth we've made this compact with ourselves. After all, we know the roots of the great economic deals we're getting. They come from workers forced to settle for lower wages and benefits. They come from companies that shed their loyalties to communities and morph into global supply chains. They come from CEOs who take home exorbitant paychecks. And they come from industries that often wreak havoc on the environment.

Unfortunately, in the United States, the debate about economic change tends to occur between two extremist camps: those who want the market to rule unimpeded, and those who want to protect jobs and preserve communities as they are. Instead of finding ways to soften the blows of globalization, compensate the losers, or slow the pace of change, we go to battle. Consumers and investors nearly always win the day, but citizens lash out occasionally in symbolic fashion, by attempting to block a new trade agreement or protesting the sale of U.S. companies to foreign firms. It is a sign of the inner conflict Americans feel—between the consumer in us and the citizen in us—that the reactions are often so schizophrenic.

Such conflicting sentiments are hardly limited to the United States. The recent wave of corporate restructurings in Europe has shaken the continent's typical commitment to job security and social welfare. It's leaving Europeans at odds as to whether they prefer the private benefits of global capitalism in the face of increasing social costs at home and abroad. Take, for instance, the auto industry. In 2001, DaimlerChrysler faced mounting financial losses as European car buyers abandoned the company in favor of cheaper competitors. So, CEO Dieter Zetsche cut 26,000 jobs from his global workforce and closed six factories. Even profitable companies are feeling the pressure to become ever more efficient. In 2005, Deutsche Bank simultaneously announced an 87 percent increase in net profits and a plan to cut 6,400 jobs, nearly half of them in Germany and Britain. Twelve-hundred of the jobs were then moved to low-wage nations. Today, European consumers and investors are doing better than ever, but job insecurity and inequality are rising, even in social democracies that were established to counter the injustices of the market. In the face of such change, Europe's democracies have shown themselves to be so paralyzed that the only way citizens routinely express opposition is through massive boycotts and strikes.

In Japan, many companies have abandoned lifetime employment, cut workforces, and closed down unprofitable lines. Just months after Howard Stringer was named Sony's first non-Japanese CEO, he announced the company would trim 10,000 employees, about 7 percent of its workforce. Surely some Japanese consumers and investors benefit from such corporate downsizing: By 2006, the Japanese stock market had reached a 14-year high. But many Japanese workers have been left behind. A nation that once prided itself on being an "all middle-class society" is beginning to show sharp disparities in income and wealth. Between 1999 and 2005, the share of Japanese households without savings doubled, from 12 percent to 24 percent. And citizens there routinely express a sense of powerlessness. Like many free countries around the world, Japan is embracing global capitalism with a democracy too enfeebled to face the free market's many social penalties.

On the other end of the political spectrum sits China, which is surging toward capitalism without democracy at all. That's good news for people who invest in China, but the social consequences for the country's citizens are mounting. Income inequality has widened enormously. China's new business elites live in McMansions inside gated suburban communities and send their children to study overseas. At the same time, China's cities are bursting with peasants from the countryside who have sunk into urban poverty and unemployment. And those who are affected most have little political recourse to change the situation, beyond riots that are routinely put down by force.

But citizens living in democratic nations aren't similarly constrained. They have the ability to alter the rules of the game so that the cost to society need not be so great. And yet, we've increasingly left those responsibilities to the private sector—to the companies themselves and their squadrons of lobbyists and public-relations experts—pretending as if some inherent morality or corporate good citizenship will compel them to look out for the greater good. But they have no responsibility to address inequality or protect the environment on their own. We forget that they are simply duty bound to protect the bottom line.

The Rules of the Game

Why has capitalism succeeded while democracy has steadily weakened? Democracy has become enfeebled largely because companies, in intensifying competition for global consumers and investors, have invested ever greater sums in lobbying, public relations, and even bribes and kickbacks, seeking laws that give them a competitive advantage over their rivals. The result is an arms race for political influence that is drowning out the voices of average citizens. In the United States, for example, the fights that preoccupy Congress, those that consume weeks or months of congressional staff time, are typically contests between competing companies or industries.

While corporations are increasingly writing their own rules, they are also being entrusted with a kind of social responsibility or morality. Politicians praise companies for acting "responsibly" or condemn them for not doing so. Yet the purpose of capitalism is to get great deals for consumers and investors. Corporate executives are not authorized by anyone—least of all by their investors—to balance profits against the public good. Nor do they have any expertise in making such moral calculations. Democracy is supposed to represent the public in drawing such lines. And the message that companies are moral beings with social responsibilities diverts public attention from the task of establishing such laws and rules in the first place.

It is much the same with what passes for corporate charity. Under today's intensely competitive form of global capitalism, companies donate money to good causes only to the extent the donation has public-relations value, thereby boosting the bottom line. But shareholders do not invest in firms expecting the money to be used for charitable purposes. They invest to earn high returns. Shareholders who wish to be charitable would, presumably, make donations to charities of their own choosing in amounts they decide for themselves. The larger danger is that these conspicuous displays of corporate beneficence hoodwink the public into believing corporations have charitable impulses that can be relied on in a pinch.

By pretending that the economic success corporations enjoy saddles them with particular social duties only serves to distract the public from democracy's responsibility to set the rules of the game and thereby protect the common good. The only way for the citizens in us to trump the consumers in us is through laws and rules that make our purchases and investments social choices as well as personal ones. A change in labor laws making it easier for employees to organize and negotiate better terms, for example, might increase the price of products and services. My inner consumer won't like that very much, but the citizen in me might think it a fair price to pay. A small transfer tax on sales of stock, to slow the movement of capital ever so slightly, might give communities a bit more time to adapt to changing circumstances. The return on my retirement fund might go down by a small fraction, but the citizen in me thinks it worth the price. Extended unemployment insurance combined with wage insurance and job training could ease the pain for workers caught in the downdrafts of globalization.

Let us be clear: The purpose of democracy is to accomplish ends we cannot achieve as individuals. But democracy cannot fulfill this role when companies use politics to advance or maintain their competitive standing, or when they appear to take on social responsibilities that they have no real capacity or authority to fulfill. That leaves societies unable to address the tradeoffs between economic growth and social problems such as job insecurity, widening inequality, and climate change. As a result, consumer and investor interests almost invariably trump common concerns.

The vast majority of us are global consumers and, at least indirectly, global investors. In these roles we should strive for the best deals possible. That is how we participate in the global market economy. But those private benefits usually have social costs. And for those of us living in democracies, it is imperative to remember that we are also citizens who have it in our power to reduce these social costs, making the true price of the goods and services we purchase as low as possible. We can accomplish this larger feat only if we take our roles as citizens seriously. The first step, which is often the hardest, is to get our thinking straight.

Want to Know More?

Robert B. Reich argues that the effectiveness of democracy has waned in the face of the modern global market in *Supercapitalism: The Transformation of Business, Democracy, and Everyday Life* (New York: Alfred A. Knopf, 2007). He blogs regularly about global economics and politics at robertreich. blogspot.com.

Milton Friedman's classic *Capitalism and Freedom* (Chicago: University of Chicago Press, 1962) established economic freedom as a key precondition for political freedom. In *The Great Risk Shift: The Assault on American Jobs, Families, Health Care and Retirement—And How You Can Fight Back* (New York: Oxford University Press, 2006), Jacob S. Hacker examines a prosperous United States where citizens increasingly feel politically powerless. Martin Wolf refutes the allegation that the global economy undermines democracy in *The Morality of the Market* (Foreign Policy, September/October 2003).

For links to relevant Web sites, access to the *FP* Archive, and a comprehensive index of related Foreign Policy articles, go to www. ForeignPolicy.com.

ROBERT B. REICH, former U.S. secretary of labor, is professor of public policy at the University of California, Berkeley. This article is adapted from his book, *Supercapitalism: The Transformation of Business, Democracy, and Everyday Life* (New York: Alfred A. Knopf, 2007).

Grassroots Diplomacy

How corporations can change the way people think about America.

GAIL DUTTON

Do people trust you and your company? You'd certainly like to think so. You've done all you can to leave an ethical, positive impression of your business. But despite your efforts, consumers worldwide are losing trust in you. The unlikely cause of such distrust: your own government.

According to a recent poll by GMI, a Seattle-based market-research company, 80 percent of European and Canadian consumers distrust the U.S. government. Even if your company didn't launch the Iraq war—or make any other policy decision of the past few decades—those consumers aren't separating corporate and government interests as much as you might hope: Fully half of survey respondents don't trust American corporations.

It'd be foolish to hope for a surge of good feeling toward U.S. foreign policy anytime soon from Europeans and Canadians, but companies can't afford to let public opinion toward them deteriorate further. It's time to start thinking about corporate diplomacy—taking the lead in improving views of American companies and, along the way, America itself.

"Companies must develop a series of positive images and behaviors that shows respect and understanding for international cultures and generates respect for us," notes Keith Reinhard, chairman of DOB Worldwide and president of Business for Diplomatic Action, a coalition of marketing communications executives spearheading the corporate-diplomacy movement. Still in their infancy, such efforts are gaining the interest of multinationals and their CEOs, who see corporate diplomacy as a way to soften America's image and burnish the image of their own brands. Indeed, U.S. corporations are de facto diplomats representing the United States.

Negative perceptions of the United States took at least two decades to materialize, driven by controversial and sometimes-belligerent foreign policy and encroaching globalization heralded by such iconic brands as McDonald's and Starbucks. Those perceptions will take at least as long to dissipate—if such resolution is even possible. In addition, a number of other trends have either contributed or facilitated the growing anti-Americanism:

- The worldwide goodwill toward America for its support of Allied powers during World War II has waned among all but the oldest generations.

- The image of the United States as a promised land—distant, exotic, and glamorous—has faded in the onslaught of familiarity with U.S. products, the media portrayed image of America, and the vast numbers of people who have traveled here.

- Recent business scandals have eroded the honor and integrity of not just the likes of Enron and Andersen but the nation as a whole. The international business community has focused on the scandals themselves rather than on the fact that they have been brought to light and addressed. Corporations that enter another country content with what they can take—tax credits, for example—and uninterested in corporate citizenship in their new community further sully their and our country's name.

- Finally, "there has been a great deal of powerful, negative media working against U.S. exports," says U.K. brand expert Simon Anholt, who advises several governments on public diplomacy, Anholt specifically cites the best-selling books *No Logo* and *Fast Food Nation* and the films *Fahrenheit 9/11* and *Bowling for Columbine* as contributing to America's negative image. "The general appetite for this kind of fare appears to be snowballing. It's feeding people's desire to find the fault in America's massive presence in so many global arenas. America is now widely considered to be largely dysfunctional."

Before companies can practice corporate diplomacy, they must examine what messages they are receiving. For example, when Anholt asked young Muslims about their feelings toward America, a topical response was: "I hate America; I spit on the flag." Yet when he asked about their post-school ambitions, they often responded: "Oh, to go and study at MIT or Harvard."

"They are predictably savage when the question refers to America as a political concept, yet entirely moderate when the question refers to American products" or institutions, Anholt says. Indeed, he adds that "consumers aren't dumb. They are perfectly capable of distinguishing between 'the government,' which devises and executes foreign policy, 'the people,' some of whom vote for the government but, ultimately, can't—and shouldn't—be held responsible for its actions, and 'the products,' which people usually think of as morally and politically neutral, except in extreme circumstances."

A Lesson from . . . Latvia?

If there are doubts that a nation can transform itself in the eyes of the world, look no further than Latvia, which is developing a national branding strategy that aligns foreign-policy goals with tourism, investment, and general recognition of the country. Although American and Latvian companies face different challenges—we're often perceived as brash, pervasive, loud, and certainly not an underdog—the strategies being honed by Latvia are just as relevant to American businesses as they are to Latvian companies.

While Latvia faces no negative foreign-policy-based perceptions, it must overcome its history as a Soviet satellite. "We stress that Latvia has always been a European country, with European values, traditions, and history, despite fifty years of Soviet occupation," says Ojars Kalnins, former Latvian ambassador to the United States and current director of the Latvian Institute, which helps Latvian businesses advance their images—and consequently, those of their home country.

To that end, businesses emphasize their nation's close ties with Scandinavia, Latvia's strategic location on the Baltic Sea, and the cosmopolitan dynamics of Riga, the country's eight-hundred-year-old capital. Latvia is also positioning itself as a nation that understands both Russian and Western thinking, making it a potential intermediary to help Western businesses trade with former Soviet-bloc countries—much like Hong Kong is a go-between for China.

Kalnins believes that the best way to promote his country is through its culture and cultural figures. So he helps tailor programs, such as concerts and art exhibits, to support the nation's goals—most recently, membership in NATO and the EU. "Businesses are also using Latvian artists and musicians in their presentations and materials," he says.

Additionally, Kalnins' organization arranges interviews for foreign media with non-government spokespeople, including "businessmen, professionals, and average people" who help further Latvia's foreign-policy goats by supplementing what is said by politicians or government officials. And Kalnins points out that many business leaders incorporate foreign-policy goals when participating in international conferences or seminars.

Latvian companies also promote foreign-policy goals through their membership in and sponsorship of non-government organizations. American companies might do the same through such organizations as the American Chamber of Commerce abroad, the U.S. Council on Foreign Relations, and local World Affairs Councils.

These approaches are working for Latvia. It is now usually referenced as "a new EU member state" rather than as "a former Soviet republic," and there is a growing recognition that Latvia is a modern, democratic, Western European country. The country's business community deserves a good deal of the credit for the shift. —G.D.

How extreme? Very. And such circumstances are already upon us. Consumers may not be dumb, but they do seem to be growing angrier—and taking out that anger on U.S. companies. Slipping sales aren't the only result—hostility may make it more difficult for those companies to gain necessary regulatory approvals abroad and to attract and retain the best and brightest employees.

U.S. corporations can no longer separate themselves from government politics. Beyond fostering a better image for America, good corporate diplomacy is essential to protecting your brand, as more evidence pours in linking politics to consumer behavior. In a January GMI survey of twenty thousand international consumers, some 17 percent of respondents said they would consciously avoid U.S. companies and products "because of discontent over U.S. military action and foreign policies." And in addition to sporadic boycotts of American goods, such as Levi's, KFC, and Ford, foreign consumers have targeted some less obvious products. One-third of respondents to a GMI survey last fall said they would avoid purchasing Mattel's Barbie because of her American origins, and sales of the doll fell 13 percent worldwide in the third quarter of 2004.

Corporate bottom lines are feeling the impact. Indeed, antipathy toward America may be one reason why top brands—including Coca-Cola (which earns 80 percent of its profits overseas), Marlboro, McDonald's, Wal-Mart, Disney, and Gap—have reported weak or falling sales in European markets.

"What could we do anyway?," an Altria executive asked the *Financial Times* in response to a decline in Marlboro's sales in France, "Fly the French flag?" Perhaps not, but U.S. businesses have enormous power to counter negative sentiments toward their home country—and toward themselves, A week after the South Asian tsunami in February, a GMI poll of twenty thousand consumers worldwide found 59 percent so pleased with American corporations' relief efforts that their impressions of those companies' brands had improved.

Simple approaches may prove more enduring: employing local spokespeople, contributing to local charities, or using the example of what Starbucks has done in Germany. To foster goodwill with Germans, the coffee giant has replaced cultural references to the United States on products with those of German tourist sites. Furthermore, McDonald's recently co-hosted a seminar at its management-training center to discuss ways for American companies to be better "world citizens."

Fluor Corp. is another company practicing corporate diplomacy. Its stance against corruption in the public works and construction industries—the second most corrupt sector, behind arms and defense, according to Transparency International, a watchdog group—is an example of how values play out on the ground. The company, which heads the World Economic Forum's Engineering and Construction sector, developed anti-corruption

If Germany and Japan Can, So Can We

The United States is hardly the first country to face image problems. World War II left the world scarred by the savagery of Germany and Japan toward civilian populations and reported on newsreels throughout the world. Yet only a few decades later, Americans began driving Hondas and Toyotas and equipping their kitchens with Krups and Braun appliances. Why? Because these companies' reputations for quality and ethical dealings soon overshadowed the memories of what their countries did during the first half of the twentieth century.

After the war, the Japanese and German governments encouraged fledgling industries to expand their industrial bases. Especially following the collapse of the Soviet Union, German corporations continued to expand into Eastern Europe, where they renovated factories, trained workers, and worked with governments to develop democratic, market-based policies. Today, Germany continues to hone its image.

The country's long-range plan, Agenda 2010, was devised two years ago to present Germany as an innovative nation and a logical development partner.

Likewise, Japan is attracting many start-up companies in the biotech sector because of available financing and a growing venture-capital market. And Japanese companies have been active on the world stage, carefully providing logistical support, equipment, and funding for humanitarian activities throughout the world. Consequently, much of the world now sees Japan as a compassionate country willing to involve itself in world affairs.

"There's no doubt that the commercial brands have achieved an enormous amount in building a more helpful, more attractive image of both countries," says U.K. brand adviser Simon Anholt. U.S. corporations, too, have a lot to offer the world, but America's biggest challenge, says Keith Reinhard, president of Business for Diplomatic Action, "is to demonstrate in tangible ways that America is about a lot more than foreign policy."

—G.D.

principles that have been adapted by twenty-five global engineering and construction firms. Results, so far, have been positive.

A few years ago, Fluor's integrity was challenged in an international meeting attended by representatives of a number of companies, Alan Boeckmann, the company's chairman and CEO, recounts one attendee's remarks about Fluor's presence in a Third World country: "How could you work there?," he asked. "You have to be corrupt to do business there!" To which Boeckmann replied, "We've been there fifty years, profitably and successfully, and maintain values that are unassailable." At the same meeting, another man with operations in that country added that in working with Fluor, he learned it was an honest company, and, many years later, his business was still working with them. "So you *can* have an effect," Boeckmann says.

Fluor's guiding principle has been integrity, not methodology. Part of the problem people have with the United States, according to Allyson Stewart-Allen, co-author of *Working With Americans,* is that U.S. companies often "insist on imposing the American way of doing things on their international markets" and show little respect or understanding of other cultures. America prides itself on being a melting pot—or at least a stew—in which myriad cultures and ways of thinking co-exist with a high degree of harmony. However, our "take charge" national personality doesn't necessarily blend well with cultures accustomed to a more sedate, deliberate, decision-making process. That, predictably, leads to charges of arrogance and impertinence from U.S. trading partners.

Yet another corporate diplomat is UPS, "In foreign affairs, corporate diplomacy is as important as political diplomacy," says CEO Mike Eskew. "We learned very early in our international development that our business ran best when we empowered local people and made long-term commitments." When UPS entered the European market in 1976, only academics were envisioning what became the European Union, but UPS understood that a single economic entity was inevitable. It planned for that and built a network of companies, often in concert with local carriers, giving up some control in exchange for greater flexibility and local knowledge.

It is imperative that you identify with the local culture—not merely fit in—and to that end, the UPS success story is built on careful listening to international employees and letting the business grow naturally under the guidance of the people who intimately know the local culture, business practices, and legal system. Since the company first entered Europe, it has learned to integrate the UPS way of doing things into the local ways. For example, Buddhist shrines are common in UPS facilities in Thailand, and pictures of the Madonna are allowed in Latin America. However, in applying the same values to business decisions and actions abroad as at home, UPS knows when not to bend to other cultures customs. For instance, even though many Germans enjoy a beer with lunch. UPS Deutschland frowns upon the practice.

Multinationals have a potential "diplomatic corps" of some 8.2 million people outside the United States. Though some are Americans, most are locals. In fact, of UPS's forty thousand employees overseas, fewer than forty are American. The local workers, by virtue of working at a U.S.-based company, are exposed to American business principles and corporate ethics. Consequently, each worker is for good or ill, a spokesperson for that company. As such, corporations offer credibility that governments cannot and can pursue consumer-friendly policies that aren't always feasible in the harsh realities of international political and economic relations. "It's hard for the government to always be friends with everyone," Anholt says, "but companies can be perfectly lovely all day long if they choose."

GAIL DUTTON is a business and technology writer who recently returned to the United States from a two-year stint in Canada

Mixed Messages

Consumers all over the world are saying that U.S. foreign policy is making them less likely to purchase your brands. They're saying they don't trust you. But maybe it's you that shouldn't believe what they say, because their actions seem to speak otherwise. A recent Associated Press poll reveals that U.S. foreign policy hasn't had much impact on how foreigners view American consumer goods, and there's been no significant shift in attitude since prior to the war in Iraq, says the poll. In addition, 20 percent of French people would rather buy U.S. products than any others, assuming price and quality were equal. Likewise, the American Chamber of Commerce in Germany reports seeing no evidence of Germans avoiding American products.

"There is considerable slippage between people expressing anti-American sentiment and translating that into action at the point of sale," explains John Quelch, Harvard Business School's senior associate dean of international development. Quelch points out that while many surveys are tracking consumer attitudes, they're not actually indicating behavior. Nor are they demonstrating a clear cause-and-effect relationship between anti-Americanism and buying decisions.

If foreign consumers aren't buying American goods, it's not necessarily because they don't like America. "The factors affecting the competitiveness of U.S.-owned global brands precede and are much larger than reactions to U.S. foreign policy of the last few years," says Earl Taylor, chief marketing officer at Marketing Science Institute, a nonprofit think-tank. "Focusing on the likely minimal and short-term impact of recent U.S. foreign policy may distract us from understanding the larger forces at work." One such force has been a general economic downturn in Europe, which has been experiencing high interest rates, high unemployment, and low growth. As a result, says Quelch, people are choosing less expensive local brands rather than paying premium prices for their American counterparts. And even local brands, including Unilever and Nestlé, are facing their own share of hardships.

U.S. companies also seem hesitant to fault anti-Americanism for their troubles abroad. For instance, Coca-Cola blames new bottling laws for its 16 percent sales decline in Germany during last year's third quarter. Likewise, Marlboro attributes its 18.7 percent drop in sales in Germany and 24.5 percent drop in France to higher cigarette taxes in those countries. However, an even closer look reveals that these taxes resulted in a decline in total category sales—Marlboro's market share actually remained unchanged.

Then again, not all American brands are all that "American." In a poll last November, market research firm GMI asked eight thousand international consumers whether they considered certain brands American and whether they plan to avoid purchasing these brands. Those deemed least American and least likely to be boycotted were personal-hygiene ones, such as Kleenex, Gillette, Pampers, and Estee Lauder. Additionally, brands like MasterCard and Visa were also perceived as less American, perhaps due to the fact these companies have made efforts to localize their cards—for example, German Visas deal with German banks. And though tech firms like IBM and Microsoft were seen as very American, consumers weren't likely to avoid them (perhaps because firms like Microsoft have few competitors).

On the other hand, General Motors, Marlboro, AOL, and—this will come as no shock—McDonald's were all perceived as extremely American and at high risk for boycotts. As was Chrysler—never mind that it's actually owned by a European company. Yet once again, just because consumers say they'll quit eating Big Macs doesn't mean they will. "These companies employ local workers and managers and use local raw materials," Quelch points out "Boycott them, and you are boycotting your own neighbors."

"Most consumers do not let their political opinions affect their brand-choice behavior. When they shop, they are searching for the best value for their families. They are not looking to make political statements."   —V.L.

From *Across the Board*, May/June 2005. Copyright © 2005 by Conference Board, Inc. Reprinted by permission.

New Tech, Old Habits

Despite world-class IT networks, Japanese and Korean workers are still chained to their desks.

Moon Ihlwan and Kenji Hall

Masanori Goto was in for a culture shock when he returned to Japan after a seven-year stint in New York. The 42-year-old public relations officer at cellular giant NTT DoCoMo logged many a late night at his Manhattan apartment, using his company laptop to communicate with colleagues 14 time zones away. Now back in Tokyo, Goto has a cell phone he can use to send quick e-mails after hours, but he must hole up at the office late into the night if he needs to do any serious work. The reason: His bosses haven't outfitted him with a portable computer. "I didn't realize that our people in Japan weren't using laptops," he says. "That was a surprise."

A few hundred miles to the west, in Seoul, Lee Seung Hwa also knows what it's like to spend long hours chained to her desk. The 33-year-old recently quit her job as an executive assistant at a carmaker because, among other complaints, her company didn't let lower-level employees log on from outside the office. "I could have done all the work from home, but managers thought I was working hard only if I stayed late," says Lee.

These days, information technology could easily free the likes of Goto and Lee. Korea and Japan are world leaders in broadband access, with connection speeds that put the U.S. to shame. And their wireless networks are state of the art, allowing supercharged Web surfing from mobile phones and other handhelds, whether at a café, in the subway, or on the highway. But when it comes to taking advantage of connectivity for business, Americans are way ahead.

For a study in contrasts, consider the daily commute. American trains are packed with business people furiously tapping their BlackBerrys or Treos, squeezing a few extra minutes into their work days. In Tokyo or Seoul, commuters stare intently at their cell phone screens, but they're usually playing games, watching video clips, or sending Hello Kitty icons to friends. And while advertising for U.S. cellular companies emphasizes how data services can make users more productive at work, Asian carriers tend to stress the fun factor.

Why? Corporate culture in the Far East remains deeply conservative, and most businesses have been slow to mine the opportunities offered by newfangled communications technologies. One big reason is the premium placed on face time at the office. Junior employees are reluctant to leave work before the boss does for fear of looking like slackers. Also, Confucianism places greater stock on group effort and consensus-building than on individual initiative. So members of a team all feel they must stick around if there is a task to complete. "To reap full benefits from IT investment, companies must change the way they do business," says Lee Inn Chan, vice-president at SK Research Institute, a Seoul management think tank funded by cellular carrier SK Telecom. "What's most needed in Korea and Japan is an overhaul in business processes and practices."

Time, Not Task

In these countries, if you're not in the office, your boss simply assumes you're not working. It doesn't help that a lack of clear job definitions and performance metrics makes it difficult for managers to assess the productivity of employees working off site. "Performance reviews and judgments are still largely time-oriented here, rather than task-oriented as in the West," says Cho Bum Coo, a Seoul-based executive partner at business consulting firm Accenture Ltd.

Even tech companies in the region often refuse to untether workers from the office. Camera-maker Canon Inc. for instance, dispensed with flextime four years ago after employees said it interfered with communications, while Samsung stresses that person-to-person contact is far more effective than e-mail. In Japan, many companies say they are reluctant to send workers home with their laptops for fear that proprietary information might go astray. Canon publishes a 33-page code of conduct that includes a cautionary tale of a worker who loses a notebook computer loaded with sensitive customer data on his commute. At Korean companies SK Telecom, Samsung Electronics, and LG Electronics, employees must obtain permission before they can carry their laptops out of the office. Even then, they often are barred from full access to files from work. And while just about everyone has a cell phone that can display Web pages or send e-mails, getting into corporate networks is complicated and unwieldy.

Bound by Tradition

Despite fast wireless and broadband networks, Korean and Japanese companies aren't getting the most out of technology. Here's why:

FUN FACTOR Smart phones are viewed more as toys than tools.

FACE TIME If you're not in the office, no one thinks you're working.

INFO-FEAR Companies worry that laptop-toting commuters could misplace sensitive data.

The result: Korean and Japanese white-collar workers clock long days at the office, often toiling till midnight and coming in on weekends. "In my dictionary there's no such thing as work/life balance as far as weekdays are concerned," says a Samsung Electronics senior manager who declined to be named. Tom Coyner, a consultant and author of *Mastering Business in Korea: A Practical Guide,* says: "Even your wife would think you were not regarded as an important player in the office if you came home at five or six."

These factors may be preventing Japan and Korea from wringing more productivity out of their massive IT investments. Both countries place high on lists of global innovators. For instance, Japan and Korea rank No. 2 and No. 6, respectively, out of 30 nations in terms of spending on research and development, according to the Organization for Economic Cooperation and Development. And the Geneva-based World Intellectual property Organization says Japan was second and Korea fourth in international patent filings. But when it comes to the productivity of IT users, both countries badly lag the U.S., says Kazuyuki Motohashi, a University of Tokyo professor who is an expert on technological innovation. "Companies in Japan and Korea haven't made the structural changes to get the most out of new technologies," he says.

Still, a new generation of managers rising through the ranks may speed the transformation. These workers are tech-savvy and often more individualistic, having come from smaller families. Already, some companies are tinkering with changes to meet their needs. SK Telecom abolished titles for all midlevel managers in the hopes that this would spur workers to take greater initiative. Japan's NEC Corp. is experimenting with telecommuting for 2,000 of its 148,000 employees. And in Korea, CJ 39 Shopping, a cable-TV shopping channel, is letting 10% of its call-center employees work from home.

Foreign companies are doing their bit to shake things up. In Korea, IBM has outfitted all of its 2,600 employees with laptops and actively encourages them to work off site. The system, which was first introduced in 1995, has allowed the company to cut back on office space and reap savings of $2.3 million a year. One beneficiary is Kim Yoon Hee. The procurement specialist reports to the office only on Tuesdays and Thursdays. On other days, calls to her office phone are automatically routed to her laptop, so she can work from home. "It would have been difficult for me to remain employed had it not been for the telecommuting system," says Kim, 35, who quit a job at a big Korean company seven years ago because late nights at the office kept her away from her infant daughter. "This certainly makes me more loyal to my company."

Is U.S. Business Losing Europe?

Sure, there's hostility. But how deep—and what can be done about it?

STUART CRAINER AND DES DEARLOVE

It's no secret that if Europeans had a vote in last November's election, few would have cast theirs for George W. Bush. Across the Atlantic, the president is viewed with great suspicion; even his February "charm offensive" tour of European capitals and his April visit to Vatican City failed to thaw the chill. And Europeans don't reserve their scepticism and hostility for Bush and his administration—the feelings reach far beyond politics.

Dismissed by the Bush administration as "old Europe" and unable to slow the march to war, Western Europeans have focused their ire on the government's nearest representatives: American businesspeople.

"If you are an American doing business with Europeans, you want to go into any possible relationship and negotiations with a positive image," says Allyson Stewart-Allen, a London-based American consultant and co-author of *Working With Americans.* "If you're being asked to explain America's foreign policies and deal with their frustration, the cost to doing business is already significant. It's a distraction that wastes time and valuable relationship-building opportunities."

The stakes are undoubtedly high. Annual trade between the United States and the European Union totals about $380 billion. But there is more to this than American companies and brands feeling the commercial pinch.

This Time It's Personal

In the past, for Americans working in Europe politics was seen as separate from business; today, the two are inextricably linked. It is becoming personal. "I was actually involved in organizing one of the antiwar protests," a longtime European resident told us. "I realized how things had changed when someone at the protest refused to take orders from me because I was an American."

"It is something that comes up in relatively relaxed settings—such as over cocktails, dinner, small talk," says John McAuliffe. Moscow-based president of the KOM Group. "I'm not sure I would label it 'anti-Americanism'—it is more an automatic opposition to any action of the Bush administration and a general suspicion of American motives in the international arena, I have heard some amazing conspiracy theories about American foreign and business policy. There is also a certain level of distrust that I have never experienced before." In Russia, this

was manifest in suspicions that the U.S. government, seeking to install a friendly leader in Kiev, engineered Viktor Yuschenko's electoral victory in Ukraine.

Journalist and business commentator Joshua Jampol is another veteran expat who is feeling the climate change. "I've lived in Europe for over twenty years, and I can't ever recall such outright hostility toward the U.S. of A.," he comments. "There is a tendency now to associate Americans—all Americans—with what the Bush administration is doing. When I meet new business contacts, I seem to spend the first hour just defusing the tension."

Another long-term overseas American describes working with an Arab organization, helping it set up an advisory committee for international development. Previously, it would have been automatic to include an American or two on the committee, but in the current climate, the organization expressly asked to exclude Americans altogether, purportedly for their own benefit—they'd have felt uncomfortable.

"Attitudes have changed," confirms Marjorie Thompson, an American management consultant who has been based in Europe for twenty-two years. "I came here when Ronald Reagan was president, but at that time, people separated the administration from Americans here on business. Now, there is a sense that we are held responsible."

Anglo-American Nigel Andrews of Internet Capital Group provides a useful perspective: He criss-crosses the Atlantic constantly. "There is no doubt that the Iraq war was divisive—as wars always are—and that it can be awkward and difficult to be an American in Europe," he says. "It can become very edgy and some subjects are best avoided with certain people."

So what are Americans doing in response to the climate change in Europe? Three trends are apparent. First, at the individual level, almost all the Americans with whom we spoke agreed that, obviously, tub-thumping, flag-waving nationalism is counterproductive. Second, at the corporate level, the new climate is speeding up a process that was already under way: Increasingly, U.S. companies are looking to Europeans, not Americans, to run their European operations.

The recent scandals have sapped the credibility of U.S. management principles.

An American in Paris

Michael M. Cooper is a film executive based in Paris. The son of an American expat executive, he was raised in Europe and attended school in the United States. After graduating from Dartmouth College, he worked for the French broadcaster TF1, then as a research analyst, before attending Tuck Business School. In 1992, he moved to Paris, where he is now a freelance producer, writer, and founder of consulting and project-management firm Afinexis SARL

How has the climate changed since the 2004 presidential election?

It's brought out the worst in many French and Europeans. In short, just about anyone now feels they can tell you what they think of America right to your face, whether they know you or not. We're all guilty by association for being American, and we're learning what it's like to be on the receiving end of bigotry.

Is this anti-Americanism significant? I'm not so sure. We have so much trade and so much influence that it would really take a cultural tsunami—even more hostility—to significantly affect how we're perceived and how we prosper in Europe.

When Bush was elected the first time, I remember predicting to friends and colleagues that now they were going to have a better reason to be anti-American. Now they were going to know why they hate us. And there certainly has been a surge in expressed sentiment, people really going out of their way to vocalize their criticisms of America. But I am not sure that the French hate America and/or Americans any more than previously. Back home, we're getting just as vocal in our criticism of the French.

There was a lot of shock and disbelief when John Kerry failed to get elected, and now there seems to be a pregnant silence. The French are adjusting, perhaps taking a step back, and trying to be less emotional and more cerebral about all this. It's important to remember that we are living in very particular and unusual times, and Americans on the front lines are always going to be exposed.

How do these sentiments manifest themselves?

Often in stupid and provocative comments and questions. It's counterproductive to doing business. You have to politely acknowledge these anti-American expressions without being goaded into lengthy discussions, because it's equally important to keep your chin up. A lot of the time, the people who seem the most anti-American are in fact, deep down inside, hugely admiring of America, what it stands for, in the finest sense. As the French say, *Qui aime bien, chatie bien*—who loves well punishes well. So if you happen to be the type of person who is readily going to agree with any criticism that's leveled at the United States and join in on dumping on your country, that's not going to elicit much respect from your opponent. You have to stick to your guns without drawing them.

What does this mean for you personally and your business?

My French collaborators are extremely admiring of American filmmaking, but they often get hot around the collar when it comes to politics. In France you can't just nod your head—everyone has an opinion. If you don't have an opinion, it means either that you have a speech impediment or that you have stopped breathing. So all this anti-Americanism is business as usual for me, and I suspect it is, to varying degrees, the same for my other long-term expatriated compatriots. In more conventional businesses, it's probably more black-and-white, but I'm aware of a lot of strife and inefficiencies that arise owing to the inability of U.S. executives to bridge the language and cultural divides in their everyday operations.

What do you see as the most serious effects over time?

It's the beginning of a new era in U.S.-European relations, and the ground rules are just being worked out. From a business perspective, I think the serious effects will be that we as Americans will be forced to be ever more innovative, ever more competitive. Which is as it should be. We Americans thrive on competition, and now we have some.

—S.C. and D.D.

Finally, at the national and international level there are signs that the U.S, model of globalization is losing popularity and momentum. The American corporate approach, based on turning iconic U.S. brands into global brands, is under attack; and the recent scandals have sapped the credibility of U.S. management principles—the same ones that dominated the first phase of globalization.

Sense and Sensibility

At an individual level, it's clear that Americans in Europe are treading carefully and tuning in to cultural differences more keenly than ever before. Pride and prejudice have given way to sense and sensibility.

Americans report that they are becoming adept at allaying suspicions. "I always need to be ready to respond to questions about the American people electing Bush, to create an atmosphere that shows I'm sensitive to their bewilderment and perhaps even make a few jokes myself about how and why the United States is at an all-time low in terms of general popularity," says Allyson Stewart-Allen.

"I watch what I say whenever conversations touch on international relations," observes Moscow resident John McAuliffe. "And not only with Russians and Europeans—with Americans too. People seem touchier nowadays than they were ten years ago."

American execs now tend to carefully distance themselves from their U.S. roots. This can mean paying attention to seemingly unimportant issues, such as their appearance. One American executive who regularly travels to Europe quips that she leaves her stars-and-stripes earrings at home.

Judy Vezmar, CEO of LexisNexis Group Europe, spent the bulk of her career in the United States with Xerox—starting out as a sales rep—before joining LexisNexis in 2001. She is based in London, "It comes down to individual attitude," she says. "I think of myself as a guest in other countries. You can be very effective if you show some sensitivity and show respect."

Robert Gogel came to Europe twenty years ago; he lives in France and works in London. CEO of Xchanging Global Insurance Solutions Ltd., he is editor of *Chief European Officer,* a new book exploring the role of managers in the European operations of U.S. multinationals, and a member of the European Executive Council, a network of executives who run the European operations of U.S. multinationals, Gogel favors applied common sense. "It's always been a good time to be a quiet American, but the Americans, like the Brits, don't tend to do that," he says. "Americans tend to be loud; Europeans tend to be more discreet. To anyone crossing the Atlantic in either direction, my advice would be: Until you understand the culture, keep a low profile. Go native as quickly as you can. Learn the language and mix with local people: don't live in a U.S. enclave."

Neil McArthur is vice president and regional director of operations at the U.S. consulting company Booz Allen Hamilton, and another member of the European Executive Council. Based in Amsterdam, he is responsible for Booz Allen Hamilton's European operations and is a member of the company's global leadership team. McArthur cautions that American executives in Europe need to understand that although Europe is one Europe with the enlarged EU, there are still very distinct local cultures. "Understanding cultural differences and how they apply to various products and services is really essential for anyone coming to do business in Europe," he says.

Dwindling Expats

The second trend, and one that has accelerated since George W. Bush moved into the White House, is a decline in the number of U.S. companies sending American expats to Europe. It may also involve deliberately changing corporate structures so that Americans do not run European subsidiaries.

This is already happening, Robert Gogel says. "The days of sending hordes of American managers to run European activities are gone. Companies now require executive talent that is both far more business-savvy than in the past and ultra-sensitive to every cultural nuance." Technology and rising costs have already cut the numbers of expats.

Anti-American sentiment may be hastening the change. But it was already in the pipeline. "Twenty years ago," Gogel says, "there was still an attitude that said, Let's send the Americans overseas. The reality is, there is enough knowledge transfer and bright local people, so now the only compelling reason for sending American expats is if they have specialized knowledge or experience."

McArthur confirms the change, "We certainly don't use as many expats as we did historically," he says of Booz Allen Hamilton. "There are only a small handful of U.S. partners.

We recruit for top European talent at the leading American and European business schools. But we've also just made offers to a number of Americans who want to start their careers in Europe. However, the vast majority now are Europeans studying in the United States or Europeans at top European business schools."

Many American executives who do cross the Atlantic stay only two years—and are keen to finish what they see as their European tour of duty, Gogel has some sympathy with this attitude but sees it as an obstacle to cultural enlightenment. "The reason most expats stay for just two years," he says, "is that after that, it is hard to fit back in. You lose your network in the States. Once you're out of the loop, it's hard to go back. Also, if you go back in year four, the person who sent you may have moved on and the organization may have changed. Your family is a bit older. Your wife says, I've been living in Paris—how will I fit in? That's why people send their kids to the American schools—so they can fit back in.

"If you're coming over for some real knowledge transfer, then you ought to plan for a longer-term assignment. The message I'd send back to HQ is: Don't forget the poor people you sent overseas. It ain't as easy as it looks. It ain't all cheese and wine."

Other American expats are concerned that a declining expat population in the old world could have significant implications. "You've got to remember that the expat community has always been the eyes and ears of America," says London-based Booz Allen Hamilton consultant David Newkirk. "Now they feel disconnected."

A New Brand of Globalization

The final factor in this climate change is at a macro level. America has long been the iconic and economic driving force of globalization, but its iconic force is no longer as pervasive. "There's a whole generation of Europeans which is not going to be influenced by the United States in the way that previous generations were. While it retains its economic power. America has lost some of its moral and intellectual leadership," Newkirk says.

Clearly, this could have important implications for American brands and globalization. "A lot of business people in the United States now see the fallibility of the American approach to globalization and are de-Americanizing their global efforts," says Nigel Andrews. "There's a temptation to think that this has to do with recent events. But I think it has longer-term roots and ramifications which can be traced back to the postwar years."

Globalization appears to be entering a more mature stage. Instead of being globalization with a U.S. face, it is more genuinely global—but still backed by greenbacks. The positive story is that U.S. corporations are now more attuned to the competitive global environment than ever before. They have asked themselves hard questions and are emerging as more sensitive and more competitive global players. And there is some more good news. As Allyson Stewart-Allen puts it: "The appetite to make money from Americans and in America seems undiminished."

Can Europe Compete?

CARL SCHRAMM AND ROBERT E. LITAN

This year marks the 50th anniversary of the Treaty of Rome, the agreement that created the European Economic Community, the precursor to today's European Union. Conferences, festivals, and summits have been held across the continent to celebrate a half-century of peace and growing cooperation. As many observers have noted, it now seems almost archaic to think of France and Germany as enemies—an achievement for which European integration, initiated in the wake of the devastation of World War II, deserves substantial credit.

In recent years, the EU has expanded eastward to include most of the countries of the former Soviet bloc, and it has also grown in institutional heft. The European Parliament, though toothless in many respects, has established itself as an influential voice on issues of common political concern; the European Central Bank has become a major player in international finance; and the European Court of Justice is of growing importance in international law. Perhaps most impressive has been the introduction of a common currency, the euro, which has reduced the costs of trade and capital flows within Europe and, of late, has risen sharply in value relative to the dollar.

Despite these positive developments, however, there is no avoiding the gloom that has hovered over the anniversary. Most Europeans have decidedly mixed feelings about the EU, and have resisted further integration. In 2005, voters in France and the Netherlands, two countries firmly wedded to the European project, expressed their ambivalence by rejecting a proposed European constitution. This past June, chastened European leaders agreed to support a mere "treaty" giving the EU many of the same powers, but it remains to be seen whether their citizens will be any more receptive to this "constitution in drag," as some have called it.

Much of the backlash can be traced to the lackluster economic performance of most European economies, especially as compared with those of the U.S. and Asia. The countries of the EU have prospered, to be sure, but not nearly as much as Europeans expected in the heyday of their joint enterprise. Nor were they alone in their hopes for an integrated, liberalized continent. In the early 1990's, the economist Lester Thurow of MIT wrote a best-selling book, *Head to Head*, in which he forecast, among other things, that Western Europe would soon overtake the United States economically.

But the threat never materialized, and now Europe's citizens and political leaders openly worry about the future. Put simply, they wonder: can Europe compete?

Today's 27-member EU is an outgrowth of the European Coal and Steel Community, formed in 1951 with just six members—Germany, France, Italy, Belgium, the Netherlands, and Luxembourg. The early focus of the community was on eliminating barriers to the cross-border flow of goods, services, and capital. The point was to promote trade and growth, but the broader political aim was to reduce the economic tensions that, in the previous 40 years, had contributed to the onset of two European wars.

As an exercise in opening borders, the European project has been a remarkable success, creating a single market that now extends from London and Lisbon to Helsinki and Athens. Today, it is possible, at least in principle, for any citizen of an EU country to work in any other EU country. With most of the Eastern European countries having already been absorbed after the fall of the Berlin Wall, the next round of accessions is slated to include Croatia and Macedonia. (More controversial is Turkey's prospective membership, which has aroused passionate debate and opposition.)

As for the EU's economic performance, here, too, there has been some good news. The unemployment rate in the Western European countries (the so-called "EU-15"), after hovering in the 10-percent range for most of the 1990's, has dropped steadily to roughly 7 percent. Inflation has remained low, in the 2-percent range, as in the United States.

The great disappointment has been lagging growth in living standards. After approaching the American level of per-capita income in the 1980's, Western Europe has since fallen back somewhat (with the exception of booming Ireland). Labor-force productivity, which is the main driver of living standards, has inched forward at less than 1 percent annually since 2000, compared to a pace of 2.5 percent in the U.S. A study published earlier this year by Eurochambres, the European business lobby, concluded that, in terms of its place in the world economy, the "EU is progressing at an insufficient pace."

What accounts for the EU's economic sluggishness? In the first place, there is a profound demographic problem. Aging is a far more serious challenge for Europe than for the United States. By 2030, a quarter of Western Europe's population will be at least sixty-five years old, twice the share of children under fifteen. Though the birthrate in a few EU member states—France, Denmark, Ireland—has bounced back in recent years, approaching the replacement rate of two-plus children per family, it would have to climb much more in these countries and elsewhere in Europe to offset the rapid increase in the ranks of senior citizens. The U.S. will also age during this period, with the elderly comprising close to 20 percent of the population, but they will still be outnumbered by children under fifteen.

As an economic matter, Europe's aging population will make it much more expensive for governments to finance the pension and health-care benefits that they have promised. Unless Europe can find a way to grow much faster, this will mean having to raise taxes or cut benefits, or both, none of which, to say the least, will be highly popular. To make matters worse, countries with aging populations tend to resist change and, lacking a large supply of young people, to fall short in the energy and zeal needed for innovation. Still worse, if continental Europe fails to provide opportunities for its most ambitious young residents, they will continue their already substantial migration across the English Channel—to the healthy economies of Great Britain and Ireland—thus making it even more difficult for their countries to support the aging populations left behind.

Western Europe would find it much easier to manage this challenge if it adopted more liberal policies on immigration, but this is highly unlikely. Much of the continent already faces significant difficulties in absorbing its existing immigrant population, as suggested by the riots among young Islamic immigrants in France two years ago and the ongoing tension between natives and Muslim newcomers in the historically tolerant Netherlands. European countries have yet to figure out how to assimilate this potentially valuable pool of young people into the economic and social mainstream.

Another barrier to growth is that European workers seem content to have traded competitiveness for comfort and security. In 2004, a French government employee wrote a best-selling book called *Bonjour, Paresse* ("Hello, Laziness"), which extolled the virtues of not working hard. This "avoidance of work" ethic has become a serious cultural problem across Western Europe, manifesting itself in a noticeable drop in the average number of hours worked per year by employed individuals. As recently as the late 1960's, Europeans spent more time at work than Americans did. Yet, according to data compiled by the Organization for Economic Cooperation and Development (OECD), by 2004 the average European worked between 35 and 40 weeks a year, compared with 46 weeks in the U.S.

Economists continue to debate the reason for these differing work ethics. Some argue that high European taxes over the past several decades have created disincentives. More convincing are the economic analyses that pin most of the blame on the restrictive labor rules that compel European firms to limit the number of hours their employees work. Indeed, the rallying cry among unions throughout much of Europe since the mid-1970's has been "work less, work all." Judging by the numbers, at least the first part of the slogan has come true.

Debilitating as these factors may be, the most serious challenge confronting the economies of Western Europe lies still deeper—in the basic-model of capitalism that they have embraced. Much like the United States in the first two decades after World War II—when what was good for General Motors was said to be good for the rest of the country—today's Western European economy is dominated by large firms. These firms were crucial to Europe's recovery after the war, but today they are holding the continent back. Economies dependent on such behemoths eventually slow down; they suffer from the sclerosis that sets in when unions and big government—the institutions established to balance the power of large firms—stifle enterprise and change.

The U.S. experienced this sort of malaise in the 1970's and early 1980's until a wave of entrepreneurial innovation—centered on the personal computer and later the Internet—helped to transform the economy. Companies that did not exist 30 years ago—Microsoft, Cisco, eBay, Google, Amazon—helped to accomplish the revolution. But in Europe this kind of entrepreneurialism is absent. To be sure,

some large European firms—Nokia, to take a prime example—have come up with radically new and exciting products or ways of doing business. But the American experience shows that the most reliable source of such change is new, vibrant firms that do not have a vested interest in preserving existing markets.

Why does Europe have such a hard time generating new Nokias? It certainly does not lack for brains. Its people are well-educated (better-educated, arguably, than Americans). Much of the problem lies in regulations that make it difficult for firms above a certain size (typically ten to 50 employees, depending on the country) to fire or lay off redundant or underperforming employees. Although defended as a way of "saving jobs," these protections ironically have the opposite effect: if firms cannot shed workers in response to market conditions, they will be reluctant to hire new workers in the first place.

Even more important, these labor regulations inhibit the formation and growth of new firms. Why should someone take the risk of launching an enterprise that, just as it starts to grow into a more substantial business, would become subject to rules sharply limiting his control over employees? Why should venture capitalists back a company that, at some point, would lose the incentive, and perhaps the ability, to grow?

These difficulties help to explain why the few highly successful new European ventures like Skype (which pioneered Internet-based telephone calls) sell out (to eBay, in Skype's case) rather than expand internally. In a rapidly changing technological environment, Skype's founders probably did not want to incur the fixed costs of a workforce that would have difficulty adapting to new tasks in the very competitive international telecommunications industry. Similar fears help to explain why would-be European entrepreneurs (like the Paris-born Pierre Omidyar, one of the founders of eBay) move abroad to start their companies, rather than building them in their home countries.

To their credit, Europe's leaders are aware of these structural problems and have tried to address them. Meeting in Portugal in 2000, they announced the "Lisbon Agenda" for fundamentally reforming European economies, with the goal of making the EU into the "most competitive and dynamic knowledge-based economy in the world." Many of the items on their laundry list of recommendations—reducing the cost of registering new companies, teaching entrepreneurship in technical schools and universities, expanding small-business loans—were intended to promote the creation of vigorous new enterprises.

By European standards, the Lisbon Agenda was radical, but it fell far short of what many American—and, indeed, some European—observers have been advocating for years. Martin Baily, the former chairman of President Clinton's Council of Economic Advisers, and his colleagues at the Peterson Institute for International Economics have outlined a series of much more ambitious reforms for Europe, aimed at boosting productivity, making labor markets more flexible, and giving governments greater latitude in fiscal and monetary policy during downturns. Such measures go far beyond anything the European Council or EU member states have envisioned.

Advocates of radical economic reform for Europe typically urge that the various components of liberalization be adopted simultaneously, like the "shock therapy" adopted (on the advice of Western economists) by several former Soviet-bloc countries after the fall of the Berlin Wall. But such a strategy would be a political nonstarter in Western Europe, whose many entrenched interests are fully capable of blocking thorough-going change. The vast majority of employed adults on the continent are earning more than they probably ever expected to, and (if they are in large firms) believe that they will continue working at their current jobs until they move into comfortable, state-supported retirements. There is little political support for reforms that would threaten these expectations.

Consider the experience of Angela Merkel, who was elected chancellor of Germany in 2005 by the barest of margins. Voters refused to give her Christian Democratic Union a majority in part because they feared the economic reforms, especially in labor law, that Merkel had discussed during the campaign. She was forced to cobble together a multiparty coalition that has so far shown little appetite for her controversial proposals.

Nicolas Sarkozy's recent election to the French presidency may indicate a new readiness for change among the French. Sarkozy was unabashed in his enthusiasm for reducing the tax and regulatory burdens and loosening the labor rules that have constrained growth and left many workers feeling like second-class participants in the world economy. Polling indicates that he won a majority among voters twenty-five to thirty-four, perhaps a sign that they are dissatisfied with their dim economic prospects. But Sarkozy is aware of Merkel's experience, and knows the limits of his own mandate. Indeed, at the EU summit in June, he seemed to back away from his commitment to unfettered competition in favor of continued support for French (or European) "national champions"—that is, state-supported large firms—in key industries.

None of this is to say that entrepreneurialism is dead in Europe. Though the continent as a whole remains handicapped in many ways, there are "hot spots" worth noting. The leading example is Ireland, which only 30 years ago was looked down upon as the poor cousin of Europe, and now boasts one of the highest standards of living in the world. Lacking the burden of a costly social safety net, Ireland was able to launch its magical economic ride on the strength of a low corporate tax rate, heavy investment in education, and an "open door" policy for foreign direct investment (along with, it should be noted, some very large temporary subsidies from the EU).

Another European success story can be found in Estonia, which has used its Soviet-era scientific expertise and well-educated workforce to become a leading center of information technology and biological sciences. Wales, too, is an economic success-in-the-making. Once dominated by coal mining, it has become a force in the European aerospace industry. Indeed, on a larger scale, the whole United Kingdom has been able to depart from the continental norm, thanks to privatization, looser labor rules, and a strong commitment, under Tony Blair's "third way," to market economics. The results can be seen in the numbers. From 1990 to 2004, per-capita output actually grew a bit faster in the UK than in the U.S.—a fact that did not go unnoticed in the rest of the world. In 2006, the UK raked in $170 billion in foreign direct investment, putting it close behind the U.S. even though its population is roughly one-fifth the size of our own.

As for the rest of Europe, some of the best prospects for serious economic reform can be found in the lower- and medium-income countries, like Spain, Romania, and Poland, which feel a strong need to catch up to the living standards of the continental core. If reform proceeds faster on the fringe, a sense of rivalry—and

envy—may help to shake France, Germany, and Italy into adopting more radical measures. Sarkozy's recent victory is a welcome harbinger in this respect, even if he is forced by political realities to take a more modest approach than his election rhetoric suggested.

Any reform package with a chance of success in these calcified economies will have to do its work at the margins. Under the current regime, when firms grow beyond a certain threshold number of employees, they become subject to a panoply of additional regulations, and thus have strong incentives to remain small. The way to address this "notch" problem (as economists call it) is to allow new firms formed after a certain date to operate under liberalized labor rules and perhaps a lighter regulatory burden in other areas as well. Additional incentives for new-business formation might also be considered, like lowering income-tax rates for some initial period.

If Western Europeans need a model for such an incremental program, there is an obvious one: China. Rather than administering the "shock therapy" of privatizing state-owned enterprises all at once, as happened in post-Soviet Russia and Eastern Europe, China by and large left them alone, while allowing new firms to form and grow. Although this strategy was not, of course, the only contributing factor, the result has been two decades of astonishing growth.

A "new deal for new firms" would not be a silver bullet for Europe's lethargic economies. But, in combination with other proposals now on the table, like streamlining rules for business registration and teaching the value of entrepreneurialism, the total package could begin to change the way Europeans think, encouraging more of them to see their futures in creating new, high-growth businesses of their own rather than in working for someone else for a lifetime.

Would a set of reforms targeted only at encouraging the formation of new firms stand a chance politically? Could it overcome the ingrained cultural habits and economic expectations of the continent? Perhaps not. After all, even more modest efforts to liberalize Europe's labor and tax structure have been denounced as representing the proverbial "camel's nose under the tent." If the critics and proponents of such measures agree on one thing, it is that the ultimate goal of reform is the dismantling of the rules and privileges that have defined European economic life for decades.

This, however, is precisely what Europeans, especially the parents of children who cannot find jobs in today's rigidified system, should want. Indeed, young people themselves are the obvious potential beneficiaries of more dynamic economies. Whether such far-sightedness can prevail in the streets of Berlin and Paris, and in the bureaucratic enclaves of Brussels, is the great open question. Europe has no time to waste.

CARL SCHRAMM is the president of the Kauffman Foundation and a Batten fellow at the Darden School of Business at the University of Virginia. **ROBERT E. LITAN** is vice president for research and policy at the Kauffman Foundation and a senior fellow at the Brookings Institution. They are co-author, along with William Baumol, of *Good Capitalism, Bad Capitalism, and the Economics of Growth and Prosperity* (Yale), from which some of the ideas in this essay are drawn. This is their first contribution to Commentary.

Unequal Access

India's lower castes are seeking a toehold in the global job market.

EMILY WAX

As a Dalit, Pratibha Valmik Kamble is part of the poorest and most ostracized community in this subcontinent's ancient caste system, a group of people so shunned that they are still known as untouchables. Her mother is a maid, her father a day laborer.

Yet here in this prospering city, Kamble, 24, was recently applying to an Indian firm called Temp Solutions to go to Philadelphia for a well-paying social service job there. During the interview, she twisted her hands nervously in her lap, knowing that if she landed the position, she would not only make more money than both of her parents combined, she would enhance their social status, and her own.

India has long had an affirmative action program for federal government jobs, setting aside 23 percent of positions for the most oppressed castes. Now activists are campaigning to open the private sector to them as well, whether the employer is Indian or multinational. Prime Minister Manmohan Singh recently said he favors that goal.

So does Temp Solutions co-owner Michael Thevar, himself a member of a low-ranking caste. He gave Kamble the job. "I'm so proud of you," he told her after delivering the good news. "I know so well how much you struggled. That's why I am that much more impressed."

Kamble's eyes went wet as she straightened her mustard-colored outfit and smiled, appearing to be almost embarrassed by his praise.

Recruiting drives aimed at hiring members of India's underprivileged castes, who make up 70 percent of the population, remain rare in the subcontinent's booming service sector. But as India hurtles into world markets, such hiring has touched off a larger debate over the country's 3,000-year-old caste system.

In much of India, the system organizes people into a rigid social order by accident of birth, determining everything from professions to marriage partners.

While the caste system is outlawed by the constitution, low-caste Indians still experience severe discrimination. Dalits are regarded as so low that they are not even part of the system. To this day, they are not allowed to enter many Hindu temples or to drink water from sources used by higher castes.

So far only two major companies—Bharti Enterprises and Infosys—have announced they would set aside jobs for Dalits and other oppressed castes.

Ramesh Bajpai, executive director of the New Delhi-based American Chamber of Commerce in India, says the issue of affirmative action for oppressed castes has not been raised among his members—an indication, some Indian workers contend, that many U.S. companies are not fully aware of the caste system and its complex legacy of discrimination.

India-based executives for IBM and Microsoft, which are among the top foreign employers in this country, declined to comment for this article.

"Things are changing in India and, I believe, changing for the good," says Bajpai. "As far as we know, our member companies try to hire across the spectrum of Indian society. But since the government has started talking about this issue, we in the industry will follow. It is a complex and interesting discussion."

An estimated 86 percent of technology workers at multinationals and large Indian outsourcing firms come from upper castes or wealthy middle castes, according to a study released in August 2006 by the government and activist groups.

At the same time, the vast majority of Indians living in the United States and Britain come from upper castes, partly because they have better access to work and education visas and can afford expensive plane tickets.

"Caste should not be globalized, and as India rises economically, that is the real fear," says Thevar. "I think this is the moment in India for us all to stand up and tell the world that we are capable. There is no longer such a thing as untouchable in the world."

Thevar and Dalit activists have even lobbied the U.S. Congressional Black Caucus, with whom they see common cause and a shared experience in discrimination.

Congress has taken notice, and in July passed a resolution calling for the United States to work with India to address the problem of untouchability by "encouraging U.S. businesses and other U.S. organizations working in India to take every possible measure to ensure Dalits are included and are not discriminated against in their programming."

"It is now time for this Congress to speak out about this ancient and particularly abhorrent form of persecution and segregation—even if it is occurring in a country considered to be one of America's closest allies," Republican Rep. Trent Franks of Arizona said during a speech last spring on the House floor. Franks went on to call Dalits "one of the most oppressed peoples on Earth."

The 2006 study found that public health workers refuse to visit 33 percent of Dalit villages, while mail is not delivered to the homes of 24 percent of Dalits.

The reason for the neglect, the study said, is that some in the upper castes believe lower-caste people are dirty and lack dignity in their labor as latrine cleaners, rickshaw drivers, butchers, herders and barbers.

The debate on affirmative action in India is similar to the one in the United States in terms of discrimination and ways to end it. But in India, those who experience discrimination, especially in rural areas, are the majority and are ruled by an elite.

The issue here is complicated by India's turbulent history of race, class and caste. Centuries-old customs of arranged marriages and inherited professions perpetuate caste divisions, which are further reinforced by some interpretations of Hinduism, India's dominant religion, which sanctions the caste system.

The country's education system also hardens caste. Lower castes largely attend public schools, which teach local languages, while private schools attended by upper castes teach English—the most important criterion to be hired at a call center, where young employees spend their nights helping customers phoning from the United States.

Opponents of affirmative action argue that government set-asides should have lasted only 10 years after independence in 1947, not the six decades that they have. In the workplace and in colleges, affirmative action programs breed resentment, the critics say, because they dilute merit-based hiring that should, in theory, reward the most qualified job candidates, regardless of caste.

Creating quotas for the private sector would be a "disaster," says Shiv Khera, an author who opposes set-asides on the grounds that they call too much attention to caste. "We shouldn't even be asking what caste people are."

He also says that affirmative action will not fix what he sees as the roots of caste divisions: deeply impoverished public schools that don't teach English or even have enough funding for up-to-date books. The government should fix those schools, Khera says, "not worry about the private sector," a view echoed by others.

Still, affirmative action has helped pull tens of thousands of people out of abject poverty and into universities and government jobs, while creating a small Dalit middle class that many hope will expand along with India's economy. It also has given rise to a new kind of struggle, as other low-ranking groups known here as the "backward castes" protest that their government designation isn't "low-caste enough" to make them eligible for job set-asides, Khera says.

"That just shows you that set-asides don't work," Khera adds. "It just makes the people more aware of caste and who's getting what job and why."

But inside the interview room, the young professionals applying for jobs with Temp Solutions said they would have never gotten an education without set-asides. The interviews were held at the Manuski Center, part of a Buddhist monastery. Hundreds of thousands of Dalits have converted to Buddhism in an attempt to escape the caste system.

Sitting in a circle as they waited to hear whether they would get jobs, Kamble and the other students talked about the often harrowing discrimination they faced.

"I knew there was hatred in the world and in India, when as a child I watched some upper castes refuse to sell my mother lentils and rice in the nicer part of the market because we were 'dirty,' and from a backward caste," said Vivek Kumar Katara, 22, who has a master's degree in social work focusing on helping the mentally ill. Without quotas, Katara said, "I honestly don't know if professors would have even let me sit in the same class as upper castes."

After awarding jobs to Kamble, Katara and others, Thevar said they would be expected to return to India once their visas expired and to help hire from their own communities.

"It will be our responsibility to tell the world about caste and fight it," Kamble said as a group of chosen candidates raced downstairs to call or tell their parents, who were anxiously waiting. She is to work for a child social services agency in Philadelphia.

Pacing downstairs, Kamble's gray-haired father, Valmik, put his thick, callused hands over his eyes and wept when he found out his daughter would be working for a major company. "I'm so happy and so proud," he said, hugging her. "I never dreamt of such a thing for our family."

When Greens Go Corporate

They start wondering whether the gain to their wealth and clout is worth the tossing at night.

WILLIAM UNDERHILL

As partnerships go, the current team-up between WWF International, one of the world's best-known champions of the environment, and French multinational Lafarge, the world's largest supplier of building materials, is an unlikely one. Under a three-year pact, WWF reportedly receives a sum of $2 million a year to advise Lafarge on shrinking its carbon footprint. Lafarge gets plenty of favorable publicity. The big question is what, if anything, the environment gets. Lafarge has a questionable record on greenhouse gases, and figures published last year showed that its CO_2 emissions had risen 19 percent since 1990, boosted by the recent acquisition of a string of cement plants in China.

Small wonder that WWF occasionally agonizes about its policy of corporate engagement, now shared by many of its fellow nonprofits. "It's based on an economic assessment of how the market works and where is the best leverage point," says Maria Boulos, head of business and industry relations. "But we do sometimes wake in the middle of the night wondering what we are doing."

Indeed, it's a tough call. In the new green-tinted world, business and environmental groups are edging ever closer, with collaboration replacing confrontation as the favored means of saving the planet. Pressure from big investors and consumers, as well as a stream of new regulation, means companies can no longer afford to ignore eco-concerns. That has opened up a new and sometimes lucrative niche, offering businesses help in such areas as developing sustainable supply chains or cutting emissions. The value of global trade in environmental goods and services is forecast to rise 45 percent to $800 billion by 2015, and not all beneficiaries will be corporations. "In the past you were either an environmentalist or you were in the business of making money," says Paul Gilpin, a onetime Greenpeace boss now running a Sydney-based consultancy, with the U.S. chemical giant Du Pont and the Ford Motor Co. among its customers. "Now those artificial lines have faded." Gilpin and many others argue that corporate funding of green NGOs makes sense. But befriending the old enemy entails tricky compromises that hardline greens still hesitate to accept.

It is a mark of how far the trend has come that the green NGO Environmental Defense now has an office inside Wal-Mart's Bentonville, Arkansas, corporate headquarters (Wal-Mart shoppers who now buy fresh fish from sustainable stocks have the nonprofit to thank). "More and more companies are seeing this as a success story and want to get onboard," says ED's director of corporate partnerships, Gwen Ruta.

The lure of such relationships is obvious. Get alongside Wal-Mart at the senior level and there's an opportunity to influence the 60,000 companies worldwide that stock its warehouses. "One lesson that we have learned is the power of the supply chain," says Glenn Prickett of the U.S.-based NGO Conservation International, which has worked with the Starbucks coffee chain for almost 10 years. "It can send signals all round the world." Thanks to CI, some 60 percent of Starbucks coffee now comes from growers pledged to meeting a set of conservation and social goals.

Corporate money can also cross-subsidize other work. When Ikea wanted advice on sourcing timber it turned to Rainforest Alliance, an NGO that now derives about 25 percent of its annual revenue from certifying sustainable supplies, useful cash for its conservation work around the world. WWF in 2006 received more than $30 million from corporate funds, whether as gifts or in return for services. Pragmatism rules. "Sometimes we're like a consultancy, but we're working to a conservation agenda," says Prickett. If the company is committed to change, its cash is acceptable. In return for a "generous donation" to help save bee habitats, CI recently helped McDonald's with the launch of a "Bee Movie" Happy Meal, encouraging kids to study the environment in their own backyards.

But integrity and independence are always at stake. Can NGOs continue to campaign against corporate wrongdoing when they are taking corporate funds? If the arguments for collaboration are compelling for NGOs, they may be less clear to the public. "It's like pop stars appearing with politicians," says Tom Woollard, of the international consultancy Environmental Resources Management. "The politicians get a temporary increase in their street credibility; the pop stars appear slightly less cool."

Among larger NGOs, Greenpeace is rare in that it still depends wholly on private donations to fund its work. Yet many others remain ambivalent about getting into bed with business. Friends of the Earth will deal only with the most planet-friendly companies (one recent arrangement allowed the Eurostar high-speed rail service to use FoE's endorsement in its advertising). Environmental Defense won't accept donations from companies in sectors like automobiles or waste management, and total corporate contributions are limited to 3 percent of the operating budget. "The environment is our only client," says Gwen Ruta. "Business is our ally."

But business is an ally to be treated with extreme caution, say the skeptics. Well-meaning NGOs are too easily duped, says Michael Marx of the U.S. lobbying group Corporate Ethics. Smart companies will use the link to burnish their environmental reputation while making no changes in other areas. "Wal-Mart is now leveraging its good public relations around the environment to neutralize its bad public relations around labor relations and its treatment of communities." And there's a danger of unhealthy financial reliance as the NGOs seek to widen their role and must compete for funds. "A lot of NGOs are now almost totally dependent on corporate funding," according to the leading British eco-campaigner, George Monbiot.

Saving the planet will certainly prove an expensive business. The total budget for WWF in 2006 ran to $636 million, with more than 1,300 projects, including tree planting and World Bank lobbying. Multinationals, most agree, should pay their share. But persuading business to change its ways will take more than partnerships. When it comes to twisting arms in the boardroom, governments still have more muscle than NGOs.

UNIT 4

International Business Operations

Unit Selections

Key Points to Consider

- What do you think is the impact of China on the world economy now and in the future?

- What do you think is the impact of the other BRIC economies on business now and in the future?

- How do you think the businesses participating in the global market are going to be able to cope with the different accounting systems that are used around the world?

- There still remains abuse in the labor market, especially in developing countries. How do you think corporations should respond to this? And how should consumers respond to this?

- Outsourcing and off-shoring are some of the most controversial aspects of globalization. Do you think something should be done about it, and if so, what? Is there something that you personally can do? If yes, what do you think will be the possible results of your action?

Student Web Site

www.mhcls.com/online

Internet References

The Development Gateway
http://www.developmentgateway.org/
Harvard Business School
http://www.hbs.edu
International Business Resources on the WWW
http://globaledge.msu.edu/ibrd/ibrd.asp

Operating a multinational business organization is very different from the operation of a domestic firm. Even if a domestic organization relies heavily on imported goods, the operation of facilities outside of one's own home market and society is a very different task than the operation of facilities that function only in one country, one society, and one economy. International business operations are far more complex than those of a purely domestic organization.

Developing a global business strategy is a necessary task for multinational organizations. To be truly successful and to be able to justify themselves, organizations need to be able to be more than just the total of the sum of their parts. Multinationals need to be able to take advantage of the strengths of being a multinational corporation, when competing with other kinds of organizations.

China represents one of the greatest opportunities for business at present in the future. But, China is a unique country with its own way of doing business. Many have gone into China, thinking they could quickly take advantage of this expanding market, only to learn that the Chinese are not so quick as Americans to establish business relations and that the signing of a contract is only the beginning of the relationship, not the culmination. There are many opportunities in China, which is the fastest growing major economy in the world. But, to be able to make it in China, you have to be patient and you have know the rules as discussed in "Making It in China".

The traditional way of importing and exporting goods still represents a major portion of global trade. Establishing a manufacturing facility oversees for meeting the demand of the American domestic market or simply off-shoring manufacturing is one way to deal with high domestic costs, but there are certainly other options too as seen in "The China Factor."

Foreign direct investment has been one of the primary ways by which developing countries have been able to grow; having wealthy countries invest in them improves their industry, infrastructure, creates jobs, and generally, enhances prosperity and increases economic growth. This was one of the chief ways in which the United States accumulated its capital during the 1800's. But, in order to do this, foreign investors need an assurance of political stability in the country they wish to enter and a reasonable expectation of a return on their investment. That is what is beginning now in Indonesia with the installation of a new government that is friendlier to foreign investment than previous governments were. "A Whiff of New Money" is starting to be present in Indonesia for the first time in a long time.

Most foreign direct investment does not take place in developing countries, rather, it takes place between developed countries and can even take place in a developed country by a developing country as when the Chinese computer maker Lenovo purchased IBM's PC division for $1.75 billion. Foreign direct investment is a two-way street, and it is sometimes difficult to determine exactly who owns what.

One of the problems facing global corporations has been the reforms in the international accounting area. The International Financial Reporting System (IFRS) and the American Financial Accounting Standards Board (FASB) have undergone major reforms over the past several years. Reconciling these two standards is going to be a major task for corporations doing business in the United States and abroad as discussed in "Found in Translation."

Operations, supply chaining and R&D have been some of the most active areas of development in global trade. The supply chain has been the key to the success of such major corporations as Wal-Mart, which has created one of the most efficient supply chains in the world, to get the products from the producer to the consumer. Research and development has also proven to be a key for many corporations. The way to stay ahead of the competition in a hyper-competitive environment is to produce goods that are better, faster, and less expensive than the competitor's, and the way to do that is through research and development. Those firms that skimp on this part of their business do so at the peril of being left behind the rest of their competitors due to inferior products resulting in declining sales and profitability.

As global firms look for new markets, they historically neglected the poor of the developing world. These people want the same kinds of things that everyone else wants, and there is a market for goods and services waiting to be addressed. The traditional methods may not be the way to address these markets and new ways may need to be found to explore this area.

International human resource management represents one of the most difficult aspects of managing a global organization. Each country has a different set of laws and expectations, and employees from different countries likewise have different expectations as to how they will be treated by their employer. However, there are certain minimum standards that should be met by all corporations wherever they do business, and some companies may not be doing that as outlined in "International OHS."

The practice of outsourcing and off-shoring, both low- and high-skilled work that was once done in developed countries, to much lower cost venues has stirred concern and controversy as seen in, "Worrying Trends for the Global Outsourcing Industry" and "Roots of Insecurity". One thing is certain, however, global businesses are in a hyper-competitive environment that demands the highest possible quality of goods, while at the same time, using draconian measures to cut costs and keep them low. This provides their customers with the classic benefits of free trade—high-quality goods at low cost, but puts increasing pressure on the classic factors of production of labor to produce more for less. The paradox is that the final customers of the products are the workers producing the goods. One of the great challenges for governments and industries in the coming decades will be to solve this problem not only in the developed world but in the developing world as well.

Making It in China

American entrepreneurs are overcoming cultural, regulatory, and other barriers to build fortunes in one of the greatest booms in history. Here's how they've done it, and how you can do it too.

G. Pascal Zachary

Seeing Barrett Comiskey lounging in the rooftop beer garden of Shanghai's fabled Peace Hotel at twilight, sipping his cool Tsingtao and gazing down at the hurly-burly street scene below, you may be tempted to call out, "Hey, buddy. You're dreaming." A year ago, Comiskey, 29, came to China to seek his fortune. He brought with him a Stanford MBA and not much else. He speaks some Mandarin, and he has a Taiwanese wife, Jojo Tsai, who is fluent. But for much of the time he's been here, he's hardly had 2 yuan to rub together, and he owes $100,000 on his school loans. His business partner, Andy Mulkerin, seems at first even more out of his depth; he arrived four days ago with a freshly minted Harvard MBA, but he's also deep in gradschool debt and speaks not a word of Mandarin. Weirder still, he just turned down a job at McKinsey that would have paid him more than $100,000 a year. Why? So he could come to China—the new land of opportunity.

The idea they've come up with as their ticket to riches sounds like a serious stretch, and might even strike some folks back home as vaguely distasteful. They've formed a company that seeks to persuade small U.S. manufacturers—the kind that may not have thought that outsourcing was right for them—that they too can shift production jobs to China, just like the big multinationals. "People think everything is made in China already, but many things are still made in America," Comiskey explains. He and Mulkerin plan to profit by brokering deals with Chinese factory operators for American manufacturers of offbeat things like, say, vending machines and hearing aids.

It's quite the scheme, and given Comiskey and Mulkerin's resources and inexperience, it would be tough to pull off anywhere. But in China?

True, the Middle Kingdom has become the global epicenter of wild-and-woolly capitalism. We've all read the stories about how China's exploding economy is now the world's second-largest, behind that of the United States. China is growing so fast, it's expected to be in a league of its own well before midcentury. Yet the place is commonly regarded as a mausoleum

for the broken dreams of fresh-faced foreign entrepreneurs like Comiskey and Mulkerin—people who caught China fever only to be laid low by the country's impenetrable business culture, its barbed-wire bureaucracy, its endemic corruption. Many of America's saviest corporate giants have straggled to cash in on the China boom too. Pepsi has never made a profit in China despite 20 years of trying. A big Kraft cheese venture melted down. Even titans of the new economy have been humbled here: Amazon.com bought a Chinese online bookseller last year but recently warned that success is "many years" away. With household names flailing in China, what chance could entrepreneurial greenhorns possibly have?

Quite a good chance, actually. As unlikely as it might seem, Comiskey and Mulkerin now have a modest stable of paying clients, including sizable manufacturers of, yes, vending machines and hearing aids. Their progress bespeaks a little-noticed aspect of China today: The hard-luck stories of failed fortune seekers have done nothing to slow the stream of American entrepreneurs into China, and each wave of new arrivals learns from the mistakes of predecessors. Today there are thousands of Americans who, through pluck, ingenuity, and perseverance, have managed to decode the mysteries of Chinese capitalism. They are creating their own businesses at a furious pace, and some aren't simply surviving: They're getting rich.

Idea No. 18—Tap the developing world's mobile communications boom.

How? Their stratagems are numerous, varied, and as full of contradictions as Lao-tzu's *Tao Te Ching:* Some of the entrepreneurs immerse themselves deeply in Chinese culture and language, while others learn most of what they know from reading Lonely Planet books on the flight over. Some are transplanting American consumer culture, from coffee to hip-hop clubs, while others are inventing entirely new products, like the perfect clothing hanger. Some are getting rich quick, while others have 10-year plans. Taken together, the experiences of today's American entrepreneurs in China provide a sort of guidebook for anyone who dreams of getting in on the phenomenal wealth and opportunity being generated by an epic boom. "To come to a new land, with a new language and a new focus—that may seem aggressive for an American," Comiskey says. "But this is a buyer's market for what we're after."

Court Powerful Partners, but Get Out of Their Way

Five years ago, as the dotcom boom was peaking in the United States, a platoon of American Internet pioneers descended on China, assuming that with its massive population (1.3 billion at last count), the country would become fertile ground for cutting-edge digital businesses, especially those based on the Web and wireless communications. Those predictions of China's growth came true: Today 350 million people spend an average of $10 a month on cell-phone service. The Web has evolved more slowly, with about 100 million people using it regularly, partly because of China's political restrictions on Internet content.

But many of the early China trailblazers lost their shirts. Derek Sulger didn't—and how he avoided that fate holds crucial lessons. Sulger started his business in 1999, on his first day in China. He was on the verge of quitting a high-paying job as a Goldman Sachs investment banker in London to pursue his belief that China was about to be swept up in the cell-phone revolution. "Everyone at Goldman thought I'd lost my marbles," he recalls. But Sulger and his American business partner, also a former Goldman banker, did have all their marbles—and more.

They had capital, for starters. Each partner invested $250,000 of his own money to form Linktone, a startup that aimed to sell ringtones and other content to Chinese mobile-phone customers. They also had a good sense of how business works, and set about analyzing China's telecom market, identifying the most powerful players. Their breakthrough, however, was Sulger's idea of immediately stacking his startup with Chinese talent, people who knew how to navigate the murky sloughs of Chinese capitalism, and using them to forge ties to powerful telecoms and other partners. Never mind that Sulger was 27 at the time and didn't speak a word of Chinese. His Wall Street pedigree and the fact that he and former colleagues at Goldman had cash to invest impressed his early hires—many of them recent graduates of English training as well as Shanghai businessmen—enough to get them to sign on to his untested venture. "I don't think anyone would have ever come to work for us if I hadn't convinced them that Goldman made me Qualified to build a business," Sulger says.

The local team then set its sights on the real power players. Sulger's first target was China Mobile, the country's largest telecom, but his managers persuaded him that he had to win over the company's regional divisions to have any hope of a broad alliance. Deals with Zhejiang Mobile and Shanghai Mobile opened the door, and soon Sulger was hooking up not just with China Mobile's national operations but with dozens of other carriers, content providers, and cell-phone makers, including Nokia. The big players' access to customers assured Linktone an immediate and steady source of revenue. And the startup's growth was meteoric: Sales rose from $1 million in 2001 to $50 million last year. In March 2004 the company became the only American-spawned Chinese high-tech firm to float a public offering, listing its shares on Nasdaq. The IPO brought in $86 million; Sulger's stake was worth about $30 million.

The score, by all accounts, makes Sulger the biggest equity-market winner to date among American entrepreneurs in China. But he's not cashing in his chips. Even before Linktone went public, Sulger founded Smartpay, which enables bill payments over cellular networks. Smartpay already has 175 employees and eight offices, and Sulger, now the company's CFO, says it will thrive if it grabs even a tiny share of the mushrooming number of mobile-phone payment transactions in China. He expects to eventually take Smartpay public too.

Sulger's initial insight—putting a local face on the company as soon as possible—also helped counter a problem that undid many other American wireless and Web entrepreneurs. The Chinese are masters at rapidly mimicking almost any newly established service or product and using guanxi—connections and cronyism—to basically steal away customers. That problem confronts almost every American in China at some point, regardless of industry or niche. By rapidly converting a foreign startup into a Chinese company, with mostly Chinese managers and employees, Sulger in effect created his own guanxi. He's taking the same approach at Smartpay; Sulger is its only American employee. He feels pretty good about his future in China. "Not a lot of Americans have made it big here," he says. "I did it once, and I can do it again."

Go Native, but Think Different

One man has single-handedly produced the three top-grossing native-language films of all time in China. His name is Peter Loehr. He's a New Yorker.

Loehr, 37, has become the unlikely king of China's film industry by essentially turning Chinese. Like a growing number of outsiders, he has mastered the language and absorbed the culture to gain a deep knowledge of the idiosyncratic ways of Chinese business—and to reduce or eliminate altogether his dependence on local partners.

Idea No. 19—Sell services to remote offices of global corporations.

As a teenager in Brooklyn, Loehr was fascinated by Asia and filmmaking—particularly the work of the Japanese master Akira Kurosawa. Loehr moved to Japan after college and caught the attention of Japanese media execs impressed with his artistic bent. By the time he arrived in Beijing in 1996, Loehr had already produced television programs in both Japan and Taiwan. He'd also studied Mandarin intensely, ultimately reading entire film scripts in the language. Initially bankrolled by a Taiwanese media company, Loehr formed indie studio Imar Film with the goal of nurturing local talent. He plucked out of obscurity a novice director named Zhang Yang; their first movie, *Spicy Love Soup,* was made for $362,000 and grossed 10 times that, making it the top domestic release at the box office in 1998. Loehr later broke with his Taiwanese backers and set up his own company, Ming Productions, which has produced two films so far and has three more in the pipeline.

Loehr's success, while inspired by art, is built on a keen grasp of how Chinese business really works. He is widely considered to have been the first of a new generation of moviemakers in China to recognize the importance of distribution in a country where provincial exhibitors tend to run their turf like personal fiefdoms. When China's few national distributors declined to handle *Spicy Love Soup,* Loehr toured 28 cities by train, lugging along two steel boxes containing his film. He wooed local distributors in all-night drinking and karaoke sessions. "I learned to hold my liquor," he says. He also came away with 40 deals.

Loehr understands Chinese traditions, but he also breaks new ground. In 1997 he became the first to advertise a film on television—and on radio and bus billboards. Recently he formed a new joint venture, Dragon Studios, to handle the needs of foreign filmmakers who want to use China as a shooting location. In a shrewd move, he's offering Hollywood (with which he has links through dealmaker CAA, where he's a consultant) a turnkey solution: He provides not only technical talent but also local actors. His company has deals to assist on four foreign films this year. Loehr says he regularly turns down seven-figure offers, mostly from Asian investors, for a piece of his empire. "I'd rather go it alone," he says.

Try to Get Rich Quick, but Prepare to Put in the Time

The business education of Chris Barclay took 11 years. It started inauspiciously, shortly after Barclay arrived in Beijing in 1994. China wasn't as alien to him as it is to some Americans—he spoke good Mandarin and had lived in Taiwan. But he didn't have much of a clue about Chinese business, and the stories he heard about it curled his toes. One of his first local acquaintances was an American who wanted to make a speedy killing by becoming the hot dog king of China. The guy got a license from Beijing officials to sell wieners from street carts. He bought 1,000 carts and one morning unleashed an army of hot dog peddlers. Within a few hours, the police had impounded his carts. "I have a permit," the American protested. The police laughed. "You have one permit," a police official told him. "You need one for each cart." The would-be hot dog king was 999 permits short, and the dream died then and there.

Barclay took many lessons from the episode, but one stood out: Don't try to get rich quick in China. Sure, it happens. "But longevity is key," he says, "You've got to survive your failures."

He endured several himself, including an ill-fated attempt to sell basketballs, before arriving at an insight that has proven valuable for many American entrepreneurs. The easiest way to make money in China today, Barclay says, is to serve the thousands of large American and European corporations flooding into the country. In 1995, with $10,000 in cash, Barclay started a company that offers management training for local Chinese employees of Adidas, Coca-Cola, ConocoPhillips, Sun Microsystems, and other multinationals. To enhance his training business, he opened a hotel on a mountainside near the southern city of Guangzhou, where he supplements workshops with outdoor activities like rock climbing and hiking. Together, the ventures bring in about $2 million a year and earned about $400,000 in profit in 2004. Barclay has 30 full-time employees. He's the lone foreigner. He recently received a seven-figure offer from a U.S. consulting firm for his training business alone, and he's considering selling that branch of his business.

But Barclay wants to expand his resort company, which is why on a recent afternoon he stands beneath a leaky umbrella near the famed Simatai section of the Great Wall. He has come to negotiate with a group of farmers over the lease of five acres of idle land on which he hopes to build a 25-room hotel for Wall tourists. "The farmers might not be interested," he says. "They might not even show up."

He is unfazed by the prospect, but the farmers do show eventually. One man steps forward and names his price: $1,200 a year. Five minutes later another farmer arrives and explains that the first farmer is not authorized to negotiate. Barclay rolls with it, and soon a deal is struck: He'll pay $833 a year for five lush acres. But another snag later develops: The farmer doesn't have the government clearance required to take farmland out of circulation. Shades of the hot dog king. Barclay says he'll keep the resort expansion project on low boil until the paperwork comes through. "I won't make any big plans until I can see the documentation," he says.

Idea No. 20—Get a job with a multinational to spot startup opportunities.

The Fung brothers likewise believe in patience as a business strategy. Micky Fung, a Chinese American whose home base is Brooklyn, N.Y., has been doing business in China since the 1980s, moving from one niche to another. These days he's leading a pioneering effort to supply every taxicab in the country with a flat-panel TV screen that, controlled by a computer under the front seat, will broadcast advertisements (and potentially other content) to its captive audience of passengers. Shanghai has been chosen for a large-scale trial of the technology. Fung has signed up 10,000 Shanghai taxis and will roll out the system later this year. Heineken, Nokia, and Virgin are already on board as advertisers. Fung's brother has bought an entire fleet of taxis to help exploit the opportunity. "It's a landgrab, pure and simple," says Adam Bornstein, an American financier in China and one of Fung's backers.

Fung says he's never seen as many foreigners looking to get rich quick as there are in China today. But that's the wrong play, he says; he's looking for lasting relationships. "A common mistake made by outsiders is to avoid long-term deals," Fung explains from his Shanghai office. "Then they have a hit product or service that they can't capitalize on because they are vulnerable to simply being replaced." Long-term deals offer a way around this problem. Fung, for instance, is signing 10-year deals with his taxi owners.

"In 10 years, a whole lot can change," including the basic technology behind his company, he says. "But by then I'll have made my money, and I'll have a position worth defending."

Feel Free to Change the World, but Don't Think You Can Change China

One tried-and-true way to hit the ground running in China is to enter the country as an employee of a big multinational and then strike out on your own. But it's wise to check your idealism at the door. Terry Rhoads, an Oregon native, was sent to China in 1994 by Nike and ran marketing for the shoe giant before starting his own company, Zou Marketing, with a fellow Nike alum. Today, Zou is the nation's leading sports marketing company, with 33 employees and annual revenue of $5 million. The company advises China's fledgling pro basketball league and runs the National Football League's ambitious program to export the all-American sport to China.

Rhoads says pragmatism is a must to do business in China. For example, the government remains a huge presence in professional sports, which are only now developing, and Rhoads privately questions some of its policies. Top basketball players, for instance, are forced to play meaningless games for the country's Olympic and national teams, often leaving them exhausted. (Houston Rockets center Yao Ming is widely considered a victim of this practice.) But Rhoads isn't about to campaign for better treatment of athletes. That's because he needs the cooperation of China's official sports agencies to land deals. A Chinese star who plays for the NBA's Miami Heat refused to play for the national team at last year's Olympics and is now persona non grata not only to the Chinese government but also to the entire sports marketing establishment. Rhoads empathizes with the player but won't have anything to do with him, fearful of provoking retaliation from the government. "We retain our credibility, our influence, so we can work behind the scenes for the right things," he says.

Idea No. 21—Cash in on American cachet by making yourself a celebrity.

Simeon Schnapper also had to lose some illusions on the road to entrepreneurial success in China. A 32-year-old American convert to Buddhism who visited the country in 2003 to help a nonprofit that's rebuilding Tibetan monasteries damaged by Chinese attacks in the 1960s, Schnapper eventually decided to relocate permanently to Shanghai. He joined a team of Germans who were trying to build the tallest skyscraper on the planet as the centerpiece of Shanghai's 2010 World's Fair. Despite a year of cultivating guanxi, the Germans didn't get the deal. Schnapper was crushed. "I was wallowing in my own ash heap of disillusion and remorse," he says. But by then he had a spacious high-rise apartment full of Tibetan art, and he didn't want to leave China for good. So he flew to New York and met a friend who now works at the Home Shopping Network. Over a drink they concocted an unlikely mission: figuring out how to supply one of HSN's star housewares brands, Joy Mangano, with a new line of branded hangers. It turns out that every year, consumers buy Joy Mangano Huggable Hangers from HSN by the millions.

Forthwith, Schnapper became a hanger expert. He found several factories outside Shanghai that could produce a strong, cheap plastic hanger with a special felt covering to keep clothes properly situated. Schnapper also learned that the current generation of hangers carry "Made in China" stickers that get caught on clothes, irking customers. Schnapper asked factories to stamp the country of origin into the plastic, eliminating the tag. That innovation clinched the deal: HSN ordered millions of hangers from Schnapper's company. If he meets his production targets this year, he will earn millions of dollars from hangers. Pondering the possibility, Schnapper shakes his head. "Only in China," he observes.

Focus Not on America's Cultural Values, but on the Value of Its Culture

As in much of the world, Americans and American culture are often viewed in China with a mixture of repulsion and fascination. Andrew Ballen has ridden the second part of that equation to improbable heights.

Ballen arrived in China four years ago "on a whim," he says. A native of New York, Ballen, now 32, had dropped out of Duke University's law school, angering his father, a high-achieving Jamaican immigrant who is a physician in North Carolina. Ballen wanted to get far away from the scene of his failure, and China seemed about as far away as he could go. He didn't know a soul in China. He didn't speak a word of Chinese.

To cushion his landing, he took a job at one of China's leading for-profit language schools. After a month, he realized two things. First, he'd never earn enough money as an English teacher to live well in China. Second, Chinese youth were mesmerized by hip-hop. "As an American black kid, I knew something about hip-hop," Ballen says.

He'd never done serious performing in America, but Ballen quickly started his own weekly Thursday night hip-hop show in Shanghai, renting out a club, paying a flat fee to the Chinese owner, and keeping the $4 entrance fee and a slice of the bar take. He canvassed top universities, distributing fliers to students to announce his opening night. He did the same in expat neighborhoods, concentrating on women. "Get the hot women, and the hot men follow," Ballen says, summarizing his marketing strategy.

Three hundred people turned out to hear Ballen rap and DJ on opening night, and kids keep coming back, in increasingly large numbers. On a recent Thursday night, Ballen takes in $3,200 from the gate, and the bar soaks up more than $10,000. In the four-year history of the show, Ballen has grossed nearly $2 million.

The rap gig launched a burgeoning multimedia empire. A few months after his debut in the club, Ballen started an English-language radio talk show where he spoke frankly about romance and the anxieties of youth. The talk show led to a deal with Motorola; Ballen became "the voice" for some cell-phone services. Next he started a popular TV travel program, striking an innovative deal with one of Shanghai's leading stations that allowed him to sell advertising and keep the lion's share of the take.

Andrew Ballen is now a star in China. He moves around the country with two Chinese assistants, one of them on hand simply to answer his mobile phone. The endorsement deals keep coming; even his old employer, the language school, pays him more than $1,000 a month to be a pitchman. He is frequently stopped on the street by Chinese who want to shake his hand or buy him a beer.

On a recent Friday, after staying up all night at the hip-hop club, Ballen snatches a few hours of sleep, then goes into a studio to do a radio commercial. Next he grabs a late breakfast and gulps down two cups of coffee before locking himself away to write a script for his next TV episode. Between paragraphs, he ponders how someone who never ran a business in the United States could launch so many, so quickly, in a country he still barely comprehends. "I have nothing," he says, "but my imagination."

A lot of people thought Stuart Eunson had too much imagination when he arrived in China in 1993. Craving his java, he decided to try to trigger an American-style coffee craze. "Don't you know they drink tea in China?" asked one doubter—his mom. After getting off the ground in 1994, for five years Eunson's company, Arabica Coffee Roasters, barely stayed afloat. "I almost starved," he says. But around 2000, as China became increasingly intrigued by all things Western, the American custom of chugging lattes began to catch on. Now Eunson supplies high-end restaurants and hotels with premium roasted coffees and adds value by teaching clients how to make a good cup of cappuccino.

China's economic transformation may ultimately rank as one of the greatest producers of business opportunity ever. But the process won't last forever. Indeed, some experts think that within a decade, many niches will have been filled, industries will have dominant players, infrastructure will have been built. There will be much less room then for foreign entrepreneurs—which is another reason young guns like Comiskey and Mulkerin are taking their shot in China now.

In another expat bar on another Shanghai evening, Comiskey and Tsai are raving about the possibilities unfolding all around them. "He's mad for China," says Tsai, who is a third partner in the outsourcing enterprise. She worries that her husband may be overoptimistic, and that the windows of opportunity might snap shut, leaving American entrepreneurs scrambling. But Comiskey seems to thrive on scrambling. And if things fall apart? Comiskey's been traveling around the region a bit lately, scoping things out. If China doesn't work out for him, well, there's always India.

G. PASCAL ZACHARY (gzachary@business2.com) is a senior writer at *Business 2.0.*

The China Factor

Navigating Risk in a Land of Opportunity

For manufacturers struggling to map their future in a global economy, where the signs and landmarks shift with dizzying speed, the question of the moment is this: What will be the impact of China?

Manufacturers know that China will transform how they do business in the future. To be successful in the global marketplace, it is important that they devise a strategy that not only addresses near-term challenges but longer-term opportunities as well. A successful approach to China requires enhancing an understanding of how China differs from other markets they are accustomed to and how China is evolving, both internally and as a player in the global economy. Using that understanding, manufacturers can put together the right strategy, structure, people and processes to achieve their vision.

Manufacturers must consider that China-related opportunities are growing and diversifying. China is no longer just a low-cost source of goods but also an increasingly sophisticated manufacturing center and consumer market in its own right. The facts are both heartening and sobering. Competing successfully in today's China is directly tied to remaining competitive everywhere else.

Manufacturing at a Crossroads

Having become the world's factory and the leading destination for global foreign investment, China's economy has boomed. Not only is China the preferred location for sourcing goods but also its domestic market is quickly achieving critical mass, driving global companies to increasingly target Chinese consumers. With strong productivity gains, increasing deregulation and privatization, reduced trade barriers and excellent labor force development, China is now the place to be and be with.

For the world's leading companies, this means that China is an increasingly important part of what they do. The sheer size of China's economy means that policy decisions made in Beijing will have ramifications for the rest of the world. For manufacturers, that means keeping a close eye on China, even if they don't have operations there. Finally, China's path to greater affluence and power will not be without volatility. Understanding the risks and planning for them will be critical for any company doing business in China.

The China Opportunity

Few corners of the world are more promising for manufacturers—or more intimidating—than China. China's entry into the World Trade Organization, continuing industrial consolidation, and social and economic reforms have rapidly brought China's industry to global prominence, if not preeminence. In fact, industry in China is evolving at a pace so rapid that it almost defies comprehension—yet to remain competitive, every manufacturing executive must understand this large and nimble competitor.

According to a recent study by *IndustryWeek* and the Manufacturing Performance Institute, manufacturers now play in a highly competitive global marketplace, and many of them look to China not only to purchase low-cost components but also to establish new world-class facilities of their own. Yet China's domestic players are not standing still.

Revenue projections for China's manufacturers in 2005 make an impressive case: 84 percent expect their revenues to increase. And China's impact on the profitability of U.S. manufacturers is undeniable: Across an array of industry sectors, 25 percent or more of U.S. plants reported decreased profitability last year.

A comparative analysis of the investment patterns of U.S. manufacturers versus their Chinese counterparts is revealing:

- U.S. manufacturing plants spent 3 percent of sales on capital equipment in 2004; the figure for China was 20 percent.
- In the United States, 53 percent of manufacturing plants were expected to increase their capital-equipment spending in 2005; the comparable number for China was 72 percent.
- IT spending was expected to increase at 42 percent of U.S. plants in 2005; in China, 75 percent of plants were expected to increase their spending on IT.

A comparison of human resource expenditures is even more stunning: Median monthly manufacturing wages (160 hours) are $2,160 in the United States and just $120.80 in China.

In short, the study indicates that China has a manufacturing base that is more cost-efficient today and investing more heavily in the capital equipment and IT that will enable it to become more innovative tomorrow.

Additional figures paint a larger picture: Manufacturing now accounts for 53 percent of China's GDP (versus 14 percent for the United States), 90 percent of its exports (versus 62 percent for the United States), 85 percent of its imports and 70 percent of its inbound investment. China is now the world's fourth-largest producer (after the United States, Japan and Germany); it was eighth only a decade ago. In addition to a skilled low-cost industrial labor force of almost one hundred million, China is also graduating 350,000 engineers each year. This is six to seven times the number in the United States. These engineers are now joining a manufacturing sector that is far less dominated by state-owned enterprises. State-owned enterprises now account for just over one-fifth of China's industrial output, down from 51.5 percent in 1992 and over 80 percent in the late 1970s.

Clearly, the country is well on its way to becoming the "world's factory." U.S. manufacturers must be prepared for the challenge.

Navigating Opportunities and Risks

Despite the myths, U.S. manufacturers can make money in China. A 1999 survey by the American Chamber of Commerce in China found that just 10 percent of U.S. companies operating in China had margins above their global average that year. By 2004, that figure had risen to 42 percent, with another 31 percent reporting profit margins comparable to global margins. China is also the United States' fastest-growing export market. The taste for U.S. consumer goods, whether produced locally or shipped from the United States, is growing by leaps and bounds.

U.S. manufacturers are responding by expanding their understanding of opportunities in China beyond its role as the "world's factory" to include other contexts as well:

- China as a major buyer;
- China as a global investor; and
- China as a vast consumer market.

China has become the third largest importer and America's fastest-growing import market, with imports skyrocketing from $4.1 billion in 1970 to over $561 billion last year.

At the same time, China's outbound foreign direct investment topped $3.6 billion last year, which brought the cumulative total close to $45 billion from just $400 million in 1990. As Chinese companies seek their fortunes abroad, U.S. manufacturers can avail themselves of new opportunities for collaboration and partnerships.

And how vast is China's consumer market? For starters, of course, there is its population of 1.3 billion—21 percent of the world's people. Over 120 Chinese cities have a population of a million or more residents. The United States, with its population of 295 million, has only nine such cities. More importantly, an urban Chinese middle class is emerging with significant levels of disposable income. New regulations extending full trading and distribution rates to foreign manufacturers make this market more accessible then ever.

While the Chinese business environment creates opportunities, it also poses new challenges—legal and regulatory, social and cultural, as well as issues related to physical infrastructure. In order to navigate the risks associated with doing business in China, U.S. companies should seek to develop two basic understandings about the business environment:

- The gap between home and China; and
- The general direction of change.

Once this has been achieved, companies can begin to adapt their strategies, structures, people and processes to suit the China environment and begin the process of identifying and containing risk.

A wide range of best practices can then be evaluated improving operational efficiency in areas such as supply-chain management, customer service, finance, tax and IT; establishing shared service centers; getting serious about identifying and retaining human talent; organizing effective government relations offices; and so on.

Over time, a comprehensive strategy that accounts for the idiosyncrasies of China must be carefully developed.

Seizing the Opportunity

For global companies with an interest in China, the prospects for success must be viewed against the backdrop of risk. China's road to prosperity, like that of others before, will be bumpy. Navigating that road will require an understanding of the risks and the flexibility to deal with potential hurdles. A successful China strategy will require a sound understanding of the operating environment in China as well as the corporate-wide implications of conducting business there. Yet despite the scale and speed of China's economic transition, unparalleled by any country in history, U.S. manufacturers can still navigate their way through a thicket of financial and operational risk to discover the land of opportunity that China is now—and promises to remain throughout the 21st century.

If you would like to know more about developing an effective China strategy, please contact Clarence Kwan, National Managing Partner, U.S. Chinese Services Group, Deloitte & Touche USA LLP, at uscsg@deloitte.com.

If you would like to view additional material on the China Factor, please go to www.iwchinafactor.com

A Whiff of New Money

President Yudhoyono has Indonesia growing again, and investors are back. Can he keep up the momentum?

BRIAN BREMNER AND ASSIF SHAMEEN

Indonesia is a society on edge. You can see it in the eyes of security guards brandishing automatic weapons in front of all the Jakarta business hotels, poised to ward off potential terrorist attacks. Or check out the headlines: Gas and power shortages have surfaced in East Java because cash-strapped state oil giant Pertamina can't afford to import enough fuel, and the nation's energy assets have been terribly managed. In Aceh province, home to a violent separatist movement, life is still a struggle in the wake of the tsunami that killed 128,000 Indonesians and left 500,000 homeless.

Yet behind these grim realities, you sense something more in this sprawling archipelago: the scent of money. The Jakarta composite index has shot up 65% over the past year, and the economy is growing at its most rapid clip since 1996, up a surprising 6.4% year-on-year in the first quarter. Foreign direct investment commitments, which had collapsed after the fall of Suharto in 1998, have nearly doubled in the first four months of the year from the same period in 2004, to $5.5 billion. A consumer spending revival coupled with robust global demand for palm oil, coal, tin, and apparel, is fueling growth. "Whoever puts their foot in here is going to make money over the next three to five years," says Henk Mahendra, Jakarta-based president-director of Orient Technology Indonesia, which on May 30 signed a $250 million government contract to build and operate an international port in southern Sumatra.

The new optimism owes much to President Susilo Bambang Yudhoyono. The retired-general-turned-political-reformer, who earned a PhD in economics last year at the age of 55, took power in October. He beat weakened incumbent Megawati Sukarnoputri in the first direct general election in the nation's history. Yudhoyono has won international praise—and a state visit to the White House in May—for his response to the tsunami and for his blunt talk about Indonesia's problems, including terrorism and human rights abuses by the military. But what really has the markets smoking is a five-year, $145 billion spending plan he unveiled in January to upgrade the country's creaky infrastructure—everything from a $178 million Jakarta airport extension to a $1.5 billion gas pipeline. Although cash-strapped Indonesia can ill-afford such spending, Yudhoyono says foreign investors will provide at least $90 billion, then lease the facilities out to cover costs and earn a profit.

Yudhoyono has also made ending Indonesia's endemic graft a personal crusade. The country has been ranked the most corrupt in Asia for four years running, according to Hong Kong-based Political & Economic Risk Consultancy Ltd. In an interview with *BusinessWeek,* Yudhoyono said he received 5,000-plus complaints about corruption and red tape when in mid-June he invited Indonesians to call him on his personal mobile-phone number, which he made public. His phone soon crashed, but he got the message: If Indonesia doesn't clean up its act, "we will lose the battle to attract foreign capital and stimulate our domestic economy," Yudhoyono said.

Indonesia enters that battle with serious handicaps. It has been hit by two major al Qaeda-inspired bombings since 2002. Red tape has made it an expensive, frustrating place to do business, despite a large labor force and factory wages of roughly $80 per month. The country's port-handling fees are the highest in Southeast Asia. And it takes foreign businesses about five months to get a license to operate, vs. one month in Thailand, according to the World Bank.

Yudhoyono is committed to changing all that. State money is already wending its way through the economy as the government has signed off on the first of some $22 billion in expected infrastructure deals in 2005. Yudhoyono is promising 6.6% annual growth—about what's needed to create jobs for the 2.5 million young people who enter the labor force every year. Otherwise, he may not meet his goal of reducing the jobless rate from 9.5% to 5.1%.

Some observers say it'll be hard to meet those targets. Morgan Stanley economist Daniel Lian figures growth will hit 5.4% this year, with government investment accounting for four-fifths of that. It will take steady foreign investment in all sectors to give Indonesia the "structural lift" it needs, Lian figures.

Red tape has made Indonesia a frustrating place to do business

The good news is, Indonesia is back on the investment radar. Yudhoyono has met with foreign investors and pressed the bureaucracy to speed up license approvals. That has paid off. Malaysia's Maxis Communications ponied up $100 million for Lippo Telecom in February, while Hong Kong's Hutchison Telecom spent $120 million for mobile carrier Cyber Access Communications in March. That same month, Philip Morris International Inc. agreed to a $5.2 billion takeover of No. 3 cigarette maker Hanjaya Mandala Sampoerna.

Easily Tarnished

Yet keeping that kind of momentum going will be hard. Yudhoyono is popular, but his legislative clout is limited. His coalition controls less than half of the Parliament, and few in the opposition like Yudhoyono's strategy of kick-starting growth with big-ticket infrastructure projects when government money is tight. "The quality of the growth is the big question," says Rama Pratama, a Parliament member from the Islamic Justice & Prosperity Party. If the economy doesn't grow fast enough to improve the lives of ordinary citizens, Yudohoyono's halo might start to tarnish. "I am afraid people's patience will end, and then we will have trouble," says former President Abdurrahman Wahid, a longtime rival.

Another big terrorist attack could unwind the economic gains. "We are conducting massive intelligence and police operations to find the cells," says Yudhoyono, though he concedes that the threat of an attack is "very real." Given everything that the country has been through, Indonesians desperately hope Yudhoyono can bring them prosperity and stability—and even let the security guards relax their white-knuckled grip on those rifles.

BRIC Crumbling?

Corruption in Russia and a Brazilian economy that continues to protect domestic producers are just two reasons to question the investment attention U.S. manufacturers have been giving to the BRIC countries—Brazil, Russia, India and China. But pulling out in favor of Eastern Europe or Vietnam may not be the answer for many manufacturers either. Time to reconsider Mexico? Here's what you need to know to determine whether the business risks remain acceptable.

JOHN S. MCCLENAHEN

N ordson Corp., a Westlake, Ohio-based maker of systems that apply adhesives, sealants and coatings during manufacturing, is considering increasing its presence in Russia, a country where corruption corrodes the business climate.

What is Edward P. Campbell, Nordson's chairman and CEO, thinking? Campbell is thinking strategically.

Nordson is "considering forming a direct subsidiary in Russia—although we've not made a commitment to do so," says Campbell. "What we're talking about is a very limited investment; the exposure we would have is not large in financial terms," he stresses.

Nordson is considering a wholly owned subsidiary as a base for providing local service to its equipment customers in Russia and for partnering with some of its customers in developing specifications for next-generation Nordson products. "We're not talking about manufacturing; we're not talking about sourcing any components for our factories in the West," Campbell emphasizes. For about a decade, Nordson, an $838 million company with 67% of its sales outside the U.S. in 2005, has primarily served the Russian market from Europe, with its "direct investment" in Russia limited to not more than a couple of employees at any one time, Campbell notes.

For about five years, Russia has been one of the four so-called "BRIC" nations—the others are Brazil, India and China—that have attracted substantial interest, and sometimes substantial investment, from U.S.-based manufacturers. But with the Czech Republic, Poland, Hungary, Vietnam, and, again, Mexico emerging as significant markets and places of production, is BRIC crumbling? Not really. Rather there seems to be less hype and more reality about BRIC's place in a world in which manufacturers are chasing lower costs of production and distribution and seeking new markets.

Update, by Country

Brazil. Has a history of high inflation, high interest rates and high import duties to protect domestic industry. But "the macroeconomic climate has been fairly stable . . . under [President Luiz Inácia] Lula [da Silva]," notes Thomas Duesterberg, president and CEO of Manufacturers Alliance/MAPI, an Arlington, Va.-based business and public policy research group with about 450 member companies.

The ethanol industry is growing, and Brazil has a lot of iron ore, to which the Chinese increasingly are trying to get access, says Duesterberg. Nordson has had sales and service operations in Brazil for 15 years, but no manufacturing.

Brazil is closer to the U.S. than China, meaning goods arrive faster, but the cost of labor is higher because of Brazil's currently booming economy, says Kurt Cavano, CEO of New York-based TradeCard Inc., a firm that offers technologies to automate trade transactions. Brazil is in the same time zones as the U.S., meaning "you don't have to be up all night or have an agent there," he adds.

Auto companies and consumer packaged goods producers have built operations in Brazil, and "they've been fairly successful," observes Kevin Prouty, senior director for manufacturing solutions at Symbol Technologies Inc., a Boston-based provider of mobility solutions. Brazil is "just such a large, economically stable population you really can't ignore it," he asserts. The country is a "reasonably good" place in the long run, adds Conrad Winkler, a Chicago-based vice president of consulting firm Booz Allen Hamilton who focuses on manufacturing and supply chain strategies.

Russia. "A good choice" if you're shipping into Europe rather than the U.S., believes TradeCard's Cavano. "Probably not a low-cost producer for [manufacturers in] the United States,

[but] it would probably be a low-cost producer for Western Europe," says Symbol's Prouty.

Russia's big negatives are logistics problems and organized crime, states Cavano. The Russians "appear to want to control the extractive industries pretty closely. [And] even some of the other major industries, like telecommunications, appear in recent years to have come under the sway of the authorities, the groups closely tied to the centers of political power," says the Manufacturers Alliance's Duesterberg. "We hear very little among our members about investment in Russia," he relates.

Of the four BRIC countries, the risk of the government taking away a company's business—or that someone will take away the business and the government won't protect the company—is probably highest in Russia, believes Booz Allen's Winkler.

Outside the energy sector, U.S. companies have been slow to locate in Russia, confirms Dan McCarthy, distinguished professor of global management and innovation at Northeastern University's School of Business in Boston. "For the most part, because of the obsolete condition of the manufacturing sector in general in Russia, [U.S. manufacturers] have to go in through another [company's] greenfield [investment]," adds Sheila Puffer, another professor at Northeastern's business school.

India. Of the four BRIC countries, India "has the most long-term potential," claims Prouty. "They have a fairly stable economy. They still have a significant amount of protectionism in place, but that slowly has been loosening. In the next 10 to 12 years you will probably see [India] outpace China in true manufacturing economic growth—both as a low-cost producer and as a consumer."

Nordson has had sales and service operations in India for a decade—and has added product development and software development activities. But for Nordson, India represents lower rates of demand and growth for its products than does China.

"Indian companies have accepted the fact that they are never going to catch the Chinese on low-cost manufacturing," says Michael Treacy, a founder and chief strategy officer at Boston-based Gen3 Partners Inc. "India is challenged by basic infrastructure issues like roads," cautions Manoj Kumar, a Mountain View, Calif.-based director of PRTM Management Consultants. TradeCard's Cavano agrees, noting difficulties in getting goods off the coast. Then there's the distance from the U.S., he adds. Having a reliable power supply is another issue, adds Booz Allen's Winkler.

China. "China clearly is the most mature outsourcing location for manufacturing today," contends PRTM's Kumar. In China, labor is cheap, logistics between China and the U.S. are good, and in China there are partners U.S. manufacturers can work with "to make things happen," states TradeCard's Cavano. What's more, "if you're selling components for goods that are going to get re-exported," China is a pretty easy place from which to get your money out," he judges.

During the past five years or so, China has been creating more scientists and engineers, and that's starting to draw more foreign direct investment in R&D centers than the other three BRIC countries, says New York-based Gary Coleman, global

Where to Locate?

The questions you need to ask to assess risk.

1. What is the socio-economic climate of the region like? What's the work ethic? How about skills? Can I get good labor? Is labor reliable? What is the pay rate?

2. Is the area safe from terrorists? Are employees likely to be affected by diseases and pandemics? Is this an area that encounters floods, hurricanes and tsunamis frequently?

3. What transportation modes are available in, out and around the region? Roads? Rail? Seaports? Airports? How reliable is the power grid?

4. What sources of supply are available? Are they of the quality you need to make your products? Are they reliable? Need to qualify a secondary source? Does the length of the supply chain create reliability, time and cost issues?

5. What's the legal and regulatory environment? How stable is the government? What's the extent of ownership allowed? Taxation? Duties? How about intellectual property rights—and their enforcement?

managing director, manufacturing industries, at Deloitte Services LLP. And as a consumer market, "blink an eye and China will be Hong Kong," says Gen3's Treacy.

On the other hand, China "is really far away," which puts the supply chain at added risk from such events as natural disasters and port closures, Cavano warns.

"China has said it does not want to be just a low-cost producer for manufacturing. So they've started to make it a little more difficult to invest in manufacturing in China," states Symbol's Prouty. Another negative: China "is still a dictatorship," reminds Deloitte's Coleman. "The laws can be rewritten overnight."

Beyond BRIC

Nordson's Campbell continues to see "good rates of growth" for its products in Mexico and in Spain, where he reports "excellent growth . . . on a consistent basis."

"Mexico is a very attractive way to serve the U.S. market with any product that needs to be made to order. It is a very effective low-cost location. It's so close to whole swaths of the U.S. market like the Southwest, Texas and California," says Winkler. "I don't expect electronics to come back to Mexico, but for other industries it could make a lot of sense—building products, automotive supplies," he says.

"If you have larger components that have obvious shipping constraints, then maybe you ought to think about sourcing closer to home" than China, adds Pittsburgh-based Pat Furey, senior category manager in the global sourcing operations at Ariba Inc., a technology-based business-to-business services firm.

Among Manufacturers Alliance/MAPI members, "the Czech Republic seems to be a favorite place," says Duesterberg. "We hear more and more about Poland because it's not a bad environment and the domestic market is big," he adds. "Interestingly enough we hear a bit about the so-called Baltics—Estonia, Latvia and Lithuania. All have surprisingly good governance, with maybe Estonia coming out on top. [They have] low taxes and a lighter hand on regulations."

"We are hearing a bit more about southeast Asia, especially Vietnam," Duesterberg continues. "Low cost. Big domestic market. Still very poor, but increasingly attractive in terms of its stability. Economy growing. Large population so it can be something of an export platform. Think about the potential domestic market as well." He doesn't think Vietnam will develop into another Asian Tiger, but that being said, "Vietnam is going to start to grow pretty fast." Symbol's Prouty foresees some of the low cost of production investment in China being shifted to Vietnam.

The Brave New World of IFRS

IFRS have been widely accepted, and are expected to enhance international financial reporting transparency, comparability and investment patterns. This progress will not come, however, without some unintended impacts on companies, countries and capital markets.

EVA K. JERMAKOWICZ AND SYLWIA GORNIK-TOMASZEWSKI

The year 2005 should be proclaimed "The Year of International Financial Reporting Standards (IFRS)." Thousands upon thousands of companies around the world are getting ready to prepare their 2005 financial statements, and at least one year of comparatives, according to a set of accounting standards they have never used before. IFRS were promulgated by the International Accounting Standards Board (IASB), headquartered in London.

A worldwide consensus has been building for many years on the need for high-quality global accounting standards that would better serve investors and facilitate more efficient allocation of capital. This is why the European Union (EU) introduced a regulation requiring all companies listed on a regulated market, including banks and insurance companies, to prepare their consolidated financial statements in accordance with IFRS from 2005 onwards. EU member states have the option to extend this requirement to unlisted companies and to unconsolidated financial statements.

Everywhere IFRS are being implemented, organizations are struggling to come to grips with the new system. The situation is particularly difficult in the EU, where companies are overwhelmed with a multitude of new regulatory demands coming into effect almost simultaneously—requirements under the impending Basel II Accord, a new Prospectus Directive and others resulting from the implementation of the Financial Services Action Plan. In addition, companies listed in the U.S. have to comply with the Sarbanes-Oxley Act.

Transition to IFRS—Much More Than an Accounting Issue

Implementing IFRS brings the need for change in the format of accounts, different accounting policies and more extensive disclosure requirements. In many EU countries, technical differences between local generally accepted accounting principles (GAAP) and IFRS are numerous, and the costly and resource-consuming conversion process could last up to 24 months.

Many organizations are experiencing a shortage of well-trained personnel, and there are necessary IT system changes and enhancements to be made. For many, it is not a matter of just replacing one accounting system with another, but rather the addition of a new accounting system on top of the existing one still to be used for statutory purposes.

Most companies adopt IFRS not only for the consolidated accounts, but also for internal management use in the parent and subsidiaries. Harmonization and streamlining of internal and external reporting by creating a single accounting language across the business is often listed among the most important benefits of conversion. The new accounting system may affect bonus and reward schemes, treasury options, business combinations, measurement and treatment of intangible assets, leases, financial instruments, tax liabilities and debt covenants.

Some European companies in EU member states are exempted until 2007 from adopting IFRS. This exemption is for companies that are listed in both the EU and in another non-EU jurisdiction (such as the U.S.) and that are following another internationally recognized set of accounting standards (such as U.S. GAAP).

One key challenge in adopting IFRS is their use of fair value as the primary basis of asset/liability measurement.

"The IASB advocates its fair value approach on the grounds of relevance; the board quite simply considers fair value to be the most relevant measurement basis," says Allister Wilson, senior technical partner with Ernst & Young. "We are concerned that the IASB has placed too much emphasis on 'relevant' information and has given insufficient consideration to the other attributes [of accounting information], in particular reliability and understandability," he adds.

Also, banks and insurance companies have been the biggest opponents of the controversial International Accounting Standard 39 (IAS 39) *Financial Instruments: Recognition and*

Measurement, which requires the use of fair values for financial instruments such as derivatives.

This valuation approach may bring increased volatility in the reported values of assets as well as earnings. Under pressure from the banking sector, the European Commission (EC) deleted certain sections of IAS 39. Now, management will have to take actions to manage the volatility associated with conversion to IFRS.

An initial period of volatility in accounting numbers, lasting a few years, is expected and comparisons among companies will not be always an easy task. Common sense suggests that investors should look beyond net income forecasts to gauge how accounts will be affected by the switch to IFRS this year.

Growing Prominence of IFRS

All 25 EU member states and a number of other countries are implementing IFRS, indicating their growing prominence. IFRS already represent the standard, or the basis of standards, in many countries worldwide. Australia has decided to adopt national equivalents of IFRS (so-called A-IFRS) by the 2005–2006 fiscal year. Among other countries that have indicated they will or may move to IFRS are South Africa, China and Russia. It is estimated that about 15,000 listed companies will produce annual financial statements in compliance with IFRS this year.

Authorities in European countries are considering whether to extend the application of the EU regulation to unlisted companies and individual accounts. So far, most of the countries have permitted or even required IFRS for the consolidated statements of all, or at least some, unlisted companies.

More difficult decisions are to be made as to individual accounts. Some member states will permit at least some listed companies to prepare individual accounts under IFRS. But the extension of the regulation to individual accounts is not expected in the near future in countries such as Germany, France or Belgium, where individual accounts are traditionally used for statutory purposes, such as for determination of taxable income.

The impact of the changes taking place abroad on U.S. standard-setters and regulators is remarkable. In 2002, the U.S. Financial Accounting Standards Board (FASB) and the IASB signed the Norwalk Agreement committing them to converge their accounting standards.

In April 2005, the process of convergence received a new impetus as the U.S. Securities and Exchange Commission (SEC) and the EU reached an agreement on a roadmap that sets out steps the SEC will take to eliminate the need for non-U.S. companies using IFRS to reconcile to U.S. GAAP in order to access U.S. capital markets, possibly as soon as 2007, but no later than 2009. All major stock exchanges across the world accept IFRS, except those in the U.S. and Japan.

EU regulation on implementing IFRS will have significant implications for international corporations as well. U.S. subsidiaries of parent companies located in the EU, as well as U.S. companies with operations in the EU, will need to file IFRS-based reports. International joint ventures will also be affected by IFRS.

Areas for Future Exploration

Although IFRS will continue to evolve, in their current form, the standards are shorter and less detailed than U.S. GAAP. It is expected that the demand for more interpretations and detailed implementation guidance may increase significantly after 2005 as the number of companies applying IFRS increases. This means that initially, judgment will be used often, so application of the standards could be slightly inconsistent across the market.

A lot will depend on the auditing function. The EC proposed a new Directive on Statutory Audit of Annual Accounts and Consolidated Accounts. The proposal would adopt international standards on auditing and many other measures improving audit quality throughout Europe.

Enforcement is also extremely important. High-quality financial reporting depends on it, but at the present time, securities regulation in Europe is jurisdiction-specific and varies among countries. Moving toward IFRS may create the need for a single EU enforcement body.

National authorities in continental European countries will need to find solutions for organizing the tax computation in the future. A significant disharmony may arise between individual and consolidated accounts; companies will need to maintain complex and costly parallel running of the two or even three accounting systems, creating barriers to corporate development and competition between companies.

Questions also remain about what to do with small and medium-sized entities (SMEs). For example, in the EU, IFRS will be required for consolidated financial statements of approximately 7,000 listed companies in 2005, while about 5 million unlisted SMEs will most likely follow national standards. The IASB has an active project on IFRS for SMEs, with the likely result that these entities will eventually have the option of using a set of standards aimed specifically at smaller entities and aligned with IFRS.

IFRS has been accepted widely, since it is expected to enhance international financial reporting transparency, comparability and investment patterns, resulting in an efficient global financial market and increased economic growth. Some indicate that the EU regulation will have various unintended and unexplored impacts on corporate, economic and social life. IFRS impacts on corporate governance, human resource management, strategy or macroeconomic planning should be investigated.

Eva K. Jermakowicz, Ph.D., CPA (Ejermako@usi.edu) is Professor of Accounting in the Department of Accounting and Business Law at the University of Southern Indiana. Sylwia Gornik-Tomaszewski (gornikts@stjohns.edu), DBA, CMA, CFM is assistant Professor in the Department of Accounting and Taxation in the Peter J. Tobin College of Business at St. John's University.

From *Financial Executive,* November 2005. Copyright © 2005 by Financial Executives International (FEI). Reprinted by permission from FEI, 200 Campus Drive, Florham Park, NJ 07932-0674, ph. 973.765.1000; www.fei.org.

Found in Translation

A Guide to Using Foreign Financial Statements

Susan M. Sorensen and Donald L. Kyle

Your Monday is off to a reasonably good start. The improvements you made last year to your company's financial reporting system are paying off. You're getting data faster and your boss, the president, is delighted with the new reports you created. But this morning's call is not a request for yet another report.

"Did you see what we're paying for bearings for the new 800s?" blurts your boss. "Every time we turn around, our domestic supplier hikes prices. I've found a new supplier, and it's for sale."

"Good," you reply "Where is it located?"

"Ukraine," he says. "And I want you to take a look at its financials. They're in English."

If you have not already experienced this situation, you may soon. Globalization, once the exclusive realm of America's largest companies, is now a reality for companies of all sizes—so all financial managers and CPAs must be prepared to work with foreign financial statements. You may need to include information from foreign statements in your own statements or tax returns, or to rely upon foreign financials when making investment decisions, securing credit or using foreign outsourcing firms. CPAs in industry may find themselves dealing with foreign subsidiaries or working for a subsidiary of a foreign company

As CPAs, you have expectations about language, currency, accounting practices, methods and presentation when reading and analyzing U.S. GAAP statements. When dealing with foreign or transnational statements—even if they are presumed to be prepared using U.S. GAAP—be ready to adjust your expectations.

Know Common Approaches

When providing statements to foreign users, companies adopt a variety of approaches based on factors such as language, currency and accounting practices. These cover the spectrum from not changing the primary foreign statement at all to preparing primary statements using U.S. GAAP (see exhibit 1). The specific approach may not be obvious and may vary from year to year. The options include:

Doing nothing. If a company chooses to provide its primary statements without making any changes, it often

Understanding IASs and IFRSs

International Accounting Standards (IASs) were issued by the International Accounting Standards Committee (IASC) from 1973 to 2000. Although the IASC Foundation continues as the parent body of the International Accounting Standards Board (IASB), in 2001 the IASB took over the IASCs standard-setting activities. The IASB has amended some IASs and proposed to amend others, proposed to replace some IASs with new International Financial Reporting Standards (IFRSs) and adopted or proposed certain new IFRSs on topics for which there were no previous IASs. Through committees, both the IASC and the IASB also have issued interpretations of standards. Financial statements may not be described as complying with IFRSs unless they comply with all the requirements of each applicable standard and interpretation.

Source: Deloittes's IAS Plus Web site. www.iasplug.com/standard/standard.htm.

will be apparent because the statements will be written in a foreign language.

Primary statements under U.S. GAAP. Many foreign companies choose to prepare primary statements using U.S. GAAP.

Convenience translation. Companies may translate the language into English, but provide no information about the accounting practices and currency Volvo's balance sheet in exhibit 2, is an example of a convenience translation. The currency is the Swedish krona (SEK) and the format does not follow U.S. GAAP.

Convenience statements. These contain translated language and, often, converted currency. They still lack information CPAs need about accounting practices, the translation method and bow the currency was converted. Do not assume they are in or comparable with U.S. GAAP. Even large companies may choose to use convenience statements. Suzuki Motor Corp., for example,

Exhibit 1 Behind the Numbers

Common approaches foreign businesses take when providing financial statements to U.S. investors/creditors.

Approach	Language	Currency	Accounting Principles	Selected Items Reconciled to U.S. GAAP	Statements Reconciled to U.S. GAAP
Do nothing	Foreign*	Foreign*	Foreign	No	No
Primary statements prepared under U.S. GAAP	English	U.S.	U.S. GAAP	N/A	N/A
Convenience translations	English	Foreign	Foreign	No	No
Convenience statements	English	U.S.	Foreign	No	No
Limited restatements	English	U.S./Foreign	U.S./Foreign	Yes	No
Reconciliation to U.S. GAAP (Minimum required by SEG–Form 20-F)	English	U.S./Foreign	U.S./Foreign	Yes	Yes
Secondary statements–country-specific for U.S.**/Secondary statements– universal	English/ Commonly in English	U.S./U.S. or foreign	U.S. GAAP/May use IFRS/IAS	N/A/ No	N/A/ No

*The term *foreign* does not preclude the possibility that English may be spoken, the company's primary reporting language may be English, the primary reporting currency may be the U.S. dollar or the foreign company's statements may be prepared using U.S. GAAP.
**Meets SEC requirements.

Executive Summary

- **More CPAs are finding themselves working** with foreign statements. As progress is made in convergence and harmonization between FASB and the IASB, the interpretation of foreign financial statements should become easier. CPAs in the United States should watch these developments carefully and familiarize themselves with IFRSs.
- **Users should be ready to adjust** their expectations about language, currency, accounting practices, methods and presentation when working with foreign statements.
- **Even if a company's statements** have been audited, CPAs should be aware that the sophistication and enforcement of accounting rules vary significantly by country.
- **Approximately half of the countries** in the world have adopted international standards for publicly listed companies. Although the United States is not one of them, FASB and the IASB are working on convergence projects.
- **Many domestic CPA firms can,** through their international alliances and networks, help U.S.-based CPAs in business and industry understand foreign financial statements.
- **Cultural differences often make foreign statements** prepared using U.S. GAAP quite different from statements of U.S.-based companies. CPAs should not accept anything at face value.

prepares statements that show both Japanese yen and U.S. dollars. Amounts are converted to U.S. dollars at the year-end exchange rate.

Limited restatements. These attempt to provide more information by reconciling some significant items to U.S. GAAP. Critics argue they allow companies to selectively choose items that improve their financial picture.

Reconciling to U.S. GAAP. Companies that cross-list their stock on foreign and U.S. exchanges must, at a minimum, prepare a reconciliation of their home-country statements to U.S. GAAP. These companies file Form 20-F in lieu of Form 10-K with the SEC; the filings are available on the SEC Web site at www.sec.gov/edgar.shtml.

Secondary statements. These may be country-specific or universal. A U.S. country-specific secondary statement would be prepared using U.S. GAAP; universal statements may use International Accounting Standards/International Financial Reporting Standards (IASs/IFRSs). (See "Understanding IASs and IFRSs")

Determine the Approach

If the reporting approach is not disclosed in the notes or referred to in the auditor's report, CPAs can contact the company and make a detailed inquiry. The lack of notes to the financial statements explaining how they were prepared may show a lack of accounting sophistication on the foreign company's part.

Even if the statements have been audited, be aware that the sophistication and enforcement of accounting rules vary signifi-

Exhibit 2 Volvo Group Balance Sheet for 2005

Consolidated Balance Sheet December 31

SEK M	Volvo Group 2004	2005
Assets		
Intangible assets	17,612	20,421
Property, plant and equipment	31,151	35,001
Assets under operating leases	19,534	20,839
Shares and participations	2,003	751
Long-term customer-financing receivables	25,187	31,184
Long-term interest-bearing receivables	1,741	1,433
Other long-term receivables	6,100	7,021
Inventories	28,598	33,937
Short-term customer-financing receivables	26,006	33,282
Short-term interest-bearing receivables	1,643	464
Other short-term receivables	29,647	35,855
Marketable securities	25,955	28,834
Cash and cash equivalents	8,791	8,113
Total Assets	223,968	257,135
Shareholders' equity and liabilities		
Shareholders' equity[1]	70,155	78,768
Provisions for post-employment benefits	14,703	11,986
Other provisions	14,993	18,556
Loans	61,807	74,885
Other liabilities	62,310	72,940
Shareholders' equity and liabilities	223,968	257,135
Shareholders' equity and minority interests as percentage of total assets	31.3%	30.6%

[1]Whereof minority interests SEK 260 M (229).

cantly by country. Some foreign accounting firms register with the Public Company Accounting Oversight Board (PCAOB) so they may conduct or participate in audits of companies filing with the SEC; they therefore are subject to PCAOB rules and oversight. About one-third of the more than 1,500 public accounting firms listed on the PCAOB Web site (www.pcaobus.org) are foreign.

More than 90 countries permitted or required their domestic-listed companies to report under IFRSs in 2005, and the list is growing rapidly. Summaries of IFRSs are available at www.iasplus.com/standard/standard.htm. Although the summaries are inherently incomplete, they offer a quick read for the beginner. Be cautious, since implementation and enforcement of IFRSs vary from country to country. An updated list of adoption status by country is available at www.iasplus.com/country/useias.htm.

Although Japan and the United States have not yet adopted IFRSs, both have committed significant resources toward international convergence. For the United States, progress is being made on harmonization under an agreement between FASB and the IASB. Significant differences, however, remain between IFRS and U.S. GAAP.

Exhibit 3 U.K. vs. U.S. Reporting Terminology

U.K. terminology	U.S. equivalent or definition
Accounts	Financial statements
Debtors	Accounts receivable
Hire charges	Rent
Stocks	Inventories
Turnover	Sales and other operating income

Source. BP's 2004 Annual Report.

Watch for Presentation Differences

Some countries present items differently. For example, the Volvo balance sheet in exhibit 2 lists long-term assets before short-term assets and shareholders' equity before liabilities. This format is consistent with the IAS-compliant model financial statements for 2005 available at www.iasplus.com/fs/2005modelfs.pdf. CPAs also should seek information about accounting practices such as the grouping or netting of accounts and the definition of current vs. noncurrent. These types of differences make it important to read the footnotes and to obtain country-specific information.

Information about doing business in specific foreign countries can be obtained from sources such as HLB International (www.hlbi.com/DBI%_flist.asp) and the Tax and Accounting Sites Directory (www.taxsites.com). HLB International is a global network of accounting firms and business advisers whose Web site includes information on currency and languages, investment factors, business organizations and taxation. The Tax and Accounting Sites Directory provides links to a variety of other international information Web sites.

It's also important to know whether a company's foreign statements reflect historical cost or contain inflation adjustments. Two common models for inflation adjustment are the general price-level-adjusted (GPLA) model and the current cost-adjusted (CCA) model. Information about the accounting methods and presentation rules may be disclosed in the supplemental information included with the statements. If the information is difficult to locate, a source of last resort may be the accounting principle disclosures or the reconciliation to U.S. GAAP in the statements of multinational corporations based in that country.

Do not assume common accounting terms have the same meaning outside the United States. For example, although some companies in the United Kingdom have adopted IFRSs, many continue to use terminology that can be confusing to CPAs in the United States (see exhibit 3).

Determine the Currency

The currency used in the financial statements may not be obvious, as shown in exhibit 2. The SEK M above the "Assets" caption shows the statements are in the Swedish

Bridging the Culture GAAP

The foreign financial statements you're examining may have been prepared using U.S. GAAP, but was it applied in the same way it would have been in the United States?

"In a lot of cases, probably not," says Gregory S. Miller, CPA, a professor at Harvard Business School, "Conservatism [in financial reporting] is driven by the litigation environment." Even if a foreign company is cross-listed on a U.S. exchange, it does not run the same risk of investor lawsuits as a U.S.-based company. Furthermore, research suggests there are country-specific biases, Miller says. For example, a company in Germany is far more likely than a company in Italy to interpret the same results negatively.

Paul Neubelt, CPA, chairman of BDO International's China region, agrees that accounting principles are applied differently according to the culture of the country where the statements are prepared. "Anyone looking to invest in another country needs to know something about the cultures of the country," he says. That caution extends to choosing your own translators, who can explain the meaning behind the words.

Changes to U.S. GAAP may present other problems with financial statements of foreign companies. "A company may say it knows U.S. GAAP and may have someone on staff who has lived in the United States, but it's often not up to date," Neubelt says.

Even if you hire an expert in the country in question, ultimately you've got to have the courage and conviction that you understand the numbers yourself, Miller says. "The same [cultural] factors that make it difficult to understand the accounting can make it difficult to understand a local consultant."

—Matthew G. Lamoreaux is a senior editor of the JofA. Mr. Lamoreaux is an employee of the AICPA, and his views, as expressed in this article, do not necessarily reflect the views of the Institute. Official positions are determined through certain specific committee procedures, due process and deliberation.

Exhibit 4 Translation Methods and Rates Used for Asset Accounts

- **Current rate method:** Assets are translated at the current rate.
- **Current/Noncurrent method:** Current assets are translated using current rates and noncurrent assets are translated using historical rates.
- **Monetary/Nonmonetary method:** Monetary assets are translated using current rates and nonmonetary assets are translated using historical rates.
- **Temporal method:** Monetary assets such as cash and receivables are translated using current rates. Nonmonetary assets such as inventory and long-term investments are translated using current rates if they are carried on the books at current value. Other assets are translated using historical rates.

Multinational enterprises have been dealing with translation issues for many years because their foreign divisions and subsidiaries often keep records in the local currency. Exhibit 4, lists four common methods of translation. Each uses a different combination of the following three rates: the historical rate in effect on the date of the transaction, the rate in effect at the end of the current year and the weighted average rate for the period.

Translation rules are addressed by FASB Statement no. 52 in the United States and by IAS 21 in the international standards. Current and historical exchange rate information is available from Web sites such as the Federal Reserve Bank (www.federalreserve.gov/releases/H10/hist) or the Federal Reserve Bank of St. Louis (http://research.stlouisfed.org/fred2/).

Many accounting firms belong to international networks or alliances to expand their resources. Your domestic CPA firm may be able to help arrange for an accounting firm in the foreign country to provide assistance in interpreting the financial statements. Exhibit 5, contains a list of some of the larger networks and alliances that provide international resources to accounting firms.

krona. Remember that Canada, Australia and Jamaica also call their currency "dollars" and many currencies use the familiar $ symbol.

Translated financial statements are meaningful only if the reader knows the method used to convert foreign currencies to U.S. dollars. A basic convenience statement may be prepared by multiplying all the amounts on the income statement and balance sheet by the translation rate in effect at the balance sheet date. In that case there would not be any translation gains or losses, and the statements would not provide any information about the effects of rate changes over time.

What's Next?

The global integration of national economies is well under way and will accelerate over the next two decades. The result is that U.S.-based CPAs will see more financial statements originating in foreign countries. Foreign investment in the United States also is likely to increase, and many financial executives in the United States may soon he required to report results in compliance with IFRSs. As progress is made in convergence and harmonization between FASB and the IASB, the interpretation of foreign financial statements should become easier. CPAs who develop expertise in the international reporting arena will be in increasingly high demand.

Practical Tips

- Understand the common approaches foreign companies take when they provide statements to users in the United States.
- Understand the effects of currency translation on financial statements and the common conversion methods.
- Become familiar with IASs/IFRSs, since more than 90 countries have adopted these international standards.
- Line up sources of help in advance.

Exhibit 5 CPA Firm Networks and Alliances

- Baker Tilly International, **www.bakertillyinternational.com**
- BDO International, **www.bdointernational.com**
- BKR International, **www.bkr.com**
- CPA Associates International, **www.cpaai.com**
- CPAmerica International, **www.cpamerica.org**
- DFK International, **www.dfkintl.com**
- GMN Enterprise, **www.gmnen.com**
- HLB International, **www.hlbi.com**
- IGAF Worldwide, **www.igafworldwide.org**
- Moores Rowland International, **www.mri-world.com**
- NACPAF, National Associated CPA Firms, **www.nacpaf.com**
- PKF North American Network, **www.pkfnan.org**
- RSM McGladrey Network, **www.rsmi.com**

AICPA Resources

CPE

International Versus U.S. Accounting: What in the World is the Difference? (# 731662JA).

For more information or to make a purchase, go to **www. cpa2biz.com.**

JofA Article

"Financial Reporting Goes Global," JofA, Sep.04, page 43.

Other Resources

Web Sites

- Deloitte IAS Plus list of IFRS/IAS adoption status by country, www.iasplus.com/country/useias.htm.
- Deloitte's IFRS-compliant model financial statements, www.iasplus.com/fs/fs.htm.
- Federal Reserve Bank, www.federalreserve.gov/releases/H10/hist, or the Federal Reserve Bank of St. Louis, http://research.stlouisfed.org/fred2/, for current and historical exchange rate information.
- HLB International information about doing business in foreign countries, www.hlbi.com/DBI%_flist.asp.
- International financial reporting standards summaries, www.iasplus.com/standard/standard.htm.
- PricewaterhouseCoopers' Similarities & Differences—A comparison of IFRS and U.S. GAAP, www.pwcglobal.com.
- Tax and Accounting Sites Directory links to international information Web sites, www.taxsites.com.

Susan M. Sorensen, CPA, PhD, has 30 years of public accounting experience and is an assistant professor of accounting and Donald L. Kyle, CPA, PhD, is a professor of accounting, both at the University of Houston-Clear Lake. Their e-mail addresses are sorensen@uhcl.edu and kyle@uhcl.edu, respectively.

Shaping the Future of Manufacturing

A tour through manufacturing's recent history reveals clues of what's to come.

PATRICIA PANCHAK

B ill Gates was five years from founding Microsoft, and Michael Dell was 15 years from starting Dell Computer Corp., but Gordon Moore and Robert Noyce were in their second year running Intel Corp., and Sam Walton was in his eighth year running a new discount retail chain called Wal-Mart (20th if you count back to the original store).

The year was 1970, and the manufacturing sector was about to enter a period of profound change in which these and other new companies played key roles. Though they couldn't have predicted with certainty the events that were about to unfold, the editors of a magazine named STEEL clearly sensed something new afoot as they retooled their magazine and renamed it INDUSTRYWEEK.

Now in its 35th year, IW continues to tell the story of manufacturing, but this year we're taking the time to review the trends, technologies, strategies and ideas of the past that shaped today's—and will continue to shape tomorrow's—manufacturing sector. It's fascinating: The undulating cycle of history turns up perennial problems that each new generation declares will variously sink, save, stall or speed the sector's growth. Even a cursory look through the pages of IW since its beginnings turns up stories that could have been written today: Healthcare and energy costs soared throughout the '70s, '80s and '90s too; skilled labor was dangerously short; and U.S. manufacturing dominance was being threatened. For every new development today, it seems, there's a precedent 10, 20 or 30 years ago.

Yet punctuating these seemingly mundane recurrences are events that dramatically altered the course of manufacturing history—that set off a chain of events and a change of thinking that will resonate far into the future. As we careen through the first decade of the 21st century, a brief pause to look back at these events will provide clues to our future.

Globalization

Yes, we know this is a no-brainer, but just because it's obvious doesn't mean we can ignore it or can't learn from it. Besides, when you stop to look at the trend toward globalization over the past 35 years, you'll wonder why so many manufacturers seem ill prepared for China's "overnight" success.

Still, the idea of a global economy was but a glimmer in the most visionary manufacturing executive's eye when IW's Bill Miller became the first business journalist to report from China in the Spring of 1973. Following then-President Richard M. Nixon's historic trip to China the previous year, Miller's reporting from the Canton Trade Fair found high prices, reluctant buyers and inefficient manufacturers along with U.S. manufacturing executives eager to do business there.

But make no mistake: What would become known at the close of the century as "globalization" and China's sudden emergence as a manufacturing powerhouse had begun long before Miller's trip. "We tended to be global to a much greater extent than people realize," says Jerry Jasinowski, president of The Manufacturing Institute, the research arm of The National Association of Manufacturers in Washington, D.C. Argentina, Brazil and Mexico had all passed through the first phase of industrialization decades before, and in the '60s many U.S. companies had begun buying materials and components from low-cost Asian countries.

But it was Japan, not China, that first flexed its industrial muscle, and by 1971 an IW special report wondered, "Is there still time to save U.S. manufacturing?" It described the imports flooding into the U.S. and reported that poor productivity, high labor costs and unfavorable trade rules hampered U.S. competitiveness. By 1980 Japan topped the world in automobile production, making 11 million of 38.6 million and taking 30% market share in the U.S. The U.S. dropped to second place for the first time since 1904. By the mid-'80s Japan Inc. seemed to threaten U.S. manufacturing's very existence.

It didn't take long for U.S. manufacturing to respond—by the early '90s the tables had turned and U.S. manufacturing thrived—but the manufacturing environment was forever changed. Entire industries—computer memory chips, most consumer electronics, shoes, apparel and textiles—had migrated overseas, and new industries began to take their places. A January 1993 cover story welcomed the biotechnology industry "out of the lab and into reality," and in 1995, U.S. companies led the world in manufacturing personal computers, semiconductors and chip manufacturing equipment.

Meanwhile, other economies sought their share of the manufacturing pie. Most prominently, Taiwan, South Korea, Hong Kong and Singapore catapulted from third-world to first-world status in a matter of decades on the strength of export-driven growth, only to suffer an economic setback in the 1997 Asian Crisis.

By the late '80s manufacturers were anticipating the European Communities' attempt to create a single, unified and open market by 1992. Later in the decade Eastern European countries emerged as the low-cost production center of Europe after the breakup of the Soviet Union.

By the dawn of 2000, India and, most especially, China, had burst onto the global manufacturing scene. While it may seem as if China arrived without notice, IW regularly featured articles on the country's increasing role in manufacturing. In November 1981, IW reported on the return of the first U.S. Ambassador to the People's Republic of China. His analysis: "Once it's economically healthy, the internal demand for goods and services should be tremendous." In 1986 "Beyond Japan: the Trade Crises to Come," IW noted that China was the world's fourth largest exporter of textiles to the U.S. and quoted a business professor saying, "China is 'probably the biggest' future competitor to U.S. business." A 1993 cover story later declared: "The China Boom: This Time It's for Real."

But globalization didn't just happen. Business and government leaders' push for free trade drove global expansion and led to "a very clear trend line for passing free trade agreements of one sort or another, whether regional or bilateral," says Tom Deusterberg, president and CEO of Manufacturers Alliance/MAPI, an Arlington, Va.-based business and public policy research organization. Indeed, the world's government and business leaders had long before turned their attention to expanding free trade and making it easier for developing countries to participate in the global economy. From the General Agreement on Tariffs and Trade (GATT) in 1948, to the first United Nations Conference on Trade and Development in 1964, to the World Trade Organization in 1995, and the hundreds of bilateral and regional trade pacts penned in the last five years, globalization is a trend that's likely to accelerate in the coming years.

Production

The emergence of Japan as a manufacturing leader brought to the sector more than just a new, formidable competitor to U.S. dominance. It brought entirely new management strategies that many manufacturers today still struggle to understand, let alone perfect: The Toyota Production System (now called lean manufacturing), with its focus on "make to order" and just-in-time deliveries; and Total Quality Management, with its belief that quality should be built into the manufacturing process. Indeed, while information technology tends to get most of the credit for the dramatic productivity improvements that helped U.S. manufacturing meet competitive challenges from Japan and elsewhere, these new plant-floor production management techniques deserve some of the credit, says Jasinowski. "We did overcome the Japanese threat, and we did it by incorporating some of their production ideas in our plants." IW noted the trend throughout the late '80s and in 1990 prepared a special report on "world-class manufacturing," which highlighted such specific production strategies as TQM, JIT, work teams, continuous improvement, total productive maintenance, close supplier links, and performance measurement and reward." In 1995, the magazine launched IW's Best Plants, an annual awards program that celebrates world-class manufacturing and evaluates plants based on their successes with the new production strategies.

Just as important as the changes to *how* production was done, are changes to *where* it was done. In the search for improved productivity, manufacturers started moving from the traditional manufacturing strongholds to cheap-labor countries and rural refuges. Even as early as the 1950s transnational companies had explored the possibilities of splitting up the production processes, making possible the sourcing of materials and components in different countries.

Meanwhile, within the U.S. factories started their migration from the Midwest and Northeast toward the right-to-work states in the South, and more recently the West. An early '70s IW article notes that the Southeast had become the fastest growing area of the country, with "plentiful cheap land, lower taxes, lower wages and lower construction costs." It also noted: another stimulus "for moving southward is 'union problems.'"

Information Technology

It's difficult to overstate, however, the role information technology played in U.S. manufacturing's resurgence in the late '80s and throughout the '90s. In the '70s, CAD/CAM had begun to fundamentally change how products are designed and manufactured. And the first ERP systems, which promised standardized software for real-time, enterprise-wide business processing, were introduced. A flurry of software applications followed, promising productivity leaps, quality improvements and, best of all, customer-supplier integration. By the mid-'80s, IW reported that desktop computers, introduced a decade before, had flooded the business world, and described how digital networks—electronic and voice mail and facsimiles (the short term, fax, apparently not in common use yet)—give companies a competitive advantage.

By the time the Internet became commercially viable, interest in IT had reached a fever pitch, and the Internet boom—now known as the Internet bubble—was born. IW editors, caught up in the hype, struggled to distinguish between "vapor ware," (newly introduced, untested software whose developers' promised capability never materialized) from software that companies had implemented and benefited from. As early as 1990, Wal-Mart, which had grown to be the dominant retailer in the nation, offered manufacturers "Retail Link" direct access via a secure Internet Web site to internal information, one of the first implementations of a new strategy dubbed value-chain management strategy. For manufacturers it was a mixed blessing: The ability to ship to the giant came with the realization that control over the buying-selling process had shifted to the retailer.

123

By 1996, Cisco Systems Inc. and Dell Computer Corp. had pioneered business-to-business and consumer selling, respectively, over the Internet. Compared with these companies and a few Web-only retailers such as bookseller Amazon.com, companies with brick-and-mortar plants and stores seemed like obsolete relics of the costly and slow-selling process of the past. Also, Dell's supply-chain strategy demonstrated the efficiencies that were possible with an integrated supply network, earning founder and then-CEO Michael Dell IW's CEO of the Year for 1998. From 1996 to 1999, IW expanded its IT coverage to accommodate the flood of new technologies introduced each year.

By the end of the century, information technology was both revered and feared, as companies raced to update their systems to avoid the dreaded Y2K meltdown. For nearly two years before the turn of the century, IW published warnings and possible solutions to the impending problem, including the 1998 cover story, "The Real Year 2000 Nightmare." What happened, however, was a different kind of meltdown, as the financial collapse of Internet companies wiped out billions of dollars of shareholder value, helping set off an economic recession in the U.S. Manufacturers' expectations of IT and the Internet fell back toward earth, with the realization that neither software nor the Internet would be the panacea they'd hoped, or been led to believe—but that it would continue to be a powerful tool for a host of challenges.

Somewhat overlooked amidst all the IT excitement were advances in industrial automation, though a 1988 article reported that "81% of electronic components are now assembled automatically compared to 48% in 1983." On the back of these new production strategies, IT and industrial automation, productivity skyrocketed—hitting a 3.6% annual growth rate in 1990s, and 4.7% so far in the new century—leaving no doubt that manufacturers will continue to seek out and perfect the implementation of the latest strategies and technologies in the future.

So many other significant events transpired in the past 35 years that it's difficult to summarize them all. The increased role of government in the '70s when the creation of an entire alphabet soup of regulatory agencies—OSHA, EPA, EEOC, ERISA—ultimately forced manufacturing executives to play a greater role in public policy making, and caused manufacturing associations to move to Washington, from New York and Chicago. Manufacturers moves to exploit new non-production-oriented "value creation" strategies, such as providing services with (think GE) and branding their products (think Intel). The metamorphosis of the CEO from being a "corporate statesman" in the '70s, concerned about the community and society, to being a celebrity in the '80s, to being as mistrusted as a politician in the '90s. Yet even as these words are being written, new challenges are gathering, new strategies are being formulated, new industries and the companies that will lead them—the Microsofts, Dells, Wal-Marts and Intels of 2050—are being created. None of the new will spring forth without precedent. The clues are here, now, all around us and in our generation's history: in the labs, in the halls of academia, in the boardrooms of companies. We just need to pause and pay attention.

The Rise of BRIC

How Brazil, Russia, India and China Are Reshaping the Marketing World

NOREEN O'LEARY

What used to be considered the developing countries of the Third World are quickly becoming the emerging economies of the next world. BRIC: Brazil, Russia, India and China are four markets with unique characteristics, but are nonetheless fled together by the potential created after changes in their political systems unleashed the consumer demand of 43 percent of the world's population. Already, five of the planet's top 10 cities—centers of wealth generation for consumers climbing the economic ladder—are located in the burgeoning BRIC.

The term entered into business parlance in 2003 after Goldman Sachs global economist Jim O'Neill outlined his future world view. He believed BRIC possessed the economic potential to become the world's four most dominant economies by 2050, which could be larger than that of the U.S. and Western Europe combined.

Recent headlines about the bailouts of major U.S. financial institutions and speculation about the dollar's fall from global dominance underscored the shift in power towards Asia that has been well under way. China and India, along with Russia, are expected to be among the fastest-growing economies in the world this year (although a U.S.-triggered global downturn could impact the BRIC economies, which are still heavily driven by exports).

Even before the coining of BRIC, WPP Group CEO Martin Sorrell identified the potential in such emerging markets, an expansion strategy often noted by Wall Street analysts when recommending WPP's stock. WPP agencies are now at the top of the agency food chain in the BRIC countries and command the lion's share of media buying in populous giants India and China. While 82 percent of WPP's revenue is generated by Europe, the U.K. and the U.S, the company believes that by 2015, 40 percent of its revenue will come from Asia alone.

From a marketing perspective, not all countries are weighted evenly within the BRIC equation. With their explosive growth and massive populations, China and India are dominant factors, often described as Chindia. But the two cultural mind-sets couldn't be more different.

"India boasts a developed managerial mind-set while China's entire economy is production based," says Tom Doctoroff, CEO of JWT China. "This fundamental difference springs from very divergent cultural orientations. Indians are Brahmanist conceptualizers and theorists while the Confucian Chinese are, and have always been, bureaucratic and incremental pragmatists."

One of the biggest challenges for marketers and their agencies is the sheer scale of the BRIC countries and the difficulty in reaching far-flung consumers with different cultures, languages and traditions. The marketing infrastructure in countries like China, India and Russia is still under development, and Western aspects of doing business that are taken for granted elsewhere—such as national retailers—are still in the making.

Companies like Unilever now derive over 40 percent of their sales in developing and emerging markets, compared to 26 percent in the '90s. To manage such dispersed operations, the packaged-goods giant had to centralize its brand-development efforts while tailoring its brand building locally. "We had ended up with 100 Unilevers around the world in the mid-'90s all doing their own thing with little central direction," explains company rep Trevor Gorin. "We needed a global approach to branding, to utilizing the synergies of a $40–50 billion company's marketing organization."

At Kimberly-Clark, sales in its "BRICIT" markets (the company includes Indonesia and Thailand in the group) have grown more than 15 percent over the past four years.

"The biggest challenge in these markets is to anchor your brand with a premium positioning," says Robert Abernathy, group president, developing and emerging markets for K-C. "It's tempting to position it otherwise because many of these people are low-end consumers. But it's important to establish yourself as a marketer of high-performance, premium products and then come back with multiple price points."

For agencies, developing a strong presence in countries like China and India has become a necessity. Global account consolidations increasingly turn on the strength of agency operations there; holding company stock prices increasingly reflect the extent of business derived from these markets. Thanks to acquisitions like Saatchi and Bcom3's Leo Burnett, Publicis has become a more competitive player in these countries. Omnicom has trailed its industry peers and is now investing heavily to catch up.

China and Russia are now among the world's top luxury markets as newly affluent consumers want Western badges of status to signal their arrival into prosperity. And because rapid change has become the norm in BRIC countries, consumers are becoming fast adopters of technology.

"Technology is leapfrogging the normal product life cycle in the West where you tend to have in-home media, radio, billboards, PCs, laptops," says ZenithOptimedia CEO Steve King. "That comfortable life cycle isn't happening in these markets. In the old days, we could export our best (headquarters) knowledge into these markets. Now there are new opportunities with media owners, with embedded advertising and content. Mobile, which already outnumbers landlines, is becoming a huge growth platform. It's leapfrogging media, eliminating desktops and laptops."

King cites Shanghai Media Group as an example of the pace of innovation. The media company handles TV production, and owns portals, radios and magazines. It streams programming on mobile phones with embedded advertising that can't be fast-forwarded. "It used to be we were dealing with Third World media," he says. "Now, it's 'God, this is frightening, they're already developing things we haven't thought of yet.'"

The high growth rates in countries like Russia and China have driven up media inflation, with prices rising five to 10 times faster than in the West.

The biggest investment—and challenge—for any company doing business in BRIC countries lies in people. Training local staff has become an imperative and retaining them is difficult, and often expensive, as the limited pool of homegrown talent regularly trades up for bigger paychecks and titles.

Staffing issues exist on the client side as well. "We've had to build a relationship with local advertisers, based on equal footing, people who are not used to working in a market economy or used to marketing tools," says Publicis CEO Maurice Lévy. "We have to educate them and make them understand that out of the millions they give us, we have to pay salaries. We also need to get them to respect intellectual property because it has value and creative work has value."

As the dimensions of the consumer world quickly change, Goldman Sachs has already coined "N11," a shorthand for the "next 11" countries nipping at the heels of the BRIC markets as investment opportunities. They are Bangladesh, Egypt, Indonesia, Iran, South Korea, Mexico, Nigeria, Pakistan, the Philippines, Turkey and Vietnam.

The newly dynamic countries of Central and Eastern Europe are also remapping the world for marketers. Alex Herdt, CEO of Ogilvy Group's operations in those countries, argues that with the 10 new Eastern countries that have joined the European Union (forming a "Corporate Europe"), the EU has an economic value comparable to the U.S.

Marcel Fenez, a Hong Kong-based global managing partner at PricewaterhouseCoopers, expects global ad spending to increase by more than $100 billion in the next five years, fueled by the Web, TV distribution, video games and casinos. (China's Macau has now surpassed Las Vegas as the world's largest gambling center.) Fenez also expects that a quarter of that growth will come from the BRIC countries. Still, he cautions that global marketing dollars alone won't guarantee success with BRIC consumers.

Brazil
The Most Western and Mature BRIC

A country known for images of its poor living in shantytowns now boasts the highest level of home ownership among the BRICs. The past three years have been good for Brazilian consumers. After years of hyper-inflation, the country's fortunes have been boosted by hard-won macroeconomic stability and government social assistance to those living at the lowest economic tiers.

"For the first rime in recent Brazilian history the middle class grew and the consumption indexes of the bottom of the pyramid showed significant improvement," says Marlene Bregman, director of marketing services, Leo Burnett Publicidade. "The impact of this shift is big. . . . We are talking about 20–30 million people consuming more and/or entering the marketplace."

Ironically, that expansion of a consumer class has occurred even as Brazil's economy has slowed in recent years. In fact, Brazil's economic growth is tepid compared to the other BRIC countries and it is more different than similar to those emerging economies. It is the most Westernized of the group for one thing, and has a more mature marketing communications business, with an ample supply of talent and award-winning advertising.

Today, some 35 percent of Brazil's population of 180 million are considered middle class. One telling sign: The use of credit cards has soared 200 percent since 1999. Brazil has the highest concentration of car ownership among the BRIC countries and its consumers are moving beyond buying basic necessities and demanding more sophisticated products like cell phones and computers. (Interestingly, Brazil lags China and Russia in PC ownership.)

"Around 30 percent of Brazilians [still] buy 80 percent of the announced products," says Eddie Gonzalez, chairman, Young & Rubicam Brands, Latin America. "Therefore, the Brazilian communication industry is highly sophisticated when speaking to that group and less innovative when the focus is the remainder of the population."

Sergio Amado, chairman, Ogilvy Group, Brazil, is more blunt: "The majority of the brands in Brazil are not able to talk with the lower-income consumers."

Unlike its BRIC counterparts, Brazil's advertising—in particular, print and outdoor—is known outside Silo Paulo creative corridors, thanks to award wins at shows like Cannes. In the '90s, the country's agencies went through a creative renaissance similar to what happened in New York in the '60s. Now as the country's advertising goes more mainstream, some wonder if it is losing a touch of its previous edge.

That renaissance "led to creatives heading up agencies and as a consequence a lack of creativity [based in] strategy," says Y&R's Gonzalez, who adds that by 2000, the local industry struck more of a balance. "This fact, when looked at single-handedly, can give the impression of a loss of the creative capacity, but, in fact, it is exactly the opposite—there was a huge gain in efficiency."

Sergio Valente, CEO of DDB, which bought local hot shop DM9 in 1997, adds, "Although there has been local talk about a creativity crisis, I do not believe this. The economic stability we now have brought a somewhat 'settled' advertising. Brazilian advertising is highly eclectic; it has humor, it has emotion, it is powerful."

Multinational agencies dominate Brazil. In the last five years international networks partnered with or bought local agencies accounting for nearly all of the 10 biggest shops. Other multinationals like McCann, led by globetrotting clients like Esso, have been there for 73 years. Advertising is a glamorous, well-paid job in Brazil, and the social moves and love lives of certain executives are tabloid fodder. Y&R Brazil president Roberto Justus stars in ad campaigns and hosts the Brazilian version of The Apprentice. One of the industry's most high-profile executives, Washington Olivetto of W/Brasil, drew international headlines after he was kidnapped in December 2001 and held in captivity for nearly two months.

By law, media agencies are not allowed to operate in Brazil, a provision that has prevented media unbundling which agencies say allows them to prevail in channel planning. But one executive at a global media company says that law has also prevented the kind of media clout that forces price negotiation: "The Brazilian media market is a cozy cartel controlled by the country's two biggest media owners who don't want us there."

Those two vendors are Editora Abril, with about 70 percent of magazine ad budgets, and Rede Globo, with about 70 percent of TV's ad dollars. (Muti-channel subscriber TV has yet to make an impact and media fragmentation is still nascent.).

"If you want to buy very good [TV] slots, best positions, you have to buy in September for the full following year," says Luca Lindner, McCann Worldgroup regional director, Latin America/Caribbean.

Brazil may be one of the only markets in the world where agencies, per a 1998 law, have to be paid 15 percent commissions.

Globo's dominance also impacts the country's TV production values.

"Globo drives the agenda, the way serials are shot, the way commercials look. Creative experimentation is not very strong," says Stefano Zunino, CEO, JWT, Brazil. "It's not that Globo is controlling, it's just that consumers are used to one kind of TV advertising."

Even though Brazil's more mature economy isn't growing at the rate of other BRIC countries, multinational marketers have been rewarded for their investment. Brazil was one of the first countries targeted by Farine Lactee Nestlé and provided the inspiration for the company's first global brand: Nestlé. (Nestlé is now the country's largest food company.)

"Omo [detergent] is Brazil's biggest brand, bigger than Coe," says Unilever's Gorin, who says the company has been in Brazil for over 75 years. "It's considered a Brazilian brand. The same is true of Dove. It's fantastic for an advertiser—people feel you are part of their consumer texture."

Brazilian Highlights

- Population: 180 million
- 2008 Estimated GDP Annual Growth: 4.5%
- 2007 Ad Spend: $8.3 bil. '08: $8.8 bil.
- Brazil has the largest number of MSN Messenger users worldwide, as well as the most members in Orkut, the Google-sponsored social networking site.
- About 35% of Brazilian families are middle class, representing 50% of total consumption.
- Some 68% of the Brazilian population owns their house. Of these, 80% own houses, 20% apartments.

The growing dynamism of the market is driving the creation of strong local companies. In 2004, the merger of Belgium's Interbrew and AmBev of Brazil created InBev, the world's largest brewer by volume. One year later, Latin America alone accounted for almost 50 percent of the new group's earnings.

"During a long time, Brazil had a closed, protected market, causing a huge repressed demand on automobile, high technology, luxury and other imported items," says DDB's Valente. "In the '90s, the market opened its doors to imports and their high quality pushed local industry to achieve higher quality standards, for competition increased."

Russia
Corruption Gives Way to Consumerism

In 1998, the head of Publicis' Moscow office was beat up by local racketeers trying to sell him a protection contract. The agency immediately pulled out of Russia. The local industry was virtually demolished that year as other agencies bailed out of a country whose business practices were becoming increasingly corrupt and dangerous for foreign executives.

Since Vladimir Putin was elected president in 2000, Russia has benefited from structural economic reforms as well as higher global oil prices stoking the country's petro-economy. One indicator of that change: Publicis reopened in that market and, bolstered by its absorption of D'Arcy Masius Benton & Bowles, is now the largest multinational. All the holding companies are again represented in Russia and WPP, which formed a joint venture with Video International in 2004, is now the largest entity.

Much is made of the country's flashy new oligarch money. Russia now has 53 billionaires, and Moscow alone is home to 88,000 millionaires. On any given night they drop tens of thousands of dollars on drinks in the ultra exclusive lounges in Moscow's nightclubs, rubbing shoulders with a new generation of wealthy youth who have no recollection of Soviet-era food lines. Russia has already become the world's fourth-largest luxury market, which is expected to ring up $13 billion this year, nearly twice the amount of just two years ago. Outside of cities like Moscow, what was formerly a pastoral dacha area is now home to Barvikha Luxury Village with retailers like Giorgio Armani, Tiffany, Prada, Ferrari and Lamborghini. For the last three years, Moscow has hosted the Millionaire Fair where, in 2006, 38,000 people came to look at jewel-encrusted pencils, helicopters and dresses stitched with dollar bills. Those who can't afford such extravagances like Cartier watches or Chanel couture settle for Cartier cigarettes or Chanel perfume.

"Luxury products gradually cease to serve as show-off elements only and are more and more used for personal pleasure," observes Dmitry Korobkov, chairman, ADV Marketing Communications. "In Russia the number of people who exploit luxury brands to demonstrate their status is still high, yet there is a noticeable tendency to shift motivation towards personal pleasure."

If not yet on that luxury threshold, the plight of Russia's rank and file is improving. Workers' salaries have doubled since 2003 and the country is also home to a newly developing middle class. While one in five Russians still lives in poverty, others are enjoying newfound discretionary income. (Due to privatization, many Russians now own their homes, the government subsidizes utilities, and citizens pay a fiat 13 percent tax.) By some estimates, Russians are now spending 70–80 percent of their per capita income at retail. Consumption grew by 27 percent, in U.S. dollars, in 2006 and sales in the retail, consumer goods, finance and construction sectors are expected to increase 40 percent over the next several years, according to investment bank Renaissance Capital.

Not surprisingly, Western marketers like Coca-Cola, Ikea, American Express, Nestle, Wrigley, Procter & Gamble and Unilever are rapidly expanding there. As a result, Russia is also one of the fastest-growing ad markets, with spending increasing in excess of 20 percent year over year.

But for all of its prospects, marketers and agencies find Russia's complex scale and diversity extremely challenging.

Crossing vast steppes and tundra, the country covers 11 time zones and is home to dozens of peoples, cultures and languages. How tough a job do marketers have? Consider KhantyMansiysk, Russia's fourth-richest city, which has the highest per-capita income in the country. But its 18,000 inhabitants are isolated in northwestern Siberia where tough winters make mail deliveries difficult and they don't get all of the country's terrestrial TV channels.

Television is the predominant media in tackling the country's scope of consumers and the number of channels has doubled since 2000, enabling marketers to better reach those diverse audiences. Media is still largely in the hands of the state. WPP partner Video International—a media sales group founded by a Putin advisor—controls 80 percent of TV sales.

Russia's rapidly growing consumer culture is stoking media inflation, with prices up 40–50 percent the last couple of years and expected to increase similarly this year: TV costs have risen by 237 percent between 2005 and 2008. In 2006, the government reduced the number of minutes of ads per hour from 15 to 12. This month, they were further reduced to nine minutes.

Perhaps not surprisingly, certain marketing disciplines are harder to implement. Conventional public relations, for instance, doesn't work as it's widely understood that businesses pay for editorial coverage. Lack of data precludes sophisticated direct marketing efforts. Harking back to the closed society of the Soviet era, official consumer data is often inaccurate and income statistics have been underreported due to tax fears and threats from organized crime. But now that research companies like WPP's TGI and TNS Gallup have entered the country, consumer information is becoming more reliable.

Russians are embracing new technologies. A full 60 percent of Russians now use mobile phones compared to 5.1 percent in 2001. PC ownership has risen to 31 percent, up from 12 percent seven years ago, and 21 percent of the population now use the Internet.

"Increasing use of mobile phones and computer penetration are creating new opportunities. Russian consumers are not only advertising and marketing literate, but they're also very receptive to it. They're less cynical than consumers in the U.S. and the U.K.," says John Farrell CEO, Publicis Groupe specialized agencies and marketing services.

Russia doesn't have a long history of advertising. In the Soviet era, the Ministry of Foreign Trade ran an agency, Vneshtorgreklama, which was a clumsy effort at foreign trade advertising. Early post-Perestroika efforts from local entrepreneurs were essentially notices of product availability and pricing. Multinational agencies, following their global clients, largely created the industry as they moved into Russia in the '90s.

"With Perestroika, we had a very strange revolution," says Sergey Koptev, CEO, PGM Eurasia in Moscow. "We were not consumers, we were buyers and often products were not available. When products became available, we had the evolution to becoming consumers and as young consumers, it is trial, trial and trial. Even for very well-established brands, people are not brand loyal at all—it's all very exciting. Whether it's an old lady with her sausages or a new brand of milk or the wealthy with a new expensive toy, if they can afford it, they try it." No doubt Russia is among the world's fastest growing ad markets. But unlike China, where its growing economic prospects are more widespread (that country's highest GDP growth is in its third- and fourth-tier markets), Russia's growing affluence tends to be located around areas involved in the oil business whose fortunes fluctuate with global pricing. Marketers face other uncertainties as well. In a country with fragile Democratic traditions, politics may be unsettled; Putin's future role is still unclear as the outgoing president seeks to maintain control. Though there's been stabilization, Russia has had a rocky transition to a market economy: GDP has grown steadily since the late 1980s, but Russia's economy deteriorated after Mikhail Gorbachev's reforms, and the marketing communications business has not steadily built its presence the way it has developed in China.

Many foreigners in Moscow still find it a chaotic Wild West business culture, requiring a great deal of local knowledge and contacts. In the era of Sarbanes-Oxley, dealing with some local clients is simply off limits for multinational agencies.

What might be viewed as corruption in other markets is just standard business procedures in Russia. One exec at a multinational agency recalls an ultimatum made as his company was merging two of its agencies: "You need a 'roof in Russia, an institutional requirement to have some level of protection, to pay people to look after you in business. [During the merger] I had my managing director held up at gunpoint by a 'roof rep who advised him to pick the right 'roof in the merged organization."

Russian Highlights

- Population: 141.8 million
- 2008 Estimated GDP Annual Growth: 6.3%
- 2007 Ad Spend: $9.1 bil. '08: $11.3 bil.
- Russia's oil and gas industry accounts for nearly a quarter of the country's GDP; its tax revenue, one-third of all state income.
- Car sales are growing 70% annually and this year sales in Russia are expected to surpass those in Germany.

Just last September, Moscow's Central District Police Department arrived at BBDO's offices, claiming software licensing violations and asking for $1 million in fines. The agency had just completed a KPMG audit and knew that wasn't the case. The police department lowered its fine to $500,000, then $250,000. BBDO held strong and ended up paying 50 rubles pertaining to some graphics software that had been bought by an employee for his laptop that happened to be in the office.

The most essential problem is the image of Russia, which still leaves much to be desired, says ADV's Korobkov. "Companies and public opinion tend to extrapolate general opinions to the advertising market. The other side of the same problem is that Western colleagues often underestimate the professionalism of the Russian ad makers, while the algorithm of creative agency work has been the same in Moscow, New York and Hong Kong for a long time already," he says.

India
'A Marketing Man's Dream'

In India, creative personalities like McCann's Prasoon Joshi and Ogilvy's Piyush Pandey are stars on par with Bollywood celebrities. In fact, India's film business—which this year will produce more movies than Hollywood—borrows freely from the country's ad business and many agency execs also dabble in the film biz.

Inevitably, Mumbai agency execs traverse both worlds as they gush about the pace of change and opportunity in India.

"India is a place even Spielberg couldn't have thought of in his wildest dreams," says Colvyn Harris, CEO, JWT India. "Land here and wonder how someone could have imagined a set like this."

It's hard to imagine how fast that social backdrop is changing. Twenty years ago more than 90 percent of Indians lived on less than a dollar a day; now the country boasts more millionaires than the U.S. The ranks of desperately poor have been reduced to 54 percent of the population, from 93 percent, according to McKinsey & Co. The perception of a country blighted by poor rural villages and urban slums is being replaced by the new glass and steel buildings of Bangalore—India's Silicon Valley.

While China's stratospheric growth has captured the imagination of marketers, India's grassroots revolution is expected to yield larger results, long term. Goldman Sachs estimates that India's growth rate will be the highest of the BRICs in coming years and the country will overtake Japan as the world's second-largest economy by 2032.

Of all of the BRIC markets, India arguably has the best potential for a stable middle class. Indians place a high premium on education and the country's knowledge-based economy has reduced the income extremes that have long characterized its social strata. Since the early '90s, with India's shift away from Socialism, the country has become more of a Westernized economy open to free-market ideas, with a parliamentary government and contract law. But perhaps the most compelling aspect of sociological change is the country's youthful optimism: Half of India's population is 25 years old or younger.

"The sooner people understand how young a country we are, the better they'll do here," says Anil Kapoor, DraftFCB regional president, Asia/Pacific and Africa. "We have a lot of happy people looking forward to the future. The economy is moving strongly, markets are growing rapidly. It's truly the land of opportunity, a marketing man's dream."

Joshi, McCann's executive chairman, India, concurs. "India is emerging as a more confident country. People who used to talk about dreams now talk about hope . . . Building aspirations around products used to be the mantra here. In the new India consumers are very confident. They want promises that are achievable," he says.

India's middle class currently numbers some 50 million people. But McKinsey estimates that number will grow to 583 million by 2025, about 40 percent of the population. Compare that to 20 years ago when much of the country depended on government subsidies just to consume enough calories each day.

For industry multinational marketers and agencies, India has built-in advantages not found in China and Russia. Despite its many languages, it has more of an affinity to English because of its colonial past. It's a data-rich country, thanks in part to India's pervasive IT business. Bollywood has influenced production technology and experimentation. "The Advertising Agencies Association of India is 75 years old and India's Audit Bureau of Circulations is 70 years old. There is a long-standing professional class."

"The actual depth of talent is much deeper in India than in China," observes Lowe CEO Steve Garfield. "The country has a longer tradition of an agency sector. It has to do with Hindustan Lever, which benefited its agencies."

Hindustan Unilever, which has been in the market since 1933, is the largest consumer products company in India. (It is two-to-three times the size of the next biggest marketer in India.) The company is a corporate gold standard in India and is a first-work choice among new graduates from India's best universities. The multinationals who have worked for the client—JWT, Ogilvy & Mather, McCann Erickson and Lowe—are still the country's strongest players.

India has a staggering array of media. WPP's MindShare unit, which buys media for Unilever, has a firm grasp on the market, controlling more than 40 percent of India's media billings.

Indian Highlights

- Population: 1.1 billion
- 2008 Estimated GDP Annual Growth: 7.9%
- 2007 Ad Spend: $5.8 bil. '08: $6.7 bil.
- There are 250 million consumers now considered middle class.
- India added over 17,000 millionaires in 2006.
- It also has the highest growth in high net-worth individuals, after Singapore.
- India is one-quarter the size of America with four times the population.
- The country has over 200 TV channels and more than 10,000 publications in at least 18 languages.

By Lowe Lintas' reckoning, India has about 300 TV channels, 12,000 newspapers, 60,000–65,000 magazines, 12,000–13,000 cinemas and 1,000 radio stations. Almost 65 percent of the population lives in rural areas and six out of 10 consumers still don't have access to mass media.

That variety of media underscores the diversity of the country, which has 22 official languages, with Hindi its most predominate. In tackling rural India, marketers would have to deal with 16 languages and more than 2,000 dialects, according to Ashish Bhasin, Asia regional director, integrated marketing, Lowe Lintas. "Different parts of India are like different countries. The north of the country is completely different from the south, with different races, subdivisions and fragmentation. It's very complicated."

To tackle that complexity, Lowe Lintas employs 10,000–15,000 field service personnel. Tile agency has collected extensive geographic data covering 650 districts, 4,500 towns and 6,000 villages in India and has created digital maps for marketers that are more precise than even the ones used by the Indian Army, says Bhasin. As marketers plan their field campaigns, Lowe customizes the data to suit their objectives. Some marketers might want to focus on activities near a road, where areas are more built up; some might prefer a location near a haap, a weekly shanty market, or a nela, one of the 60,000 annual fairs and festivals.

"You can sit in Bombay and plan, but how do you know what's happening in the field?" asks Lowe's Bhasin. "We have field force supervisors who upload photography and information from cyber cafes and post offices and clients can see in real time how the campaign is progressing and take corrective steps, if necessary."

Despite such sophistication in problem solving, India still poses considerable challenges. Harkening back to its Socialist past, the country still has tight controls on foreign investment, strong unions and a restrictive retail environment.

"When you walk into India, the infrastructure is appalling," says DraftFCB's Kapoor. "The country's hardware still leaves a lot to be desired while its software is tremendous. The good news? Almost 20 percent of the world's population lives here. The bad news? We still have miles to go. But in the next 10–15 years, it will all be fixed."

China
Olympian Leap to New World Image

To appreciate the pace of change in China, consider this: Fifteen years ago an advertising community hardly existed. Last year, American entrepreneur Fredy Bush's Xinhua Finance Media went on a buying spree, scooping up mobile, outdoor, advertising and production assets to focus solely on China's high net-worth consumers, with liquid assets of at least RMB 1 million ($138,081). Bush says there are already 140 million in this group and another 365 million about to join their gilded ranks.

Brand China goes on display this summer during the Olympics and with it, the staggering change under way in the world's most populous country. This year, China's GDP will make it the world's third-largest economy and for the first time, Chinese demand will become the main impetus for world economic growth, overtaking America.

China now has 163 cities with populations of more than 1 million people. By comparison, Western Europe has 24 of the same size and the U.S., 12. Major marketers are moving beyond China's most affluent areas, if they haven't already done so, and are shifting their focus deeper into tier 2 and 3 areas, adding a new level of complexity to a market that is already one of the industry's most challenging.

"The realization of how different these cities can be from each other is hitting home. There is no homogenous 'Chinese consumer,'" says Carol Potter, CEO, BBDO/CNUAC, Shanghai. "While local Chinese agencies still lag behind the international agencies in their strategic and professional capabilities, international agencies have a hard time setting up and getting representation outside of Beijing, Shanghai and Guangzhou because they are not making enough money as it is. They cannot afford to invest in regional offices to get that kind of local understanding."

Last year, there were more ad industry acquisitions than in the previous five years combined, according to Asian industry consultants R3. In addition to field marketing operations, holding companies snatched up digital shops.

Strengthening resources on the Mainland has become critical: R3 said China played a critical role in the outcome of recent global reviews like Nokia, Johnson & Johnson, Dell, Samsung and Wrigley. China has become a center of product development for marketers, with some of those innovations, launched globally. Agencies like Ogilvy & Mather are already producing advertising in its Beijing office that is being used elsewhere in the world.

"Next year China is expected to overtake Japan as the second-largest ad market," says Miles Young, chairman, Ogilvy Asia Pacific, which runs the largest mainland group. "And how much longer, after, before it overtakes the U.S.? This part of the world has to be as sophisticated as the West. Now you have agencies here with the same global standards as anywhere else."

With the evolution of the Chinese marketing communications industry, clients are demanding more accountability.

"More and more marketers are now conducting media and financial audits in China to validate agency performance than ever before," says Greg Paull, principal at R3, Beijing. "In recent

Key Insights

1. The biggest challenge is to anchor your brand with premium positioning and then introduce multiple price points.
2. Because rapid change is the norm, consumers are fast adopters of technology.
3. Global account consolidations increasingly turn on the strength of agency operations in China.

Chinese Highlights

- Population: 1.3 billion
- 2008 Estimated GDP Annual Growth: 10.1%
- 2007 Ad Spend: $16.6 bil. '08: $20.9 bil.
- China had 210 million Internet users at the end of 2007 and in 2008 will surpass the U.S. as the country with the most Web users.
- China is already the world's largest mobile phone user population, with 500 million owning the devices.

years, the market has become so critical globally for companies and they are bringing in the world's best practices into their operations."

Advertising related to the Olympics began over a year ago and is set to boom as the August games approach. In November at the raucous annual China Central Television auction of prime-time slots, the country's biggest traditional medium reeled in nearly $11 billion in ad spending this Olympics year, about 20 percent higher than in 2007. One new development was the amount of local money at the auction, where multinational marketers were actually outbid by more aggressive Chinese companies.

The state-owned national network is a power unto itself in China, censoring ad content before it airs. CCTV is facing new competition from other media, including provincial stations which have hit shows and digital media. As a voice of the Communist Party, CCTV is subject to restrictions and limits on programming, so it is somewhat limited in the kind of innovation it can attempt.

"The major challenge for marketers in China is to reach consumers through the increasingly cluttered media environment which is surrounding the consumer," says Paul Pi, vp, marketing, Adidas, Greater China, an Olympic partner. "The digital platform is becoming increasingly important to the marketing mix within China."

This year, for instance, China will surpass the U.S. as the country with the largest number of Internet users.

As the only Chinese company to be an Olympic worldwide sponsor, PC maker Lenovo will be the first sign of the arrival of China Inc. on the world stage just as the 1964 Tokyo games introduced Japanese companies to a larger global audience. In recent years, Western auto companies have capitalized on China. Now the country has become the world's second-largest car market with local companies like Chery (this being China, the company's name mimics Chevy) beginning to sell branded vehicles in the U.S., Europe and Latin America through an alliance with Chrysler.

One of China's most fascinating recent client developments occurred in December. Appliance maker Haler Group hired exMotorola and ad agency exec, American Larry Rinaldi as its first global chief brand officer. Like most state-run companies, Haier—which already sells products through U.S. and European retailers—has focused more on tactical promotions than corporate brand building.

"This could be a watershed. If Haier becomes successful, a lot of Chinese companies could follow suit," says Tom Kao, chairman, Y&R, Greater China, who worked on Haier. "A lot of Chinese brands are ambitious and want to become worldwide brands. But there are few Chinese brands that have become successful in becoming a more global organization."

While some Chinese marketers seek a global profile, others are focused first in expanding in their own booming backyard.

"We're seeing more of the rise of the mid-sized local marketer," says JWT's Doctoroff. "They're eager to establish a marketing framework."

Those multinationals have their work cut out. Grey Group Asia has found that across the region the majority of consumers surveyed, 73 percent, are interested in advertising—with the glaring exception of China.

"Only 27 percent believe there is any excitement [in ads], and [15 percent] feel it is not exciting, and only 5 percent believe their advertising is world class," says Mike Amour, CEO, Grey Global Group, Asia Pacific. "There is a truism that advertising is a window into a country's culture. So the Chinese people's desired view of their own country, and the view portrayed by advertising, may be out of synch. It's clearly a huge opportunity for marketers."

And it's clearly a time of social change. There's a growing number of working-age "empty nesters" as China's first generation of "little emperors" leave home. Those parents—estimated at 265 million and growing—have much more disposable income since they already own most of their household needs.

Those little emperors, who are swelling the ranks of China's first professional class, are already redefining status in the world's third-largest luxury market.

"Ten years ago wealth was the most important aspect of status, but now lifestyle is the expression of the newly arrived," notes T.H. Peng, CEO, McCann Worldgroup, Greater China. He says the "old Chinese" way equated wealth with materialistic luxury and power.

And despite the considerable cultural differences that make that journey unique within each of the BRIC countries, brands are increasingly the common language consumers share in articulating that arrival.

International OHS

Through the Looking Glass of the Global Economy

In late 2007, a multinational group of EHS professionals traveled to Mexico to observe working conditions at a giant open-pit copper mine in Cananea. What they found shocked them.

GARRETT BROWN

The occupational health and safety conditions at the giant open-pit copper mine in Cananea, Mexico displayed how workplace safety in the global economy can best be understood through the intersection of transnational corporations, a "race to the bottom" in working conditions and growing labor internationalism.

The historic, open-pit mine and processing plants in Cananea, Mexico are operated by the family-owned, transnational conglomerate Grupo Mexico, which acquired the mine for pennies on the dollar during the privatization of Mexico's state enterprises in the 1990s. Grupo Mexico also ended up owning several of Mexico's railroads, as well as copper mines in Peru, and it recently bought the bankrupt ASARCO (American Smelting and Refining Co.), which has mine and smelter properties in Arizona. Cananea is just 30 miles south of the Arizona border.

Like other transnational corporations in the global economy, Grupo Mexico has been on a relentless drive to reduce production costs, including weakening or eliminating labor unions, to boost corporate profits. Two years ago, Grupo Mexico began sustained attempts to replace unionized mine workers in Cananea with lower-cost, non-union contractor employees.

When Local 65 of the Mexican Miners union—one of the oldest and strongest in Mexico—refused to allow non-union maintenance and housekeeping contract employees into the mine, Grupo Mexico literally disassembled the dust collectors in the multi-building Concentrator Department and piled the duct work on the ground next to Area 23, one of the enclosed buildings processing the copper coming from the open-pit mine.

From that time forward, there has been a contest of wills between Grupo Mexico and the miners over how much silica-containing ore dust the mine workers are willing to breathe—given that the company disconnected the local ventilation systems—and how important it is to the miners to prevent their union from being steadily eaten away by increasing numbers of non-union contract employees. Some 400 contract workers already are on the job along with 1,200 unionized mine workers.

Over the last 2 years, the mine's concentrator buildings have been filled with dense clouds of rock dust, forming snowdrift-sized piles of settled dust two to three feet high through the plants. A bulk sample of the accumulated dust taken in October 2007 and sent to an AIHA-accredited laboratory in the United States found the dust was 23 percent crystalline silica, with 50 percent of particles in the respirable range of less than 10 microns in diameter.

Finally, in July 2007, the miners union struck the Cananea mine over health and safety issues, foremost among them being hazardous exposures to silica, a known human carcinogen and the cause of debilitating and usually fatal silicosis. The union miners also were reacting to an attempt by Grupo Mexico to establish a rival, company-friendly union (with only 85 members compared to the historic union's 1,200 members) as the sole legal union on site.

When the Cananea miners went on strike on July 30, the United Steel Workers (USW) union in the United States launched a solidarity campaign. The USW represents copper miners in Arizona working for ASARCO, now owned by Grupo Mexico, and, "thinking globally," has tried to build bridges to both the Mexican and Peruvian miners unions as all three unions have members employed by Grupo Mexico.

The Peruvian miners union also has conducted several strikes at Grupo Mexico-owned facilities over the last year, in part in response to Grupo Mexico's attempt to impose 12-hour shifts, instead of 8-hour days, on the mines. The unions consider 12-hour shifts in mining operations to be a serious safety hazard due to accidents caused by worker fatigue.

Reaching Out for Help

In September 2007, USW passed along to the all-volunteer Maquiladora Health & Safety Support Network (MHSSN) a request from Local 65 of the Mexican Miners union for an independent evaluation of the working conditions in the Cananea mine and the health status of the mine workers.

In 2 weeks, the MHSSN pulled together a volunteer team of eight occupational professionals to go to Cananea to conduct extensive interviews with 70 miners, perform lung function tests (spirometry) on the miners and spend 4 hours touring both the open-pit mine and the processing plants.

The OHS survey team consisted of three Mexicans (two occupational physicians and an industrial hygienist), four U.S. citizens (an occupational doctor, a registered nurse, an industrial hygienist and a Mexican-American pulmonary technician) and a third industrial hygienist from Colombia. A Southern California local union of the USW put up the $3,500 needed for travel expenses and all the professionals donated their time.

The OHS survey team spent a day and half interviewing and testing mine workers, who were recruited to participate by Local 65 of the Mexican Miners union, at the miners union hall in downtown Cananea. The afternoon of the second day was spent driving through the giant open-pit mine and walking through the multiple processing plants, where the bulk samples of settled rock dust were collected.

The multi-national OHS survey team was shocked at the level of disrepair and non-existent housekeeping in such a large facility operated by a major transnational corporation. The team concluded the Cananea mine and processing plants were being "deliberately run into the ground," according to the report issued by the survey team in November. Among the team's other findings, based on the worker interviews and spirometry test results, were:

- Semi-quantitative calculations indicate workers in the concentrator area are exposed to dust levels of at least 10 milligrams per cubic meter of air (mg/m3). The respirable quartz silica component of this dust would be at least 1.2 mg/m3, or 10 times greater than the Mexican Maximum Permissible Exposure Limit (LMPE) of 0.1 mg/m3;
- There are substantial elevations in the prevalence of respiratory symptoms in a population that should be healthier than the general, non-industrial worker population. These symptoms include shortness of breath, wheezing, cough and sputum production, which appears to be related to dust exposure estimates. These symptoms reflect past exposures, and likely underestimate the burden of disease that will occur in this population if the current exposures continue;

The group found that Grupo Mexico, in violation of existing Mexican workplace safety regulations, failed to:

- Conduct sufficient industrial hygiene monitoring to identify, evaluate and later control health hazards to miners including exposure to mineral dusts (including silica), acid mists, airborne solvents, high noise levels, high vibration levels and hot and cold conditions;
- Install effective ventilation and source pollution controls for silica-containing dust in the concentrator buildings and in the two ESDE plants to prevent hazardous exposures to sulfuric acid mists. The presence of high levels of acid mist is indicated by the fact that the floors and structural steel frame of ESDE II building have been eaten away;
- Conduct a comprehensive medical surveillance program to determine the health status of workers exposed to airborne contaminants (silica, heavy metals like lead, acid mists, solvents) and physical hazards such as noise and vibration;
- Provide the training required by Mexican law to workers with hazardous exposures that trigger the training requirement. Despite high noise levels, exposure to chemicals and exposures to energized machines, 91 percent of the interviewed miners had not received noise training, 58 percent had not received chemical hazards training, 70 percent had not received electrical hazards training and 75 percent had not received training on lockout/tagout procedures for operating and repairing energized equipment; and
- Correct serious electrical, machine-guarding and other safety hazards created by industrial-scale mining, crushing and pulverizing, acid leaching and electro-plating and milling operations to produce fine powder copper ore from refrigerator-sized rocks blasted out of an open-pit mine.

The OHS survey team could not verify the exact circumstances of the 50 separate accidents reported at the site in the past 12 months. The anecdotal reports of broken limbs, amputations, electrocutions, falls, burns and at least one fatality suggest these incidents were the result of unsafe working conditions, poorly maintained machinery and equipment and inadequate safety procedures. The investigators also found the enterprise's required Joint Management-Labor Safety Committee is small—six members total—and unable to conduct or oversee effective safety inspections, hazard corrections, accident investigations and employee training.

In April 2007, before the strike closed the facility, two inspectors from the Mexican Department of Labor (STPS) also inspected the mine and processing plants over 2 days. At the end of the site visit, the inspectors issued a report ordering Grupo Mexico to implement 72 separate corrective actions. The STPS findings confirm the reports of unsafe working conditions made by workers interviewed in October by the MHSSN team.

Among the 72 corrective actions prescribed by the STPS include orders to: 1) re-assemble and use dust collectors in the concentrator buildings; 2) repair the malfunctioning brakes on a 10-ton and a 15-ton crane in Area 30 of the concentrator; 3) install guards on moving parts and energized equipment; 4) correct numerous electrical hazards; 5) repair or replace damaged or missing wall and roof panels; and 6) implement a major housekeeping effort to clean up accumulated dusts throughout the plant.

Report Issued

In November 2007, the MHSSN team publicly issued its report at a press conference in Mexico City with miners from Local 65 in Cananea, representatives of the national office of the Mexican Miners union and USW members from the Arizona ASARCO mines and USW's Pittsburgh headquarters. (English and Spanish language versions of the MHSSN report, and photographs from the Cananea mine, are posted at *http://www.igc. org/mhssn.*)

Following the press conference, the joint MHSSN-union delegation met with STPS officials to request the creation of a tripartite (government-management-labor) commission to verify working conditions at the Cananea mine. Grupo Mexico, for its part, denied there were any unsafe conditions or worker illnesses at the mine.

A day later, the STPS responded by stating that the MHSSN study was not "legally valid," but refused to either follow up its own April 2007 inspection or establish a special fact-finding commission to resolve conflicting reports of actual conditions in the mine and processing plants.

The next step of this international OHS project will likely include filing a complaint under the labor side agreement of the North American Free Trade Agreement (NAFTA) in January 2008 by MHSSN and interested unions and labor rights organizations in Mexico and the United States. Efforts also are being made to raise funds for a more comprehensive health study of active and retired mines to determine the prevalence of respiratory diseases like silicosis.

The "new world order" of occupational safety and health in the globalized economy is evident even in this small project. A transnational corporation operates facilities in three countries, and, as many other transnationals do, exerts downward pressure in each country to maximize operating revenues and profits. The mine workers in the three countries are building bridges of solidarity and working toward "coordinated bargaining" with their common employer. And at the same time, occupational health professionals from three countries are volunteering their time and expertise to prevent a "race to the bottom" in workplace safety from undermining working conditions and workers' health throughout the global economy.

GARRETT BROWN, MPH, CIH, is coordinator of the Maquiladora Health & Safety Support Network and was a member of the OHS survey team in Cananea. The Cananea report and photos are posted at http:// www.igc.org/mhssn.

Out of Work

KANAGA RAJA

The number of people unemployed worldwide remained at an historical high in 2006 despite strong global economic growth, according to the International Labor Organization's (ILO's) January report, "Global Employment Trends Brief 2007."

The ILO reported that even though more people are working globally than ever before, the number of unemployed remained at an all-time high of 195.2 million in 2006, a global rate of 6.3 percent. This rate was almost unchanged from the previous year.

The ILO report counts workers in the informal sector, self-employed persons and unpaid family members as employed.

The ILO also reports only modest gains in lifting some of the world's 1.37 billion working poor—those working but living on less than the equivalent of $2 per person, per day—out of poverty. It stresses that there aren't enough decent and productive jobs to raise them and their families above the $2 poverty line.

"The strong economic growth of the last half decade has only had a slight impact on the reduction of the number of workers who live with their families in poverty and this was only true in a handful of countries. In addition, growth failed to reduce global unemployment," says ILO Director-General Juan Somavia.

"What's more, even with continued strong global economic growth in 2007, there is serious concern about the prospects for decent job creation and reducing working poverty further."

The report says that to make long-term inroads into unemployment and working poverty, it is essential that periods of high growth be better used to generate more decent and productive jobs. Reducing unemployment and working poverty through creation of such jobs should be viewed as a precondition for sustained economic growth.

Jose Salazar Xirinachs, the ILO's executive director of the employment sector, says that an integrated approach is needed to increase the job content of growth.

Policymakers need to balance high-productivity sector growth and labor-intensive growth, he says. In the area of macro-economic policy, they should avoid a preoccupation with inflation leading to overly restrictive fiscal and monetary policy, he says.

Another area of importance, he adds, is trade policy. In this period of trade negotiations and bilateral agreements, Xirinachs says, it is important to pay attention to gradualism and orderly adjustments. There is also a need to take into account the employment effects of trade agreements.

Xirinachs also points to the need to pay attention to the role of small and medium sized enterprises (SMEs). It is crucial to have policies to promote the SME sector, as in many countries it is the SME segment that is more dynamic in job creation.

He also highlights institutional and labor market interventions as another important area, in terms of finding the right balance between flexibility in labor market regulations and protection for workers.

According to the ILO report, at the end of 2006, 2.9 billion people aged 15 and older were in work, up 1.6 percent from the previous year.

How many of the new jobs created in 2006 were decent jobs is difficult to estimate, but given that the share of working poor in total employment decreased from 54.8 percent in 1996 to 47.4 percent in 2006, it is likely that at least some of the jobs were productive enough to help people work themselves and their families out of poverty, the ILO says.

Among the main findings of the report is that, for the last decade, economic growth has been reflected more in rising levels of productivity and less in growing employment. While world productivity increased by 26 percent, the global number of those employed rose by only 16.6 percent.

The last decade has also witnessed a decline in the share of the world's working-age population (aged 15 years and older) that is in employment. This employment-to-population ratio stood at 61.4 percent in 2006. This was 1.2 percentage points lower than 10 years earlier. The decrease was larger among young people (aged 15 to 24). Within this group, the ratio decreased from 51 percent in 1996 to 46.8 percent in 2006.

The increasing proportion of young people in school may in part explain this reduction, said the ILO.

Unemployment hit young people the hardest, with 86.3 million young people accounting for 44 percent of the world's total unemployed in 2006.

The gap between men and women continued, with 48.9 percent of women employed in 2006, compared with 74 percent of men. A decade earlier, in 1996, 49.6 percent of women and 75.7 percent of men were employed.

In 2006, the employment share of the service sector in total global employment progressed from 39.5 percent to 40 percent and, for the first time, overtook the share of agriculture, which fell from 39.7 percent to 38.7 percent. The industry sector represented 21.3 percent of total employment.

The report said that in most of the regions, unemployment rates did not change markedly between 2005 and 2006.

East Asia's unemployment rate was 3.6 percent, the lowest in the world. For the fifth consecutive year, East Asian economies have had GDP growth of over 8 percent. This was underpinned by China's growth rate of more than 10 percent. Despite such solid economic expansion, the total number of unemployed increased in 2006 by more than the previous year. The change was small enough, however, for the unemployment rate to rise by only 0.1 percentage points, to 3.6 percent.

Current estimates suggest that the number of people in East Asia working but still living with their families on below $2 a day fell to 347 million (or 44.2 percent of those in work) in 2006.

Slightly positive labor market trends in recent years in Latin America and the Caribbean are partly the result of three successive years of economic growth of over 4 percent. The unemployment rate decreased fractionally from 8.1 percent to 8 percent in 2006, which was about the same level as 10 years earlier.

Positive labor market trends are also reflected in a decrease in working poverty. The total numbers, as well as the share of those working but still living in poverty with their families, have decreased both at the $1-and $2-a-day poverty levels ever since reaching a high in 2003. Still, in 2006 almost one-third of those employed lived in households where each family member had to live on less than $2 a day.

According to the report, the Middle East and North Africa remained the region with the highest unemployment rate in the world, at 12.2 percent in 2006. Sub-Saharan Africa's rate stood at 9.8 percent, the second highest in the world. Sub-Saharan Africa also had the highest share in working poverty, with eight out of 10 women and men living on less than $2 a day with their families.

The ILO estimates that the global number of employed people earning $1 a day or less declined between 2001 and 2006. However, in Sub-Saharan Africa, it increased by another 14 million; the number held constant in Latin America and the Middle East and North Africa.

"Nowadays, the widespread conviction is that decent work is the only sustainable way to reduce poverty, which is why the target of 'full, productive and decent employment' will be a new target within the Millennium Development Goals in 2007. Therefore, it is now the time for governments as well as the international community to make sure that the favorable economic conditions in most parts of the world will be translated into decent job growth," the report concludes.

KANAGA RAJA, Third World Network Features/South-North Development Monitor (SUNS). KANAGA RAJA is a researcher with Third World Network based in Geneva, Switzerland.

Worrying Trends for the Global Outsourcing Industry

Barbara Wall

Outsourcing companies are raking in profits as fears spread that there will be a global recession, but their reputation as haven investments should be taken with a grain of salt, analysts advise.

The two largest Indian outsourcing groups in information technology, Tata Consultancy Services and Infosys Technologies, brought a smile to the faces of shareholders this month when they reported revenue growth in excess of 20 percent for the financial year that ended March 31. Their competitor, Wipro, was equally upbeat in its annual management statement, which suggested that businesses were still prepared to farm out activities to try to reduce operating costs and improve company focus.

Unfortunately, behind the glad tidings lie some worrying trends.

Revenue growth is slowing as Indian outsourcing companies weather an economic downturn in their main market, the United States. The Indian National Association of Software and Services Companies forecast revenue growth of 21 percent in 2008, down from 28 percent in 2007.

Those who believe that investing in Indian outsourcing is still a winning bet have dismissed the figures as inconsequential, but Frances Hudson, an equities strategist with Standard Life in Edinburgh, figures that outsourcing firms in the Asia-Pacific region will struggle to reverse the downward trend in revenue growth as economic and political headwinds build.

"There is a logical limit to the outsourcing story," she said. "High wage inflation is a growing problem for IT vendors in India. Experienced workers are moving jobs more frequently in a bid for better salary packages and this is having an impact on business models."

Wage inflation could not have happened at a worse time for the Indian outsourcing industry. "Both Infosys Technologies and Tata Consultancy have reported order delays from key clients in the financial services sector who are increasingly reluctant to commit to large-scale IT projects," Hudson said. Considering that both companies derive more than 30 percent of their business from banks, insurance companies and asset management groups, shareholders could be forgiven for feeling jumpy.

Anti-globalization sentiment could be the last straw. "As the global economy stalls and protectionism rears its head, we could see a significant number of companies move operations back onshore," Hudson said. "Businesses are becoming a lot more risk-averse and there is a sense that outsourcers in India and China will have to redouble their efforts to win new contracts."

With revenue growth slowing at information technology vendors like Infosys, Tata and Wipro, while revenue growth at multinational companies like IBM and Accenture continues, it's clear that someone is losing out.

International Business Machines and Accenture have won large contracts in recent months from U.S. financial services providers. Accenture posted its best-ever revenue growth figures—20 percent—for the three months ending May 31. Earnings per share grew 36 percent, another company record. Accenture has also raised its outlook for earnings per share.

Multinational IT outsourcers are in a better position to cope with the downturn, Hudson said, because buyers are increasingly passing over providers that offer delivery from just one country: Increasingly risk-averse clients, she said, are more comfortable with big-name companies that have operations in many countries. More significantly, multinationals tend to offer a fuller package and more tailored services in business processing and consultancy, according to Hudson. She said Indian IT vendors needed to move up the value chain if they were to compete effectively.

Outsourcing is a broad category covering IT, public services, security and product testing, among other activities. Hudson recommended that investors focus on businesses with long contracts, strong organic growth potential and high barriers to entry.

Serco Group might not be the most exciting company given its business, which includes taking people to prison. In terms of share price performance, however, "it is as safe a haven as is possible to find in the current economic climate," said Julian Cater, an analyst in London for Collins Stewart. "The majority of Serco's contracts are long-term agreements at a fixed price, so they are fairly immune to the economic cycle."

Analysts figure that there is plenty of scope for growth in public services outsourcing in Britain and mainland Europe.

This view is supported by the Public Services Industry Review, published in July, in which DeAnne Julius wrote: "Evidence suggests that private provision in the public services sector is generally cheaper than public provision, without sacrificing the quality of services provided. We anticipate an increase in outsourcing in areas such as health care, education and business processes."

Julius suggested companies that were already leaders in these areas—she mentioned VT Group, Capita Group, Serco Group and Interserve Group—could easily roll out their expertise internationally. Many countries in mainland Europe, including France and Spain, continue to rely on the civil service to deliver public services.

Developing markets also offer rich opportunities for outsourcing groups like Interserve, which provides maintenance and other building services and makes around 35 percent of its revenue from the Middle East. Analysts at Panmure Gordon, a London stockbrokerage firm, expect the stock to do well this year, having come back significantly since April.

Another group that is likely to benefit from the trend toward public sector outsourcing is a social housing contractor, Connaught Group. "Local authorities are under pressure to cut costs," said Henry Carver, an analyst at Panmure Gordon. "The rents they charge are fixed but the cost of services is rising. Large social housing contractors such as Connaught Group are attractive propositions because they can afford to undercut small, local competitors."

Cater of Collins Stewart singled out Healthcare Locums, a British temporary staffing agency that places doctors and other health professionals in hospitals across Europe and the United States, as a potential beneficiary of the drive to cut costs in health care services. Healthcare Locums has a market capitalization of just $200 million but size has not been a barrier to growth.

Outsourcers in the testing and inspection subsector have piqued the interest of Alice Evans, a portfolio manager with Henderson Global Investors in London.

"The amount of testing that is being carried out on food, consumer products and the environment is increasing at a phenomenal pace," she said. "A lot of the growth is being driven by concerns from customers about minimizing litigation risk, and these concerns are being supported by government legislation." Pressure is also coming from consumers, she said, in the wake of tainted-food incidents that have increased the need for purveyors to show the purity of their products.

The global testing and inspection industry is worth $50 billion a year. Evans favors Intertek Group, which reported 10 percent organic revenue growth last year and a return on capital in excess of 25 percent.

Testing and inspection is the preferred subsector for Morgan Stanley within business services, because of its relatively defensive revenue base. The firm recently initiated coverage on the big players Intertek, SGS and Bureau Veritas, which outperformed the business services sector and wider market during the past 12 months.

As testing and inspection becomes more complex, high-tech companies like Eurofins Scientific, a leader in bioanalytical services, or the testing of pharmaceutical and hygiene products, food and the environment, should benefit, according to Evans. "The testing industry is highly fragmented, with significant scope for consolidation," Evans said.

Roots of Insecurity

Why American Workers and Others Are Losing Out

HORST BRAND

In 2004 the International Labor Office (ILO) published a voluminous though mistitled report called "Economic Security for a Better World." This is in fact a treatise about the economic insecurity that has been afflicting the world's working people for the past several decades. It is also an argument criticizing the "liberalization context" of insecurity and the policies that have deliberately fostered it. Liberalization, says the ILO, is the objective of policies formulated by international financial institutions in concert with the U.S. Treasury—policies that are based on the "Washington Consensus."

The ILO defines liberalization in terms of certain "key policy commitments," all of which affect the situation of workers, though at times only indirectly. One of the crucial commitments is a reduction in the size and role of the public sector of given countries, which usually results in cutbacks in public employment and productive public assets and the elimination of much of the state's regulatory capacity. Other key commitments include unobstructed capital mobility, regardless of the effects on the value of a country's exchange rate and ability to finance domestic business (hence to sustain employment levels), and labor market "flexibility," a euphemism for removing (or restricting) such labor market "distortions" as trade unions and minimum wage laws and, in brief, subjecting workers to the dictates of supply and demand.

The Washington Consensus does not, in fact, govern the economies of the leading industrial countries, but its doctrines are broadly shared by their leading economists. The rights of labor and various labor standards are seen as "rigidities," to be modified or if possible removed. In his *Global Labour Flexibility*, Guy Standing, a senior economist with the ILO, writes, "In the 1980s . . . those favoring the cold bath approach were back in ascendancy, and it is no coincidence that in the latest era of insecurity no fewer than eight Nobel Prizes have been awarded to economists from the University of Chicago, where . . . the Chicago school of law and economics depicted regulations as impediments to growth . . . . In the 1980s and 1990s, security has been derided as the source of "rigidity" and dependency . . . ." This "neo-classical paradigm" is the very antithesis of what the ILO stands for—thus another ILO writer: "It essentially ignores the value of labor standards as instruments of social justice."[1]

Nelson Lichtenstein notes the disdain with which this concern is viewed by top government representatives. "At a 1998 meeting of the G-8 industrial nations in Cologne, a delegation of trade unionists, representing virtually all the big labor confederations in the developed world, found themselves completely stymied when they tried to put international labor standards, financial market regulation, and compensatory help to displaced workers on the agenda. In any national context, such initiatives would have been long-standing elements of mainstream politics." These ideas were now "considered anathema . . . to the principles of free trade . . . and even to political parties—like those then running Great Britain, Germany, and the United States—that relied on the labor vote for their very survival."

The attitude of the G-8 officials is more explicitly conveyed by Alan Greenspan, then chair of the Federal Reserve's Board of Governors, in words that go to the roots of job insecurity—though this was not their intent. At a symposium in 2000, attended by high officials of international financial institutions and economists, Greenspan said that it was "remarkable how far economic opinions . . . have shifted since the 1970s. At the risk of some oversimplification, there has been a noticeable reversion in thinking toward nineteenth century liberalism, with the consequence that deregulation and privatization have become policies central to much government reform." Greenspan further remarked that although "the value standards of our societies that developed out of the Great Depression" have given rise to "some government regulations practiced virtually everywhere," it is now well understood that "government actions often hinder incentives to investments by increasing uncertainties, boosting risk premiums, and raising costs. . . . Many attempts to tame such regimes are not without cost in terms of economic growth and the average living standards of a nation."[2]

The "regimes" in that last sentence, which we once thought needed taming, are the "unbridled forms of capitalism." But "unbridled" is now a good thing: Greenspan immediately proceeded to discuss the contrast between the lower level of high-tech capital investment in Europe and Japan relative to the United States. And he attributed Europe's lower level of such investment to legislative protection of its workers against the "presumed harsher aspects of free-market competition."

The difference between Europe and Japan on the one hand and the United States on the other is all the more important, he averred, inasmuch as the return (profit margin) from newer technologies results chiefly from a reduction of labor costs. When firms cannot "really implement" such reductions—that is, "release" workers—rates of return will be lower. And this will blunt incentives to invest and result in lower productivity gains—gains that are "clearly evident in the United States and other countries with fewer impediments to implementation."

Indeed, few impediments to "releasing" employees exist in the United States. It is the only advanced industrial country that does not legally constrain employers to hire or fire at will (except on grounds of race or gender). The 1988 Worker Adjustment and Retraining Notification Act hardly provides even a modicum of job security. It mandates notification of plant closing or mass layoff where fifty or more employees are affected; it does not bar the discharge of employees. Without labor-management contracts restricting an employer's right, "workers have little entitlement to protections against loss of work."[3]

But layoffs also occur for reasons other than technological changes that make workers redundant. "Shareholder value" has motivated some large-scale discharges. For example, a Kodak company spokesperson explained why a planned layoff was raised from ten thousand to sixteen thousand persons because of Wall Street dissatisfaction with the previously announced lower number. "You cannot ignore important constituencies like shareholders," he said, according to the *New York Times*. That the "constituency" of property owners should take precedence over the interests of productive working people and their livelihood—and this case is by no means unusual—betrays a corruption of some fundamental moral values.

As regards Greenspan's claim that rates of return on technologically advanced plants and equipment in the United States have exceeded comparable rates in the European Union (EU)—although pertinent data are not at hand, it is unlikely that this is related to the greater protection of European workers. According to data published by the Economic Policy Institute in *The State of Working America, 2004/2005*, the growth rate of labor productivity (output per hour worked) averaged 1.7 percent annually between 1989 and 2000 for the United States, which is about the same as in France, Germany, Italy, and the United Kingdom. Nor did *levels* of the gross domestic product per hour worked differ significantly when figured in relation to the United States. For a number of EU countries (such as France and Germany), those levels exceeded that of the United States.

Deregulating Terms of Employment

These European countries, however, have been plagued by very high rates of unemployment—which have been attributed largely to labor market "rigidities" and to the relatively generous income supports for unemployed workers. Since the 1980s, these supports and the conditions of their availability have become increasingly restrictive (see below). More important, government and employer efforts have succeeded, if gradually and against much resistance, in making working conditions more "flexible." These developments have intensified employment and labor-market insecurity in the EU, particularly in France.

It has been argued that the hiring of workers was impeded in the EU by legal and administrative difficulties and attendant expense of dismissal. The American employment-at-will doctrine is not acceptable there and could not be enforced. But this difficulty has been widely circumvented by the use of temporary help and of term contracts. Temporary employment in France, Germany, and the Netherlands runs to near 15 percent of total employment and to some 30 percent in Spain. Moreover, there is a tendency to replace permanent employees, as these quit or retire, with temporary workers. It is in part this prospect that caused French youth to revolt against the law (eventually rescinded) that would have permitted employers to fire workers aged twenty-six and under without notice or explanation—thus invalidating part of the protective clauses of existing labor law.

Despite its subsequent rescission, the law exemplifies legislative tendencies in European countries seeking to deregulate or destandardize existing terms of employment and dismissal, thus facilitating a more "flexible" labor market. In Germany, for example, small and newly established firms have been relieved from certain worker protective rules. Part-time workers are excluded in determining the number of employees of a firm, thus "allowing more firms to remain below the size threshold for which protective rules apply." The "social plan that employers must negotiate in case of an economic downturn has been modified so that up to 20 percent of employees may be dismissed before a plan is worked out, rather than only 5 percent.[4] In general, protective statutes are evaded or circumvented. Outsourcing, for example, affects a substantial part of the labor force. Larger companies outsource work to small or semi-independent firms to whom conventional statutory regulations don't apply or don't fully apply. Guy Standing writes that "(T)he current era has seen a regrowth of casualization."[5]

Degrading Unemployment Compensation

In the advanced industrial countries, labor-market security—fundamentally assured by policies of full or near full employment—included the understanding, until the 1980s or 1990s, that income support would be available in case of job loss, and that such support would not be conditional on accepting the first job offered. It was a social right, if somewhat encumbered bureaucratically. It was part of a range of income supports to promote "the decommodification of labor." Now decommodification has turned into its opposite. The conditions for unemployment compensation have become stringent and exacting. Income maintenance programs have been designed to "activate beneficiaries," and the criteria for "suitable work"—which an unemployed person must accept—have been broadened well beyond the occupational status of previous employment.

Entry to social protection has been restricted, says Neil Gilbert, and exit has been accelerated.[6] According to the ILO report, income insecurity linked to unemployment has "unquestionably increased." Qualifying periods for benefit eligibility have been lengthened in many countries and the duration of benefits reduced; income replacement ratios have declined.

More generally, social protection in many, perhaps most, countries remains severely inadequate and is becoming even more inadequate under budgetary and privatization pressures. In the absence of reliable quantitative data, the ILO has developed a database derived from descriptive and budgetary information for 102 countries. It concludes that only one in three countries offers schemes covering the conventional social risks—among them, sickness, maternity, old-age disabilities, the plight of survivors, injury, and unemployment. One in six countries covers only one half or fewer of these risks. Only one in two pays unemployment benefits—and even then coverage is sparse, payouts low. Estimates of the adequacy of risk protection or of eligibility allow an evaluation of effectiveness: Only 17 of the 102 countries examined meet ILO criteria satisfactorily; 34 countries, mostly in Africa and Latin America, meet none of the criteria.

Pensions have been under strong privatization pressure. Moreover, there is a significant movement from defined benefits to defined contributions—a shift of investment risks to employees. As a result, income security in old age is in jeopardy. In addition, current earnings of workers bear a greater and greater burden of pension costs. Contribution rates have risen in half the countries surveyed by the ILO; the legal retirement age is being steadily increased; the number of years in which workers must contribute before they are entitled to state pensions is also being increased. Mandatory private insurance schemes (such as the one in Chile) intensify income insecurity.

The ILO report, in an unusually acerbic statement, says, "As income inequality grows, social policy is likely to become regressive . . . . The reality is that in the early years of the 21st century powerful interests are pressing governments all over the world to cut public social spending, and in doing so reduce the income security provided by the State."

The Curse of "Informal Labor"

"Labour relations are being informalized," says the report. Often the majority of working people, or a large minority of them, lack secure employment; they have no status as wage workers; no fixed workplace, such as a shop, factory, or office; and as often as not they lack social protection, such as health insurance or old-age pensions. The ILO estimates that 50 percent to 70 percent of those countries' labor force engages in informal activities—they are self-employed or casual workers or they work with or for their families. "About 40 percent of people in the developing world live in absolute poverty . . . obliged to take on the most rudimentary form of work or labor to ensure a basic subsistence."

Informal workers maintain work or market exchange relationships with semiformal or, indirectly, with formal enterprises. The *New York Times* of May 23, 2006, tells about Teresa Janoras, who scavenges for discarded food from hotels and restaurants in a Manila dump (where 150,000 people rummage through the daily delivery of 6,700 tons of garbage to find articles for recycling). Mrs. Janoras sells her "goods" to a broker as feed for pigs. On a good day (that is, a very long day), she earns three dollars. The relationship between her and the broker is not uncommon. "Informalization" is perpetuated by chains of subcontractors reaching upward from street and garbage dump collectors to, say, paper, plastic, and glass buyers, who have the stuff cleaned and sorted, then sell it to wholesalers, who in turn sell it to a manufacturer who probably employs a formal work force.

Alejandro Portes argues that "a high proportion of the informal labor force is in reality composed of 'disguised' wage workers who toil for modern firms" but have no status as "regular" employees.[7] Protective labor legislation, often modeled on the laws of industrially advanced countries, will not or cannot be enforced. "The fundamental difficulty in the application of protective legislation in Third World nations is the existence of a large mass of surplus labor," Portes writes. Non-enforcement of such legislation, however, is also part of a deliberate policy.

Portes himself has shown that industrialization in a number of Latin American countries increased at one-third again the rate of the gross domestic product, which itself doubled between the 1950s and 1980s even while their informal work force did not decrease; its proportion to the formal work force was unchanged. Furthermore, spokespersons for developing countries have opposed labor-standard clauses written into trade treaties, because such clauses would reduce the "comparative advantage" that plentiful cheap labor presumably bestows on them. Similarly, they justify the nonenforcement of the core ILO standards (for example, the right to free association and union organization). Considering that property and investment rights are stringently guarded under domestic and international laws, there should certainly be an effort to absorb informal workers in a modernizing economy based on a statutory conception of the labor market. This is clearly a political issue.

The conditions under which masses of workers exist recall Alan Greenspan's words about the "reversion in thinking toward nineteenth century liberalism." It might be relevant to quote a passage from E.J. Hobsbawm's *The Age of Capital, 1848–1875*, bearing upon labor market conditions in that century:

If any single factor dominated the lives of nineteenth-century workers it was *insecurity*. They did not know in the beginning of the week how much they would bring home at the end. They did not know how long their present work would last or, if they lost it, when they would get another job or under what conditions. They did not know when accident or sickness would hit them, and though they knew that sometime in middle age—perhaps in the forties for unskilled labourers, perhaps in the fifties for the more skilled—they would become incapable of doing a full measure of adult physical labour, they did not know what would happen to them between then and death. . . .

There was no certainty of work even for the most skilled: during the slump of 1857–58 the number of workers in the Berlin engineering industry fell by almost a third (Italics in original).

Although Greenspan and others may deny that the passage reflects the "vision" of nineteenth-century liberalism they have in mind, a large literature, including papers by World Bank staffers and the "Eurosclerosis" school, have argued for years, and with some success, about the adverse consequences of protective labor regulations. Standing writes that "there has been a considerable erosion of protective labor regulation in industrial, industrializing and low-income countries, in response to the growing openness to international trade and the changing international division of labor, under pressure from governments pursuing explicit and implicit protective deregulation or as a consequence of enterprise-level restructuring of employment relations towards 'external' labor flexibility.[8]

Attacking Organized Labor

Widespread hostility to unions has further impaired the capacity of workers to improve their conditions. This probably reflects deeper trends, summarized by the labor historian Henry Phelps Brown in the early 1990s: "The dissolution of the labor movement is . . . the counter-revolution of our time."[9]

Neither international competition nor advances in production technology fully explain the pressures on wages and benefits that American workers have been experiencing. In his *State of the Union: A Century of American Labor*, Nelson Lichtenstein points out, "Union labor's most significant difficulties first appeared not in manufacturing but in the construction industry." And the problems faced by municipal labor beginning in the 1970s were likewise "entirely homegrown," with the federal government refusing to relieve the fiscal crisis that older American cities underwent at the time owing to deindustrialization and a stagnant tax base. Regarding construction labor, the big companies using such labor acted in concert to resist wage demands. Contractors hired more and more non-union labor, and "the great exurban construction boom of the late 1980s and mid-1990s has been largely union-free. 'We're paying less than Wal-Mart,' acknowledged the president of a non-union construction group in Alabama."

A more recent example of labor-cost cutbacks unrelated to international competition is the policy of Caterpillar, an otherwise "healthy and profitable company," according to Louis Uchitelle, in the *New York Times* of February 6, 2006. After years of strikes and job actions at the company, the United Auto Workers union was compelled to accept the two-tier wage and benefit arrangements that had become emblematic of collective bargaining since the early 1980s. Newly hired workers would now receive lower rates of compensation and lower increases than their seniors. The average level of labor costs would thus decline as older workers quit or retired. "The long standing presumption that factory workers at successful companies can achieve a secure, relatively prosperous middle class life for themselves and their families," writes Uchitelle, "is evaporating."

Caterpillar imposed what it termed a "market-competitive payscale" in the localities or regions where it operates. Although workers in the lower tiers have a chance to work their way up, "the union mind set" of gaining annual increases doing minimally skilled jobs must be "shed," according to company officials. Uchitelle doesn't say so, but that policy may in time make the union irrelevant.

During the mid-twentieth century, labor in the industrial countries enjoyed rising real wages, a degree of job security, and an extension of its rights—tendencies that Scandinavian social democrats called decommodification—the distancing of labor, however gradual, from "the whip of the market." It was in line with the ILO's 1944 dictum that "labor is not a commodity"—an idea that had originated with John R. Commons and the Wisconsin school of labor relations. Moreover, labor standards were similar among the industrial countries' major trading partners, hence were neutral in regard to international competition. Yet, Lichtenstein rejects the notion that a "social contract" between labor and management existed during the mid-twentieth century, which was presumably abrogated in the 1980s. He points to the steep barrier to organizing in the South erected by the 1947 Taft-Hartley legislation and to the bitter strikes that occurred during the 1950s and 1960s. Beginning with Taft-Hartley, labor was forced onto the political defensive.

Standing similarly holds that there was no "Golden Age." The economic security of the few decades following the Second World War could not last. Deepening insecurity already lay ahead for large numbers of workers—an erosion of their rights, a recrudescence of commodification—for the supposed Golden Age, writes Standing, "was based on an inequitable and unsustainable international division of labor . . ." That was not the only reason why economic security crumbled. The postwar boom was ending, an era of much-slowed growth and productivity began. Worker demands for better conditions were resisted more strongly. Welfare-state budgets became harder to finance and met increasing opposition. But the fundamental event that brought about the end of the era of economic security was the transformation of the international division of labor.

The older division of labor was based, roughly speaking, on the manufacturing preeminence of the West and the agricultural and raw-materials economies of the South. With the end of colonialism and of Western dominance after the Second World War, this dependency relationship was no longer tolerable. The steady reduction of tariffs and import restrictions that industrial countries negotiated with one another in the postwar period (but which applied universally under the most-favored-nation principle) promised trading opportunities to some industrializing poorer countries.

Export- or trade-based economic growth, urged by the International Monetary Fund and the World Bank, spelled intensified global competition based on low labor costs. Low labor costs were enforced by repressive wage and worker association policies, as in Korea, until the late 1980s and other Southeast Asian countries. In China such policies have not abated. Even where such repressiveness has eased, labor cost differentials persist and keep attracting foreign capital—though, as product upgrading requires some skill improvement and as internal markets develop, such cost differentials will probably diminish to some degree.

The inequality of the international division of labor that marked the nineteenth and much of the twentieth centuries has undoubtedly lessened. This has been in large measure the result of an expanding world market—an expansion driven by capitalist enterprise, financial interests, reduction of trade barriers, and not least, since the 1960s, increasing pressures by developing countries. This same world market, however, has been the arena of widespread deprivation of fundamental labor rights and standards. The "liberalization context of insecurity" described in the ILO report has embraced efforts by international financial institutions to break down the collective bargaining power of labor as part of their deregulation project. These efforts have probably perpetuated the "informalization" of much of the working-age population in developing countries—the more so as the privatizing of public services and enterprises has inevitably meant layoffs.

"Liberalization" doesn't refer only to a pattern of regressive social policies; it is linked to powerful political forces that have material and ideological interests in privatizing public assets and services, and whose influence extends worldwide. There is little likelihood that these regressive forces will be overcome any time soon. Nor does a party of social democracy exist that appears capable of producing or enforcing a new vision of social justice—or, more particularly, of eliminating global poverty. The struggle for social justice will not cease, but, as yet, it cannot count on more than marginal success.

References

1. Roger Plant, *Labour Standards and Structural Adjustment.* (International Labour Office: Geneva, 1994), p. 9.
2. Alan Greenspan, "Opening Remarks—Global Integration: Opportunities and Challenges," in a symposium sponsored by the Federal Reserve Bank of Kansas City (Jackson Hole, WY, August 24–26, 2000).
3. Raymond Hogler, *Employment Relations in the United States: Law, Policy and Practice.* (Sage Publications, 2004), p. 162.
4. G. Bosch and W. Sengenberger, "Employment Policy, the State and the Unions in the Federal Republic of Germany," in *The State and the Labor Market*, Samuel Rosenberg, ed. (Plenum Press, 1989), p. 96.
5. Guy Standing, *Global Labor Flexibility: Seeking Distributive Justice* (St. Martin's Press, 1999), p.107.
6. Neil Gilbert, *Transformation of the Welfare State: The Silent Surrender of Public Responsibility* (Oxford University Press: New York, 2004), p. 66.
7. Alejandro Portes, "When More Can be Less: Labor Standards, Development, and the Informal Economy." In *Labor Standards and Development in the Global Economy* (U.S. Department of Labor: Washington, 1990), p. 28.
8. Guy Standing, "Structural adjustment and labour market policies: Towards social adjustment?" in *Towards Social Adjustment*, Guy Standing and Victor Tokman, eds. (International Labour Office: Geneva, 1991), p. 36.
9. Quoted in *Global Labour Flexibility*, op. cit., p. 2.2

HORST BRAND writes on economics for *Dissent*.

UNIT 5

International Business and the Future

Unit Selections

Key Points to Consider

- What do you think will be the future of oil in the global economy?

- Over the next century, Asia will rise to be an important economic and political power in the world. The Pacific Rim countries will be more important than they are today. What do you think of this development? How do you think it will affect Europe and the United States?

- What are some of the ways that other industries besides the auto industry can go green by? In what way could this step be important? And how do you think this could be accomplished?

- How do you think the changes in the global business environment will impact you and your career?

Student Web Site

www.mhcls.com/online

Internet References

The Economic Times
http.//www.The economic times
International Business Times
http.//www.ibtimes.com
Private Sector Development Blog of the World Bank
http.//www.psdblog.worldbank.org
Outsourcing Center
http.//www.outsourcing center.com

The one factor that will characterize the economy in the future is globalization. With increased communication, better transportation, logistical techniques, and with more integrated financial markets than they have ever been in the past, it seems only natural that the globalization of the world economy will continue at an increasing pace in the future.

In today's world economy, Boston is as far away from New York as Singapore is. Workers in the United States are competing, not just with other Americans, as was the case a generation ago, for jobs, status and position with in and outside of their organizations, but with people from all over the world. Because of the end of the Cold War, new markets and sources of supply have opened for the first time in decades. This represents the entry of over 1.5 billion new people into the world economy, who up until the end of the Cold War, were not a part of this market. They have brought with them enormous talent and energy along with the desire for the things that by rights, should be provided to them. Their entry into the global economy has made it a far more competitive place, yet it has also provided business and industry far greater opportunities to those who have enough courage and imagination to take advantage of these new opportunities.

These events, however, are not without risk. There is the possibility that things could go terribly wrong in the next ten years and that the promise of globalization could turn into the nightmare the protectionists predict. In "Countdown to a Meltdown," the worst possible scenario that could happen in the next ten years is explored. It is a presentation of what might happen if things were to really go bad in the economy as well as some other aspects of the society.

In "A New World Economy" the argument is made that as China and India continue to grow and prosper, they will begin to dwarf the European countries in terms of size and productivity. While the European countries are seeking to unite themselves in the form of the European Union, long-term demographic trends seem to be working against Europe. Birth rates in Europe are so low that the population is going to grow progressively older and eventually start to decline, unless these trends are reversed. The population of Russia is already declining at a rate of about one million a year. Bulgaria, Estonia, Lithuania, Romania, Moldova, Hungary, The Czech Republic, Serbia, Montenegro, Germany and Poland are already experiencing declining populations. This aging of the population in Europe will put a nearly impossible strain on Europe's social safety net that will make America's problems with Social Security look trifling, unless draconian reforms are put in place now, something that Europeans seem little interested in doing.

India and China are the countries with the largest population on the planet, each with over one billion people. The next country in terms of population is the United States with about 300 million people, followed by Indonesia with about two-thirds as many as the United States and then Brazil with a little more than half as many as the United States. While all of Europe together, from Iceland to the Urals exceeds the American population, given the current trends, this will be reversed by 2050. In the meantime, India is expected to exceed China's population by 2050.

As the economies of India and China continue to grow and prosper, they will exceed the United States and Europe in terms

© Eric Audras/Photoalto/PictureQuest

of potential. There will be almost three billion people in India and China by 2050, but only about 400 million in the United States. Even if an expanded European Union is added, India and China are likely to have a total market, including demand for goods and services as well as labor force that is three times that of Europe and the United States combined. If Japan, Taiwan and Korea, which are already highly developed, as well as Indonesia, and the rest of Asia are added, it is easy to see that over the next fifty years, the economic center will be moving in the direction of the Pacific and away from the Atlantic.

The next century will bring new challenges to the environmental movement to help preserve the globe and environmentalists will face new hurdles. Most people agree that human beings have been, at the very least, lax in the stewardship of the earth and that people need to take a more active role in presenting and protecting the environment. But, this is a worldwide endeavor. What happens in terms of pollution in China affects the environment in the United States and Europe. For example, even the auto industry is attempting to become more environmentally friendly, and not just by finding alternative fuels to gasoline, but by finding alternative materials with which to actually manufacture the vehicles.

What all this means is that globalization, for good or for bad, is here to stay. It means a far more competitive world than the one that existed just a few years ago. But it also means more opportunities for more people than ever before. People are going to have to be smarter than they were and they are going to have to be more aware of the world around them and the changes that are taking place in that world. The days of going to work to the same company and retiring with a gold watch and a pension after forty years of service are over. People are going to have to change companies simply because many of the companies are not going to be around for forty years. These issues are addressed in "Globalization and You," which deals with the fact that you are not only competing with the person next to you, but with people you will never meet or ever see.

The present world, highly competitive and exciting, is just waiting for people with the right ideas and who are willing to hard work, to seize it.

Countdown to a Meltdown

America's coming economic crisis. A look back from the election of 2016.

JAMES FALLOWS

January 20, 2016, Master Strategy Memo Subject: The Coming Year—and Beyond

Sir:

It is time to think carefully about the next year. Our position is uniquely promising—and uniquely difficult.

The promise lies in the fact that you are going to win the election. Nothing is guaranteed in politics, but based on everything we know, and barring an act of God or a disastrous error on our side, one year from today you will be sworn in as the forty-sixth president of the United States. And you will be the first president since before the Civil War to come from neither the Republican nor the Democratic Party.[1] This is one aspect of your electoral advantage right now: having created our new party, you are already assured of its nomination, whereas the candidates from the two legacy parties are still carving themselves up in their primaries.[2]

The difficulty, too, lies in the fact that you are going to win. The same circumstances that are bringing an end to 164 years of two-party rule have brought tremendous hardship to the country. This will be the first time since Franklin Roosevelt took office in 1933 that so much is demanded so quickly from a new administration. Our challenge is not just to win the election but to win in a way that gives us a chance to address economic failures that have been fifty years in the making.

That is the purpose of this memo: to provide the economic background for the larger themes in our campaign. Although economic changes will be items one through ten on your urgent "to do" list a year from now, this is not the place to talk about them in detail. There will be plenty of time for that later, with the policy guys. Instead I want to speak here not just as your campaign manager but on the basis of our friendship and shared efforts these past twenty years. Being completely honest about the country's problems might not be necessary during the campaign—sounding pessimistic in speeches would hurt us. But we ourselves need to he clear about the challenge we face. Unless we understand how we got here, we won't be able to find the way out once you are in office.

Politics is about stories—the personal story of how a leader was shaped, the national story of how America's long saga has led to today's dramas. Your personal story needs no work al all. Dwight Eisenhower was the last president to enter office with a worldwide image of competence, though obviously his achievements were military rather than technological. But we have work to do on the national story.

When it comes to the old parties, the story boils down to this: the Democrats can't win, and the Republicans can't govern. Okay, that's an overstatement; but the more nuanced version is nearly as discouraging.

The past fifty years have shown that the Democrats can't win the presidency except when everything goes their way. Only three Democrats have reached the White House since Lyndon Johnson decided to leave. In 1976 they ran a pious sounding candidate against the political ghost of the disgraced Richard Nixon—and against his corporeal successor, Gerald Ford, the only unelected incumbent in American history. In 1992 they ran their most talented campaigner since FDR, and even Bill Clinton would have lost if Ross Perot had not stayed in the race and siphoned away votes from the Republicans. And in 2008 they were unexpectedly saved by the death of Fidel Castro. This drained some of the pro-Republican passion of South Florida's Cuban immigrants, and the disastrous governmental bungling of the "Cuba Libre" influx that followed gave the Democrats their first win in Florida since 1996—along with the election. But that Democratic administration could turn out to have been America's last. The Electoral College map drawn up after the 2010 census removed votes from all the familiar blue states except California, giving the Republicans a bigger head start from the Sunbelt states and the South.

As for the Republicans, fifty years have shown they can't govern without breaking the bank. Starting with Richard Nixon, every Republican president has left the dollar lower, the federal budget deficit higher, the American trade position weaker, and the U.S. manufacturing workforce smaller than when he took office.

The story of the parties, then, is that the American people mistrust the Republicans' economic record, and don't trust the Democrats enough to let them try to do better. That is why—and it is the only reason why—they are giving us a chance. But we can move from electoral to governmental success only with a clear understanding of why so much has gone so wrong with the economy. Our internal polls show that nearly 90 percent of the public thinks the economy is "on the wrong track." Those readings should hold up, since that's roughly the percentage of Americans whose income has fallen in real terms in the past five years.

The story we will tell them begins fifteen years ago,[3] and it has three chapters. For public use we'll refer to them by the names of the respective administrations. But for our own purposes it will be clearer to think of the chapter titles as "Cocking the Gun," "Pulling the Trigger," and "Bleeding."

1. Cocking the Gun

Everything changed in 2001. But it didn't all change on September 11.

Yes, the ramifications of 9/11 will be with us for decades, much as the aftereffects of Pearl Harbor explain the presence of thousands of U.S. troops in Asia seventy-five years later. Before 2001 about 12,000 American troops were stationed in the Middle East—most of them in Kuwait and Saudi Arabia. Since 2003 we have never had fewer than 100,000 troops in CENTCOM's theater, most of them on active anti-insurgency duty. The locale of the most intense fighting keeps changing—first Afghanistan and Iraq, then Pakistan and Egypt, now Saudi Arabia and the frontier between Turkey and the Republic of Kurdistan—but the commitment goes on.

Before there was 9/11, however, there was June 7, 2001. For our purposes modern economic history began that day.

On June 7 President George W. Bush celebrated his first big legislative victory. Only two weeks earlier his new administration had suffered a terrible political blow, when a Republican senator left the party and gave Democrats a one-vote majority in the Senate. But the administration was nevertheless able to persuade a dozen Democratic senators to vote its way and authorize a tax cut that would decrease federal tax revenues by some $1.35 trillion between then and 2010.

This was presented at the time as a way to avoid the "problem" of paying down the federal debt too fast. According to the administration's forecasts, the government was on the way to running up $5.0 trillion in surpluses over the coming decade. The entire federal debt accumulated between the nation's founding and 2001 totaled only about $3.2 trillion—and for technical reasons at most $2 trillion of that total could be paid off within the next decade.[4] Therefore some $3.6 trillion in "unusable" surplus—or about $12,000 for every American—was likely to pile up in the Treasury. The administration proposed to give slightly less than half of that back through tax cuts, saving the rest for Social Security and other obligations.

Congress agreed, and it was this achievement that the president celebrated at the White House signing ceremony on June 7. "We recognize loud and clear the surplus is not the government's money," Bush said at the time. "The surplus is the people's money, and we ought to trust them with their own money."

If the president or anyone else at that ceremony had had perfect foresight, he would have seen that no surpluses of any sort would materialize, either for the government to hoard or for taxpayers to get back. (A year later the budget would show a deficit of $158 billion; a year after that $378 billion.) By the end of Bush's second term the federal debt, rather than having nearly disappeared, as he expected, had tripled. If those in the crowd had had that kind of foresight, they would have called their brokers the next day to unload all their stock holdings. A few hours after Bush signed the tax-cut bill, the Dow Jones industrial average closed at 11,090, a level it has never reached again.[5]

In a way it doesn't matter what the national government intended, or why all forecasts proved so wrong. Through the rest of his presidency Bush contended that the reason was 9/11—that it had changed the budget as it changed everything else. It forced the government to spend more, for war and for homeland security, even as the economic dislocation it caused meant the government could collect less. Most people outside the administration considered this explanation misleading, or at least incomplete. For instance, as Bush began his second term the nonpartisan Congressional Budget Office said that the biggest reason for growing deficits was the tax cuts.[6]

But here is what really mattered about that June day in 2001: from that point on the U.S. government had less money to work with than it had under the previous eight presidents. Through four decades and through administrations as diverse as Lyndon Johnson's and Ronald Reagan's, federal tax revenue had stayed within a fairly narrow band. The tax cuts of 2001 pushed it out of that safety zone, reducing it to its lowest level as a share of the economy in the modern era.[7] And as we will see, these cuts—the first of three rounds[8]—did so just when the country's commitments and obligations had begun to grow.

As late as 2008 the trend could have been altered, though the cuts of 2003 and 2005 had made things worse. But in the late summer of 2008 Senate Republicans once again demonstrated their mastery of the basic feints and dodges of politics. The tax cuts enacted during Bush's first term were in theory "temporary," and set to expire starting in 2010. But Congress didn't have to wait until 2010 to decide whether to make them permanent, so of course the Republican majority scheduled the vote at the most awkward moment possible for the Democrats: on the eve of a close presidential election. The Democratic senators understood their dilemma. Either they voted for the tax cuts and looked like hypocrites for all their past complaints, or they voted against them and invited an onslaught of "tax and spend" attack ads in the campaign. Enough Democrats made the "smart" choice. They held their seats in the election, and the party took back the presidency. But they also locked in the tax cuts, which was step one in cocking the gun.[9]

The explanation of steps two and three is much quicker: People kept living longer, and they kept saving less. Increased longevity is a tremendous human achievement but a fiscal challenge—as in any household where people outlive their savings. Late in 2003 Congress dramatically escalated the fiscal problem by adding prescription-drug coverage to Medicare, with barely any discussion of its long-term cost. David M. Walker, the government's comptroller general at the time, said that the action was part of "the most reckless fiscal year in the history of the Republic," because that vote and a few other changes added roughly $13 trillion to the government's long-term commitments.

The evaporation of personal savings was marveled at by all economists but explained by few. Americans saved about eight percent of their disposable income through the 1950s and 1960s, slightly more in the 1970s and 1980s, slightly less and then a lot less in the 1990s. At the beginning of this century they were saving, on average, just about nothing.[10]

The possible reasons for this failure to save—credit-card debt? A false sense of wealth thanks to the real-estate bubble?[11] stagnant real earnings for much of the population?—mattered less than the results. The country needed money to run its government, and Americans themselves weren't about to provide it. This is where the final, secret element of the gun-cocking process came into play: the unspoken deal with China.

The terms of the deal are obvious in retrospect. Even at the time, economists discussed the arrangement endlessly in their journals. The oddity was that so few politicians picked up on what they said. The heart of the matter, as we now know, was this simple equation: each time Congress raised benefits, reduced taxes, or encouraged more borrowing by consumers, it shifted part of the U.S. manufacturing base to China.

Of course this shift had something to do with "unfair" trade, undereducated American workers, dirt-cheap Chinese sweatshops, and all the other things that American politicians chose to yammer about. But the "jobless recovery" of the early 2000s and the "'jobless collapse" at the end of the decade could never have occurred without the strange intersection of American and Chinese (plus Japanese and Korean) plans. The Chinese government was determined to keep the value of its yuan as low as possible, thus making Chinese exports as attractive as possible, so that Chinese factories could expand as quickly as possible, to provide work for the tens of millions of people trooping every year to Shanghai or Guangzhou to enter the labor force. To this end, Chinese banks sent their extra dollars right back to the U.S. Treasury, in loans to cover the U.S. budget deficit; if they hadn't, normal market pressures would have driven up the yuan's value.[12] This, in turn, would have made it harder for China to keep creating jobs and easier for America to retain them. But Americans would have had to tax themselves to cover the deficit.

This arrangement was called "Bretton Woods Two," after the regime that kept the world economy afloat for twenty-five years after World War II. The question economists debated was how long it could last. One group said it could go on indefinitely, because it gave each country's government what it really wanted (for China, booming exports and therefore a less dissatisfied population; for America, the ability to spend more while saving and taxing less). But by Bush's second term the warning signals were getting louder. "This is starting to resemble a pyramid scheme," the *Financial Times* warned

early in 2005.[13] The danger was that the system was fundamentally unstable. Almost overnight it could go from working well to collapsing. If any one of the Asian countries piling up dollars (and most were doing so) began to suspect that any other was about to unload them, all the countries would have an incentive to sell dollars as fast as possible, before they got stuck with worthless currency. Economists in the "soft landing" camp said that adjustments would be gradual, and that Chinese self-interest would prevent a panic. The "hard landing" camp—well, we know all too well what they were concerned about.

2. Pulling the Trigger

The 2008 election, like those in 2000 and 2004, could have gone either way. If Fidel Castro had died two years earlier, the second Bay of Pigs tragedy and related "regime change" difficulties might have been dim memories by Election Day. Or if he had died a year later, the Cuban-American bloc of Florida voters would have been as reliably Republican in 2008 as in the previous fifty years. Since the red state-blue state divide was otherwise the same as in 2000 and 2004, if the Republicans had held Florida they would presumably have held the White House as well—despite mounting unease about debt, deficits, job loss, and rising U.S. casualties in Pakistan.

But by dying when he did, at eighty-two, and becoming the "October surprise" of the 2008 campaign, Castro got revenge on the Republicans who had for years supported the Cuban trade embargo. Better yet, he got revenge on his original enemies, the Democrats, too.[14] Castro couldn't have planned it, but his disappearance was the beginning—the first puff of wind, the trigger—of the catastrophe that followed.

Or perhaps we should call it the first domino to fall, because what then happened had a kind of geometric inevitability. The next domino was a thousand miles across the Caribbean, in Venezuela. Hugo Chavez, originally elected as a crusading left-winger, was by then well into his role as an outright military dictator. For years our diplomats had grumbled that Chavez was "Castro with oil," but after the real Castro's death the comparison had new meaning. A right-wing militia of disgruntled Venezuelans, emboldened by the news that Castro was gone, attempted a coup at the beginning of 2009, shortly after the U.S. elections. Chavez captured the ringleaders, worked them over, and then broadcast their possibly false "confession" that they had been sponsored by the CIA. That led to Chavez's "declaration of economic war" against the United States, which in practice meant temporarily closing the gigantic Amuay refinery, the source of one eighth of all the gasoline used on American roads—and reopening it two months later with a pledge to send no products to American ports.

That was when the fourth—and worst—world oil shock started.[15] For at least five years economists and oilmen alike had warned that there was no "give" in the world oil market. In the early 2000s China's consumption was growing five times as fast as America's—and America was no slouch. (The main difference was that China, like India, was importing oil mainly for its factories, whereas the United States was doing so mainly for its big cars.[16]) Even a temporary disruption in the flow could cause major dislocations.

All the earlier oil shocks had meant short-term disruptions in supply (that's why they were "shocks"), but this time the long term was also in question. Geologists had argued about "peaking" predictions for years, but the concept was on everyone's lips by 2009.[17]

The Democrats had spent George Bush's second term preparing for everything except what was about to hit them. Our forty-fourth president seemed actually to welcome being universally known as "the Preacher," a nickname like "Ike" or "Honest Abe." It was a sign of how much emphasis he'd put on earnestly talking about faith, family, and firearms to voters in the heartland, in his effort to help the Democrats close the "values gap." But he had no idea what to do (to be fair, the man he beat, "the Veep," would not have known either) when the spot price of oil rose by 40 percent in the week after the Chavez declaration—and then everything else went wrong.

Anyone who needed further proof that God is a Republican would have found it in 2009. When the price of oil went up, the run on the dollar began. "Fixed exchange rates with heavy intervention [in essence, Bretton Woods Two] have enormous capacity to create an illusory sense of stability that could be shattered very quickly," Lawrence Summers had warned in 2004. "That is the lesson of Britain in 1992, of Mexico in 1994, of emerging Asia in 1997, of Russia in 1998, and of Brazil in 1998." And of the United States in 2009. It didn't help that Hugo Chavez had struck his notorious then-secret deal with the Chinese: preferential future contracts for his oil, which China needed, in return for China's backing out of Bretton Woods Two, which Chavez wanted.

There had been hints of how the falling dominoes would look as early as January of 2005. In remarks made at the World Economic Forum in Davos, Switzerland, Fan Gang, the director of China's nongovernmental National Economic Research Institute, said that "the U.S. dollar is no longer seen as a stable currency."[18] This caused a quick flurry in the foreign-exchange markets. It was to the real thing what the World Trade Center car bomb in 1993 was to 9/11.

W hen we read histories of the late 1920s, we practically want to scream, *Stop! Don't buy all that stock on credit! Get out of the market before it's too late!* When we read histories of the dot-com boom in the late 1990s, we have the same agonizing sense of not being able to save the victims from themselves: *Don't take out that home-equity loan to buy stocks at their peak! For God's sake, sell your Cisco shares when they hit 70, don't wait till they're back at 10!*

In retrospect, the ugly end is so obvious and inevitable. Why didn't people see it at the time? The same clearly applies to what happened in 2009. Economists had laid out the sequence of causes and effects in a "hard landing," and it worked just as they said it would.

Once the run on the dollar started, everything seemed to happen at once. Two days after the Venezuelan oil shock the dollar was down by 25 percent against the yen and the yuan. Two weeks later it was down by 50 percent. By the time trading "stabilized," one U.S. dollar bought only 2.5 Chinese yuan—not eight, as it had a year earlier.[19]

As the dollar headed down, assets denominated in dollars suddenly looked like losers. Most Americans had no choice but to stay in the dollar economy (their houses were priced in dollars, as were their savings and their paychecks), but those who had a choice unloaded their dollar holdings fast.[20] The people with choices were the very richest Americans, and foreigners of every sort. The two kinds of assets they least wanted to hold were shares in U.S.-based companies, since the plummeting dollar would wipe out any conceivable market gains, and dollar-based bonds, including U.S. Treasury debt. Thus we had twin, reinforcing panics: a sudden decline in share prices plus a sudden selloff of bonds and Treasury holdings. The T-note selloff forced interest rates up, which forced stock prices further down, and the race to the bottom was on.

Because interest rates had been so low for so long, much of the public had forgotten how nasty life could be when money all of a sudden got tight.[21] Every part of the cycle seemed to make every other part worse.

Businesses scaled back their expansion or investment plans, since borrowed money was more expensive. That meant fewer jobs. Mortgage rates went up, so buyers who might have bid on a $400,000 house could now handle only $250,000. That pushed real-estate values down; over time the $400,000 house became a $250,000 house. Credit-card rates were more onerous, so consumers had to cut back their spending. Some did it voluntarily, others in compliance with the Garnishee Amendments to the Bankruptcy Act of 2008. Businesses of every sort had higher fixed costs: for energy, because of the oil-price spike; for imported components, because of the dollar's crash; for everything else, because of ripple effects from those changes and from higher interest rates. Those same businesses had lower revenues, because of the squeeze on their customer base. Early in Bush's second term economists had pointed out that the U.S. stock indexes were surprisingly weak considering how well U.S. corporations had been doing.[22] The fear of just these developments was why.

Americans had lived through a similar self-intensifying cycle before—but not since the late 1970s, when many of today's adults were not even born. Back in those days the sequence of energy-price spike, dollar crash, interest-rate surge, business slowdown, and stock-market loss had overwhelmed poor Jimmy Carter—he of the promise to give America "a government as good as its people." This time it did the same to the Preacher, for all his talk about "a new Democratic Party rooted in the oldest values of a free and faithful country." When he went down, the future of his party almost certainly went with him.

The spate of mergers and acquisitions that started in 2010 was shocking at the time but looks inevitable in retrospect. When the CEOs of the three remaining U.S. airlines had their notorious midnight meeting at the DFW Hilton, they knew they were breaking two dozen antitrust laws and would be in financial and legal trouble if their nervy move failed. But it worked. When they announced the new and combined AmFly Corporation, regulators were in no position to call their bluff. At their joint press conference the CEOs said, accept our more efficient structure or we'll all declare bankruptcy, and all at once. The efficiencies meant half as many flights (for "fuel conservation") as had been offered by the previously competing airlines, to 150 fewer cities, with a third as many jobs (all non-union).[23] Democrats in Congress didn't like it, nor did most editorialists, but the administration didn't really have a choice. It could swallow the deal—or it could get ready to take over the routes, the planes, the payrolls, and the passenger complaints, not to mention the decades of litigation.

Toyota's acquisition of General Motors and Ford, in 2012, had a similar inevitability. Over the previous decade the two U.S. companies had lost money on every car they sold. Such profit as they made was on SUVs, trucks, and Hummer-style big rigs. In 2008, just before the oil shock, GM seemed to have struck gold with the Strykette—an adaptation of the Army's Stryker vehicle, so famous from Iraq and Pakistan, whose marketing campaign attracted professional women. Then the SUV market simply disappeared. With gasoline at $6 a gallon, the prime interest rate at 15 percent, and the stock and housing markets in the toilet, no one wanted what American car makers could sell.[24] The weak dollar, and their weak stock prices, made the companies a bargain for Toyota.[25]

For politicians every aspect of this cycle was a problem: the job losses, the gasoline lines, the bankruptcies, the hard-luck stories of lifetime savings vanishing as the stock market headed down. But nothing matched the nightmare of foreclosures.

For years regulators and financiers had worried about the "over-leveraging" of the American housing market. As housing prices soared in coastal cities, people behaved the way they had during the stock-market run-up of the 1920s: they paid higher and higher prices; they covered more and more of the purchase price with debt; more and more of that debt was on "floating rate" terms—and everything was fine as long as prices stayed high and interest rates stayed low.

When the market collapsed, Americans didn't behave the way economic theory said they should.[26] They behaved the way their predecessors in the Depression had: they stayed in their houses, stopped paying their mortgages, and waited for the banks to take the next step. Through much of the Midwest this was a manageable problem: the housing market had gone less berserk to begin with, and, as in the Great Depression, there was a longer-term, more personal relationship between customers and financiers. But in the fastest-growing markets—Orlando, Las Vegas, the Carolina Research Triangle, northern Virginia—the banks simply could not wait. The deal brokered at the White House Security-in-Shelter Summit was ingenious: federal purchase of one million RVs and mobile homes, many of them built at idle auto or truck factories; subsidies for families who agreed to leave foreclosed homes without being evicted by marshals, such that they could buy RVs with no payments for five years; and the use of land at decom-

missioned military bases for the new RV villages. But it did not erase the blogcam live broadcasts of families being evicted, or the jokes about the "Preachervilles" springing up at Camp Lejeune, the former Fort Ord, and the Philadelphia naval shipyard.

Here is how we know that, a sitting president is going to lose: he is seriously challenged in his own party's primaries.[27] So if the economic tailspin had left any doubts about the prospects for the Preacher and his party, they were removed by the clamor to run against him in the Democratic primaries of 2012. The party's biggest names were all there: the senators from New York, Illinois, and Florida; the new governors of California and Pennsylvania; the mayor of New York, when it looked as if the Olympic Games would still be held there that fall; and the actor who in his three most recent films had captured Americans' idea of how a president should look and sound, and who came closest to stealing the nomination from the incumbent.

He and the rest of them were probably lucky that their campaigns fell short—not that any politician ever believes that. The Democratic nomination in 2012 was obviously a poisoned chalice, but a politician can't help thinking that a poisoned chalice is better than no chalice at all. The barrier none of them could have overcome was the financial crisis of state and local government.

All that befell the federal budget during the collapse of 2009–2012 happened to state and local governments, too, but more so. They had to spend more—on welfare, Medicaid, jails, police officers—while taking in less. One by one their normal sources of funding dried up.[28] Revenues from the multi-state lottery and the FreedomBall drawings rose a bit. Unfortunately, the surge of spending on casino gambling in forty-three states and on legalized prostitution in thirty-one didn't benefit state and local governments, because except in Nevada those activities were confined to Indian reservations, and had only an indirect stimulative effect.

And many governors and mayors faced a reality the president could avoid: they operated under constitutions and charters that forbade deficit spending. So they had no practical choice but to tighten the clamps at both ends, cutting budgets and raising taxes. The process had begun before the crash, as politicking in most state capitols was dominated by "intractable" budget disputes.[29] When the downturn really hit, even governors who had never heard of John Maynard Keynes sensed that it was a bad idea to raise taxes on people who were being laid off and evicted. But they were obliged by law to balance their budgets. All mayors and governors knew that it would be dicey to renege on their basic commitments to education, public safety, public health, and public infrastructure. But even in hindsight it is hard to know what else they could have done. California did too much too fast in closing sixty-three of its 110 community colleges[30] and imposing $9,500 annual "user fees" in place of the previous nominal fees. Its solution to the financing crisis on its high-end campuses was defter—especially the "Great Pacific Partnership" between the University of California and Tsinghua University, in Beijing. This was a win-win arrangement, in which the Chinese Ministry of Education took over the funding of the UC Berkeley physics, computer-science, and biology laboratories, plus the genomics laboratory at UC San Francisco, in exchange for a 51 percent share of all resulting patents.

State and local governments across the country did what they could. Fee-for-service became the norm—first for "enrichment" programs in the schools, then to underwrite teachers' salaries, then for emergency police calls, then for inclusion in routine police and fire patrols. First in Minnesota, soon after in Michigan, New York, and Pennsylvania, there were awkward moments when the governor, exercising his power as commander in chief of the state National Guard, ordered the Guard's medical units to serve in hospitals that had furloughed nurses and emergency-room doctors. The Democratic president decided not to force the question of who had ultimate control over these "citizen soldiers." This averted a showdown in the short term, but became one more attack point for the Republicans about weak and vacillating Democrats. Cities within 150 miles of the Mexican border opened police-service and trash-hauling contracts to companies based in Mexico. The state of Georgia, extending a practice it had begun in the early 2000s, said that it would hire no new public school teachers except under the "Partnership for Excellence" program, which brought in cut-rate teachers from India.[31]

The chaos in public services spelled the end for the administration, and for the Democratic Party in the long run. The Democrats couldn't defend the unions. They couldn't defend pensioners. They couldn't even do much for their limousine liberals. The nation had never been more in the mood for firm leadership. When the "Desert Eagle" scored his astonishing coup in the Saudi Arabian desert just before Christmas of 2011, America knew who its next leader would be. For a four-star general to join his enlisted men in a nighttime HALO32 special-operations assault was against all established practice. The Eagle's determination to go ahead with the stunt revealed him to be essentially a MacArthuresque ham. But the element of surprise was total, and the unit surrounded, captured, and gagged Osama bin Laden before he was fully awake.

The general's news conference the next day had the largest live audience in history, breaking the record set a few months earlier by the coronation of England's King William V. The natural grace of this new American hero was like nothing the world had seen since Charles Lindbergh landed in Paris. His politics were indistinct, but if anything, that was a plus. He was strong on defense; urgent (without details) about "lighting smart against our economic enemies"; and broadly appealing on "values"—a devout Catholic who had brought the first openly gay commandos into a front-line combat unit. ("When we were under fire, I never asked who they loved, because I knew they loved our flag.") Political pros had always assumed that America's first black president would be a Republican and a soldier, and they were right. He just didn't turn out to be Colin Powell.

The only suspense in the election was how big the win would be. By Labor Day it was clear that the Democrats might lose even the District of Columbia, whose rich residents were resentful about their ravaged stock portfolios, and whose poor residents had been cut off from Medicaid, welfare, and schools. As the nation went, so went the District, and after fifty-seven presidential elections the United States had its first across-the-board electoral sweep.

3. Bleeding

The emergencies are over. As our current president might put it, it's a war of attrition now. His administration hasn't made anything worse—and we have to admit that early on his ease and confidence were like a balm. But he hasn't made anything better, either. If not fully tired of him, the public has grown as fatalistic about the Republicans' ability to make any real difference as it already was about the Democrats'. The two-party system had been in trouble for decades. It was rigid, polarizing, and unrepresentative. The parties were pawns of special interests. The one interest group they neglected was the vast center of the American electorate, which kept seeking split-the-difference policies. Eight years of failure from two administrations have finally blown apart the tired duopoly. The hopes of our nation are bleeding away along with our few remaining economic resources.

Here is the challenge:

- Our country no longer controls its economic fundamentals.
- Compared with the America of the past, it has become stagnant, classbound, and brutally unfair.
- Compared with the rest of the world, it is on the way down. We think we are a great power—and our military is still ahead of China's. Everyone else thinks that over the past twenty years we finally pushed our luck too far.

To deal with these problems once in office, we must point out basic truths in the campaign. These truths involve the past sources of our growth: savings, investment, education, innovation. We've thrown away every one of these advantages. What we would do right now to have back the $1 trillion that Congress voted away in 2008 with the Freedom From Death Tax Act![33] A relatively small share of that money might have kept our aerospace programs competitive with Europe's[34]—to say nothing of preparing us for advances in other forms of transportation. A little more might have made our road and highway system at least as good as China's.[35] With what was left over, our companies might have been able to compete with Germany's in producing the superfast, quiet, efficient maglev trains that are now doing for travel what the jet plane did in the 1950s. Even if we couldn't afford to make the trains, with more money at least some of our states and regions might have been able to buy them, instead of just looking enviously at what China, India, and Iran have done.[36]

Or we could have shored up our universities. True, the big change came as early as 2002, in the wake of 9/11, when tighter visa rules, whatever their effect on reducing terrorism, cut off the flow of foreign talent that American universities had channeled to American ends.[37] In the summer of 2007 China applied the name "twenty Harvards" to its ambition, announced in the early 2000s, to build major research institutions that would attract international talent. It seemed preposterous (too much political control, too great a language barrier), but no one is laughing now. The Chinese mission to Mars, with astronauts from Pakistan, Germany, and Korea, indicates the scope of China's scientific ambition. And necessity has pushed China into the lead in computerized translation technology, so that foreign students can read Chinese characters. The Historic Campus of our best-known university, Harvard, is still prestigious worldwide. But its role is increasingly that of the theme park, like Oxford or Heidelberg, while the most ambitious students compete for fellowships at the Har-Bai and Har-Bei campuses in Mumbai and Beijing. These, of course, have become each other's main rivals—whether for scores on the World Ingenuity Test or in the annual meeting of the teams they sponsor at the Rose Bowl.

Or we could at last have begun to grapple with healthcare costs. We've managed to create the worst of all worlds—what the Democrats call the "30–30 problem." Thirty percent of our entire economy goes for health and medical costs,[38] but 30 percent of our citizens have no regular contact with the medical system. (Except, of course, during quarantines in avian-flu season.) For people who can afford them, the "tailored therapies" of the past decade represent the biggest breakthrough in medicine since antibiotics or anesthesia. The big killers—heart disease and cancers of the colon, lung, breast, and prostate—are now manageable chronic diseases at worst, and the big moral issues involve the question of whether Baby Boomers are living "too long." But the costs are astronomical, which raises questions of both efficiency and justice. Google's embedded diagnostic technology dramatizes our problem: based on nonstop biometric testing of the thirty-seven relevant enzymes and organ-output levels, it pipes into cell-phone implants instructions for which treatment, pill, or action to take next. The system is extremely popular—for the 10 million people who can afford it. NetJet flights to the Bahamas for organ replacement illustrate the point even more sharply, although here the breakthrough was less medical than diplomatic. The World Trade Organization, after the most contentious proceeding in its history, ruled that prohibiting commerce in human organs for transplant was an unjust trade barrier. The ruling may have caused the final, fatal split in the Republican Party (libertarians were jubilant, religious conservatives appalled), but it became the foundation of an important Caribbean industry after threats of violence dissuaded many transplant centers from operating within the United States. Meanwhile, despite the Strong America–Strong Americans Act of 2009, which tied income-tax rates to body-mass index and cigarette consumption, smoking and eating junk food have become for our underemployed class what swilling vodka was for the dispossessed in Boris Yeltsin's Russia.

All these issues involve money, and we can't avoid talking about money in this campaign. But your ability to address an even harder issue will largely determine whether you can succeed in the job the voters are about to give you.

That problem is the sense of sunset, decline, hopelessness. America has been so resilient as a society because each American has imagined that the sky was the limit. Obviously it was not for everyone, or always. From the beginning we've had a class system, and a racial-caste system, and extended periods—the 1890s, the 1930s, the 1970s, the past few years—when many more people than usual were struggling merely to survive. But the myth of equal opportunity has been closer to reality here than in any other society, and the myth itself has mattered.

My father, in explaining why it was so painful for him to see a lifetime's savings melt away after the Venezuelan crisis, told me about a political speech he remembered from his own youth. It was by Daniel Patrick Moynihan, a Harvard professor who later became a politician. In the late 1960s, when American prosperity held despite bitter political turmoil, Moynihan told left-wing students why preserving that prosperity should be important even to them. We know Europe from its novels, Moynihan said: the old ones, by Austen and Dickens and Stendahl, and the more recent ones, too. We know it as a static society. Young people, seeking opportunity, have to wait for old people to die. A whole life's prospects depend on the size of an inheritance. People know their place. America, Moynihan said fifty years ago, must never become a place like that.

That is the place we have become. Half this country's households live on less than $50,000 a year. That sounds like a significant improvement from the $44,000 household median in 2003. But a year in private college now costs $83,000, a day in a hospital $1,350, a year in a nursing home $150,000—and a gallon of gasoline $9. Thus we start off knowing that for half our people there is no chance—none—of getting ahead of the game. And really, it's more like 80 percent of the public that is priced out of a chance for future opportunity. We have made a perfect circle—perfect in closing off options. There are fewer attractive jobs to be had, even though the ones at the top, for financiers or specialty doctors, are very attractive indeed. And those who don't start out with advantages in getting those jobs have less and less chance of moving up to them.

Jobs in the middle of the skill-and-income distribution have steadily vanished if any aspect of them can be done more efficiently in China, India, or Vietnam. The K-12 schools, the universities, the ambitious research projects that could help the next generation qualify for better jobs, have weakened or dried up.[39] A dynamic economy is always losing jobs. The problem with ours is that we're no longer any good at creating new ones. America is a less attractive place for new business because it's a less attractive place, period.[40]

In the past decade we've seen the telephone companies disappear. Programming, data, entertainment, conversation—they all go over the Internet now. Pharmaceuticals are no longer mass-produced but, rather, tailored to each patient's genetic makeup. The big airlines are all gone now, and much of publishing, too. The new industries are the ones we want. When their founders are deciding where to locate, though, they'll see us as a country with a big market—and with an undereducated work force, a rundown infrastructure, and a shaky currency. They'll see England as it lost its empire. They'll see Russia without the oil reserves, Brezhnev's Soviet Union without the repression. They'll see the America that Daniel Patrick Moynihan feared.

This story is now yours to tell, and later I'll turn to notes for the stump speech. But remember that the reality of the story reaches backward, and that is why I have concentrated on the missed opportunities, the spendthrift recklessness, the warnings America heard but tuned out. To tell it that way in public would of course only make things worse, and we can't afford the recriminations or the further waste of time. The only chance for a new beginning is to make people believe there actually is a chance.

Notes

1. The last one was Millard Fillmore, a Whig. We will not emphasize this detail.

2. Also, though I never thought I'd say it, thank God for the Electoral College. In only two states, Michigan and Maine, are you polling above 50 percent of the total vote—in Michigan because of the unemployment riots, in Maine because that's what they're like. But you will probably have a strong plurality in at least forty other states, yielding a Reagan-scale electoral-vote "mandate."

3. Nothing in history ever quite "begins." Did America's problems with militant Islam begin in 2001? Or twenty years earlier, when we funded the anti-Soviet mujahideen in Afghanistan, who later turned their weapons against us? Or sixty years before that, with the breakup of the Ottoman Empire after World War I? Or during the Crusades? Similarly, warning signs of today's economic problems were apparent in the mid-1960s. But the big change started fifteen years ago, at the beginning of this century.

4. The federal debt consists of bills, notes, and bonds that come due at different periods—thirteen weeks, five years, twenty years. The main way to retire debt is to pay off holders on the due date. Only $2 trillion worth of debt would have matured within a decade, so only that much could be paid off. That is why the Bush administration's first budget message said, "Indeed, the President's Budget pays down the debt so aggressively that it runs into an unusual problem—its annual surpluses begin to outstrip the amount of maturing debt starting in 2007."

5. In 2005 Ben White, of *The Washington Post,* noted the coincidence of the Dow's peak and Bush's signing of the tax-cut bill.

6. Late in January of 2005 the CBO calculated that policy changes during Bush's first term had increased the upcoming year's deficit by $539 billion. Of that amount about 37 percent could be attributed to warfare, domestic security, and other post-9/11 commitments; 48 percent resulted from the tax cuts; and the rest came from other spending increases.

7. This CBO chart (omitted) illustrates the pattern. The big dive is the result of the 2001 and 2003 tax cuts.

8. In 2003 Congress approved a second round of tax cuts. In 2005, after a fifty-fifty deadlock, the Senate failed to enact a "pay as you go" provision, which would have required the administration to offset any tax cuts or spending increases by savings in the budget.

9. Through the early 2000s the Government Accountability Office issued warnings about the consequences of extending the tax cuts. This chart (omitted), from 2004, showed what would happen to the budget if the tax cuts were locked in.

10. "In the last year, the net national savings rate of the United States has been between one and two percent," the economist and then president of Harvard Lawrence Summers said in 2004, a year before the rate hit its nadir. "It represents the lowest net national savings rate in American history and, I believe, that of any major nation." Summers gave the speech five years after his appointment as Treasury secretary and five years before his nomination as chairman of the Federal Reserve Board.

11. Robert Shiller, an economist at Yale, was ahead of most other observers in predicting the collapse of the tech-stock bubble of the 1990s and the personal-real-estate bubble a decade later. In a paper for the National Bureau of Economic Research, published in 2001, he and two colleagues observed that the housing boom intensified the savings collapse. Every time homeowners heard that a nearby house had sold for an astronomical price, they felt richer, even if they had no intention of selling for years. That made them more likely to go out and spend their theoretical "gains"—and not to bother saving, since their house was doing it for them. "The estimated effect of housing market wealth on consumption is significant and large," Shiller and his colleagues concluded. If people felt rich, they spent that way.

12. As background for the speechwriters, here is the longer version of what was happening.

In normal circumstances economic markets have a way of dealing with families, companies, or countries that chronically overspend. For families or companies that way is bankruptcy. For countries it is a declining currency. By normal economic measures the American public was significantly overspending in the early 2000s. For every $100 worth of products and services it consumed, it produced only about $95 worth within our borders. The other $5 worth came from overseas. Normally an imbalance like this would push the dollar steadily down as foreigners with surplus dollars from selling oil or cars or clothes in America traded them for euros, yuan, or yen. As demand for dollars fell and their value decreased, foreign goods would become more expensive; Americans wouldn't be able to afford as many of them; and ultimately Americans would be forced to live within the nation's means.

That is in fact what happened in America's trade with Europe-and to a large extent with the oil-producing world. The euro skyrocketed in value against the dollar, and oil prices—which until the crisis of 2009 were fixed in dollars—went up too, which preserved Saudi and Kuwaiti buying power for European goods.

It didn't work this way with China. Americans bought and bought Chinese goods, and Chinese banks piled up dollars—but didn't trade them back for yuan. Instead China's central bank kept the yuan-to-dollar exchange rate constant and used the dollars to buy U.S. Treasury notes. That is, they covered the federal budget deficit. (Since Americans, on average, were saving nothing, they couldn't cover it themselves.) To a lesser extent Korean and Japanese banks did the same thing.

10. This was different from the situation in the 1980s and 1990s, when foreigners earned dollars from their exports and used those dollars to buy American companies, real estate, and stock. In those days foreigners invested heavily in America because (he payoff was so much greater than what they could get in Frankfurt or Tokyo. In an influential paper published in 2004 the economists Nouriel Roubini, of New York University, and Brad Setser, of Oxford University, demonstrated that this was no longer the case. Increasingly it was not individuals or corporations but foreign governments—in particular, state-controlled banks in Asia—that were sending money to America. And America was using it to finance the federal budget deficit.

13. The paper showed how foreign money was supporting U.S. spending.

14. We now know from the memoirs of his eldest son, Fidelito, that Castro never moderated his bitter view of the Kennedy brothers—Jack for authorizing the Bay of Pigs invasion. Bobby, for encouraging the CIA to assassinate Castro—and, by extension, their Democratic Party, Castro told his children that if the United States and Cuba ever reconciled, he dreamed of doing two things: throwing an opening-day pitch at Yankee Stadium, and addressing a Republican convention in prime time. (From *Mi Papa: The Castro I Knew,* Las Vegas: HarperCollins, 2009.)

15. The first one, starting in 1973, transformed the world more than most wars do. It empowered OPEC; enriched much of the Middle East; brought on five years of inflation, slow growth, and stock-market stagnation in the United States; pushed Japan toward a radically more energy-efficient industry; and more. The second, after the Iranian revolution of 1979, caused the inflation that helped drive Jimmy Carter from office, and spilled over into the recession of Ronald Reagan's first two years. The third, after Iraq's 1990 invasion of Kuwait, disrupted world trade enough to lay the groundwork for Bill Clinton's "It's the economy, stupid" attack against George H.W. Bush. And seven years after the shock of 2009 began, we are still feeling its effects.

16. After the first oil shock U.S. oil consumption actually fell in absolute terms. In 1973, as the first shock began, Americans consumed 35 "quads," or quadrillion BTUs, of oil. Ten years later, with a larger population and a stronger economy, they consumed only 30. But from that point on total consumption moved back up. In 2003 Americans consumed 39 quads—and two thirds of that oil was for transportation. Consumption for most other purposes, notably heating and power generation, actually went down, thanks to more-efficient systems. Industrial consumption was flat. So bigger cars and longer commutes did make the difference.

17. Every oil field follows a pattern of production: Its output rate starts slow and keeps getting faster until about half the oil has been pumped from the field. Then the rate steadily declines until the other half of the oil is gone. Since total world production is the aggregate of thousands of fields, it is presumed to follow a similar pattern. In 2005 the research and engineering firm SAIC released a report commissioned by the U.S. government on best guesses about the worldwide peak and what would happen when it came. "No one knows with certainty when world oil production will reach a peak," the report said, "but geologists have no doubt that it will happen." Of the twelve experts surveyed for the report, six predicted that the peak would have occurred before 2010, and three more that it would happen by 2020.

The world was not going to "run out" of oil—at least not immediately. Even at the peak, by definition, as much as had ever been pumped in history was still there to be extracted. But the rate of production, barrels per day and per year, would steadily lessen while the rate of demand kept increasing. The report was released when oil crossed $50 a barrel; we are long into the era of oil at 30 euros, or $90.

18. "That turned out to be the next-to-last convening of the Davos conference, before the unproven but damaging accusations that it was a front for the A. Q. Khan combine.

19. What happened to America almost exactly repeated what had happened ten years earlier to Thailand, Indonesia, and other countries during the Asian panic of 1997–1998. South Korea lost 50 percent of the value of its currency in two months; Indonesia lost 80 percent over the course of a year. As in America, the collapse of each currency led to equally deep stock-market declines. The Asian crash also turned into a foreign-policy nightmare for the United States, with Prime Minister Mahathir of Malaysia leading the denunciation of U.S.-based financiers, including the "moron" George Soros, for the "'criminal'" speculations that destroyed the economies of smaller nations like his. Since Malaysia and Indonesia are largely Muslim, and the financiers could be cast as part of the great shadowy U.S.-Zionist cabal, the crash worsened U.S. relations with the Islamic world.

20. Once the foreigners knew that the dollar had hit bottom, they came back to buy shares at bargain prices. But the currency run of 2009 showed the same pattern as the tech-stock crash of 2000 and, indeed, the generalized market panic of the 1930s: prices stayed depressed for years, because investors who had suffered heavy losses were understandably slow to return.

21. Let's make up flash cards for the speechwriters, so they are clear about the role of interest rates.

When interest rates go up, these things go down: stock-market prices, bond prices, housing prices, overall economic growth rates, overall investment, overall job creation.

The most important thing that goes up when interest rates rise is the value of the dollar. We'll save the cause and effect for our policy guys, but make sure the writers have these points straight.

For the speechwriters' benefit, let's spell this out too: Why did the dollar panic raise interest rates? Two related reasons. First, interest rates are ultimately set by supply and demand. If the Treasury can't sell enough notes at four percent to cover the deficit, it will keep raising the rate—to five, six, ten percent—until it gets the money it needs. Second, the main way a government can keep up the value of its currency is to raise interest rates, hoping to attract investments that would otherwise be made in yuan, euros, or yen.

22. In the spring of 2005, as stock averages slid week by week, W. Bowman Cutter, a managing partner of the investment-banking firm Warburg Pincus, asked, "Why are we not in a bull market now?" He said that if you looked at the traditional measures of economic strength—high corporate investment, rapid productivity improvements, strong overall growth rates—"you

would have to say that 2004 was the best year of the past twenty." Interest rates at the time were still very low. "If you transposed this to any other era in history." Cutter said, "you would have a very strong bull market. Why not now? Because the market is looking to the long-term structural problems." If the market couldn't go up when conditions were promising, it had no cushion when the crisis began.

23. Jobs in the airline industry had been plummeting for years. In 2000 the eight largest carriers employed 432,000 people. Four years later a third of those jobs were gone. That meant the loss of 136,000 mainly unionized, mainly high-wage jobs, offset by a small increase in lower-paid jobs at regional and discount airlines.

24. U.S. auto companies and the U.S. auto-buying public suffered in different ways from the "slowness" of America's industry compared with Japan's, China's, and Korea's. It took Detroit companies three years to shift production from trucks and SUVs to hybrid cars; by that time the Asian brands owned the market. Also, it took the American fleet as a whole a surprisingly long time to change. The average car on America's roads is nine years old, and in the course of a decade only half of all cars are replaced. It takes a long time to work the older gas-guzzlers out of the system.

25. The rising value of the euro and the troubled state of the airline market might well have made Boeing a similar target for the new Airbus-Mitsubishi consortium—but for the Transformational Air Mobility Industrial Base Act of 2011, which converted Boeing's factories to national-defense production facilities on a par with Navy shipyards.

26. Through the boom years speculators would borrow the entire cost of a house. If they could flip" it in a year or two, the profit on the sale would offset the interest they'd paid. But after mortgage rates "floated" up above 10 percent, the calculation changed. The house's value was heading down, and the cost of covering the mortgage was heading up. If the house were just another asset, the rational choice would be to move out and give it back to the bank. But houses aren't normal assets, and that's not what people did.

27. The pattern goes back to the very beginning of the modern primary system, after World War II, and it has no exceptions. If an incumbent faces a serious, vote-getting rival for his party's nomination, he goes on to lose the White House. If not, he stays in.

28. State and local governments tax income, which was falling; property, whose value was plummeting; and retail sales, which were down as well. The blue states were somewhat cushioned against the shocks in comparison with the many red states that had declined to impose state income taxes. Those states depended on property taxes, a fast-disappearing revenue source. Also, since the Nixon years red and blue states alike had relied on federal revenue sharing. This was slashed as part of the Emergency Budget Act of 2012.

29. In 2002 the Rockefeller Institute of Government projected budget trends for the states through 2010, and found that forty-four of them were headed for long-term deficits like the ones plaguing the federal government. The difference, again, is that many states were obliged to change their policies to avoid the deficits.

30. This accelerated a trend that had begun a decade earlier in California. For instance, when the 2003 school year began, some 175,000 students could not find space in community colleges—which, like K-12 public schools, had previously offered enrollment to all eligible students.

31. Gwinnett County, near Atlanta, opened many school administrators' eyes to this possibility in 2004, when it brought in twenty-seven teachers from Hyderabad. In 2005 an examination board in England outsourced the grading of high-school achievement exams to workers in India.

32. For "high-altitude, low-opening" parachute jump. The jumpers leave the plane at 30,000 feet, free-fall for nearly two minutes, and open their chutes at 1,000 feet, a few seconds before impact. Because the airplanes are so high, they cannot be seen or heard from the ground; and the jumpers spend almost no time with their chutes visibly deployed.

33. In the spring of 2005 the Congressional Joint Committee on Taxation estimated that ending the estate tax would directly cut federal revenue by $72 billion in 2015. Other groups calculated that the total impact on the budget, including higher interest payments on a larger federal debt, would be $100 billion a year, or $1 trillion over a decade. All this tax relief flowed to the wealthiest one percent of Americans.

34. In 1990 the American aerospace industry employed 1,120,000 people. By 2004 that number had fallen by nearly half, to 593,000. During those same years the European aerospace industry was growing in both sales and work force. In 2003 Airbus overtook Boeing in world market share for commercial airliners.

35. In 2005 the American Society of Civil Engineers released a "report card" on the state of America's infrastructure—roads, dams, bridges, aviation, and so on. The overall grade was D, with the highest mark being C+, for solid-waste handling. According to the report, the most dramatic underinvestment involved the nation's roads. Simply maintaining the roads at the same level would cost $94 billion, the report said—or half again as much as actual yearly investment levels. Improving the roads would require about twice as much as the United States was spending.

36. In 2003 the city of Shanghai opened the world's fastest maglev line, whose trains average 267 miles per hour and arrive on schedule 99.7 percent of the time. An editor's note in the *Journal of the American Society of Civil Engineers* pointed out that half a dozen maglev proposals for American cities were "stalled in one stage or another of planning, permitting, or budgeting." The result, the journal's editor observed, was this: "Traffic congestion on U.S. roads worsens, energy prices fluctuate unpredictably, and, at least for the moment, China pulls ahead of the United States on the path to a safe, reliable, fast, and efficient means of transporting passengers."

37. Foreign enrollment in U.S. universities increased steadily from 1971 through 2002. It fell the next year, and has gone down ever since.

38. It was under 8 percent in 1990 and under 12 percent in 2000.

39. It's hard to remember or even to believe, but not that long ago the school system was a valuable social equalizer. More important, it was seen that way. Through the three golden decades, from the late 1940s

(when the G1 Bill kicked in) to the late 1970s (when Proposition 13 passed in California), the federal government and the states put more money than ever before into elementary schools, high schools, and universities. More students than ever before finished high school; more finished college; more felt they could go further than their parents had. Proposition 13 was the California ballot measure that cut property taxes by 30 percent and then capped their future growth. It prefigured the federal tax cuts of the early 2000s, because it pushed the level of revenue below its historic "band." Before Proposition 13 California's per capita spending on public schools was high, like Connecticut's or New York's. Twenty years later it was well below the national average, just ahead of Arkansas's.

40. In the early 2000s one third of American public high school students failed to graduate on time. Niels Christian Nielsen, a

member of several corporate boards in Europe and the United States, said at the University of California in 2005, "The big difference between Europe and America is the proportion of people who come out of the system really not being functional for any serious role. In Finland that is maybe two or three percent. For Europe in general maybe fifteen or twenty. For the United States at least thirty percent, maybe more. In spite of all the press, Americans don't really get the education difference. They generally still feel this is a well-educated country and work force. They just don't see how far the country is falling behind."

JAMES FALLOWS, national correspondent for *The Atlantic,* has written three cover stories on U.S. foreign policy and Iraq: "Bush's Lost Year" (October 2004), "Blind Into Baghdad" (January/February 2004), and "The Fifty-first State?" (November 2002)

Oil Frontiers

The Future of Oil

ANDY ROWELL

In January 2007, as the world's media focused on the latest dire warnings about climate change coming from leading scientists meeting in Paris, another conference passed relatively unnoticed. Called the "Arctic Frontiers Conference," it was held in Tromso, Norway.

The opening speech was given by the fresh-faced and enthusiastic Norwegian Minister of Petroleum and Energy, Odd Roger Enoksen. "Oil is a strategic commodity and no country can afford to run out of oil," he told his captive audience. "Here, the Arctic could play an important role. If the U.S. Geological Survey is right, 25 percent of the world's undiscovered petroleum reserves could be found in the Arctic."

The Arctic region could be part of the "solution to the growing energy needs of the world," Enoksen continued. Exploitation of these resources would lead to considerable economic development in the Northern areas, but such a development would also cause considerable environmental concern.

Any development in the Barents Sea, a part of the Arctic Ocean between Norway and Russia, would have a huge ecological cost. The conservation group WWF calls the Barents one of the most productive marine ecosystems in the world and among the most biologically diverse in the Arctic.

To encourage oil exploitation, Norway issued a new exploration license round in 2006. Enoksen said the area had more than six billion barrels of oil equivalents in reserves, but many more to be found. All previous exploration activity has been in the Southern Barents Sea, which opened 25 years ago. The northern Barents is unexplored and the area to the east, where there is disputed ownership with Russia, remains "geologically very much unknown."

"Over the next few years, extensive exploration activity and drilling will take place," Enoksen concluded. "I see a new petroleum province emerging."

The Norwegian company Statoil, which recently merged with Norsk Hydro in a $30 billion deal to form the world's biggest offshore operator, is leading the development in the Barents Sea. It is the operator of the Snøhvit field, which means Snow White in English.

The field is radically different from traditional offshore oil and gas fields. There is nothing to see on the surface, no drilling platform or floating production vessel, nothing. It is the first major development on the continental shelf which has no surface installations at all. All the production facilities stand on the seabed, and are remotely controlled from onshore. The oil flows to land along an underwater pipeline. Snøhvit is "just the start," says Sverre Kojedal of Statoil. Echoing Enoksen, he says, "We think of the Barents Sea as Europe's new oil and gas province."

For the oil industry, regions like the Barents Sea and the Arctic are going to become ever more important, as traditional fields mature and others remain off limits. While the global oil industry may be flush with cash at the moment, finding and competing for oil and gas reserves is becoming increasingly difficult. Now the industry has to look further and harder to find oil.

Where the Oil Is

In May 2006, Business Week ran an article titled, "Why you should worry about Big Oil." It read: "beyond the fat profits, the giants are surprisingly vulnerable worldwide."

The giants' trouble is getting access to the remaining reserves of oil. Business Week pointed out that, in the 1960s, 85 percent of known reserves were accessible to the oil majors, but now that figure is only 16 percent. Even that figure has now been rewritten. In May 2007, a new report by energy consultants, PFC Energy concluded that the multinational oil companies "own or have access to less than 10 percent of world oil resources." One part of the problem is that the more easily discoverable reserves have already been found.

Jim Mulva, chief of ConocoPhillips, says that "vast new areas will need to be opened and explored." If they are not, the International Energy Agency is warning that the world is facing an oil supply "crunch" within five years that will force up prices to record levels.

Another part of the problem for Big Oil is that nearly two thirds of known reserves are now held by national oil companies— more than 60 percent of oil reserves are in the Middle East— and a further 19 percent have limited availability.

Big Oil is running out of oil. Countries that were once subservient partners to Big Oil, such as Venezuela, are less pliable. The majors have been hit by a double whammy: first, a spate of renationalizations, such as in Bolivia and Venezuela. Second, countries such as Russia have begun flexing their muscles and demanding the rewriting of one-sided contracts.

Shell's huge project on the island of Sakhalin, off Russia's Far East coast, is an example of the risks of frontier exploration. Once a penal colony, the area is remote and hostile. Two years ago, Shell announced that the cost of the main phase of development for Sakhalin 2 had doubled to $20 billion. Further delays threatened to undermine investor confidence not only in the project, but in Shell itself.

In 2006, in a move widely regarded as a sheer power play, Moscow announced that it might revoke a crucial environmental license Shell needed to proceed with the project. In December, Shell settled the dispute by allowing the Russian state-controlled Gazprom to take control of the project by buying 50 percent plus one share. Russia had wrestled a jewel from Shell's crown.

Shell was not alone in being pressured by the Kremlin. Two months later, fearing it would lose its operational license all together, BP offered to hand over a majority stake in Kovykta, one of Russia's most exciting gas projects, to Gazprom.

These episodes have left the oil industry reeling. Industry executives know how to factor in the huge technical and financial risks of frontier exploration, but the risk of politicians demanding contract renegotiations does not fit neatly into any spreadsheet.

The industry cannot escape the fact that where the reserves are is not where the friendliest governments are. Russia is sitting on a quarter of the world's natural gas reserves. Russia's known reserves are estimated at 47.82 trillion cubic meters, compared with Norway's total of just 2.41 trillion. Russia's gas field in the Barents, Shtokman, which is still awaiting exploitation, could be 10 times the size of Norway's Snow White field.

However, every time the Russian government demands contracts be rewritten, as with Shell and BP, Western companies and their governments become wary.

This is why European governments are looking to Norway rather than Russia, even though Norway's reserves are much smaller. Norwegian gas is already meeting 25 percent of the needs of France, Germany and the United Kingdom, and its exports to Europe are predicted to rise by almost 50 percent over the next 15 years.

Pushing Boundaries

Innovation has always driven the oil industry, and its main frontier is now in ever deeper waters. It is also moving further north into harsher and harsher conditions. In these frontier areas, the ecological and cultural footprint of the industry is much greater and much more damaging.

As the technology improves, the industry goes further than was technologically possible even a year or two before. Drilling depth records keep getting broken. As the Snow White fields shows, the days of a floating oil platform are coming to an end. In time, advances in technology may even allow for exploration beneath the polar ice. However, the ecological risks are tremendous—being able to drill under the ice does not mean that companies can clean up an oil spill there.

The ultimate irony is that as the polar ice melts, more areas of ocean and land open up for the oil industry to exploit.

Meanwhile, the search continues. Across the Arctic, just days after Enoksen's speech, Shell announced that it planned to drill the deepest offshore Alaskan well ever, at a depth of 14,000 feet beneath the sea floor. It was a remarkable U-turn for the company, which abandoned U.S. Arctic exploration 21 years ago. "Shell is pretty high on the Arctic," says Keith Craik, the Shell drilling engineer leading the project. "It's a really healthy place to look for hydrocarbons." The following month, the company announced it was gearing up for an "aggressive" 2007 offshore exploration program in the Alaskan Beaufort Sea.

In February, the U.S. Minerals Management Service (MMS) gave approval to Shell to drill as many as a dozen exploration wells over two years in the Beaufort Sea. Local environmental and indigenous groups were outraged. Earthjustice, a nonprofit law firm that represents five Alaskan environmentalist groups, sued to block the approval. They argued that Shell's activity could harm endangered bowhead whales, polar bears, migratory birds and other wildlife, and that MMS did not conduct a sufficiently rigorous environmental review to meet legal requirements.

"Native communities have the right to their subsistence way of life. Shell's plans will severely impede subsistence," argues Faith Gemmill of REDOIL (Resisting Environmental Destruction on Indigenous Lands), a network of Alaskan native subsistence users and one of the plaintiffs in the case against MMS. The agency's failure to propose a full environmental impact statement with public input, she says, demonstrates "neglect in responsibility and lack of humanity by failing to listen to the people most directly affected by offshore oil and gas exploration and development."

A federal court granted a temporary stay of MMS's approval for Shell in July.

But the bad news for local wildlife and indigenous groups is that Alaskan offshore oil and gas exploration is set to increase. So far, the world's oil companies have found more than 10 billion barrels of oil in North American Arctic seas. Many of those reserves, including gas, remain locked beneath the sea floor. Despite the fact that the Trans-Alaska-Pipeline has been operating since 1977 and over 15 billion barrels of oil have flowed along it, the industry has not been able to exploit Alaska's vast gas reserves.

All that is about to change with the building of a $30 billion Alaskan gas pipeline to transport gas from Alaska across Canada to the lower 48 states. Alaska's new governor, Sarah Palin, is working on legislation to push the project forward. BP, ExxonMobil and ConocoPhillips are all said to be interested in building the pipeline.

"For BP, the North Slope is the largest known but undeveloped resource in our portfolio, and frankly, we'd like to get rid of that idea," says David Van Tuyl of BP. "BP's future is directly linked to the future of the Alaska gas pipeline."

Every Last Drop

The oil industry magazine World Oil explains that the industry is pursuing a three-pronged strategy: First, it is seeking high-potential and accessible frontier targets for exploration. Second, it is using new technology to optimize the production from existing fields and maximize the life of those fields. Third, it is developing viable new prospects in known or mature areas. Of the three, it is actually the last area that may have the greatest effect on near-term world energy supply.

Shell's Robin Hamilton, a framework studies team leader for Shell International E&P (exploration and product) in Houston, argues, "Frontier exploration is the industry champagne and caviar that grabs media headlines, but generating new prospects in known areas remains the industry's bread and butter for exploration."

So the bread and butter for the oil industry over the next few years will be squeezing every last drop out of existing mature fields in friendly areas, such as the North Sea.

—A.R.

Trouble at Sea

The oil industry is going deeper and deeper in other offshore areas, as well. Last September, a consortium led by Chevron announced a record-setting test well in the U.S. Gulf of Mexico. It drilled in 7,000 feet of water and then another 20,000 feet below the sea floor. Some analysts are predicting that the field could be the largest in the United States since Alaska's Prudhoe Bay in 1968.

But going deeper and deeper is not without huge technical and physical risks, which translate into financial risk. BP has been placing its short-term bets in the Gulf of Mexico on its high-profile Thunder Horse field, which incorporates the largest offshore platform ever built, supported by 25 sub-sea wells. When operational, it will be the largest producer in the Gulf, producing some 250,000 barrels of oil and 200 million cubic feet of gas per day.

BP originally projected that it would start production in January 2005, but those plans were delayed and then thrown into disarray by Hurricane Dennis, which forced the semi-submersible platform to list some 20 to 30 degrees. Subsequently, metal failures have been found in the field's subsea system. The start date for Thunder Horse has now been pushed back to the second half of 2008. Every day costs BP untold financial loses.

Another deep offshore project that is over two years behind schedule is Shell's Bonga field, some 120 kilometers southwest of the Niger Delta, in water more than 1,000 meters deep. It has cost Shell and its partners some $3.5 billion before a drop of oil has been produced.

What is noteworthy is that most of these areas—Barents, Alaska and the Gulf of Mexico—are geo-politically safe.

Although Bonga has been beset by technical problems, it is far from the vortex of violence that surrounds Shell's operations in the Niger Delta itself. This fact is not lost on the industry. Notes Petroleum Economist, an oil industry journal, "As well as proved reserves, which have helped position West Africa as an exploration hotspot, the isolation factor, with fields located miles from the shore, suggests a more comfortable operating climate, free from vociferous communities and sabotage."

The Gulf of Guinea, where Bonga is located, is seen as another frontier for the industry. Within the next few years, some 25 to 30 percent of U.S. oil will come primarily from Africa. The United States now sees Nigeria and the other countries in the Gulf of Guinea as the "Next Gulf"—a counterweight to the Middle East.

Nigeria is not the only offshore "hotspot"—Angola too is enjoying a deep-water boom. In early 2007, Sonangol (Sociedade Nacional de Combustives de Angola) and Total registered new discoveries in waters over 5,000 feet deep. Chevron subsidiary the Cabinda Gulf Oil Company Limited also announced a significant oil discovery in deep water off Angola.

"This important discovery underscores the value of focusing Chevron's exploration program on high-impact opportunities," says John Watson, president of Chevron International Exploration and Production. "Our continued exploratory success in Angola, combined with our commitment to developing these resources, offers great prospect for increasing Angola's oil-producing capacity."

Into the Amazon

Just as the industry goes deeper offshore, it goes deeper into forests and other protected areas. Many oil companies are looking to the Amazon as another frontier, especially in Peru, where the government remains friendly to Western multinationals.

Perupetro, Peru's state-owned oil company, is hoping to attract U.S. energy companies to highly controversial drilling concessions. In total, some 11 Amazonian blocks, covering approximately 22 million acres of highly biodiverse, intact primary tropical rainforest, are up for grabs.

Three of those blocks intrude upon official reserves set up to protect some of the last native peoples still living a traditional lifestyle in the Amazon. Three others overlap protected areas, and nine intrude upon titled indigenous lands. Only one block does not intrude on indigenous lands or protected areas. The new blocks mean that approximately 70 percent of the Peruvian Amazon will be carved into oil concessions. Just two years ago, it was only 20 percent.

Resistance is growing. In February 2007, indigenous leaders interrupted a presentation in Houston by Perupetro concerning the new Amazon oil concessions.

The indigenous leaders warned over 200 representatives of oil majors, including ExxonMobil, that their communities would vigorously oppose both the auction and exploitation of any drilling blocks intruding on their tropical rainforest homelands. The fight will be uphill, however.

The Final Frontier

Oil companies can only go so deep offshore and only so far into the forest before the economics do not add up. This means that the final oil frontier will be in unexpected areas. As conventional reserves get smaller, more remote and more costly, the reserves embedded in unconventional heavy oils and oil sands become increasingly logistically and financially attractive.

By the end of the decade, the largest source of new oil supplies will be in Canada and Venezuela. In December 2006, Jeff Rubin, the chief strategist with CIBC World Markets, a subsidiary of the Canadian Imperial Bank of Commerce in Toronto, said that most of the world's new capacity growth outside of OPEC will come from oil sands development after 2009.

"While deep water oil will account for the largest share of net additions of non-conventional capacity in the next two to three years, the oil sands will account for a larger share of incremental production growth after 2009," he argues. According to Rubin, Canada holds about 50 percent of the world's "investable reserves" for Western oil companies barred from operating in countries such as Saudi Arabia, Mexico and even Russia.

For the oil industry, unconventional oil has much going for it. It might be costly to convert to conventional oil, but that cost is calculable and largely predictable. Although Hugo Chavez's Venezuela is slightly unpredictable at the moment, it is still selling oil to the United States, and close to U.S. consumers.

In February 2007, Venezuela's President Chavez announced the nationalization of private oil assets in the Orinoco Delta, a region of heavy oil reserves. Chavez announced that the Venezuelan state would take a controlling 60 percent stake in heavy oil projects run by BP, ExxonMobil, Chevron, ConocoPhillips, Total and Statoil. He added that Venezuela doesn't "want the companies to go. . . . We just want them to be [minority] partners." By May, Chavez's government finally seized control of the last remaining oil projects controlled by U.S. and European oil companies.

In contrast, Canada is as politically safe and financially secure as they come. "In the final analysis," argues Rubin, "what makes the oil sands properties so valuable is that there are few other places where production can grow and even fewer where you can invest. Canada's oil sands may be the final frontier for investors intent on profiting from depleting conventional crude reserves."

His analysis was backed by the first major report of its kind into unconventional oil two months later. Oil consultants Wood Mackenzie predicted in February 2007 that all of the world's extra oil supply is likely to come from oil sands and heavy oils within 15 years.

According to Wood Mackenzie calculations, there are 3,600 billion barrels of unconventional oil and gas reserves in Canadian oil sands and Venezuela's Orinoco region. This is 13 times Saudi Arabia's reserves. Of these Canadian and Venezuelan reserves, only 8 percent has begun to be developed. Fifteen percent of the undeveloped reserves is actually heavy and extra-heavy oil; the remainder is even more challenging and more energy intensive to produce.

The study argues that the shift from conventional to unconventional oil may not be far away. Dr. Rhodri Thomas from Wood Mackenzie argues that, within the decade, non-OPEC conventional oil will peak and go into decline. Thomas predicts the gap will be filled by unconventional oil sources, with production from Canadian oil sands quadrupling.

The increasing reliance on unconventional oil will require a substantial reshaping of the oil industry, notes the *Financial Times*. The super-majors—Shell, Total, Exxon and Chevron—are all investing heavily in Canada and Venezuela. Others, including the Chinese oil companies, are looking at countries as diverse as Madagascar to exploit the heavy oil.

There are two downsides to the holy grail of unconventional oil. First is the huge ecological cost. Take Canada's oil sands development: Some 150,000 square kilometers of Alberta's boreal forest could be dramatically transformed into an industrialized landscape, much of it strip-mined.

Oil sands are heavy, molasses-like, and need huge amounts of energy and water to upgrade them to a refinable product. According to the Pembina Institute, Canadian oil sands operations are licensed to divert 350 million cubic liters of water a year—twice that used by the city of Calgary. Each day, enough energy to heat more than three million Canadian homes is used to produce oil sands. Producing a barrel from oil sands produces three times more greenhouse gas emissions than a barrel of conventional oil.

The second challenge is whether it is technically feasible to convert unconventional oil at a competitive price, even given the relatively high oil prices at the moment. "The ability to extract this heavy oil in significant volumes is still non-existent," argues Matthew Simmons, a leading peak-oil advocate. "It's like turning gold into lead," as pristine areas are sacrificed for little benefit.

ANDY ROWELL is contributing editor to Oil Change International's The Price of Oil, and co-author of *The Next Gulf-London, Washington and Oil Conflict in Nigeria* (Constable & Robinson).

A New World Economy

The balance of power will shift to the East as China and India evolve.

PETE ENGARDIO

It may not top the must-see list of many tourists. But to appreciate Shanghai's ambitious view of its future, there is no better place than the Urban Planning Exhibition Hall, a glass-and-metal structure across from People's Square. The highlight is a scale model bigger than a basketball court of the entire metropolis—every skyscraper, house, lane, factory, dock, and patch of green space—in the year 2020.

There are white plastic showpiece towers designed by architects such as I.M. Pei and Sir Norman Foster. There are immense new industrial parks for autos and petrochemicals, along with new subway lines, airport runways, ribbons of expressway, and an elaborate riverfront development, site of the 2010 World Expo. Nine futuristic planned communities for 800,000 residents each, with generous parks, retail districts, man-made lakes, and nearby college campuses, rise in the suburbs. The message is clear. Shanghai already is looking well past its industrial age to its expected emergence as a global mecca of knowledge workers. "In an information economy, it is very important to have urban space with a better natural and social environment," explains Architectural Society of Shanghai President Zheng Shiling, a key city adviser.

It is easy to dismiss such dreams as bubble-economy hubris—until you take into account the audacious goals Shanghai already has achieved. Since 1990, when the city still seemed caught in a socialist time warp, Shanghai has erected enough high-rises to fill Manhattan. The once-rundown Pudong district boasts a space-age skyline, some of the world's biggest industrial zones, dozens of research centers, and a bullet train. This is the story of China, where an extraordinary ability to mobilize workers and capital has tripled per capita income in a generation, and has eased 300 million out of poverty. Leaders now are frenetically laying the groundwork for decades of new growth.

Invaluable Role

Now hop a plane to India. It is hard to tell this is the world's other emerging superpower. Jolting sights of extreme poverty abound even in the business capitals. A lack of subways and a dearth of expressways result in nightmarish traffic.

But visit the office towers and research and development centers sprouting everywhere, and you see the miracle. Here, Indians are playing invaluable roles in the global innovation chain. Motorola, Hewlett-Packard, Cisco Systems, and other tech giants now rely on their Indian teams to devise software platforms and dazzling multimedia features for next-generation devices. Google principal scientist Krishna Bharat is setting up a Bangalore lab complete with colorful furniture, exercise balls, and a Yamaha organ—like Google's Mountain View (Calif.) headquarters—to work on core search-engine technology. Indian engineering houses use 3-D computer simulations to tweak designs of everything from car engines and forklifts to aircraft wings for such clients as General Motors Corp. and Boeing Co. Financial and market-research experts at outfits like B2K, OfficeTiger, and Iris crunch the latest disclosures of blue-chip companies for Wall Street. By 2010 such outsourcing work is expected to quadruple, to $56 billion a year.

Even more exhilarating is the pace of innovation, as tech hubs like Bangalore spawn companies producing their own chip designs, software, and pharmaceuticals. "I find Bangalore to be one of the most exciting places in the world," says Dan Scheinman, Cisco Systems Inc.'s senior vice-president for corporate development. "It is Silicon Valley in 1999." Beyond Bangalore, Indian companies are showing a flair for producing high-quality goods and services at ridiculously low prices, from $50 air flights and crystal-clear 2 cents-a-minute cell-phone service to $2,200 cars and cardiac operations by top surgeons at a fraction of U.S. costs. Some analysts see the beginnings of hyper-competitive multinationals. "Once they learn to sell at Indian prices with world quality, they can compete anywhere," predicts University of Michigan management guru C.K. Prahalad. Adds A. T. Kearney high-tech consultant John Ciacchella: "I don't think U.S. companies realize India is building next-generation service companies."

Simultaneous Takeoffs

China and India. Rarely has the economic ascent of two still relatively poor nations been watched with such a mixture of awe, opportunism, and trepidation. The postwar era witnessed economic miracles in Japan and South Korea. But neither was populous enough to power worldwide growth or change the game in a complete spectrum of industries. China and India, by contrast, possess the weight and dynamism to transform the 21st-century global economy. The closest parallel to their emergence is the saga of 19th-century America, a huge continental economy with a young, driven workforce that grabbed the lead in agriculture, apparel, and the high technologies of the era, such as steam engines, the telegraph, and electric lights.

But in a way, even America's rise falls short in comparison to what's happening now. Never has the world seen the simultaneous, sustained takeoffs of two nations that together account for one-third of the planet's population. For the past two decades, China has been growing at an astounding 9.5% a year, and India by 6%. Given their young populations, high savings, and the sheer amount of catching up they still have to do, most economists figure China and India possess the fundamentals to keep growing in the 7%-to-8% range for decades.

Barring cataclysm, within three decades India should have vaulted over Germany as the world's third-biggest economy. By mid-century, China should have overtaken the U.S. as No. 1. By then, China and India could account for half of global output. Indeed, the troika of China, India, and the U.S.—the only industrialized nation with significant population growth—by most projections will dwarf every other economy.

What makes the two giants especially powerful is that they complement each other's strengths. An accelerating trend is that technical and managerial skills in both China and India are becoming more important than cheap assembly labor. China will stay dominant in mass manufacturing, and is one of the few nations building multibillion-dollar electronics and heavy industrial plants. India is a rising power in software, design, services, and precision industry. This raises a provocative question: What if the two nations merge into one giant "Chindia?" Rival political and economic ambitions make that unlikely. But if their industries truly collaborate, "they would take over the world tech industry," predicts Forrester Research Inc. analyst Navi Radjou.

In a practical sense, the yin and yang of these immense workforces already are converging. True, annual trade between the two economies is just $14 billion. But thanks to the Internet and plunging telecom costs, multinationals are having their goods built in China with software and circuitry designed in India. As interactive design technology makes it easier to perfect virtual 3-D prototypes of everything from telecom routers to turbine generators on PCs, the distance between India's low-cost laboratories and China's low-cost factories shrinks by the month. Managers in the vanguard of globalization's new wave say the impact will be nothing less than explosive. "In a few years you'll see most companies unleashing this massive productivity surge," predicts Infosys Technologies CEO Nandan M. Nilekani.

To globalization's skeptics, however, what's good for Corporate America translates into layoffs and lower pay for workers. Little wonder the West is suffering from future shock. Each new Chinese corporate takeover bid or revelation of a major Indian outsourcing deal elicits howls of protest by U.S. politicians. Washington think tanks are publishing thick white papers charting China's rapid progress in microelectronics, nanotech, and aerospace—and painting dark scenarios about what it means for America's global leadership.

Such alarmism is understandable. But the U.S. and other established powers will have to learn to make room for China and India. For in almost every dimension—as consumer markets, investors, producers, and users of energy and commodities—they will be 21st-century heavyweights. The growing economic might will carry into geopolitics as well. China and India are more assertively pressing their interests in the Middle East and Africa, and China's military will likely challenge U.S. dominance in the Pacific.

One implication is that the balance of power in many technologies will likely move from West to East. An obvious reason is that China and India graduate a combined half a million engineers and scientists a year, vs. 60,000 in the U.S. In life sciences, projects the McKinsey Global Institute, the total number of young researchers in both nations will rise by 35%, to 1.6 million by 2008. The U.S. supply will drop by 11%, to 760,000. As most Western scientists will tell you, China and India already are making important contributions in medicine and materials that will help everyone. Because these nations can throw more brains at technical problems at a fraction of the cost, their contributions to innovation will grow.

Consumers Rising

American business isn't just shifting research work because Indian and Chinese brains are young, cheap, and plentiful. In many cases, these engineers combine skills—mastery of the latest software tools, a knack for complex mathematical algorithms, and fluency in new multimedia technologies—that often surpass those of their American counterparts. As Cisco's Scheinman puts it: "We came to India for the costs, we stayed for the quality, and we're now investing for the innovation."

A rising consumer class also will drive innovation. This year, China's passenger car market is expected to reach 3 million, No. 3 in the world. China already has the world's biggest base of cell-phone subscribers—350 million—and that is expected to near 600 million by 2009. In two years, China should overtake the U.S. in homes connected to broadband. Less noticed is that India's consumer market is on the same explosive trajectory as China five years ago. Since 2000, the number of cellular subscribers has rocketed from 5.6 million to 55 million.

What's more, Chinese and Indian consumers and companies now demand the latest technologies and features. Studies show the attitudes and aspirations of today's young Chinese and Indians resemble those of Americans a few decades ago. Surveys of thousands of young adults in both nations by marketing firm Grey Global Group found they are overwhelmingly optimistic about the future, believe success is in their hands, and view products as status symbols. In China, it's fashionable for the upwardly mobile to switch high-end cell phones every three months, says Josh Li, managing director of Grey's Beijing office, because an old model suggests "you are not getting ahead and updated." That means these nations will be huge proving grounds for next-generation multimedia gizmos, networking equipment, and wireless Web services, and will play a greater role in setting global standards. In consumer electronics, "we will see China in a few years going from being a follower to a leader in defining consumer-electronics trends," predicts Philips Semiconductors Executive Vice-President Leon Husson.

For all the huge advantages they now enjoy, India and China cannot assume their role as new superpowers is assured. Today, China and India account for a mere 6% of global gross domestic product—half that of Japan. They must keep growing rapidly just to provide jobs for tens of millions entering the workforce annually, and to keep many millions more from crashing back into poverty. Both nations must confront ecological degradation that's as obvious as the smog shrouding Shanghai and Bombay, and face real risks of social strife, war, and financial crisis.

Increasingly, such problems will be the world's problems. Also, with wages rising fast, especially in many skilled areas, the cheap labor edge won't last forever. Both nations will go through many boom and harrowing bust cycles. And neither country is yet producing companies like Samsung, Nokia, or Toyota that put it all together, developing, making, and marketing world-beating products.

Both countries, however, have survived earlier crises and possess immense untapped potential. In China, serious development only now is reaching the 800 million people in rural areas, where per capita annual income is just $354. In areas outside major cities, wages are as little as 45 cents an hour. "This is why China can have another 20 years of high-speed growth," contends Beijing University economist Hai Wen.

Very impressive. But India's long-term potential may be even higher. Due to its one-child policy, China's working-age population will peak at 1 billion in 2015 and then shrink steadily. China then will have to provide for a graying population that has limited retirement benefits. India has nearly 500 million people under age 19 and higher fertility rates. By mid-century, India is expected to have 1.6 billion people—and 220 million more workers than China. That could be a source for instability, but a great advantage for growth if the government can provide education and opportunity for India's masses. New Delhi just now is pushing to open its power, telecom, commercial real estate and retail sectors to foreigners. These industries could lure big capital inflows. "The pace of institutional changes and industries being liberalized is phenomenal," says Chief Economist William T. Wilson of consultancy Keystone Business Intelligence India. "I believe India has a better model than China, and over time will surpass it in growth."

For its part, China has yet to prove it can go beyond forced-march industrialization. China directs massive investment into public works and factories, a wildly successful formula for rapid growth and job creation. But considering its massive manufacturing output, China is surprisingly weak in innovation. A full 57% of exports are from foreign-invested factories, and China underachieves in software, even with 35 software colleges and plans to graduate 200,000 software engineers a year. It's not for lack of genius. Microsoft Corp.'s 180-engineer R&D lab in Beijing, for example, is one of the world's most productive sources of innovation in computer graphics and language simulation.

While China's big state-run R&D institutes are close to the cutting edge at the theoretical level, they have yet to yield many commercial breakthroughs. "China has a lot of capability," says Microsoft Chief Technology Officer Craig Mundie. "But when

A Profile of Youth in India and China

China	India
66%—of young chinese adults regard themselves as individualists	62%—of young single women say it is O.K. to have faults that others can see
23%—of young Chinese adults say it is not important to have a child	76%—of young single women say they should decide when to have a child
64%—of young adults say married men should do housework	51%—of young urban women say a big house and car are key to happiness

Data: Grey Global Group

you look under the covers, there is not a lot of collaboration with industry." The lack of intellectual property protection, and Beijing's heavy role in building up its own tech companies, make many other multinationals leery of doing serious R&D in China.

China also is hugely wasteful. Its 9.5% growth rate in 2004 is less impressive when you consider that $850 billion—half of GDP—was plowed into already-glutted sectors like crude steel, vehicles, and office buildings. Its factories burn fuel five times less efficiently than in the West, and more than 20% of bank loans are bad. Two-thirds of China's 13,000 listed companies don't earn back their true cost of capital, estimates Beijing National Accounting Institute President Chen Xiaoyue. "We build the roads and industrial parks, but we sacrifice a lot," Chen says.

India, by contrast, has had to develop with scarcity. It gets scant foreign investment, and has no room to waste fuel and materials like China. India also has Western legal institutions, a modern stock market, and private banks and corporations. As a result, it is far more capital-efficient. A BusinessWeek analysis of Standard & Poor's Compustat data on 346 top listed companies in both nations shows Indian corporations have achieved higher returns on equity and invested capital in the past five years in industries from autos to food products. The average Indian company posted a 16.7% return on capital in 2004, vs. 12.8% in China.

Small-batch Expertise

The burning question is whether India can replicate China's mass manufacturing achievement. India's info-tech services industry, successful as it is, employs fewer than 1 million people. But 200 million Indians subsist on $1 a day or less. Export manufacturing is one of India's best hopes of generating millions of new jobs.

India has sophisticated manufacturing knowhow. Tata Steel is among the world's most-efficient producers. The country boasts several top precision auto parts companies, such as Bharat Forge Ltd. The world's biggest supplier of chassis parts to major auto makers, it employs 1,200 engineers at its heavily automated Pune plant. India's forte is small-batch production of high-value goods requiring lots of engineering, such as power generators for Cummins Inc. and core components for General Electric Co. CAT scanners.

What holds India back are bureaucratic red tape, rigid labor laws, and its inability to build infrastructure fast enough. There are hopeful signs. Nokia Corp. is building a major campus to make cell phones in Madras, and South Korea's Pohang Iron & Steel Co. plans a $12 billion complex by 2016 in Orissa state. But it will take India many years to build the highways, power plants, and airports needed to rival China in mass manufacturing. With Beijing now pushing software and pledging intellectual property rights protection, some Indians fret design work will shift to China to be closer to factories. "The question is whether China can move from manufacturing to services faster than we can solve our infrastructure bottlenecks," says President Aravind Melligeri of Bangalore-based QuEST, whose 700 engineers design gas turbines, aircraft engines, and medical gear for GE and other clients.

However the race plays out, Corporate America has little choice but to be engaged—heavily. Motorola illustrates the value of leveraging both nations to lower costs and speed up development. Most of its hardware is assembled and partly designed in China. Its R&D center in Bangalore devises about 40% of the software in its new phones. The Bangalore team developed the multimedia software and user interfaces in the hot Razr cell phone. Now, they are working on phones that display and send live video, stream movies from the Web, or route incoming calls to voicemail when you are shifting gears in a car. "This is a very, very critical, state-of-the-art resource for Motorola," says Motorola South Asia President Amit Sharma.

Companies like Motorola realize they must succeed in China and India at many levels simultaneously to stay competitive. That requires strategies for winning consumers, recruiting and managing R&D and professional talent, and skillfully sourcing from factories. "Over the next few years, you will see a dramatic gap opening between companies," predicts Jim Hemerling, who runs Boston Consulting Group's Shanghai practice. "It will be between those who get it and are fully mobilized in China and India, and those that are still pondering."

In the coming decades, China and India will disrupt workforces, industries, companies, and markets in ways that we can barely begin to imagine. The upheaval will test America's commitment to the global trade system, and shake its confidence. In the 19th century, Europe went through a similar trauma when it realized a new giant—the U.S.—had arrived. "It is up to America to manage its own expectation of China and India as either a threat or opportunity," says corporate strategist Kenichi Ohmae. "America should be as open-minded as Europe was 100 years ago." How these Asian giants integrate with the rest of the world will largely shape the 21st-century global economy.

Going Green

The Challenges & the Solutions

KEVIN M. KELLY

"The conservation of natural resources is the fundamental problem. Unless we solve that problem it will avail us little to solve all others."

—Theodore Roosevelt

Roosevelt's words are a perfect summary of the problems facing automakers in relation to balancing the survival of their business and protecting the global environment. Lawmakers, scientists and activists around the globe are demanding automakers become more environmentally-conscious. Rising global temperatures, skyrocketing fuel costs and changing weather patterns are all held up as the payback for years of neglecting the environment and of the production and use of inefficient vehicles that are designed to stoke egos more than the ecosystem. While the auto industry itself is not solely to blame for the world's changing environment—livestock emit more dangerous greenhouse gas emissions than all of the vehicles on the planet and commercial buildings and homes are notorious energy wasters—the massive visibility of the automobile and ever-clogging roadways make it an easy target.

Driving Forces

Automakers are not known for their responsiveness when it comes to meeting the demands of environmentalists. This resistance has resulted in lawmakers and regulators forcing the hand of the industry to become more conscious of the impacts the automobile poses on the environment.

In the U.S., pressure has been placed on the industry by both state and federal governments. California is leading the way on when it comes to state action. The California Air Resources Board (CARB), established in 1967, has taken up the mantle by passing regulations to reduce automobile carbon dioxide (CO_2) emission levels by 22% from the 2002 fleet average by the '09 model year—equal to 323 g/mi. The regulation further requires vehicles to achieve a more stringent 205 g/mi average by 2016—a 30% reduction from the '09 levels. Taking a page from California's rule book, New York, Rhode Island, Massachusetts, Connecticut, New Jersey, and Maine have all decided to adopt similar requirements. On the national level, Congress has finalized plans to increase the Corporate Average Fuel Economy (CAFE) standard to 35 mpg by 2020, from the current 27.5 mpg average for passenger cars and 20.7 mpg for light-trucks.

Similarly, European regulators are addressing vehicle emissions with Euro 5 standards, which go into effect in 2009 for vehicles on sale in the '11 model year. The regulation calls for diesel vehicles—which account for more than 50% of the European light-duty vehicle market—to achieve carbon monoxide (CO) output levels of 500 mg/km, along with NOx emission levels of 60 mg/km—a 24% reduction from current Euro 4 standards—with particulate matter output (diesels produce soot and aerosols including ash and metallic abrasion particulates, as well as sulfates and silicates) limited to 5 mg/km—an 80% reduction from Euro 4 standards. Gasoline-powered vehicles must achieve CO targets of 1,000 mg/km, with total hydrocarbon outputs set at 100 mg/km and NOx output capped at 60 mg/km—a 25% reduction from Euro 4. The European Commission is currently drafting rules for Euro 6, slated to take effect in the '15 model year, which is likely to include a 50% reduction in passenger vehicle emissions from Euro 5, along with diesel NOx and hydrocarbon emissions capped at 170 kg/km. Beyond just looking at tailpipe emission, European regulators will require automakers to design their vehicles to support a target of 95% recyclability by weight by 2015.

Social Pressures Build

The auto industry is feeling pressure from consumers to develop higher-mileage vehicles, particularly in light of rising gas prices. According to the Bureau of Labor Statistics, the average U.S. consumer is expected to shell out an additional 12% for gasoline in 2007, while average hourly earnings are increasing at a rate of only 3.5%, meaning consumers are finding a bigger portion of their budget going out the tailpipe. The situation does not bode well for automakers, especially those relying on big trucks and SUVs to support their bottom lines. It's not only pocket book pressures influencing consumers. From news reports about seemingly aberrant weather patterns to films like *An Inconvenient Truth* and *Happy Feet*, people are learning more about the environment than ever before.

Green Beyond Automotive

The lengthy product development timeframes automakers face tends to put them behind other industries when it comes to designing products that take advantage of consumer eco-friendliness concerns. Here's what some other companies are doing:

- IBM (www.ibm.com) changed the way it applies acoustic foam to its computer panels by discontinuing the use of chemical-based adhesives and replacing them with dart-shaped connectors that hold the foam in place. This change not only helped IBM reduce the amount of greenhouse gas emissions in the production process through the elimination of the adhesive, it also provided for ease in recycling when the product reached the end of its lifecycle.
- Steelcase's (www.steelcase.com) Think office chair was designed with a focus on recycling. It can be disassembled with the use of a few hand tools in 5 minutes with 99% of its overall content able to head to the recycling heap.
- Intel's (www.intel.com) Haifa, Israel, server facility uses water to chill the room to keep the computer systems running at peak performance. Traditional practice would route the heated water at the end of the process to cooling towers to evaporate, but Intel uses the hot water to heat the adjacent buildings in the winter and provide hot water to the showers in the facility's gym.
- Sun Microsystems (www.sun.com) decided to take the LEED building concept one step further by eliminating office space altogether. As part of its Open Work program, employees can work from home if they choose. The program cut Sun's real estate costs by $67.8 million and prevented nearly 29,000 tons of CO_2 in 2006, alone.
- Otis Elevator's (www.otis.com) Gen2 lift replaces the outmoded steel cables used to lift the passenger cars with polyurethane-coated steel belts, resulting in a lubrication-free system that does not require an expensive machine room to operate. The technology also provides for regenerative drive, which returns electricity to the building when the elevator travels downward, resulting in an elevator that is 75% more efficient than traditional systems.
- Key Tech's (www.locknpop.com) Lock n' Pop water-based adhesive can be sprayed onto the bottom and top of boxes to secure them in place on top of pallets during shipping. Once they arrive at their destination, the boxes can be removed from the stacks without any damage. Lock n' Pop reduces harmful gas emissions emitted when producing or using traditional adhesives.

Scientists are also taking their message directly to the public as the latest report from the United Nations Intergovernmental Panel on Climate Change—declaring the temperature of the Earth has increased by 0.74°C from 1906 to 2005, along with a 1.8 mm/yr. rise in sea levels from 1961 to present—has been debated in print, on television and radio. Former U.S. Vice President Al Gore has become household celebrity through his relentless raising of concern over global warming. "There's a growing awareness of climate change and the rapid availability of information is driving this change in mindset," says Jacquelyn Ottman, who has been advising the U.S. Government and Fortune 500 companies on responding to the environmental movement for more than 20 years as the president of J. Ottman Consulting (www.greenmarketing.com).

Environment = Massive Commitment[2]

Although the U.S. auto industry—which has lost more than $20 billion since 2005—is developing alternative-fuel vehicles and improving the efficiency of plants and building operations, there is a general failure in developing a holistic commitment to sustainability throughout entire organizations, from the most senior executives down to the plant floor. The necessity to improve the image and performance of the auto industry in the area of sustainability cannot be accomplished in the short term, nor can it be the responsibility of engineering, manufacturing or design alone. It's time to embrace *sustainable innovation* as a core competency, aimed at changing the mindset toward improving the environmental impact of the entire industry. Suppliers also must become responsive to the needs of OEMs when it comes to sustainability, making sure their own operations are energy and resource efficient. If the industry fails to meet the challenge, the pressures will only get more pronounced. A recent study from McKinsey & Co. (www.mckinsey.com) projects annual greenhouse gas emissions in the U.S. will rise 35% by 2030 to 9.7 gigatons. Of that, the transportation sector, which contributes 2.1 gigatons each year, is expected to grow by 1.3% to 2.8 gigatons.

When thinking along the lines of sustainable innovation, automakers must change the way they balance "green" with the bottom line. The auto industry seems to lack the financial foresight to take advantage of long-term savings and goodwill that comes with being green. "We need to have a one-year payback," Tom Neelands, director of GM's Worldwide Facilities Group, Energy and Utility Services, responds when asked how GM weighs investment decisions in green technology at the plant and facility level. That short-term outlook, unfortunately, is not uncommon in the industry, and it is something that needs to be addressed. Andrew Hobbs, director of the Environmental Quality office at Ford, says his company is trying to change the way financing of green technologies are handled: "One of the things we're trying to convince the financial community to do is look at the long-term liability. We find we can make a great business case for some technologies when we think about the potential liability of not having them five, ten, or fifteen years from now."

Little Things Mean a Lot

The answers to solving the complexities of sustainability will not be solved by a silver bullet. Most progress will be made in incremental steps across all facets of each organization. Simple things, like switching to the use of compact fluorescent or LED lighting systems in office buildings, or turning off all computers and electronic equipment at the end of the workday, can make notable differences when they are added up. On the engineering side, close scrutiny of vehicle and component weight, power-train and transmission optimization along with development of hydrogen and electric drive systems, all play critical roles in helping the auto industry gain regulatory compliance and share of consumer mind when it comes to sustainability.

Vehicle design is playing an increasingly vital role in the development of green vehicles. Designers must not only develop exteriors that look jaw-dropping, but they must also pay attention to the aerodynamic performance of their designs, particularly as the industry tries to squeeze every minute mile per gallon gain out of each vehicle. Designers will also have to utilize new materials in an effort to reduce the overall weight of the vehicle, again a key demand when it comes to improving overall efficiency. One of the materials that will find more application is aluminum, due to its inherent strength and reduced weight compared to traditional steel. Aluminum's formability is another benefit. In order to fully optimize the benefits of aluminum, however, designers and engineers will have to look beyond the skin of the vehicle for maximum optimization. According to a study by the Massachusetts Institute of Technology, the body-in-white accounts for 27% of the total weight of the vehicle, providing enormous potential when it comes to improved weight efficiency. Moving from a traditional unibody to a space frame design could help optimize weight reduction and vehicle rigidity. Space frame designs have been used in low volume, niche applications for several years—Audi is the most notable proponent of the technology.

Making complex rails that maximize the benefits of improved aerodynamics can be better accomplished through space frame construction. Aluminum has failed to gain mass acceptance because of its higher raw material cost compared to traditional steel, but looking at material selection through the approach of sustainable innovation and a holistic systems approach could change the perception of its total cost in the near future. However, steel producers have developed a range of strong, lightweight materials, so the hurdles for aluminum will continue to be set high.

The use of natural materials is likely to expand in design studios as vehicle recyclability pressures build. Ford currently uses soy-based foam in the seats of its Mustang and plans to expand use of the material into other areas of its vehicle, including structural applications in A-pillars. Likewise, the company is studying ways to use natural fiber materials, such as coconut fiber, for bumper supports and interior trim pieces. These materials are easier to recycle and take less energy to produce than petroleum-based plastics. Besides recyclability benefits, using green materials as visual cues on vehicle interior and exterior applications can help boost the "environmental" image of a

Ford's Environmental Focus

Ford is taking a step-by-step approach to meeting the green challenge. And unlike other automakers that are taking a "moon shot" approach to trying to create environmental technologies, Ford is working toward making the millions of cars and trucks it builds more fuel efficient through cost-effective, common sense approaches. "We're on this path for a long time and it's a long-term commitment and it is a commitment that is best served not by technologies that you can provide in the tens or twenties or even thousands; we need plans that work on millions of vehicles and that means these plans need to be affordable and the infrastructure needs to be in place to support them," says Derrick Kuzak, Ford's group vice president of global product development.

In the near-term—from 2008 through 2012—Ford intends to improve the efficiency of its internal combustion engines through the addition of direct-injection and turbocharging technologies, resulting in a 10% to 20% improvement in fuel economy and better performance. "Fuel economy is at the top of the list for our consumers in terms of purchase considerations, and we have to respond to that quickly," Kuzak says, adding Ford also plans to launch a family of dual-clutch transmissions to support its new engine strategy and install electric power steering systems in nearly 90% of all vehicles. Once that's complete, Ford will concentrate on reducing the average weight of its vehicles anywhere from 250 to 750 lb. by doing thing like using more lightweight materials, including high-strength steels, aluminum and composites. Kuzak predicts if Ford reaches its weight savings goals and can install smaller displacement engines in its vehicles with turbo technology, fuel economy can be improved as much as 50%. Beyond weight savings, Ford will improve battery and vehicle electrical systems management, along with improving vehicle aerodynamic performance. "At the same time we will continue to progress on hybrids. We have already committed to a plug-in hybrid," Kuzak says. Further down the road—beyond 2020—Ford plans to increase electric drive systems in its vehicle. Kuzak suggests that by then, the nature of powertrains will be different: "Now the high volume becomes plug-in hybrids, or fuel cells or hydrogen-powered internal-combustion engines. We don't know which of them will win, but they will all play a role." And at that point in time, Ford will make its high-volume moves.

All of these technologies will help boost Ford's green status, but it still remains critical the company develop products that customers demand. "If our products are not relevant, we are not supporting sustainability from an economic standpoint. The most important part of sustainability is having relevant products going forward and as customers needs change we realize we need to change," says Nancy Gioia, director of Ford's sustainable mobility technology and hybrid vehicle programs group. Building green products that customers aren't interested in is possibly less environmental than not having them at all.

particular model. Chrysler, for example, is studying using bamboo and cork materials in future interiors. "If the appearance is a positive and the cost is a positive, there is no reason we shouldn't use those materials," says Brandon Faurote, head of Chrysler's advance exterior and interior design group.

Being Green Italian Style

Improved fuel efficiency is hardly something you'd expect to see on the radar at one of the most famous high-performance car brands, but Ferrari isn't taking a backseat to the high-volume producers. The company plans to improve the efficiency of its future cars with a target of reducing fuel consumption by 40% by 2012 and reducing vehicle CO_2 emissions from 400g/km to 280–300 g/km. The Mille Chili (Italian for *1,000 kg*—the target weight of the vehicle) concept provides a glimpse into plans for making its cars more efficient, complete with active aerodynamics via openings in the underbody that change size and shape, depending on vehicle speed. The chassis and bodywork are constructed from carbon fiber and composite materials; low rolling resistance tires provide added efficiency.

Beyond just looking at the vehicle, there are other approaches. Ferrari's owner, Fiat, has tasked its engineers with changing the way consumers interpret how their driving impacts the environment. The automaker has developed EcoDrive, a computer software program developed by Microsoft that records vehicle CO_2 emissions output and fuel economy on a USB key. The key can be plugged into a PC where the software will analyze the performance of the driver and provide useful tips on how to improve fuel economy and lower harmful emissions by minor changes to driving behavior.

Green Factories

Manufacturing's role is probably most crucial in helping to improve the environmental performance of the industry. The hundreds of millions of dollars spent retrofitting and upgrading assembly, stamping and powertrain facilities provide more than ample opportunity for the industry to achieve significant financial gains when it comes to being green. Clay Nesler, vice president of Global Energy and Sustainability at Johnson Controls Building Efficiency division (www.jci.com), says it's critical for the auto industry to include sustainability as part of plant upgrade expenditures. But even on-going operations can provide advantages: "We find that the highest return on investment when it comes to building efficiencies is looking at maintenance of equipment and this requires little capital outlay, but provides marked savings," he says, noting lighting is one area that provides quick returns with little outlay. According to the McKinsey study, lighting accounts for more than 19% of greenhouse gas emissions associated with buildings and retrofitting incandescent lighting systems with compact fluorescent or LED lighting systems can cut power consumption by as much as 12%.

The biggest area of potential benefit from a cost savings and emissions reduction perspective are paint shops, which represent 60 to 75% of total assembly facility operating costs, according to Gordon Harbison, Services and Solutions manager at Dürr Systems (http://www.durr.com/en/). Since paint shops use massive amounts of air to keep spray booths clean and compliant with tight climate control requirements, it's vital to find ways to reduce the amount of natural gas used to heat the air entering the booths. Dürr developed a system it installed at a few GM facilities using a process called "building-2-booth" where general shop ventilation, which is already climate controlled, is routed to the spray booth using the building itself as the duct work. The program is expected to result in saving an average of $4 per vehicle over traditional spray booth control processes with a reduction in harmful greenhouse gas emissions. Dürr is also working to promote the use of energy-curable coatings, which use ultraviolet light or electron beams to cure vehicle paint on bodies. Several pilots are being tested for use on spot repairs at the end of the assembly line and the results are promising, with less paint being discarded due to the fact that the paint does not begin to dry until it is hit with the light or beams. Using the process on full vehicle bodies has proven challenging because complex surfaces found on many vehicles cause light bending problems and uneven cures.

Providing power to the plant itself holds ample promise for reducing cost and improving efficiency. Johnson Controls' Nesler says automakers should look at using cogeneration for plant operations. Currently, most power plants vent the heat produced during electricity production through cooling towers directly into the atmosphere. Through cogeneration, the heat generated is used for climate control of the facility being powered, thus reducing the need for separate heating equipment that uses natural gas or other resources. Cogeneration plants can use multiple feedstocks to provide heat and electricity, including waste woodchips, straw or various biomass materials. "This becomes a very attractive option when you look at the rising costs of natural gas and other resources," Nesler says. Beyond cogeneration, automakers can also turn to the sun to power their facilities. While solar panels have been available for decades, the technology used to produce them is becoming more cost-effective. The cost of photovoltaic technology is expected to drop from $300 to $350 per megawatt-hour in 2005 to $90 per megawatt-hour in 2030, moving solar power penetration from a 0.5-gigawatt capacity in 2005 to 148 gigawatts in 2030, according to the McKinsey study. GM has installed photovoltaic panels on two of its parts warehouses in California under a unique business partnership with Constellation Energy (www.constellation.com), which designed, built and owns the arrays. GM agreed to a long-term contract to buy electricity generated from the solar systems, while any excess power is sent directly to the general power grid, where Constellation earns money from the state utility.

A holistic approach to green building has been developed by the U.S. Green Building Council (www.usgbc.org). Its Leadership in Energy and Environmental Design (LEED) building certification program awards points for satisfying specific building criteria in several categories: sustainable sites, water efficiency, energy & atmosphere, materials & resources, indoor environmental quality and innovation in design. Buildings are awarded either a certified, silver, gold or platinum certification level, depending on the points earned. LEED certification can be granted for existing facilities, with a focus on improved maintenance and upgrading of equipment over a set timeline. LEED has become vogue of late, with Toyota, GM, Honda and Ford being some of the biggest proponents of the program. Honda already certified two of its U.S. facilities—the Honda R&D central plant facility in Raymond, OH, and its Northwest Regional Center in Gresham, OR, at the Gold LEED level—and has plans to expand to two more facilities in 2008.

Unfamiliar Territory

Being green isn't rocket science, but it does require a significant change in thinking. Automakers should look beyond the dealer lots to see how they can truly reshape the image of the industry going forward because the pressures from environmental groups and regulators will not abate. "In the early 1990s we went through a period of 'green washing' where if you came out with one product you were green. Now, consumers know better," says green marketing expert Ottman. She suggests that auto execs may have to think as former IBM CEO Lou Gerstner did, when he changed the model from computer-maker to technology solution-provider. As urban centers get more densely populated, it may be time for the auto industry to look at itself as transportation solution providers. With more than 645 cities around the globe offering car sharing services to their residents, it may be beneficial for automakers to look at partnering with the companies that provide the shared vehicle services. What about the dealers and market share? No doubt they will shrink, but if one automaker takes the lead, there will likely be fast followers. Speaking of the automakers, Ottman says, "They have to be looking at these things in order to stay in the game long term—if they see the writing on the wall." The writing can no longer be ignored by those companies that want to survive.

Globalization and You

Your generation will have to compete for jobs with people all over the world. Will you be ready?

SEAN PRICE

Allie Wilborn, 16, was in eighth grade when her father first announced that his job might be in trouble. He works as a sales man at a sock-making company in Fort Payne, Alabama. Allies father told the family that they would have to spend less and save more. "[He] told us to be ready for anything that could happen," Allie recalls.

Such uncertainty has become normal in Fort Payne. Two years ago, more than 7,300 of the town's 15,000 people worked in sock mills. Today, the number of jobs in Fort Payne's sock industry is 5,500 and falling. What happened? The short answer is globalization.

A Smaller World

Steven J. Davis, an economist at the University of Chicago, says that the term globalization describes several worldwide trends. 'They are technological changes, mostly," Davis told JS. "But to some extent, [globalization] also means reductions in trade barriers that make the world a smaller place, in economic terms."

Some of the greatest technological leaps have occurred in communications. Thanks to the Internet, e-mail, and cell phones, business people in Los Angeles can exchange ideas with their counterparts in Hong Kong quickly and inexpensively. Companies such as FedEx have lowered the cost and quickened the pace of transporting goods. Products have also become lighter. "It's a lot easier to ship a laptop PC than it is [an old-fashioned] supercomputer," Davis says.

The world is smaller politically, too. A decade ago, the United States and other wealthy countries formed the World Trade Organization (WTO). Among other objectives, the WTO encourages countries to drop trade barriers, including **tariffs** and **quotas**.

Countries that once lagged far behind the West, notably China and India, have become economic powers. Cheap labor has been key to their success. Chinese sock workers will accept 50 cents an hour, far below the $12 to $15 per hour that many U.S. workers expect. Such competition is forcing Fort Payne factories to shut down or relocate overseas.

Education Means Survival

Globalization does not just challenge sock makers, says *New York Times* columnist Thomas L. Friedman. It is affecting even high-tech jobs in the U.S. In his book *The World Is Flat,* Friedman points out that Bangalore, India, alone has 160,000 high-tech jobs. Well-educated Indians there earn $5,000 a year at computer call centers for such U.S. companies as Dell and International Business Machines (IBM). The same job in the U.S. pays an average of $25,000.

Last May, IBM announced that it was cutting as many as 13,000 jobs in the U.S. and Western Europe, while creating 14,000 in India. Robert W. Moffat, an IBM senior vice president, told *The New York Times* that saving money was not the biggest issue. "It's mostly about skills," he said.

Friedman echoes Moffat's reasoning. "Compared with young Indians and Chinese," he writes, "too many Americans have become lazy." The U.S. educational system, he adds, is failing. High schools produce too few graduates with basic science and math skills. U.S. colleges produce too few engineers and scientists. "In the international competition to have the biggest and best supply of [skilled] workers," Friedman says, "America is falling behind."

Critics of outsourcing (sending jobs overseas) say that corporate greed is to blame for the loss of jobs. Marcus Courtney, president of the Washington Alliance of Technical Workers, says that companies like IBM want to continually lower costs for their own profits: "The winners are the richest corporations in the world, and American workers lose."

Despite complaints from workers in Fort Payne and other U.S. cities, global competition is here to stay. Davis says that a good education and flexibility are key to maintaining a competitive advantage. "You have to be ready to do more than one thing in your life in terms of work activity," he says. "Most of us will."

That is one reason why Allie Wilborn, who still worries about the loss of jobs in her hometown, is keeping up with her studies. As Friedman observes, "In a flat world, every individual is going to have to run a little faster if he or she wants to advance his or her standard of living."

Words to Know

- **quota:** a limited number or share, as of imported products.
- **tariffs:** government taxes on imports or exports

Test-Your-Knowledge Form

We encourage you to photocopy and use this page as a tool to assess how the articles in *Annual Editions* expand on the information in your textbook. By reflecting on the articles you will gain enhanced text information. You can also access this useful form on a product's book support Web site at *http://www.mhcls.com/online/*.

NAME: DATE:

TITLE AND NUMBER OF ARTICLE:

BRIEFLY STATE THE MAIN IDEA OF THIS ARTICLE:

LIST THREE IMPORTANT FACTS THAT THE AUTHOR USES TO SUPPORT THE MAIN IDEA:

WHAT INFORMATION OR IDEAS DISCUSSED IN THIS ARTICLE ARE ALSO DISCUSSED IN YOUR TEXTBOOK OR OTHER READINGS THAT YOU HAVE DONE? LIST THE TEXTBOOK CHAPTERS AND PAGE NUMBERS:

LIST ANY EXAMPLES OF BIAS OR FAULTY REASONING THAT YOU FOUND IN THE ARTICLE:

LIST ANY NEW TERMS/CONCEPTS THAT WERE DISCUSSED IN THE ARTICLE, AND WRITE A SHORT DEFINITION:

We Want Your Advice

ANNUAL EDITIONS revisions depend on two major opinion sources: one is our Advisory Board, listed in the front of this volume, which works with us in scanning the thousands of articles published in the public press each year; the other is you—the person actually using the book. Please help us and the users of the next edition by completing the prepaid article rating form on this page and returning it to us. Thank you for your help!

ANNUAL EDITIONS: International Business 09/10

ARTICLE RATING FORM

Here is an opportunity for you to have direct input into the next revision of this volume.
We would like you to rate each of the articles listed below, using the following scale:

1. **Excellent: should definitely be retained**
2. **Above average: should probably be retained**
3. **Below average: should probably be deleted**
4. **Poor: should definitely be deleted**

Your ratings will play a vital part in the next revision.
Please mail this prepaid form to us as soon as possible.
Thanks for your help!

RATING	ARTICLE	RATING	ARTICLE
	1. Globalization and Its Contents		21. Is U.S. Business Losing Europe?
	2. The Leading Economic Organizations at the Beginning of the 21st Century		22. Can Europe Compete?
	3. Trading Places		23. Unequal Access
	4. Here's the Good News		24. When Greens Go Corporate
	5. The Real Global Technology Challenge		25. Making It in China
	6. Looking Ahead to Our Place in the Next Economy		26. The China Factor
	7. A Roadmap for the New Trade Landscape		27. A Whiff of New Money
	8. Are Global Prices Converging or Diverging?		28. BRIC Crumbling?
	9. What One Hand Gives, the Other Takes		29. The Brave New World of IFRS
	10. The World's Banker		30. Found in Translation
	11. Helping the Global Economy Stay in Shape		31. Shaping the Future of Manufacturing
	12. The Bretton Woods System		32. The Rise of BRIC
	13. Wall Street in the Desert		33. International OHS
	14. Dollar Doldrums		34. Out of Work
	15. Financial Globalization		35. Worrying Trends for the Global Outsourcing Industry
	16. China's Mobile Maestro		36. Roots of Insecurity
	17. The Challengers		37. Countdown to a Meltdown
	18. How Capitalism Is Killing Democracy		38. Oil Frontiers
	19. Grassroots Diplomacy		39. A New World Economy
	20. New Tech, Old Habits		40. Going Green
			41. Globalization and You

NO POSTAGE
NECESSARY
IF MAILED
IN THE
UNITED STATES

BUSINESS REPLY MAIL
FIRST CLASS MAIL PERMIT NO. 551 DUBUQUE IA

POSTAGE WILL BE PAID BY ADDRESSEE

McGraw-Hill Contemporary Learning Series
501 BELL STREET
DUBUQUE, IA 52001

ABOUT YOU

Name   Date

Are you a teacher? ☐ A student? ☐
Your school's name

Department

Address   City   State   Zip

School telephone #

YOUR COMMENTS ARE IMPORTANT TO US!

Please fill in the following information:
For which course did you use this book?

Did you use a text with this ANNUAL EDITION? ☐ yes ☐ no
What was the title of the text?

What are your general reactions to the Annual Editions concept?

Have you read any pertinent articles recently that you think should be included in the next edition? Explain.

Are there any articles that you feel should be replaced in the next edition? Why?

Are there any World Wide Web sites that you feel should be included in the next edition? Please annotate.

May we contact you for editorial input? ☐ yes ☐ no
May we quote your comments? ☐ yes ☐ no